CIVICUS Global Survey of the State of Civil Society

CIVICUS Global Survey of the State of Civil Society

Volume 1
Country Profiles

Civil Society Index Project
2003–2006 Phase

Edited by

V. FINN HEINRICH

CIVICUS
World Alliance for Citizen Participation

Kumarian
Press, Inc.

CIVICUS Global Survey of the State of Civil Society, Volume 1: Country Profiles

Published 2007 in the United States of America by Kumarian Press, Inc.,
1294 Blue Hills Avenue, Bloomfield, CT 06002 USA

Design, production, and editorial services were provided by Publication Services,
Inc., Champaign, Illinois. The text of this book is set in Adobe Sabon 11/13.5

Printed in the United States on acid-free paper by Thomson-Shore.
Text printed with vegetable oil-based ink.

∞" The paper used in this publication meets the minimum requirements of the
American National Standard for Information Sciences—Permanence of Paper for
printed Library Materials, ANSI Z39.48-1984

Library of Congress Cataloging-in-Publication Data

CIVICUS global survey of the state of civil society/ edited by V. Finn Heinrich
    v.   cm.
    Includes bibliographical references and index.
    ISBN 978–1–56549–235–6 (pbk. : alk. paper)
    1. Civil society--Cross-cultural studies. 2. Civil society. I. Heinrich, V. Finn.
II. CIVICUS (Association). III. Title: Global survey of the state of civil society
    JC337.C534 2007
    300--dc22   2006103415

15 14 13 12 11 10 09 08   1 2 3 4 5 6 7 8 9

Contents

Foreword

When I joined CIVICUS in 1998 as its secretary general, the organization had just published *The New Civic Atlas,* a series of brief portraits of civil society in sixty countries. *The New Civic Atlas* was the latest addition to a number of publications put out by CIVICUS to meet its goal of raising the global profile of civil society, a goal we are still committed to today. Although the *New Civic Atlas* was thought to be a very useful resource, providing concise overviews of civil society in a large number of countries, we also received recommendations that a more comparative, policy-oriented, and evaluative perspective would enhance the relevance of the book in its next edition.

Based on this feedback, and at a time when indices of key global phenomena such as corruption, human development, democracy, and economic competitiveness mushroomed, we began consultations about the development of a Civil Society Index (CSI) with CIVICUS members and partners. This is not the place to describe the stimulating and challenging discussions about the idea of a CSI and its development from 1999 to now.[1] Let it suffice to say that for the organization at large and particularly, as I observed, for the many young professionals working on the project over the last seven years, the engagement in the CSI has been a most rewarding experience in terms of intellectual learning, institutional partnership building, and gaining insights into the politics of global knowledge production.

The political context within which this work has been conducted was and continues to be challenging. For starters, there are multiple definitions of "civil society." For example, in some countries the term is used interchangeably with "NGO"; however, in most countries civil society is seen as a broader rubric that includes all organized civic elements, such as trade unions and informal community organizations. In some countries political parties are considered part of civil society but in many they are not.

Some see the intellectual framing of the role of civil society as being far too dominated by intellectuals and organizations rooted in Western paradigms and logic, without sufficient sensitivity to the realities in the global South. Some focus primarily on the role of civil society in service delivery, without sufficient focus on civil society's advocacy role or its right to question issues of governance, particularly at a time of deepening democratic deficits from the local to the global level.

There are also legitimate concerns about whether research on civil society delivers real results or whether it tells people in each country more or less what they already know. This is particularly relevant given the reality that most civil society organizations are surviving in a context of increasingly fragile finances. This has been exacerbated by the current global situation in which governments invest more in national security without embracing a more comprehensive notion of human security.

The above factors raise the question of how action-research, such as the CSI, can contribute to substantive systemic change that genuinely creates an enabling environment for civil society. There is a huge challenge to how we assess the success and impact of this work. We have often drawn on the wisdom of Albert Einstein, who once said, "Not everything that counts can be measured and not everything that can be measured counts." We have cautioned against focusing too much on short-term measurable outputs and outcomes, rather than on longer-term, complex social change processes. Sadly, most resource providers, whether they are bilateral agencies or grant-making foundations, are restricted by funding guidelines that push for quick results, and there is insufficient recognition that strengthening civil society, like social development more broadly, is a process and not a product.

The *Global Survey on the State of Civil Society* is the culmination of the CSI project's past work, particularly its current implementation phase (2003–2006), which was a major collaborative effort involving more than 6,000 active participants. I am extremely happy to contribute this foreword to Volume I of the first edition of the *Global Survey on the State of Civil Society*, which I hope will initiate a long series of these reports in the coming years and decades. By providing summary assessments of the state of civil society in forty-four countries throughout the world, this volume seeks to address the void of comparative and policy-oriented descriptions of civil society. The second volume of the report, which is scheduled for publication at the end of

2007, will complement this descriptive account with comparative perspectives on key issues of civil society as they emerge from the vast amount of data collected by the project.

As described in greater detail in the introductory chapter by Finn Heinrich, who led the project during most of its history, what is presented here is by no means the ultimate global study on civil society. It is instead one among many contributions that seek to track, assess, and, eventually, better illuminate this important aspect of our societies. It will continue to evolve over the years as the approach is refined and adapted to the ever-changing environment. We at CIVICUS appreciate and invite your input and feedback in this regard.

For CIVICUS, the CSI project will remain a major cornerstone of our work, due to its foundational character within our programmatic framework and its particular approach. The CSI is the longest-standing program of CIVICUS, with the exception of the CIVICUS World Assembly, and can now claim a solid public track record. The CSI is also the first CIVICUS program of this scale and kind. It piloted a specific approach of working with country partners on implementing the project, which generated useful lessons that other programs are taking into account. The participatory nature of the CSI, which involved, on average, more than 100 civil society representatives in each country, enabled CIVICUS to access important networks for its other areas of work and also assisted in better publicizing CIVICUS's work. The CSI identifies the strengths and weaknesses of civil society in more than fifty countries around the world, giving CIVICUS a crucial needs assessment of civil societies, which can be used for strategic and programmatic planning as well as for adjusting current programmatic focus areas. Last, but not least, the CSI aims to develop specific recommendations on how to strengthen civil society in a given country and to create a local commitment to put them into practice. Where the CSI achieves these objectives, it can serve as an extremely useful starting block for any follow-up interventions by CIVICUS and its partners.

I want to use this opportunity to thank all those who have shaped the CSI project along the way and particularly those who have contributed to this volume. In comparative terms both the costs associated with the global coordination of the project and those of our national partners were modest and recognized the need for voluntary contributions of much time and effort to ensure that the objectives of the project were achieved. I would like to particularly acknowledge the sacrifice of our national partners, many of whom worked without dedicated funding during different parts of the project. As some of them pointed out to us, given the inclusive definition of civil society used by the CSI project, one important early benefit was the fostering of dialogue between different parts of civil society, which was not happening in many countries. Because the CSI is designed to lay the groundwork for initiatives to strengthen civil society, based on what is learned through the assessments, many felt taking the risk of doing this work without having all the required resources was still very much worth the effort.

Last, let me express my hope that the values of cooperation, transparency, reflection, and knowledge, which are so strongly embodied in this project and are the hallmarks of civil society itself, will continue to guide our joint efforts to strengthen civil society and its contributions to a more just, equitable, and peaceful world.

Kumi Naidoo
Secretary General
CIVICUS: World Alliance
for Citizen Participation

Notes

1. Readers interested in the trajectory of the CIVICUS Civil Society Index are referred to the following project paper, which is available on the CSI pages of the CIVICUS website at www.civicus.org: Volkhart Finn Heinrich, *Assessing and Strengthening Civil Society Worldwide. A Project Description of the CIVICUS Civil Society Index: A Participatory Needs Assessment & Action-Planning Tool for Civil Society* (Johannesburg, South Africa: CIVICUS, 2004).

Preface

This volume summarizes the results of the forty-four country assessments of the state of civil society, conducted by CIVICUS and its country partners as part of the CIVICUS Civil Society Index (CSI) Project between 2003 and 2006. The country chapters presented in this book are short summaries of the extensive country reports, which were drafted under the leadership of CSI country partners and are available on the CIVICUS website.[1]

This compendium seeks to provide an overview of the makeup and key features of civil society in these countries. Due to their limited length, these chapters cannot comprehensively describe the multifaceted and multilayered nature of civil society in each country. Rather, they aim to provide a general overview from a bird's eye view. Readers interested in finding out more about a specific country are encouraged to read the full country report.

This publication is a major product of the CSI and targets a general audience of civil society practitioners, policymakers, academics, and students interested in the current condition of civil society in the countries covered by the CSI. A second volume, which takes a more analytical and comparative perspective, will be published in the coming months. CIVICUS hopes that this two-volume *Global Survey of the State of Civil Society,* which we aim to produce for every future CSI project phase, will help to raise global awareness of the roles, strengths, and weaknesses of civil society around the world.

The CSI project as a whole, and in particular this book, has been a truly collaborative effort, involving more than 6,000 participants in fifty-three countries.[2] Although it is impossible to acknowledge every participant in this endeavor, I would like to use this opportunity to thank a number of individuals who have made a particularly significant contribution to the success of the CSI during these years.

At CIVICUS, the project was coordinated by an energetic team of international staff, who were deeply committed to the project and its principles. Between 2003 and 2006 the CSI team included Amaya Algarra-Liquete, Lorenzo Fioramonti, Beniam Gebrezghi, Tim Gibbs, Andria Hayes-Birchler, Mahi Khallaf, Amber Leaders, Regina Martyn, Jacob Mati, Muanzu Mpezo, Ruxandra Noica, Modikoe Patjane, Priscilla Ryan, Rahim Saatov, Kristinne Sanz, Janine Schall-Emden, Tracy September, Navin Vasudev, Hannelore Wallner, and Benita Young.

The CSI team received guidance from the project's International Steering Group[3] and the CIVICUS board. Here, I would like to single out the work of the chair of the board's Programme Committee, Alan Fowler, and CIVICUS's Secretary General, Kumi Naidoo, for their ongoing commitment and engagement with the project. In addition, the project benefited greatly from the work of Helmut Anheier, who developed the basic methodology and the Civil Society Diamond tool, as well as from the crucial inputs by Carmen Malena, who worked with me on refining the CSI's approach and methodology after its pilot phase in 2001. Of course, without dedicated financial support from a range of donors, this project would not have gotten to where it is now. The list of CSI supporters in the various countries where it was implemented would be too long for this preface. I would, however, like to acknowledge the support provided to CIVICUS by the Aga Khan Foundation Canada, Canadian International Development Agency (CIDA), Cordaid, International Development Resource Centre (IDRC), Irish Aid, Norwegian Agency for Development Cooperation (Norad), Overseas Development Institute (ODI), and, last, but not least, the Swedish International Development Cooperation Agency (SIDA).

A number of people were closely involved in putting this volume together and therefore deserve special mentioning. The drafting team at CIVICUS, which took on the difficult task of condensing the extensive country reports into concise and informative chapters, was aptly coordinated by Regina Martyn and also included Lorenzo Fioramonti, Mahi Khallaf, Beniam Gebrezghi, Jacob Mati, and myself. I am grateful for the meticulous work by Kristinne Sanz and Laureen Bertin as proofreaders and to Priscilla Ryan for her patience and efficiency in editing the various drafts of the book, dealing with the different writing styles of drafting team members, and guiding the lengthy process of completing the draft manuscript. In Kumarian

Press, we found a partner, which, like CIVICUS, is committed to improving the understanding of civil society.

I would also like to thank the following group of external reviewers, who sent often encouraging and sometimes critical inputs, but always extremely useful feedback on draft versions of the chapters: Edward Aspinall, Stefanie Bailer, John Beauclerk, Vanja Calovic, Asimina Christoforou, John Clark, Gerard Clarke, Jennifer Collins, Donatella Della Porta, Ozgur Ezel, Stephan Feuchtwang, Pavol Fric, Zie Gariyo, Paata Gurgenidze, Katerina Hadzi-Miceva, Laura A. Henry, Eric Hershberg, Bernhard Hillenkamp, Richard Holloway, Marc Howard, David Kalete, Arjun K. Karki, Assya Kavrakova, Tomaž Klenovšek, Marija Kolin, Umut Korkut, Berthold Kuhn, Mladen Lazic, Alejandro Litovsky, Carmen Malena, Milena Marega, Lucas C.P.M. Meijs, Ruxandra Noica, Paul Opoku-Mensah, Petr Jan Pajas, Mario Pianta, Cvjetana Plavsa-Matic, David Robinson, Necdet Saglam, Anthony Saich, Ziad Abdel Samad, S.S. Srivastava, Paul Stubbs, Yiouli Taki, Marieta Tzvetkova, Augusto Varas, Luis Verdesoto, Yücel Vural, and Annette Zimmer. Of course, the responsibility for the final versions of the chapters, and for any errors or misrepresentations therein, lies solely with CIVICUS and me as the editor of this volume.

Finally, the biggest thank you goes to the CSI country partners, whose dedication in making the CSI assessment a reality in their country was truly outstanding. Without their work in raising the necessary resources for the project, leading the implementation of its various activities, and taking on the complex task of pulling the information together in country reports, this book would not have been possible. Due to their critical role in the project, the organizations that took the lead in implementing the CSI in the fifty-three countries deserve to be listed here:

Argentina—Grupo de Análisis y Desarrollo Institucional y Social (GADIS)
Armenia—Centre for Development of Civil Society (CDCS)
Azerbaijan—International Center for Social Research (ICSR)
Bolivia—Catholic Relief Services (CRS) and Centro de Investigación y Promoción del Campesinado (CIPCA)
Bulgaria—Balkan Assist Association (BAA)
Burkina Faso—Civil Society Organization Network for Development (RESOCIDE)
Chile—Fundación Soles

Costa Rica—NGO Research Centre, Tsinghua University (NGORC) China, Fundación Acceso

Croatia—Centre for Development of Non-Profit Organizations (CERANEO)

Northern part of Cyprus—Management Center for the Mediterranean (MC-Med)

Southern part of Cyprus—InterCollege

Czech Republic—Civil Society Development Foundation (NROS)

East Timor—East Timor National NGO Forum

Ecuador—Fundación Esquel

Egypt—Center for Development Services (CDS)

Fiji—Fiji Council of Social Services (FCOSS)

Georgia—Centre for Training and Consultancy (CTC)

Germany—Maecenata Institute for Philanthropy and Civil Society

Ghana—Ghana Association of Private Voluntary Organizations in Development (GAPVOD)

Greece—access2democracy (a2d)

Guatemala—Institute of Cultural Affairs Guatemala (ICA-G)

Honduras—Centro Hondureño de Promoción para el Desarrollo Comunitario (CEHPRODEC)

Hong Kong—Hong Kong Council of Social Service (HKCSS)

Indonesia—YAPPIKA

Italy—Cittadinanzattiva

Jamaica—Association of Development Agencies (ADA)

Lebanon—International Management and Training Institute (IMTI)

Macedonia—Macedonian Center for International Cooperation (MCIC)

Mongolia—Center for Citizens' Alliance (CCA)

Montenegro–Center for Development of NGOs (CRNVO)

Nepal—Institute of Cultural Affairs Nepal (ICA-N)

Netherlands—De Nieuwe Dialoog

Nigeria—ActionAid

Northern Ireland—Northern Ireland Council for Voluntary Action (NICVA)

Orissa, India—Center for Youth and Social Development (CYSD)

Palestine—Bisan Center for Research and Development

Poland—KLON JAWOR Association

Romania—Civil Society Development Foundation (CSDF)

Russia—St. Petersburg Center for Humanities and Political Studies: Strategy

Scotland—Scottish Council for Voluntary Organizations (SCVO)

Serbia—Center for the Development of the Non-Profit Sector (CDNPS)

Sierra Leone—Campaign for Good Governance (CGG)

Slovenia—Legal-information Centre for NGOs (LIC)

South Korea—Third Sector Institute, Hanyang University

Taiwan—Center for International NGO Studies (CINGOS)

Togo—Plan-Togo/Federation des ONGs au Togo (FONGTO)

Turkey—Third Sector Foundation of Turkey (TUSEV)

Uganda—Development Network of Indigenous Voluntary Associations (DENIVA)

Ukraine—Counterpart Creative Center (CCC) and the Center for Philanthropy (CFP)

Uruguay—Instituto de Comunicación y Desarrollo (ICD)

Vietnam—Vietnam Institute of Development Studies (VIDS)

Wales—Wales Council for Voluntary Action (WCVA).

The process of overseeing the CSI assessments and putting together this volume has been as intellectually challenging as it has been fulfilling. Most of all, I am deeply grateful for the support and encouragement I have received over the course of this project from fellow civil society activists around the world.

V. Finn Heinrich
Assistant Secretary General
Programmes
CIVICUS

Notes

1. All country chapters are available on the CSI pages of the CIVICUS website at http://www.civicus.org.
2. Fifty-three countries participated in the Civil Society Index Implementation phase 2003–2006. However, at the time of publication only forty-four country reports were complete and able to be included in this volume. The nine countries not included in this volume are Armenia, Azerbaijan, Burkina Faso, Costa Rica, East Timor, Jamaica, Mauritius, Nigeria, and Palestine.
3. The International Steering Group included Helmut Anheier, David Bonbright, Ramon Daubon, Alan Fowler, Jude Howell, Saad Eddin Ibrahim, Thierno Kane, Carmen Malena, and Christine Musisi.

Acronyms

a2d	access2democracy
ACTS	Action of Churches Together in Scotland
ADA	Association of Development Agencies
ARC	Association for Community Relations
BAA	Balkan Assist Association
CBO	Community-based organization
CCA	Center for Citizens' Alliance
CCC	Counterpart Creative Center
CDCS	Centre for Development of Civil Society
CDNPS	Center for the Development of the Non-profit Sector
CDS	Centre for Development Services
CEHPRODEC	Centro Hondureño de Promoción para el Desarrollo Comunitario
CEOSS	Coptic Evangelical Organization for Social Services
CERANEO	Centre for Development of Non-Profit Organizations
CFP	Center for Philanthropy
CGG	Campaign for Good Governance
CIDA	Canadian International Development Agency
CINGOS	Center for International NGO Studies
CIPCA	Centro de Investigación y Promoción del Campesinado
CODISRA	Commission on Racism and Discrimination against Indigenous People
CONAIE	Confederation of Indigenous Nationalities in Ecuador

CNVOS	Centre for Information Service, Cooperation, and Development of NGOs
CPP	Convention People's Party
CRNVO	Center for Development of NGOs
CRS	Catholic Relief Services
CSDF	Civil Society Development Foundation
CSI	Civil Society Index
CSI-SAT	Civil Society Index Shortened Assessment Tool
CSO	Civil society organization
CSR	Corporate social responsibility
CTC	Centre for Training and Consultancy
CYSD	Center for Youth and Social Development
DENIVA	Development Network of Indigenous Voluntary Associations
ECOWAS	Community of West African States
FCOSS	Fiji Council of Social Services
FID	Forum for Intercultural Dialogue
FLRC	Fiji Law Reform Commission
FONGTO	Federation des ONGs Togolaises
FOSDEH	Honduran Social Forum for the External Debt
GADIS	Grupo de Análisis y Desarrollo Institucional y Social
GAPVOD	Ghana Association of Private Voluntary Organizations in Development
GDP	Gross domestic product
GDR	German Democratic Republic
GONGO	Government-organized NGO
HDI	Human Development Index
HKCSS	Hong Kong Council of Social Services
ICA-N	Institute of Cultural Affairs Nepal
ICA-G	Institute of Cultural Affairs Guatemala
ICD	Institute for Communication and Development
ICSR	International Center for Social Research
IDRC	International Development Resource Centre
IMTI	International Management and Training Institute
INGO	International NGO
JRF	Judicial Reform Foundation
KMT	Kuo Ming Tang regime

KPACT	Korea Pact on Anti-corruption and Transparency
KTOS	Cyprus Turkish Primary School Teachers' Union
LGBT	Lesbian, gay, bisexual, and transgender
LIC	Legal-Information Centre for NGOs
MCIC	Macedonian Center for International Cooperation
MC-MED	Management Centre of the Mediterranean
MIDES	Ministry of Social Development
MO	Mass organization
MOFA	Ministry of Foreign Affairs
MOSA	Ministry of Social Affairs
MPRP	Mongolian People's Revolutionary Party
MZL	Macedonian Women's Lobby
NAG	National Advisory Group
NATO	North Atlantic Treaty Organization
NC	Nepali Congress
NCO	National Coordinating Organization
NDC	National Democratic Congress
NFPLEA	Not-for-Profit Legal Entities Act
NGO	Nongovernmental organization
NGORC	NGO Research Centre
NICVA	Northern Ireland Council for Voluntary Action
NIT	National Index Team
Norad	Norwegian Agency for Development Cooperation
NPP	New Patriotic Party
NRM	National Resistance Movement
NROS	Civil Society Development Foundation
NU	Nahdlatul Ulama
ODI	Overseas Development Institute
OECD	Organisation for Economic Co-operation and Development
PAG	Project Advisory Group
PAPAD	Professional Alliance for Peace and Democracy
PNDC	Provisional National Defence Council
PRC	People's Republic of China
RESOCIDE	Civil Society Organization Network for Development
RTP	Rally of the Togolese People

RUF	Revolutionary United Front
SAG	Stakeholder Assessment Group
SCVO	Scottish Council for Voluntary Organisations
SIDA	Swedish International Development Cooperation Agency
SOBOCE	Bolivian Cement Society
STUC	Scottish Trade Union Congress
TADHR	Taiwan Association for the Development of Human Rights
TDF	Taiwan Democracy Foundation
THKU	Taiwan Home Keepers Union
TRNC	Turkish Republic of Northern Cyprus
TSI	Third Sector Institute
TUSEV	Third Sector Foundation of Turkey
UNDP	United Nations Development Programme
USAID	United States Agency for International Development
VAT	Value added tax
VIDS	Vietnam Institute of Development Studies
VMRO	Internal Macedonian Revolutionary Organization
VNGO	Vietnamese NGO
VSPC	Voluntary Sector Partnership Council
VUSTA	Vietnam Union for Science and Technology Association
WAHD	Women's Action for Human Dignity
WALHI	Wahana Lingkungan Hidup Indonesia
WCVA	Wales Council for Voluntary Action
WVS	World Value Survey
ZDOS	Association of Slovenian Societies
ZSU	Association of Slovenian Foundations

Introduction

~ ~

Civil Society—Important, yet Largely Uncharted Territory

Introducing the Global Survey on the State of Civil Society

Volkhart Finn Heinrich

Civil society has become a truly global phenomenon, both as a social practice and a theoretical concept. Over the last decade and a half, an associational revolution[1] has swept large parts of the world, symbolized by the extraordinary growth in citizens' associations and their increasing role in local, national, and global governance as well as development processes. Surely, people's practices of collective action have existed throughout history; political, sociocultural, and socioeconomic changes over the last decades, however, have provided a uniquely fertile ground for the emergence of new forms of civic engagement on an unprecedented scale. This qualitatively and quantitatively new phenomenon of collective citizen action, outside the confines of the family, market, and state, which is now widely described as "civil society," soon became the beacon of a more democratic, equitable, just, transparent, and peaceful world.

Despite the popularity of civil society in public discourse, its actual shape, dynamics, and contributions to social progress remain somewhat nebulous. This first edition of the *Global Survey on the State of Civil Society*, which draws on information from the CIVICUS Civil Society Index (CSI) Project, seeks to address this void and make a contribution to the analysis of existing civil societies by examining their various forms, roles, and challenges in countries around the world. This introduction briefly scans the current global environment for civil society practice and research in order to situate this report in its larger context. It then describes some of the key issues and themes emerging from CSI studies in forty-four countries.[2]

Civil Society under Increased Scrutiny

After a period of widespread belief in civil society's almost magical power to curb the world's most glaring ills in the early to mid-1990s, the first years of the new millennium saw the emergence of perspectives on civil society that were more critical. Criticism about the unchecked influence of presumably unaccountable NGOs and other forms of citizen organizations was voiced, most fervently by conservative intellectuals and politicians.[3] Also, more balanced analyses of civil society's actual contributions to development and governance sometimes arrived at ambiguous or even negative conclusions.[4] To make matters worse, in recent years, there has been a return of distinctly state-centered as well as market-dominated development approaches. More alarmingly, the world has seen a widespread undermining of civil liberties and discrediting of democratic practices, which together are likely to pose a significant threat to civil society's viability in the years to come. Thus, civil society around the world faces formidable challenges and an uncertain future.

The current state of the concept of civil society does not fare much better, as evidenced by the existing plethora of definitions of "civil society." A consensus on how to define civil society has not been reached, and a startling share of scholarly articles on the topic regularly devote an initial section to the definitional disputes, conceptual confusion, and operational vagueness of the concept. Civil society theory has also not made any significant headway in the recent past, and empirical studies rarely go beyond in-depth case studies of specific organizations or overall descriptions of specific components of civil society, such as the NGO sector or trade unions. Consequently, some authors have announced that civil society theory and research are in crisis, and some have called for expelling the concept from the repertoire of sociopolitical analysis and research if these conceptual and operational problems cannot be solved.[5]

The Need for Self-critical Analysis

It was in this context of controversy and increased scrutiny that the international civil society network CIVICUS: World Alliance for

Citizen Participation recognized the need for more and better information on the actual state of civil society, particularly outside of the so-called Western societies. It was CIVICUS' belief that this need could be met best through a self-critical assessment by civil society actors, which would promote a better understanding of civil society—as well as its contributions and limitations—among civil society itself, as well as among policymakers, academics, and the public at large. Although the economic functions of the nonprofit sector had been examined by the Johns Hopkins Comparative Nonprofit Sector Project[6] and the contours and key developments of global civil society are now outlined annually in the Global Civil Society Yearbook,[7] there was a dearth of information on the state of civil society and its key strengths, challenges, and future prospects in various countries. It was felt that the myths about civil society[8] generated by the civil society hype of the 1990s should give way to a sober, honest, and transparent assessment of civil society's actual strengths and weaknesses. Such an empirical assessment could investigate prevailing assumptions, and, it was hoped, provide sound arguments against those who aim to curtail civil society's role in public affairs. In addition, it was hoped that an empirical analysis of civil society might contribute to breaking the impasse of definitional debates at the theoretical level by presenting an examination of what civil society actually looks like in practice. CIVICUS therefore developed a civil society assessment tool called the Civil Society Index (CSI), which examines the state of civil society in countries around the world.

The CIVICUS Civil Society Index

The CSI aims to make a unique contribution to civil society's knowledge base and practice by combining in-depth research with a participatory needs assessment. In other words, it seeks to utilize knowledge for joint reflection, assessment, and action in order to ultimately strengthen civil society and its contribution to positive social change. The CSI defines civil society as "the arena, outside of the family, the state, and the market where people associate to advance common interests." To assess civil society, it makes use of the Civil Society Diamond tool,[9] which disaggregates the state of civil society into four key dimensions: structure, environment, values, and impact. The actual implementation of the project at country level is carried out by a prominent civil society organization or research institute that conducts a secondary data review and coordinates the process of collecting primary data from a variety of sources, such as a population survey, a stakeholder questionnaire and consultative meetings, a media review, and expert interviews. A key feature of the CSI approach is its participatory nature. The CSI involves a National Advisory Group (NAG), which is made up of representatives from civil society, government, the media, academia, the donor community and the private sector, stakeholder consultations in different regions of the country, and, most importantly, a national workshop, in which the main findings of the assessment are presented and discussed and key recommendations for strengthening civil society are developed.[10] For those environments where resource and time constraints did not allow for an implementation of the full CSI, CIVICUS developed and applied the Civil Society Index Shortened Assessment Tool (CSI-SAT), which relies on secondary data only.

Between 2003 and 2006 the CSI and CSI-SAT have been implemented in more than 50 countries by CIVICUS and its country partners.[11] In June 2006, an international conference was held to discuss emerging findings and begin the process of evaluating the project approach and tools. Although it is clear that the current version of the CSI is by no means a perfect tool—rather it is an initial step in the complex endeavor of assessing and strengthening civil society—its general usefulness for practice, policy, and research has been largely recognized by partners and external stakeholders.[12]

Global Survey on the State of Civil Society

This first volume of the *Global Survey on the State of Civil Society* presents, in a substantially condensed manner, some of the key outputs of the CSI project in the form of forty-four concise country chapters describing the current state of civil society, its key strengths and weaknesses, as well as major recommendations for strengthening civil society. This book casts a wide net in terms of geography, covering Asia-Pacific, Europe, Latin America, the Middle East, and Sub-Saharan Africa. It includes a variety of organizational types, such as community-based organizations, trade unions, and professional associations, while often focusing on NGOs and social movements as the most vibrant and visible subsectors of civil society. A multilevel analysis is presented by incorporating the micro-level of individual citizens, the meso-level of organizations, and the macro-level of key attributes of the civil society sector as a whole. Such a comprehensive approach to assessing civil society is likely to yield eclectic yet complementary perspectives on its current state. Yet, given the complexity and diversity of civil society, such an encompassing methodology is deemed appropriate, and even necessary, to capture the variety of forms, actions, and motivations that exist in collective citizen action around the world today.[13] As such, this first *Global Survey on the State of Civil Society* seeks to showcase civil society in all its diversity.

The list of countries included in this report is a direct consequence of the specific CSI selection process. CIVICUS does not handpick countries. To ensure local ownership of the project, CIVICUS selects country partners through an open call for statements of interest. This has led to some imbalances in the geographic representation of the project. For instance, Eastern European countries were particularly interested in applying the CSI tool and succeeded in raising the required resources, which led to an overrepresentation of this region. In contrast, Africa, despite rather strong interest, features less prominently, due particularly to resource constraints. Given the coverage of forty-four countries, this edition of the report, despite its title, does not pretend to have achieved a truly global coverage. However, the title signals CIVICUS' aspiration to expand the CSI project to a larger number of countries and therefore to increase the country coverage in subsequent editions of the report.

Emerging Themes

Specific themes, patterns, and trends, with regard to the state of civil society around the world, will be explored in detail in the second volume of the *Global Survey on the State of Civil Society*.[14] However, some of the key themes from the CSI assessments are highlighted here in brief to give the reader a flavor of the emerging findings:

- *Unity in diversity.* Not surprisingly, the forty-four chapters of this book attest to the immense diversity in the forms, roles, and contexts of civil society around the world, from the well-established civil societies in Western Europe, to the often top-down nature of organized civil society in most of post-Communist Europe, to community-driven forms of civic life in many countries in the global South. Although many country-specific adaptations of the proposed civil society definition were made, none of the partners mentioned a fundamental challenge in applying the definition, indicating the general applicability of the CIVICUS definition of civil society to different contexts and cultures.

- *Accountability challenge.* The question of civil society organizations' (CSOs) legitimacy, accountability, and transparency surfaced in almost every country's assessment. If there is one common theme across the diverse set of participating countries, it is the question of how civil society can improve its own accountability and transparency to ensure public trust, and to support and play a stronger role in governance. Although the CSI shows that civil society stakeholders have identified the problem, it also highlights the scarcity of appropriate accountability mechanisms and processes. This is clearly an area for further applied research and practical experimentation.[15]
- *Citizen engagement and organized civil society.* These two features form the backbone of assessing civil society's structure. Interestingly, these two components do not necessarily go hand in hand. Often, high levels of citizen participation in civil society activities, such as volunteering, charitable giving, and participating in CSOs or forms of nonpartisan political actions, are not coupled with a strong, organized civil society in terms of levels of organization, networks, infrastructure, and resources, and vice versa. The juxtaposition of these two structural elements also attests to the mantra that civil society is, in fact, much more than just NGOs. Particularly when examining where the bulk of people's participation in civic activities takes place, NGOs do not feature strongly at all. Aside from participating in direct forms of civic activism and in the activities of trade unions, social movements, faith-based organizations, sports, and recreational groups, people engage in a myriad of community associations, which constitute a key reference point in their daily lives. Such forms of local-level civil society are much more prevalent in the global South than elsewhere.
- *Sustainability challenges.* Spanning countries in the North, East, and South, questions about organizational sustainability remain high on the civil society agenda. The CSI assessment shows that there are no easy fixes for issues of financial sustainability and civil society's relations with its various donors. However, CSOs seem to diverge in the extent to which they seek innovative solutions to sustainability challenges. A focus on local resource mobilization—be it corporate, public, or individual—is emerging as a potential solution, as are recommendations to make professional careers in CSOs more attractive to young and educated segments of the population.

- *Service versus advocacy roles.* There also seems to be an almost global pattern of stronger roles for civil society in working with the population, such as through direct service provision, capacity-building, and public education, rather than in advocacy and monitoring functions toward the state and private sector. Although this is at least partially due to civil society's limited capacity for influencing policies, it also seems that governments are often only paying lip-service to the notion of participatory governance.[16]
- *Civil society and the private sector.* In most countries, mutual suspicion or indifference dominates the relationships between CSOs and business. When businesses engage with CSOs, they focus on cultural and recreational organizations, but generally stay away from engaging and supporting advocacy and CSOs oriented on the public good. The CSI study also noted a tendency among the private sector in many countries to dismiss its role and responsibility in community and public affairs. At the same time, civil society seems to be aware that a stronger relationship with the private sector would present both advantages as well as challenges.
- *It's the state, stupid.* A cursory analysis of the key contributing factors to a strong civil society reveals the centrality of strong state institutions that uphold the crucial pillars of a democratic society. Although there are examples of civil society *standing in* for a weak or failed state, a truly sustainable and vibrant civil society is most often found when there is a democratic and effective system of governance that respects the rule of law. Thus, a strong civil society coexists with a well-governed and strong state. In fact, these are likely to reinforce one another. The CSI analysis also suggests that in many countries it is the limited strength of the state, rather than its limited democraticness, that is the main problem. Among the countries participating in the CSI, many made significant progress on human rights and rule of law in recent years, while effective forms of governance, which make the state strong, were often lacking.

These and a number of other crosscutting themes will be explored in much greater detail in the second volume of the *Global Survey on the State of Civil Society*, which will present a comparative analysis of the emerging findings.

Limitations

The CSI has been a wide-ranging and complex undertaking and there are a number of important limitations, which need to be mentioned at the outset. First, this volume only provides country-by-country accounts of the project's main findings; comparative analysis is reserved for a second volume of the global report, which is scheduled for publication in 2008, as well as further papers and articles focusing on specific issues and regions.[17] In general, the issue of comparability of the CSI's quantitative findings in the form of indicators, subdimensions, and dimensions needs to be approached with care, since these findings essentially reflect the assessment of predominantly local stakeholders.[18]

The chapters are also a reflection of the uneven global distribution of research infrastructure and resources. While the CSI project implementations in OECD member countries and many transitional countries of Eastern Europe could tap into decades-long traditions of large-scale social research, other partners, particularly in Africa, were confronted with a *terra incognita,* where the CSI was largely the first-ever effort conducted to examine civil society.

This book is based on a new and innovative assessment tool, which necessarily has certain imperfections, such as the limited range of indicator scores, which only range from 0 to 3. CIVICUS felt that a more fine-grained assessment tool would pretend to yield a level of precise differentiation between different civil societies, which, given our limited understanding of the configurations and forms in civil society across the world, would be unfounded. Based on the large amount of information and insights generated by the project's findings, however, the development of an expanded indicator scale for future CSI applications should be possible.

A further drawback of the project relates to the limited success in preventing subjective views to enter into the assessment, particularly in the values and impact dimensions. However, as has become clear while conducting the CSI assessments, stakeholders' views and evaluations are essential in understanding the current state of civil society, particularly in generating commitment around key priorities for strengthening the sector. Thus, finding the right but difficult balance between providing objective data versus a subjective assessment is likely to remain a key task for the refined CSI methodology and approach in the years to come.

Structure of the Book

The first chapter of this book outlines the main components of the CSI's conceptual framework and research methodology. It is useful for a deeper understanding of the following forty-four country chapters, which make up the bulk of the publication.

Each country chapter is based on a comprehensive country report, which has been developed by the respective CSI country partner. Each chapter is written as a stand-alone assessment of the state of civil society and does not require an in-depth understanding of the CSI's approach and methodology. Obviously, it is extremely difficult to provide a detailed picture of the current state of civil society in such concise chapters. Although every attempt has been made to capture the essence of each civil society and to provide the most crucial information, interpretation, and recommendations of each country report, those readers who wish to learn more about civil society and the CSI application in a specific country are encouraged to read the full country reports.[19] To maximize the amount of information and analysis provided in the chapters, extensive references are not provided. The evidence presented in these chapters is either from direct primary research, conducted as part of the CSI, or from existing studies, which are properly referenced in the full country report.

Each chapter is structured as follows: it first provides a brief overview of the historical development of civil society and some key background information,[20] in an accompanying box; it then introduces the key results of the CSI's assessment, visually in the form of the Civil Society Diamond and in a more in-depth manner by describing the main aspects of civil society's structure, environment, values, and impact. Chapters that are based on the application of the full participatory CSI tool identify the key recommendations emerging from the CSI's assessment; chapters based on the CSI-SAT do not include this component. Chapters conclude with some brief general remarks. Thus, each chapter seeks to follow the CSI's dual objectives of knowledge-generation and civil society strengthening by, on the one hand, offering a basic description of the main features of civil society in a given country, and, on the other, adding an assessment on strengths and weaknesses, as well as specific suggestions for the way forward. Although CIVICUS is aware that this dual character of providing key information as well as policy recommendations is a rather unorthodox approach for a reference book, it was deemed appropriate since it reflects the specific nature of the CSI endeavor as a policy-oriented action-research project.

Although civil society is certainly not a magic bullet that is able to fix the myriad of current development and governance challenges, this report attests to the many roles and functions citizens and their associations perform in public life. Civil society is clearly such an important component of today's societies that it warrants more attention in terms of practical support, policy development, research, and analysis. CIVICUS is committed to continuing its work with civil society partners around the world to provide relevant information, critical assessments, and thought-provoking analysis on the state of civil society to make a modest contribution to deepening our understanding of civil society as the social space in which citizens confront the challenges facing humanity. It is hoped that the first *Global Survey on the State of Civil Society* is a product that showcases this commitment.

Notes

1. See Lester M. Salamon, "The Rise of the Nonprofit Sector," *Foreign Affairs* 73, no. 4 (1994):108–22, 109.
2. Fifty-three countries participated in the Civil Society Index Implementation phase 2003–2006. However, at the time of publication only forty-four country reports were complete and able to be included in this volume. The nine countries not included in this volume are Armenia, Azerbaijan, Burkina Faso, Costa Rica, East Timor, Jamaica, Mauritius, Nigeria, and Palestine.
3. See, for example, www.ngowatch.org.
4. See, for example, Omar G. Encarnacion, "On Bowling Leagues and NGOs: A Critique of Civil Society's Revival" [book review essay], *Studies in Comparative International Development* 36, no. 4 (Winter 2002):116–31; John A. Booth and Patricia Bayer Richard, "Civil Society, Political Capital, and Democratization in Central America," *Journal of Politics* 60, no. 3 (1998):780–800.
5. See Neera Chandhoke, "The 'Civil' and the 'Political' in Civil Society," *Democratization* 8, no. 2 (2001):1–24; Barry Knight, Hope Chigudu and Rajesh Tandon, *Reviving Democracy: Citizens at the Heart of Governance*, (London, UK: Earthscan, 2002):54; David Lewis, "Civil Society in African Contexts: Reflections on the Usefulness of a Concept," *Development and Change* 33, no. 4 (2002):569–86, 582; Chris Hann, "In the Church of Civil Society," *Exploring Civil Society: Political and Cultural Contexts*, ed. Marlies Glasius, David Lewis and Hakan Seckinelgin (London, UK: Routledge 2004):44–50.
6. See Lester Salamon, et al., *Global Civil Society: Dimensions of the Nonprofit Sector* (Baltimore, MD: The Johns Hopkins Center for Civil Society Studies, 1999); Lester Salamon, Wojciech Sokolowski and Associates, *Global Civil Society. Volume Two. Dimensions of the Nonprofit Sector* (Bloomfield, CT: Kumarian Press, 2004).

7. See Marlies Glasius, Mary Kaldor and Helmut Anheier (eds.), *Global Civil Society 2006/7* (London, UK: Sage, 2006).
8. See, for example, Thomas Carothers, "Think Again: Civil Society," *Foreign Policy* 117 (1999–2000):18–29.
9. The Civil Society Diamond tool has been developed for CIVICUS by Professor Helmut Anheier, then director of the Centre for Civil Society at the London School of Economics; see Helmut K. Anheier, *Civil Society: Measurement, Evaluation, Policy* (London, UK: Earthscan, 2004).
10. See Chapter 1 for a more detailed description of the CSI methodology and implementation approach.
11. Please see preface for a list of CSI country partners in the implementation phase 2003–2006.
12. See the discussion about current efforts to measure civil society in the *Journal of Civil Society* 1, no. 3; 2, no. 1; and 2, no. 2.
13. See Volkhart Finn Heinrich, *Assessing and Strengthening Civil Society Worldwide. A Project Description of the CIVICUS Civil Society Index: A Participatory Needs Assessment & Action-Planning Tool for Civil Society* (Johannesburg, South Africa: CIVICUS, 2004), for a more detailed discussion of the CSI research mix.
14. This volume is scheduled for publication by the end of 2007.
15. See CIVICUS' Legitimacy, Accountability and Transparency Programme for further information at www.civicus.org.
16. See also Monica Blagescu and John Young, *Capacity Development for Policy Advocacy: Current Thinking and Approaches among Agencies Supporting Civil Society Organisations*, ODI Working Paper 260 (London, UK: ODI, 2006).
17. For example: Lorenzo Fioramonti and V. Finn Heinrich, *Civil Society & Policy Influence: A Comparative Analysis of the Civil Society Index in Post-Communist Europe*, working paper commissioned by RAPID (London, UK: ODI, 2006).
18. See V. Finn Heinrich, "Studying Civil Society across the World: Exploring the Thorny Issues of Conceptualisation and Measurement," *Journal of Civil Society* 1, no. 3 (2005):1–18.
19. The English versions of the CSI country reports are available for download on the CSI pages at www.civicus.org. Most local language versions are available on the website of each country partner, which can be found on the CIVICUS CSI website.
20. The sources for the background information boxes include the *Encyclopedia Britannica* 2004 (country size), *2006 World Development Indicators* (population, population under 15 years, unemployment rate, and population living with less than US$ 2 a day), the *Human Development Report 2005* (urban population, seats in parliament held by women, HDI score and ranking, GDP per capita) and the *World Almanac and Book of Facts 2006* (language groups, ethnic groups and religious groups). For Cyprus, Fiji, Hong Kong, Montenegro, Northern Ireland, Orissa, Serbia, Scotland, Taiwan, and Wales, statistics provided in the respective CSI country reports were used.

Chapter 1

CIVICUS Civil Society Index—Conceptual Framework and Research Methodology[1]

VOLKHART FINN HEINRICH AND CARMEN MALENA

This chapter provides a summary of the conceptual framework and research methodology of the CIVICUS Civil Society Index (CSI) Project.[2] It begins by giving a brief account of the project's background, before outlining the methodological and conceptual foundations of the CSI. It then describes the CSI's implementation approach, the expected outcomes and outputs, and explains how the project seeks to make a contribution to bridging the gap between generating knowledge and stimulating action to strengthen civil society.

Project Background

The idea of a Civil Society Index originated in 1997, when the international NGO CIVICUS: World Alliance for Citizen Participation published the *New Civic Atlas* containing profiles of civil society in sixty countries around the world.[3] To improve the comparability and quality of the information contained in the *New Civic Atlas*, CIVICUS decided to embark on the development of a comprehensive assessment tool for civil society, the Civil Society Index.[4] In 1999, Helmut Anheier, who at the time was the director of the Centre for Civil Society at the London School of Economics, played a significant role in the creation of the CSI concept.[5] The concept was tested in fourteen countries during a pilot phase, from 2000 to 2002. Upon completion of the pilot phase, the project approach was thoroughly evaluated and refined.[6] In its first full implementation phase (2003–2005), CIVICUS and its country partners implemented the project in fifty-three countries (table 1.1[7]).

1

**Table 1.1   Countries Participating in the CSI Implementation Phase
2003–2005**

1. Argentina	19. Germany	37. Orissa (India)
2. Armenia	20. Ghana	38. Palestine
3. Azerbaijan	21. Greece*	39. Poland
4. Bolivia	22. Guatemala	40. Romania
5. Bulgaria	23. Honduras	41. Russia*
6. Burkina Faso	24. Hong Kong (VR China)	42. Scotland
7. Chile*	25. Indonesia	43. Serbia
8. China	26. Italy	44. Sierra Leone
9. Costa Rica	27. Jamaica	45. Slovenia
10. Croatia	28. Lebanon	46. South Korea
11. Cyprus**	29. Macedonia	47. Taiwan*
12. Czech Republic	30. Mauritius	48. Togo*
13. East Timor	31. Mongolia	49. Turkey
14. Ecuador	32. Montenegro*	50. Uganda
15. Egypt	33. Nepal	51. Ukraine
16. Fiji	34. Netherlands*	52. Uruguay
17. Gambia	35. Nigeria	53. Vietnam*
18. Georgia*	36. Northern Ireland	54. Wales*

*Represents the ten countries implementing the CSI-SAT.
**The CSI assessment was carried out in parallel in the northern and southern parts of
Cyprus due to the de facto division of the island. However, the CSI findings were pub-
lished in a single report as a symbolic gesture for a unified Cyprus.

During the 2003–2005 phase, in response to continuing interest
from civil society organizations (CSOs) in applying the CSI, CIVICUS
developed a shorter, less comprehensive and resource-intensive process to assess the state of civil society, the CIVICUS Civil Society
Index Short Assessment Tool (CSI-SAT). Based on the original CSI
methodology, the CSI-SAT is applicable in situations where a wealth
of secondary information on civil society is available or resource
mobilization for primary research proves to be difficult. Also, since
participation by national-level organizations in the full CSI is only
possible approximately every three years, the CSI-SAT offers a useful
tool to prepare for a full CSI and gain knowledge on the state of civil
society through an analysis of existing information.

Project Methodology

Civil society is a complex concept. The task of defining and operationalizing the concept, identifying civil society's essential features,

and designing a strategy to assess its state is a complex and potentially controversial process in itself. This section describes the key features of the CSI's civil society definition, analytical framework, and research methodology. The following principles guided the design of the CSI methodology:

1. Since the CSI seeks to assess civil society in every country around the world, there was a need to design a globally relevant and applicable framework without imposing foreign standards on specific countries.

2. Recognizing the immense variety in the forms and activities of civil society around the world, the CSI places strong importance on a flexible framework that can be adapted to fit the country-specific context. However, the international character of the project ensures that common core standards are adhered to by every participating country.

3. The primary goal for the CSI is to generate a contextually valid assessment of the state of civil society in a given country. However, responding to the interests of civil society stakeholders, who see strong benefits in comparing their state of civil society with other countries, as a secondary goal the CSI also seeks to achieve cross-country comparability of its findings.

4. Given the current lack of consensus around how to define and assess civil society, the CSI's analytical framework seeks to include a broad range of perspectives leading to a multidisciplinary approach and a comprehensive assessment framework based on seventy-four indicators.

5. Based on the view that civil society includes elements of both the civil and the uncivil, the peaceful and the violent, the CSI does not exclude any form of collective citizen action on the basis of its uncivil content. On the contrary, it seeks to reflect the (potentially uncivil) reality of civil society, rather than an ideal version of what we want civil society to look like. However, the CSI assessment is by no means value-free since it explicitly examines the extent to which civil society actually practices and promotes certain universal values, such as democracy, tolerance, or gender equity.

6. As a consequence of its action-research philosophy, the CSI assessment seeks to provide information that can easily be translated into policy recommendations and other practical actions by stakeholders.

Civil Society Definition

The CSI defines civil society as "the arena, outside of the family, the state, and the market where people associate to advance common interests."

One of the key features of this definition is the concept of civil society being an arena. The term "arena" is used to describe the particular space in a society where people come together to debate, discuss, associate, and influence broader society. Another key feature is the acknowledgment of the *fuzziness* of the boundaries between the spheres of civil society, the state, the market, and the family, since, in practice, many forms of collective citizen action are difficult to categorize into one specific sphere. The CSI emphasizes function: what is relevant is that collective citizen action is undertaken to advance common interests, rather than the specific organizational form in which the action takes place.[8] Based on the CSI's practical interest in strengthening civil society, the project also conceptualizes civil society as a political term, rather than an economic one, which would be synonymous to the nonprofit sector. The CSI focuses on collective public action in the broader context of governance and development, rather than on the economic role of nonprofit organizations in society. This political perspective leads the CSI to focus on issues of power within the civil society arena, and between civil society actors and institutions of the state and the private sector.

CSI Analytical Framework: Indicators, Subdimensions and Dimensions

The CSI uses seventy-four indicators for its civil society assessment, each of which measures an important aspect of the state of civil society.[9] These indicators are grouped together into twenty-five subdimensions, which are grouped into four dimensions: *structure, environment, values, and impact*. These four dimensions are represented graphically in the form of a Civil Society Diamond (figure 1.1).

- The *structure* dimension looks at civil society's makeup, size, and composition. This dimension examines the actors within the civil society arena, their main characteristics, and the relationships among them. It is composed of twenty-one indicators that are summarized in the following six subdimensions:

  1. Breadth of citizen participation
  2. Depth of citizen participation

Figure 1.1   Civil Society Diamond

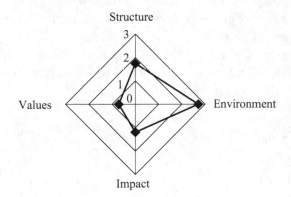

3. Diversity within civil society
4. Level of organization
5. Inter-relations
6. Resources

- The *environment* dimension examines a variety of factors influencing civil society, including political, legal, institutional, social, cultural, and economic factors, as well as the attitudes and behavior of state and private sector actors toward civil society. Although not part of civil society itself, civil society's environment is nonetheless crucial, as it might point toward root causes of potential problems. This dimension comprises twenty-three indicators that are aggregated into the following seven subdimensions:

1. Political context
2. Basic freedoms and rights
3. Socioeconomic context
4. Sociocultural context
5. Legal environment
6. State-civil society relations
7. Private sector-civil society relations

- The *values* dimension addresses the principles and values adhered to, practiced, and promoted by civil society. To date, this aspect has not received much attention, partly because civil society's values are typically predefined as positive, progressive, or democratic due to the civil society definition chosen. The CSI holds that what is crucial for judging a civil society's overall state is the ratio of civil society actors who are tolerant versus intolerant, progressive versus fundamentalist, pro-poor versus anti-poor. Values such as democracy and transparency are also critical measures of civil society's legitimacy and credibility. The values dimension is composed of fourteen indicators making up the following seven subdimensions:

1. Democracy
2. Transparency
3. Tolerance
4. Nonviolence
5. Gender equity
6. Poverty eradication
7. Environmental sustainability

- The *impact* dimension measures the impact civil society has on people's lives, policy processes, and society as a whole. Therefore, this dimension adopts a broad notion of impact, which refers not only to the end result, or how much influence civil society has had in a particular area, but also to the process, or how actively civil society was engaged in a particular area. This dimension has sixteen indicators aggregated into the following five subdimensions:

1. Influencing public policy
2. Holding state and private corporations accountable
3. Responding to social interests
4. Empowering citizens
5. Meeting societal needs

Implementation Approach

Actors Involved in the CSI Implementation

The project is implemented by national-level CSOs or research institutions that have proven research and convening abilities. These CSOs responded to CIVICUS' public call for statements of interest to take part in the project, and they underwent a thorough desk and peer review process before they were selected by CIVICUS to play the role of the National Coordinating Organization (NCO).

Figure 1.2   CSI Actors

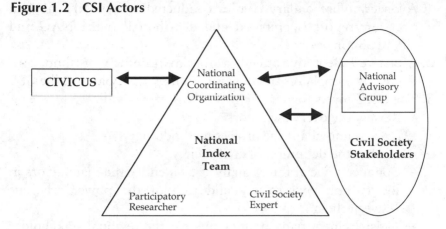

In each participating country the NCO identifies a three-person National Index Team (NIT) (figure 1.2), which includes the following members:

- Project coordinator from the NCO: coordinates the overall project implementation and acts as main contact person with CIVICUS
- Civil society expert: responsible for drafting the country report
- Participatory researcher: responsible for conducting primary research activities

The NIT carries out a preliminary stakeholder analysis and identifies the National Advisory Group (NAG), which is made up of members drawn from civil society and other stakeholder groups. The NAG's primary role is to provide overall guidance and assistance to the NIT in implementing the CSI and to score the CSI indicators. Aside from the NAG, a diverse set of stakeholders are involved in the CSI implementation through the different research activities. The aim is to include as many stakeholders as possible to guarantee a truly participatory assessment of the state of civil society within a given country. Throughout the implementation process CIVICUS advises and provides regular technical assistance and support to the NIT to guarantee a high quality implementation of the CSI project.

CSI Implementation Steps

The implementation approach can be broken down into the following steps, which were followed in the majority of countries that took part in this implementation phase:[10]

1. A review of secondary data is conducted by the NIT, and an overview report is prepared and distributed to the NAG and CIVICUS for feedback.
2. A NIT representative attends a five-day training workshop, conducted by the CIVICUS CSI team, on how to implement the CSI.
3. The NAG meets to:
   - Review the overview report
   - Discuss and adapt the project methodology
   - Discuss the definition of civil society
   - Conduct a social forces analysis to identify the main actors in society and civil society and to plot the power relations between them
   - Assist in identifying participants for the regional stakeholder consultations
4. Primary research is carried out using a mix of the following potential instruments:
   - Regional stakeholder consultations are carried out in different parts of the country in two steps. First, a select number of informed stakeholders respond to a questionnaire that covers a variety of issues related to the state of civil society. Next, they participate in a day-long stakeholder consultation to discuss the responses to the questionnaire. The group consultation is intended to scrutinize and validate individual responses, generate collective reflection, build consensus, and clarify issues of disagreement.
   - A population survey is conducted, which is designed to complement the other research methods by including data from the "grassroots," thus bringing in the voices and realities of civil society and "ordinary citizens" on the ground. Respondents are asked about their involvement in civil society and their experience with CSOs in their community.
   - Media review gathers information about civil society activities that are reported in the media and provides insight on how the media portrays civil society.
   - Desk studies consist of several research methods and studies, including a review of unpublished sources of information, key informant interviews, and two specifically designed studies to gauge the extent of corporate social responsibility and civil society's policy impact in a number of selected policy fields.
5. Findings are submitted to the civil society expert, who drafts a country report.

6. The NAG meets to score indicators, based on the draft country report and according to the project's scoring guidelines.
7. The country report is updated with results from the NAG scoring meeting.
8. A National Workshop is convened to review and validate findings, to analyze principal strengths and weaknesses of civil society, and to identify potential activities to strengthen civil society.
9. Final scores and National Workshop results are incorporated into a final country report, which is reviewed by CIVICUS, and then published.
10. A project evaluation is conducted jointly by CIVICUS and the NCO, based on the project findings and internal project monitoring

CSI Research Mix and Scoring Process

The CSI project utilizes a mix of the following data collection methods and instruments to collect information on the indicator set:

1. Secondary data review
2. Regional stakeholder consultations
3. Population surveys
4. Media review
5. Desk studies

Together these instruments help the NIT collect the data required for a narrative report on the state of civil society and for scoring the indicators. Most of the information pertaining to the seventy-four indicators is collected through more than one instrument, making it possible to apply methods of triangulation and cross-checks. The CSI research mix in a given country may include all or all or some of the methods listed above.

In order to increase comparability across countries and make the data more easily understandable and communicable, the information is categorized and used to score each indicator (from 0 to 3) according to qualitatively defined benchmarks. These numbers are then aggregated into subdimension and dimension scores, and finally used to form the Civil Society Diamond for each country.

Indicators are scored by the NAG using a citizen jury approach,[11] in which a group of citizens comes together to deliberate and make decisions on a public issue, based on presented facts. In the case of the CSI, the NAG's role is to give each indicator a score based on the evidence presented by the CSI country team, a process that is similar to passing a judgment.

Applying the CSI Research Mix

- In some countries, the *regional stakeholder consultations* drew more interest and higher levels of participation in regions outside of the capital than in the capital itself. This may be attributed to consultation fatigue among civil society stakeholders in the capital.
- The *population survey* was conducted either as a national representative sample or in a subset of diverse communities. In post-Communist countries and the Middle East the majority of CSI partners were able to raise the resources for national representative population surveys. In most other developing countries the CSI partners opted to carry out community sample surveys, due to limited financial resources and constraints in managing national representative sample surveys in vast territories, without the existence of appropriate sampling frames.
- The CIVICUS guidelines encouraged NCOs to monitor civil society news in all types of *media* (print, TV and radio). However, the majority of CSI partners monitored print media only. This was due to the flexibility that it allowed monitors, since they are not constrained to a specific time to carry out the monitoring.
- The *desk studies* recommended by CIVICUS focused on civil society's policy impact and an analysis of corporate social responsibility activities by major businesses. Additional key informant interviews were utilized only in a subset of participating countries.

The scoring exercise and the resulting Civil Society Diamond is only one part of a larger analysis of civil society captured in the comprehensive country reports. The purpose of the country report is to provide a rich picture of the state of civil society in a given country, drawing on all available information without necessarily being constrained by demands for quantifiable information and comparability.

Applying the CSI Indicator Scoring Methodology

The scoring methodology and process often proved to be somewhat difficult to apply for the NCOs. In many cases NAG members found it challenging to score the indicators based on the evidence presented by the NIT, without letting their own preconceptions and views influence their score. CIVICUS institutionalized a set of guidelines to ensure that NAG members score according to the data or provide justification in cases when they differed with the evidence.

Linking Research and Action

The CSI does not stop at the generation of knowledge; it actively seeks to link knowledge-generation with reflection and action by civil society stakeholders. To ensure this link, it uses participatory action-research methods and principles.[12]

At the heart of the CSI's knowledge-action link is the CSI National Workshop, which brings together a variety of civil society stakeholders, many of which have been actively involved in the CSI research process. The National Workshop's goal is to engage stakeholders in a critical discussion of, and reflection on, the results of the CSI initiative, in order to arrive at a common understanding of its current state and major challenges. This is a prerequisite for the use of the findings as a basis for identifying specific strengths and weaknesses, and also potential areas of improvement for civil society. If deemed appropriate, the National Workshop could culminate in the development of a specific action agenda, which is subsequently carried out by the stakeholders. This cycle of assessment, reflection, and action, coupled with the general participatory nature of the project, is at the core of CSI's attempt to successfully link research with action.

How is a participatory cycle relevant to efforts to strengthen civil society in a country? Such a mechanism can foster the self-awareness of civil society actors as being part of something larger, namely, civil society itself. As a purely educational gain, it broadens the horizon of CSO representatives through a process of reflecting upon, and engaging with, wider civil society issues that may go beyond the more narrow concerns of their respective organizations. A strong collective self-awareness among participants can also function as an important catalyst for joint advocacy activities to defend civic space or to advance the common interests of civil society.

It should be kept in mind that in many instances, civil society actors and external stakeholders will not be able to find common ground, due to irreconcilable differences in values, interests, and strategies. Even then, however, the relevance of dialogue and constructive engagement, even if it is just to agree to disagree, should not be underestimated.[13] This is especially important in countries where civil society experiences internal fragmentation, parochialism, and divisions within the sector.

There are many ways of strengthening the cohesiveness and long-term sustainability of civil society. The CSI's unique approach is to combine an *empirical assessment* with a *participatory approach* to convene, engage, and mobilize civil society's diverse actors and external stakeholders. In that sense, CIVICUS believes not only that knowledge holds little value unless put into practice, but also that knowledge is essential for meaningful action.

Notes

1. A slightly different version of this chapter has been published in a CSI paper on preliminary findings of the current implementation phase. CIVICUS Civil Society Index Team, *Preliminary Findings: CIVICUS Civil Society Index Project Phase 2003–2005* (Johannesburg, South Africa: CIVICUS, 2006).

2. For a more detailed account of the CSI, see Volkhart Finn Heinrich, *Assessing and Strengthening Civil Society Worldwide. A Project Description of the CIVICUS Civil Society Index: A Participatory Needs Assessment & Action-Planning Tool for Civil Society* (Johannesburg, South Africa: CIVICUS, 2004).

3. CIVICUS, "Legal Principles for Citizen Participation," *Toward a Legal Framework for Civil Society Organizations* (Washington, DC: CIVICUS, 1997).

4. Volkhart Finn Heinrich and Kumi Naidoo, *From Impossibility to Reality: A Reflection and Position Paper on the CIVICUS Index on Civil Society Project 1999–2001* (Washington, DC: CIVICUS, 2001); Richard Holloway, *Using the CIVICUS Index on Civil Society as a Self Assessment Tool* (Washington, DC: CIVICUS, 2001).

5. Helmut K. Anheier, *Civil Society: Measurement, Evaluation, Policy* (London: Earthscan, 2004).

6. These processes were led and managed by Finn Heinrich. The evaluation of the CSI pilot phase was undertaken by Srilatha Batliwala. Carmen Malena was contracted for the redesign of the CSI conceptual framework and research methodology.

7. This list encompasses independent countries as well as other territories in which the CSI has been implemented as of April 2006. Fifty-three countries participated in the Civil Society Index Implementation phase 2003–2006. However, at the time of publication only forty-four country reports were complete and able to be included in this volume. The nine countries not included in this volume are Armenia, Azerbaijan, Burkina Faso, Costa Rica, East Timor, Jamaica, Mauritius, Nigeria, and Palestine.

8. Volkhart Finn Heinrich, "Studying Civil Society across the World: Exploring the Thorny Issues of Conceptualisation and Measurement," *Journal of Civil Society* 1, no. 3 (2005):211–28. Norman Uphoff and Anirudh Krishna, "Civil Society and Public Sector Institutions: More Than a Zero-Sum Relationship," *Public Administration and Development* 24, no. 4 (2004):357–72.

9. For a list of indicators, see Heinrich, *Assessing and Strengthening Civil Society Worldwide*.

10. Based on the original CSI methodology, the CSI-SAT has been developed to respond to situations where a wealth of secondary information on civil society is available or resource mobilization for primary research proves to be difficult. Also, as participation by national-level organizations in the full CSI is only possible approximately every three years, the CSI-SAT offers a useful tool to prepare for a full CSI and gain knowledge on the state of civil society through an analysis of existing information. With regard to the implementation steps, the CSI-SAT does not include step 4 (primary research) and step 8 (National Workshop).

11. Jefferson Center, *The Citizen Jury Process* (Jefferson Center, 2002). Available from http://www.jefferson-center.org/index.asp?Type=B_BASIC&SEC= {2BD10C3C-90AF-438C-B04F-88682B6393BE}.

12. Paolo Freire, *Pedagogy of the Oppressed* (Harmondsworth, UK: Penguin, 1974); Orlando Fals-Borda and Muhammad Anisur Rahman, eds., *Action and Knowledge: Breaking the Monopoly with Participatory Action-Research* (New York: The Apex Press, 1991); Robert Chambers, *Whose Reality Counts? Putting the First Last* (London: IT Publications, 1997); Barry Knight, Hope Chigudu and Rajesh Tandon, *Reviving Democracy: Citizens at the Heart of Governance* (London: Earthscan, 2002).

13. Michael Edwards, *Civil Society* (London: Polity, 2004).

Chapter 2

~~

Argentina[1]

In the past few years, Argentina has recovered from the dramatic socio-economic crisis of 2001 that impoverished the population and discredited the political classes of the day. During and after this crisis, civil society played a major role in assisting the population and responding to the social needs that the state failed to address, making civil society organizations (CSOs) a widely respected group of actors in Argentinean society.

Table 2.1 Background Information for Argentina

Argentina	
Country size (square km)	2,780,092
Population (millions 2004)	38.4
Population under 15 years (2004)	26.7%
Urban population (2003)	90.1%
Seats in parliament held by women (2005)	33.7%
Language groups	Spanish (official), English, French, German, Italian, and Amerindian languages (Tehuelche, Guarani, and Quechua)
Ethnic groups	European 97%, Amerindian 3%
Religious groups	Roman Catholic 93%, Protestant 2%, Jewish 2%, other 3%
HDI score and ranking (2003)	0.863 (34th)
GDP per capita (US$ 2003)	$12,106
Unemployment rate (% of total labor force)	15.6%
Population living on less than US$2 a day (2003)	23%

Historical Overview

The origin of contemporary CSOs in Argentina dates back to the nineteenth century. As a result of a wave of immigration from Europe, a large number of associations were created to mitigate the potential alienation of immigrants, and a multiplicity of community associations, support groups, and similar organizations mushroomed throughout the country.

At the beginning of the twentieth century, economic growth and social modernization led to the proliferation of professional associations and labor unions. During the 1930s, in the midst of an ideological atmosphere oriented toward corporatism, efforts were made to regulate and monitor CSOs. Under the Peron government (1945–1955) Argentina experienced profound social, political, and economic changes toward populism and a centralized government.

The 1955 military coup triggered a period of deep social conflict and political instability, which continued for almost thirty years, until the reestablishment of democracy in 1983. This period was characterized by several military coups, which created divisions within organized civil society, with CSOs both supporting and opposing military takeovers. During this same period, two fundamental changes took place within Argentinean civil society. The first was the growth of intellectual and academic organizations, which were marginalized, or even persecuted, by the military regimes. The second was the emergence of organizations for the protection of human rights, which played a key role in the reaffirmation of democratic ideals for the sector.

The democratic process, initiated in 1983, gave way to a new phase for Argentinean civil society, and a diverse set of new CSOs came to life. Some concentrated their efforts on the promotion of human rights (for example, by demanding justice for the crimes committed by the military juntas), while others committed themselves to specific causes, such as the environment, health, education, women's rights, and poverty eradication.

The 1990s were characterized by the implementation of neoliberal policies, which entailed a severe reduction of state interventions in both the economy and social welfare. As a consequence, social conditions for most citizens rapidly worsened, unemployment escalated, and the flight of money away from the country led to the 2001 economic collapse and a severe political crisis. Although this crisis was accompanied by increased inflation, escalating poverty, and violent protests, it also opened new space for civic solidarity. CSOs played a significant role by addressing citizens' demands and assisting those in need. In the early

Figure 2.1   Civil Society Diamond for Argentina

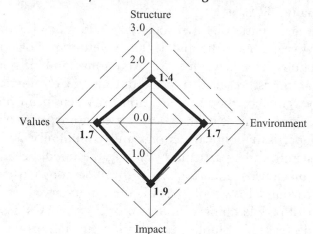

2000s, new forms of popular participation came into existence, including radical social movements, such as workers seizing control of factories abandoned by management or the so-called *piqueteros*, groups of unemployed citizens who organized roadblocks as their main form of protest. Since then, Argentinean society has gradually rebuilt itself, and relevant actors, such as the state, the private sector, and CSOs, have been exploring avenues to increase mutual dialogue and cooperation.

The State of Civil Society in Argentina

This section provides a summary of key findings of the Civil Society Index (CSI) project in Argentina. It examines the state of Argentinean civil society along four dimensions—structure, environment, values, and impact—highlighting the main weaknesses and strengths.

As visually summarized by the Civil Society Diamond (figure 2.1), civil society in Argentina has a relatively weak structure, mainly because of limited resources, but it operates in a somewhat conducive environment. Argentinean civil society is inspired by a number of important values and has played an important role in mitigating the effects of the socioeconomic crisis that hit the country in 2001.

Structure (1.4)

The structure dimension examines the makeup of civil society in terms of the main characteristics of individual citizen participation and associational life. The structure of civil society in Argentina is characterized by a significant diversity of actors, although the lack of

financial, human, and technological resources threatens the sustainability of many CSOs.

Citizen participation in civil society activities has fluctuated over
the past few years. Since the mid-1990s, several types of nonpartisan
political actions have developed in Argentina, and demonstrations
and popular unrest reached a peak during the economic crisis in
2001. However, since the normalization of Argentinean politics and
the relative improvement of the country's economy, citizen participation in nonpartisan political actions and community activities has
decreased significantly, particularly among the middle class. In 2005
only 25% of citizens undertook any form of nonpartisan political
action, and around 13% took part in community activities. Although
the number of people doing volunteer work with CSOs has also substantially decreased, volunteers still play an important role and
amount to approximately 75% of civil society's workforce.

In general, Argentinean CSOs are evenly distributed throughout
the country and represent a wide variety of social groups, including
rural and indigenous communities. Women's participation in CSOs is
significant and goes beyond those organizations specifically concerned with gender issues. Only a minority (30% to 40%, depending
on the region) of CSOs belong to an umbrella organization or network, which illustrates the struggle of Argentinean CSOs to commu-
nicate and cooperate effectively. The fact that many CSOs are
dominated by strong leaders and often lack democratic decisionmaking
processes often impedes interorganizational cooperation and the formation of effective partnerships and networks.

The CSI study found that many Argentinean CSOs have an inse-
cure financial resource base. In most cases, this leads to CSO activities
having a rather informal and ad hoc character. It also forces many
organizations to become dependent on national and international
donor agencies. Other key weaknesses of civil society's structure are
inadequate intrasectoral communication and the limited number of
formal networks within the sector.

Environment (1.7)

The environment dimension considers political, legal, socioeconomic,
and sociocultural contexts, as well as the relationships between civil
society, the state, and the private sector. In spite of the violence and
political turmoil during the socioeconomic collapse in the early
2000s, the pillars of democratic governance were not called into question and the democratic system eventually regained its credibility.

Interestingly, while the economic crisis posed an enormous strain on Argentinean society, it also triggered a stronger role for CSOs as providers of social services and propelled various local solidarity initiatives. This capacity to operate under difficult circumstances might explain why many CSOs currently manage to carry out their activities despite scarce resources. Nevertheless, it must be noted that the sociocultural environment in Argentina remains marked by low levels of interpersonal trust and public-spiritedness.

Civil society's ability to respond to critical situations is valued by various actors, and there is a growing willingness on the part of the state and the business community to develop common initiatives with CSOs. This constructive exchange has led to an increasing institutionalization of the state—civil society relationship and has created new spaces for social dialogue, such as the advisory councils for civil society representatives in the public administration. However, stakeholders involved in the CSI assessment express concern that the growing interdependence of the state and civil society, and the fairly non-transparent mechanisms governing state funding to CSOs, could lead to an erosion of civil society's autonomy.

Although the relationship between CSOs and the private sector is still in its infancy, it has potential. Most private sector representatives perceive CSOs' role in society as particularly positive, and practices of corporate philanthropy and corporate social responsibility (CSR) are becoming common among the main corporations operating in the country. However, the level of private sector funding remains limited. Only 13% of the surveyed organizations admitted to having access to any private sector funding, and for 67% of those CSOs that do receive private sector funding, this source represents less than 25% of their overall income.

Civil society's environment has been significantly transformed by the socioeconomic crisis that devastated the country in 2001 and 2002. This crisis posed challenges and offered opportunities for civil society. On the one hand, it lowered the living standards of many Argentineans and increased social inequality, but on the other hand, it helped create a sense of solidarity in the country.

Values (1.7)

The values dimension examines the extent to which civil society practices and promotes positive values. Argentinean CSOs are committed to a range of important values, such as environmental protection, poverty eradication, democratic participation, and nonviolence. The primary weakness is the scant attention paid to the practice of transparency within civil society.

Due to Argentina's recent political history, which was marked by a highly repressive military junta from 1976 to 1983, the role of civil society in promoting democratic values is of crucial importance. As part of a society-wide process to re-create a democratic culture, the last twenty years have seen a significant growth in CSOs specifically focused on civil and political rights. Throughout the 1990s, new associations arose to address issues such as political accountability, the fight against corruption, and the need to strengthen citizens' rights and increase involvement in public issues.

Furthermore, Argentinean CSOs have been active in combating poverty since this problem took center stage in the late 1990s. There are also a significant number of ecological organizations in Argentina that promote environmental preservation and sustainability. Some are local branches of international groups, but many are small associations dedicated to specific problems in local communities. They work on a wide variety of environmental issues and are active in the preservation of natural resources.

According to the CSI assessment, transparency is the only value that Argentinean civil society does not practice or promote widely. A 2004 survey by Transparency International found that NGOs and religious institutions are not seen as being free of corruption;[2] however, they received more positive ratings than the public and private sector institutions. Also, only 37% of CSOs comply with the government-required presentation of their annual financial reports. Thus, the CSI study concludes that a culture of public transparency and accountability has yet to take root in Argentinean CSOs. A number of recommendations were put forward on how civil society should instill such a culture in its own operations as well as in the public and private sectors.

Impact (1.9)

The impact dimension assesses civil society's role in governance and society at large. In Argentina, civil society's impact emerges as its most prominent strength. CSOs can rely on widespread public trust, have a strong presence in society, play a key role in meeting social needs, and have a growing influence on the policymaking processes.

After 2001, when the political system lost the credibility and capacity to address social needs, CSOs managed to mitigate the consequences of Argentina's economic disaster and helped the population recover and rebuild the country. This may help to explain why CSOs, with the exception of trade unions and political parties, are the most trusted social actors in the country. As a consequence of their actions and the government's increasing openness, CSOs are enjoying a growing role in policymaking. New models of collaboration and cooperation have been introduced at different levels of government, which could further improve civil society's contribution to policymaking, particularly in the area of social policy. At the same time, CSOs' contribution to certain policy areas, such as the national budget, is almost nonexistent, since government does not encourage the involvement of civil society in this area and few organizations have the necessary knowledge to provide input into the national budgeting process.

Two high-profile areas where CSOs' impact is significant are human rights and social policies. Examples such as the abrogation of the *ley de la obediencia debida* (due obedience laws) and *ley del punto final* (final period law), which granted amnesty or sentence reductions to many perpetrators who committed human rights violations with the military juntas, show that civil society has exerted significant pressure through years of constant activity. As a result of these popular campaigns, rallies, conferences, and demonstrations, the Argentinean public is more aware of the risks stemming from potential breakdowns of the democratic system and supports the role of civil society as a guardian of democracy.

CSOs do not show the same degree of effectiveness in holding the state and private sector accountable. Recently, however, public institutions have begun to respond to civil society's activism by introducing a number of transparency mechanisms, such as websites and formal procedures aimed at strengthening budget transparency and budget control mechanisms for citizens. Civil society's activities to monitor private corporations have only recently begun, and to date, there has been no visible impact in this area.

Argentinean CSOs are generally able to assist the population when the political system fails, and their role is recognized by the state and the private sector. In the past few years, this has led to a growing, albeit still limited, influence of CSOs in policymaking, although civil society is less effective in holding the state and, even less so, the private sector accountable.

Recommendations

The following recommendations are drawn from the CSI National Workshop held in Buenos Aires in November 2005, in which over 100 different civil society actors, academics, journalists, and state representatives participated:

- Facilitate information exchange among CSOs and increase public visibility of CSOs' actions, for example, by improving links with mass media, and by strengthening CSOs' communications skills.
- Promote greater participation by civil society in the development and planning of national strategies aimed at poverty eradication. This would ensure the participation of poor and marginalized communities. Emphasis needs to be placed on empowering these groups.
- Review CSOs' transparency and internal democracy to improve their performance and accountability to the general public. CSOs should develop common tools and mechanisms, such as performance standards and a code of ethics.
- Expand CSOs' monitoring role with regard to environmental policies, to guarantee that Argentina becomes a model of sustainable development.
- Improve dialogue between civil society and the state and the private sector. CSOs' contribution to public policy should be part of an institutionalized involvement of civil society in decisionmaking processes, and its influence should move beyond certain specific policy sectors.

Conclusion

The socioeconomic crisis that hit Argentina in 2001 and 2002 was an extremely painful blow to a society that was among the most developed in Latin America, but it also offered new opportunities for civic activism. New forms of citizen participation emerged, radical social movements such as the *piqueteros* came to the fore, and CSOs filled many gaps left by the state, by supporting people in need.

With the normalization of the sociopolitical situation, the state regained its role and popular mobilization decreased. Nevertheless, CSOs effectively exploited their newly won trust and continue to play an important role in society and governance. Thus, if government, civil society, and other relevant actors, particularly the private sector, are able to learn from past mistakes, Argentina could become an example of a country that managed to recover from widespread socioeconomic collapse and to build new forms of participatory democracy.

CSI Report

GADIS, *Civil Society from Within—Times of Crisis, Times of Opportunities: CIVICUS Civil Society Index Report for Argentina* (Buenos Aires, Argentina: GADIS, 2006).

Notes

1. The CSI assessment was implemented in Argentina by GADIS from 2004 to 2006. This chapter presents the main findings of the CSI and is based on a comprehensive country report for Argentina, which can be accessed on the CSI pages on the CIVICUS website at http://www.civicus.org.
2. They received a score of 2.9 and 3.0, respectively, on a scale from 1 (not corrupt) to 5 (highly corrupt).

Chapter 3

Bolivia[1]

Bolivia is characterized by deep social inequalities, simmering social conflicts, and weak governance institutions, which impede civil society's role in the country's development and governance processes. However, with the recent election of President Evo Morales and the installation of a pro–civil society government, Bolivian civil society may be entering a period of more cooperative relations with the Bolivian state. The Civil Society Index (CSI) project was implemented on the eve of Morales's rise to power. Therefore, it presents a picture of civil society operating under the old regime, while also pointing toward emerging opportunities resulting from the change in government.

Table 3.1 Background Information for Bolivia

Bolivia	
Country size (square km)	1,098,581
Population (millions 2004)	9
Population under 15 years (2004)	38.5%
Urban population (2003)	63.4%
Seats in parliament held by women (2005)	19.2%
Language groups	Spanish, Aymara, and Quechua (all official)
Ethnic groups	Quechua 30%, Mestizos 30%, Aymara 25%, whites 15%
Religious groups	Roman Catholic 95% (official)
HDI score and ranking (2003)	0.687 (113th)
GDP per capita (US$ 2003)	$2,587
Unemployment rate (% of total labor force)	5.5%
Population living on less than US$2 a day (2002)	42.2%

Historical Overview

Modern Bolivian civil society was spearheaded by the miners' movement. For most of the 1900s, the Bolivian economy was highly dependent on the mining industry. In 1985, after a series of military regimes, which did not leave much space for independent civic activism, a democratic government came to power. Bolivia also underwent a process of economic reform, mostly characterized by structural adjustment policies, which led to the closing of mining companies and cuts in social expenditure.

In this new context *campesino* (peasant) and indigenous movements came to the fore. Since the 1970s *campesino* and indigenous groups began a gradual process of political, cultural, and ideological emancipation, culminating in the struggle for the recognition of indigenous rights. The popularity of the *campesino*-indigenous movement was supported by the vast number of migrants who had left the rural areas in search of a better life in the cities, and who constituted the backbone of the urban proletariat. However, the prominence of the *campesino* movement within Bolivian civil society did not result in a loss of power for other organizations. Instead, throughout the 1990s, new business organizations, mainly those associated with the hydrocarbon industry, saw their power grow significantly.

In 2000 the government's credibility crisis worsened, due to tensions arising around the issue of socioeconomic rights and the provision of basic services. The *Guerra del Agua* (Water War) was sparked by the privatization of water and the rise in service fees. In February 2003 police forces joined the worker strikes and confronted the army. The conflict ended with the cancellation of the contract signed with a multinational corporation. In October 2003 the *Guerra del Gas* (Gas War) led to the resignation of the president, Sanchez de Lozada. Finally, in 2005, popular mobilization brought about the downfall of the new president, Carlos Mesa, who had succeeded Lozada eighteen months earlier. The subsequent elections in December 2005 were won by the *Movimiento al Socialismo*, in which labor organizations, affiliated with the *cocaleros* (coca growers), had organized themselves into a *campesino*-indigenous political movement. This movement and its leader, Evo Morales, now lead the Bolivian government.

The State of Civil Society in Bolivia

This section provides a summary of key findings of the CSI project in Bolivia. It examines the state of Bolivian civil society along four

Figure 3.1 Civil Society Diamond for Bolivia

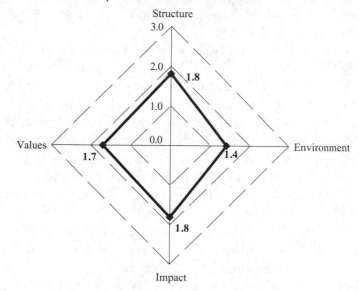

dimensions—structure, environment, values and impact—highlighting the main weaknesses and strengths.

The Civil Society Diamond (figure 3.1) indicates that civil society's structure is quite strong in Bolivia, thanks to widespread citizen participation; however, it is operating in a slightly disabling environment, mainly due to corruption-related problems and a weak state. Civil society's promotion and practice of positive values is moderate, mainly due to the limited attention paid to environmental protection and internal accountability mechanisms, while civil society's impact on society at large is relatively significant.

Structure (1.8)

The structure dimension examines the makeup of civil society in terms of the main characteristics of individual citizen participation and associational life. In Bolivia, there are significant levels of individual citizen participation, which tend to increase in times of social conflict. A large number of people give money to charity, even though the level of volunteering is lower than expected for such a participatory society. Around 70% of citizens are members of civil society organizations (CSOs), particularly faith-based organizations and community-based associations. Bolivia's civil society is especially vibrant in rural areas, where 83.9% of citizens participated in nonpartisan political actions in the last year, compared to 75.1% in the urban areas. However, some marginalized groups remain significantly underrepresented in CSO membership and leadership. In particular, the poor, sexual minorities, and women rarely lead CSOs.[2]

Most CSOs rely primarily on membership fees for their financial resources and, to a certain degree, on international donors. Financial resources are often insufficient for organizations to fully achieve their goals. Interestingly, this relatively low level of financial resources coexists with a sufficient level of human and technical resources.

Although many organizations are members of federations and networks, such as confederations of trade unions and indigenous groups, the civil society sector is rather fragmented and poorly coordinated. The stakeholders participating in the CSI assessment feel communication between CSOs is limited and unsystematic, mainly due to power disputes among CSO leaders. This results in the creation of various short-term alliances that are at times in opposition to each other, especially in situations of social conflict.

The structure of Bolivian civil society presents a mixed picture. Citizens eagerly associate and mobilize around common interests and needs, which helps enlarge the space for direct citizen participation and strengthen the role of civil society. However, organized civil society is rather weak, due to the limited availability of financial resources to CSOs and lack of cohesion within the sector.

Environment (1.4)

The environment dimension considers political, legal, socioeconomic, and sociocultural contexts, as well as the relationships between civil society, the state, and the private sector. According to the CSI assessment, Bolivian civil society is operating in a slightly disabling environment.

Bolivia is the poorest country in South America and has undergone a severe socioeconomic crisis during the past few years. The Bolivian crisis is epitomized by citizens' limited access to basic services, particularly potable water, which particularly affects rural areas with high population growth rates and areas that lack proper irrigation and sanitation systems. The impact of the socioeconomic crisis on society is amplified by the Bolivian state's weak institutional structure and by the fact that decentralization is just beginning. Thus, state institutions have a limited presence in remote areas and authoritarian political practices, such as patronage, persist at the local level.

The state's reputation is further weakened by high levels of corruption in the public administration. As reported by Transparency International, the Bolivian state is one of the most corrupt in the world and, according to the Latinobarómetro 2004 survey, more than one-third of citizens believe that police, magistrates, and public administrators are regularly bribed.

Although the National Dialogue Law of 2001 created a number of so-called social control mechanisms to enable CSOs to better interact with policymakers, these mechanisms have only proven effective at the local level, while dialogue with central government has remained limited. The legal environment also presents challenges to civil society. For example, the CSO registration process is complex, often depending on personal contacts and favoring specific sectors. However, it is difficult for government to co-opt CSOs, mainly due to the weakness of state institutions and the fact that few organizations receive public funds. Also, the private sector is largely indifferent to civil society, and corporate social responsibility (CSR) initiatives are particularly limited.

In this difficult socioeconomic and political environment, Bolivian civil society appears to have grown autonomous and distant from the state. The state has shown its incapacity to respond to societal demands, and CSOs are seen as an alternative to the discredited public administration, especially in rural areas where confidence in CSOs is particularly high.

Values (1.7)

The values dimension examines the extent to which civil society practices and promotes positive values. Bolivian civil society received a moderate rating for this dimension, mainly due to its lack of focus on environmental sustainability and gender equity, as well as its limited practice of transparency.

Bolivian civil society is particularly active in promoting democratic participation, poverty eradication, and ethnic equality, and it is generally peaceful and nonviolent. Civil society only occasionally responds aggressively to state violence, as with the riots of 2003 and 2005; however, this aspect tends to be strongly emphasized by the media. Although generally active in encouraging tolerance, only a minority of organizations promote tolerance toward sexual minorities and people living with HIV/AIDS. In Bolivian society, tolerance for these groups is low and tends to diminish during periods of social tension.

Although CSOs are extremely vocal in denouncing corruption within the public administration, many stakeholders felt that corrupt practices also exist within civil society. In their opinion, corruption in civil society is due to a lack of experience on the part of the leadership and due to members not proactively holding their leaders accountable.

Women's limited representation in civil society leadership positions may explain why CSOs only recently began to commit themselves to promoting principles of gender equality in society at large. However, in the past few years women have been taking on more significant responsibilities in CSOs. This shift was particularly visible in the *campesino* groups, in the *cocalero* movement in Chapare, and in the city of El Alto, where new women-led organizations have emerged.

It is important to point out that the participation of indigenous groups in civil society has grown significantly in recent years. Although this growth has not eliminated the problem of ethnic exclusion in society at large, CSOs have carried out a host of activities to support the rights of indigenous communities, particularly in the fields of culture, property, and political participation.

Environmental sustainability is the weakest value in Bolivian civil society. According to stakeholders, this is mainly due to a lack of information on environmental issues. Moreover, immediate socioeconomic concerns limit the significance of environmental issues on CSOs' agendas.

Impact (1.8)

The impact dimension assesses civil society's role in governance and society at large. Bolivian civil society is extremely active in the political arena, but because of the government's limited attention to most CSOs' demands and the lack of technical expertise on the part of CSOs, this rarely translates into direct impact on policy.

The few institutional channels that exist, such as the National Social Control Mechanism, are viewed by most civil society actors as ineffective, which makes mobilization and protest the most viable instruments available to exert influence on the government. However, although the adversarial relationship between civil society and the state can bring about dramatic political changes, it does not allow civil society to have a systematic role in policymaking.

Specific policy impact studies, carried out as part of the CSI study, confirm this finding. For example, civil society played a role in the downfall of President Sanchez de Lozada in 2003. Yet it was not successful in obtaining a formal incrimination of him by the judiciary. Another example is the Landless Movement, which publicly denounced the nonobservance of the Agrarian Reform Law and forced the government to begin the land redistribution process. However, to date, it has not been successful in moving the implementation process forward. Also, the influence of Bolivian CSOs on the state's budgetary process is hampered by a lack of resources and limited technical expertise. Due to such limitations and a certain level of reticence on the part of the government, only a few organizations, usually professional NGOs with the necessary technical and financial resources, are able to utilize formal venues to voice their views, generally with little impact.

These examples might explain why most stakeholders feel that CSOs are not successful in holding the state accountable. Although very active in mobilizing the affected population against state policies, very few CSOs have the technical resources and capacity to monitor government actions and act as watchdogs. The experience of the social control mechanisms established in 2001 has shown that CSOs' capacity to hold public authorities accountable is much more developed at the local level, where it benefits from a more conducive dialogue with local representatives, than at the national level, where hostility and confrontation marks the relationship between civil society and government.

The promotion of corporate social responsibility has only recently become part of civil society's agenda and the impact remains limited. Although many companies do not fulfill their social obligations and many workers enjoy limited protection and guarantees, large corporations, such as the privately owned Bolivian Cement Society (SOBOCE) and the oil company PETROBRAS, appear more eager to collaborate with CSOs when it comes to corporate responsibility toward society in general than when it relates to their own labor force.

Bolivian civil society plays an important role in informing and educating citizens, especially on crucial socioeconomic issues. Nevertheless, the ineffective public education system and high levels of illiteracy limit the overall impact of civil society's activities. Women's organizations are particularly active in empowering women in society at large and lobbying for specific laws.[3] However, their impact is limited since these laws have neither resolved the problems of social and economic inequality between men and women, nor significantly transformed discriminatory cultural attitudes.

Amid the widespread socioeconomic crisis in Bolivia, the issue of basic service provision triggered social conflict and led to the emergence of citizen movements. Examples include the uprisings in Cochabamba in 2000 and in El Alto in 2005. Another consequence of the socioeconomic situation, and particularly the lack of formal employment, is the prominence of the issue of income generation in CSOs' work. The main civil society activities in this area are implementing developmental programs in rural areas and promoting small businesses. The wide reach of these activities is evident in the fact that, according to the CSI population survey, during the past twelve months the majority of community dwellers participated in civil society initiatives aimed at generating income.

In general, civil society is active in addressing a wide range of societal needs, such as education, health, and the development of agriculture. According to a relative majority of citizens (43%), CSOs are far more reliable in providing services to marginalized groups than state institutions (14%) and private companies (14%) are. Nevertheless, some services fall under the specific responsibility of the state, such as building roads and supplying infrastructure, and these are out of the reach of CSOs.

The analysis of the impact dimension shows that civil society is particularly active in the political sphere and in providing services to marginalized groups. In spite of CSOs' significant commitment, the ineffective public administration limits civil society's impact on social development and, in various sectors, undermines the overall impact of CSOs' initiatives.

Recommendations

The following recommendations are drawn from the CSI National Workshop held in La Paz in November 2005, in which over 120 civil society actors and state representatives participated:

- Strengthen institutional dialogue structures: CSOs should improve their knowledge of the institutional dialogue mechanisms set up by the state in its legislative, executive, and judicial branches and use these to bring social demands to the forefront of the national political agenda.
- Improve CSOs' skills in influencing policymaking: CSOs should work together to improve their understanding of political processes and make more effective use of the control mechanisms, such as the social control mechanism. Civil society must also exercise its right to access public information more effectively.
- Renewed focus on education: The education system should expand its focus to include topics related to tolerance of minority groups and other civic values.
- Economic reforms and redistribution: For civil society to prosper in Bolivia, the state must improve the socioeconomic conditions and redistribute resources to guarantee social cohesion and equity.

Conclusion

Bolivian civil society is particularly vibrant and shows high levels of citizen participation, especially in rural areas, where informal forms of collective action are widespread. Similarly, the *campesino*-indigenous movement is the most prominent actor within civil society. However, its impact and public role remain limited, primarily due to antagonism in its relationship with a weak state. Although CSOs are substituting for the state in areas where the public administration is poorly institutionalized, the lack of an effective public administration limits the impact of CSOs' activities on the lives of disadvantaged groups and the country's social development.

In December 2005, Evo Morales, the leader of the progressive *Movimiento al Socialismo*, won the presidential elections. The new government, which is made up of a number of civil society leaders and which has put forward a series of significant social and political reforms, should be able to address the discordance between state institutions and CSOs. The current political change might finally make the voices of the poor and marginalized heard.

CSI Report

Cecilia Salazar, Bertha Camacho and Alcira Córdova, *Civil Society in Bolivia—From Mobilization to Impact: CIVICUS Civil Society Index Report for Bolivia* (La Paz, Bolivia: Centro de Investigación y Promocion del Campesinado [CIPCA], Catholic Relief Services USCC [CRS Bolivia], 2006).

Notes

1. The CSI assessment was implemented in Bolivia by the *Centro de Investigación y Promocion del Campesinado* (CIPCA) and Catholic Relief Services-USCC (CRS Bolivia) from December 2004 to January 2006. This chapter presents the main findings of the CSI and is based on a comprehensive country report for Bolivia, which can be accessed on the CSI pages of the CIVICUS website at http://www.civicus.org.
2. The term "sexual minorities" refers to gays and lesbians, as well as transsexuals and bisexuals.
3. Women's organizations were successful in lobbying for the introduction of initiatives such as the Law against Interfamily and Domestic Violence and the Quotas Law.

Chapter 4

Bulgaria[1]

Bulgarian civil society is currently facing a series of crucial transformations, such as the withdrawal of foreign donors and far-reaching government reforms in response to the European Union (EU) accession process. The Civil Society Index (CSI) assessment shows that together these changes pose significant challenges, but they also provide real opportunities for the sustainability of the sector. Consequently, a variety of concrete recommendations for how civil society can respond to this changing environment were made by CSI participants.

Table 4.1 Background Information for Bulgaria

Bulgaria	
Country size (square km)	110,994
Population (millions 2004)	7.8
Population under 15 years (2004)	14.1%
Urban population (2003)	69.8%
Seats in parliament held by women (2005)	26.3%
Language groups	Bulgarian (official), Turkish
Ethnic groups	Bulgarian 84%, Turk 10%, Roma 5%
Religious groups	Christians 85%, Muslim 13%
HDI score and ranking (2003)	0.808 (55th)
GDP per capita (US$ 2003)	$7,731
Unemployment rate (% of total labor force)	13.7%
Population living on less than US$2 a day (2003)	6.1%

Historical Overview

Civil society has a long history in Bulgaria, dating back to the early nineteenth century. During the National Revival period, the most common civil society organizations (CSOs) were *chitalishtes* (reading clubs), which first began appearing in 1856 and quickly grew in number to 131 clubs within fourteen years.[2] During this period, Bulgarian merchant houses were also established, and artisans in urban areas formed guild associations that actively supported educational activities and scholarships for young Bulgarians.

From 1946 to 1990, under Bulgaria's socialist regime, repressive policies suppressed any political opposition to the Bulgarian Communist Party. During this period, virtually all CSOs came under the state-controlled system. For example, Bulgarian trade unions were reorganized into the General Workers' Trade Union and youth groups were reorganized into the Dimitrov Communist Youth League. When the socialist regime began to loosen its tight grip over society in the 1980s, a range of independent civil society activities emerged. The first organized protests took place in the late 1980s, when citizens of Rousse protested against chlorine pollution in their town. The strong environmental movement played an important role in the fall of Bulgaria's socialist regime, and a host of other civic organizations and initiatives emerged during this period.

During the phase of democratic consolidation in the early 1990s, there were frequent demonstrations and strikes as the liberalization of price controls led to high inflation and unemployment. In general, this era witnessed the proliferation of new Bulgarian political parties and other civic organizations, such as labor, religious, environmental, and ethnic organizations, as well as donor-funded NGOs working on a wide range of social and political issues.

The State of Civil Society in Bulgaria

Given the current lack of consensus around the concept of civil society in Bulgaria and the global nature of the CSI project, special attention was paid to defining and operationalizing the concept to ensure that country-specific factors were taken into account. The Bulgarian project focused on the entire range of CSOs, including NGOs, informal groups, associations, and active citizens.

This section provides a summary of key findings of the CSI project in Bulgaria. It examines the state of Bulgarian civil society

Figure 4.1 Civil Society Diamond for Bulgaria

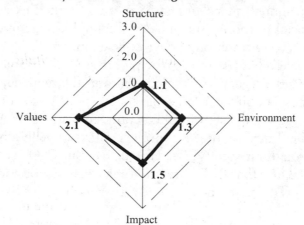

along four dimensions—structure, environment, values and impact—highlighting the main weaknesses and strengths.

The Bulgarian Civil Society Diamond (figure 4.1) visually summarizes the CSI's findings in Bulgaria. The diamond indicates a weak structure for civil society, which is hampered by weak civic engagement and civil society's high donor dependency. Civil society is operating in a slightly disabling environment characterized by positive institutional arrangements but weak support from the state, the private sector, and citizens. Civil society's values are rather strong, although concerns about CSO transparency and the donor-driven nature of its work limit civil society's reach. Consequently, the impact of Bulgarian civil society on politics and society is moderate.

Structure (1.1)

The structure dimension examines the makeup of civil society in terms of the main characteristics of individual citizen participation and associational life. This dimension receives the lowest score among the four dimensions and most notably reflects low levels of citizen participation and crucial financial vulnerabilities within the sector.

A primary barrier for civil society is the low level of citizen participation in civic activities. In 2004 only 25% of citizens belonged to a CSO and the percentage of those belonging to more than one CSO was extremely low. Participation in nonpartisan political action also remains low, with approximately 9.7% of Bulgarians having signed a petition and 9.3% having participated in meetings to resolve local problems. Only one-quarter of citizens give regularly to charity, and the average annual cash donation by citizens represents 0.5% of the average annual salary. In response to the limited extent of donations for social purposes, stakeholders highlighted the importance of reviving Bulgaria's tradition of charitable giving.

The low levels of citizen participation and charitable giving are attributed to the legacy of Communism and the tendency of citizens to view most public concerns as the responsibility of the state. Another cause is the lack of public confidence in CSOs, particularly NGOs and political parties, within the context of generally low levels of trust throughout society. The lack of trust in CSOs is likely to be linked to the fact that CSOs are often regarded as not addressing the immediate needs of the people, but rather as being driven by donor priorities.

There are also certain biases within the composition of CSO membership, in which people with medium and high socioeconomic status are overrepresented. Stakeholders identified three social groups that are particularly underrepresented: rural dwellers, the poor, and religious minorities, such as Armenians, Jews, Muslims, and Protestants. To a certain extent, this skewed makeup of CSO membership again stems from the donor-driven nature of Bulgarian civil society. In the aftermath of the socialist system, civil society's development was strongly influenced by top-down programs and foreign grant schemes, which were designed to support the institutional development of civil society. In many cases, donors developed their own agendas and priorities. Marginalized groups, such as rural dwellers, the elderly, the poor, and the Roma, became beneficiaries of projects run by urban-based CSOs, but were not involved in running CSOs themselves.

Again, as a consequence of donor priorities, organized civil society is built on a rather strong foundation of professionalism, support infrastructure, and extensive communication and cooperation among CSOs. A particular strength is the widespread presence of CSOs' self-regulatory mechanisms, even though their adherence was questioned by CSI participants.

A final key weakness of civil society's structure is its financial vulnerability. Decreasing foreign donor funding due to the upcoming EU accession and the slow growth in local sources of funding is challenging civil society to find alternative sources of income. Dependence on foreign donors has led many CSOs to focus on donors' interests ahead of the needs of local communities, which makes it difficult for CSOs to tap into individual or corporate funding sources in Bulgaria. Ironically, as foreign donors begin to withdraw their financial support, the threat of a new (over-)reliance on government funding puts at risk CSOs' ability to keep a critical distance from government and act as an independent voice for citizens' interests. However, although the financial situation is likely to remain challenging for most CSOs, Bulgaria's accession to the EU in 2007 will also open up new sources of funding from the EU Structural and Cohesion Funds.

The CSI assessment highlights a large set of challenges for civil society; however, there are distinguishable trends encouraging the development of a healthy civil society. Citizens are becoming increasingly involved in civic activities at the community level, albeit mainly outside formal CSOs. To overcome low levels of participation and further consolidate civil society's structure, CSOs are encouraged to develop projects and practices that promote citizen participation in civil society activities. The sector also needs to develop new modes of fundraising to ensure the sector's sustainability.

Environment (1.3)

The environment dimension considers political, legal, socioeconomic, and sociocultural contexts, as well as the relationships between civil society, the state, and the private sector. The assessment reveals that the environment for Bulgarian civil society is slightly disabling. Although the legal environment and the socioeconomic and political context provide somewhat favorable conditions for civil society, the sociocultural context, the nature of state–civil society relations, and the private sector's indifference to civil society were identified as unfavorable.

The political context for Bulgarian civil society is generally favorable for CSOs' operations. There is a strong legal framework to protect citizen rights and a free political environment with effective party competition. However, there are also impeding factors, which chiefly relate to low levels of confidence in the political system. For example, the CSI population survey indicates that almost 60% of citizens do not plan on voting.[3] Low levels of trust affect the political system and society at large. Approximately 74% of citizens believe that most people cannot be trusted and levels of intolerance toward marginalized groups, such as the Roma, are rather high.

The legal environment for CSOs has improved considerably over the last decade, and compared to other countries in the region it is quite favorable. The 2001 Not-for-Profit Legal Entities Act (NFPLEA) clearly outlines the CSO registration process, CSO operations, and room for state interventions in the sector. Registration is relatively simple; however, there are some administrative burdens, such as the substantial cost and time required to register small grass-roots organizations. Nevertheless, 60% of CSO representatives consider registration procedures to be quick, 68% regard the procedures to be inexpensive, and 76% feel the procedures are consistently applied without discrimination.

Although civil society remains relatively autonomous from the state, 60% of stakeholders consider the dialogue between civil society and the state to be limited. Partnerships between civil society and the national government are primarily established on a project basis. The parliament only consults through institutional mechanisms with a handful of national CSOs, such as the National Rehabilitation and Social Integration Council, the Welfare Assistance Board, the National Child Protection Council, and the National Board on Ethnic and Demographic Issues. Overall, partnerships with government are built on opportunistic goals, and cooperative projects often lack sustainability, since they are not renewed at the end of the grant term.

The majority of surveyed stakeholders view the business sector as indifferent toward civil society initiatives. There are only limited examples of partnerships between civil society and the private sector, aside from large corporations such as McDonald's and Coca-Cola, which mainly sponsor cultural and recreational activities. Seventy percent of stakeholders described corporate social responsibility (CSR) efforts among Bulgarian businesses as limited or insufficient. The prevailing perception of stakeholders is that, despite the sector's official proclamations of CSR, business does little to mitigate the impact of their operations on the environment.

Thus, although the institutional arrangements of the Bulgarian polity provide a rather conducive environment for civil society, the attitudes and behavior of key social actors, such as the state, the private sector, and citizens, toward civil society indicate a lack of interest, engagement, and support.

Values (2.1)

The values dimension examines the extent to which civil society practices and promotes positive values. In the case of Bulgarian civil society, this dimension yields a rather positive assessment, which reveals that civil society is built on widely shared values.

Democracy, tolerance, nonviolence, and gender equity are cornerstones of CSOs' practices. Despite the strong influence of top-down donor-driven approaches to their work, CSOs are contributing to building a civic culture in Bulgaria. A large number of grant-funded projects help shape public sensitivity around crucial principles, such as good governance, participation, tolerance, and the integration of disadvantaged groups.

Bulgarian CSOs typically promote positive values through the provision of services, and less through advocacy and campaigning. However, by filling in the gaps and providing services that citizens believe should be offered by the state, CSOs are often viewed as partners of the state rather than partners of citizens. Furthermore, CSOs tend to follow donor priorities and often do not respond to citizens' actual needs. Thus, civil society's values permeate society through the public nature of its projects rather than through its immediate impact on citizens.

Transparency remains problematic within Bulgarian civil society. More than half of the surveyed CSO representatives view corruption within civil society as a frequent or even very frequent phenomenon, and most CSOs' financial transparency is weak. Since public trust in CSOs is low and further weakened by corruption scandals, the lack of transparency within civil society discourages citizen involvement. Thus, increased attention to practicing and promoting transparency is necessary to limit the number of corruption scandals involving unscrupulous organizations and to boost public confidence in civil society.

Impact (1.5)

The impact dimension assesses civil society's role in governance and society at large. Bulgarian civil society receives a moderate score, which is composed of a stronger track record in the traditional fields of service delivery and policy formulation, and weaker assessments of civil society's role as a public watchdog and as a channel for representing and addressing the concerns of Bulgarian people.

Overall, civil society's policy influence is moderately strong, but it is often exerted via personal relations rather than institutionalized mechanisms, since the existing mechanisms do not encourage significant and meaningful CSO involvement in policymaking. However, recent years have seen a trend toward stronger advocacy, and, consequently, some CSOs have been successful in influencing policy, as with the amendments to the penal code and the fiscal decentralization policy.

Similarly, CSOs are increasingly active in monitoring the state, particularly in relation to the ongoing EU accession process. However, civil society appears largely unable to hold large businesses accountable, and there is little evidence of civil society efforts to monitor business practices. No significant civil litigation has taken place against private corporations, and roughly 3 out of 5 stakeholders believe that civil society is not active at all in monitoring the activities of the private sector.

Looking at civil society's standing in society at large, one notices the dismal levels of public trust in NGOs, which have lower trust levels than large companies or the press. Only political parties receive lower levels of public trust. This indicates that NGOs are seen as partners of foreign donors and the government, rather than as organizations promoting citizens' interests and needs. Most NGOs are out of touch with the population at large, particularly with poor people in rural areas. Disadvantaged groups are usually on the receiving end of projects undertaken by urban-based organizations with staff coming from different socioeconomic and cultural backgrounds. The elitist nature of these organizations inevitably affects their credibility as a voice of the people.

Recommendations

Participants at the regional stakeholder consultations and the CSI National Workshop in 2004 reflected on the CSI assessment's findings and put forward recommendations for the future of Bulgarian civil society. The following are the most crucial recommendations:

- Promote volunteering and charity: Encourage citizens to rediscover their traditional values.
- Improve civil society's public image and relationship with citizens: CSOs should pay more attention to practicing and promoting transparency. Aside from donors adopting a control system, public control mechanisms should be introduced to achieve increased transparency in the selection of projects and their implementation and in civil society's publications in the media and on the internet.
- Promote direct democracy: Promoting direct democracy is important since public confidence in politics is likely to increase when important decisions are made directly by citizens.
- Promote decentralization: There is a higher level of confidence in local legislators than in the central government. Therefore, further decentralization and a gradual increase in municipal autonomy could improve the environment in which civil society operates and lead to more favorable state–civil society relations.

- Make state funding more transparent: A task force has been set up to pressure government to establish clear rules and procedures regarding the selection of CSOs receiving state subsidies and to eliminate inequalities among legal entities in this respect.

Conclusion

After fifteen years of democratic rule, Bulgarian civil society has made major headway toward enhancing its sustainability. The external environment is relatively enabling, and CSOs have been expanding in number and scope of activities. Limited citizen participation remains the major challenge to the growth and health of civil society. The CSI finds that the public often regards CSOs as partners of the state or foreign donors rather than as true citizens' organizations, since CSOs largely developed in response to donor interests rather than through bottom-up citizen engagement and mobilization. Even when foreign donors design projects for CSOs to target marginalized groups, these groups rarely become involved in running these initiatives. Thus, CSOs' activities tend to support citizens without involving or empowering them. Developing sustainable links between CSOs and Bulgarian citizens, therefore, remains the primary challenge to civil society's sustainability.

Bulgaria's upcoming 2007 accession to the EU will likely be a milestone for civil society and present both challenges and opportunities. CSOs must develop new skills to remain competitive in the new environment and they must find new sources of funding as foreign donors withdraw. However, new opportunities for funding and policy engagement will also become available.

CSI Report

Diana Andreeva, I. Doushkova, D. Mihailov and D. Petkova, *Civil Society without the Citizens—An Assessment of Bulgarian Civil Society 2003–2005: CIVICUS Civil Society Report for Bulgaria* (Sofia, Bulgaria: Balkan Assist Association, 2005).

Notes

1. The CSI assessment was implemented in Bulgaria by Balkan Assist Association from 2003 to 2005. This chapter presents the main findings of the CSI and is based on a comprehensive country report for Bulgaria, which can be accessed on the CSI pages of the CIVICUS website at http://www.civicus.org.

2. In the nineteenth century, a movement of national revival, influenced by economic growth, the Enlightenment, and the French Revolution, sought to restore the Bulgarian national consciousness and secure a way forward for independence.

3. The Bulgarian Civil Society Sociological Survey was conducted as part of the CSI project from August to September 2004. A total of 1,000 respondents were interviewed.

Chapter 5

~~~

Chile[1]

Over the last fifteen years, Chile has achieved strong economic growth, has made a substantive reduction in poverty, and has taken important steps toward the consolidation of a democratic system of governance. In February 2006 Michelle Bachelet became Chile's first female president, the first for any South American country. President Bachelet's dedication to promoting citizen participation and civil society bodes well for the future of civil society–state relations in a country that is still grappling with the legacy of General Pinochet's dictatorship.

Table 5.1 Background Information for Chile

Chile	
Country size (square km)	756,626
Population (millions 2004)	16.1
Population under 15 years (2004)	25.5%
Urban population (2003)	87%
Seats in parliament held by women (2005)	12.5%
Language groups	Spanish (official), Araucanian
Ethnic groups	European and Mestizo 95%, Amerindian 3%
Religious groups	Roman Catholic 89%, Protestant 11%
HDI score and ranking (2003)	0.854 (37th)
GDP per capita (US$ 2003)	$10,274
Unemployment rate (% of total labor force)	7.4%
Population living on less than US$2 a day (2000)	9.6%

Historical Overview

In Chile the emergence of civil society during the nineteenth century was led by the middle class and working class and included associations of mining workers, trade unions, and anarchist groups, as well as community-based self-help groups and professional organizations. At the same time, the upper class supported many initiatives of the Catholic Church, which sought to assist the poor through orphanages and hospitals. Amid laissez faire state policies aimed at boosting the economy, to the detriment of the living conditions of the poor, civil society developed along two main trajectories. The first approach was empowering the marginalized, espoused by trade unions and self-help groups, and the second was service provision, advocated by the Catholic Church and similar groups, which was largely based on donations from the elite. In general, the development of civil society in Chile has always reflected the deep social inequalities that exist in the country, especially between the agro-industrial elite and the workers.

The electoral victory of Salvador Allende's Popular Unity party in 1970 presented a number of opportunities for progressive segments of civil society, but it also gave rise to a period of violent social conflict between groups with socialist orientations and organizations representing professional associations and business. In 1973 a military coup led by General Pinochet brutally overthrew Allende's government. The Pinochet regime dominated the country from 1973 to 1989 and had a strong impact on the economic, political, and social development of Chilean society. It systematically violated human rights and abused civil liberties, while implementing pro-market reforms that exacerbated disparities among the population. During its tenure, many civil society organizations (CSOs) lost their autonomy or disappeared altogether, and foundations and other charitable organizations were co-opted. Toward the end of the Pinochet dictatorship, a growing number of organizations, especially women's groups, mobilized against human rights abuses and spearheaded the opposition movement that would lead to the political breakthrough of 1990.

Although the return to democracy in 1990 allowed for a more favorable legal environment for civic activism, most of the socioeconomic reforms introduced by the military government remained in place and many violations committed during the military regime went unpunished. At the same time, civil society's expectation of more direct participation in public affairs was disappointed by the level of continuity in the state apparatus between the new democratic regime and its authoritarian predecessor. Still, many CSOs continued pushing to redress injustices, while others pursued sectoral activities.

The advent of democracy did not change the fact that Chilean society is marked by low levels of public trust, growing apathy, and a prevalence of individualistic attitudes. Changing the sociocultural context is therefore a key challenge for the new progressive government of President Bachelet.

The State of Civil Society in Chile

This section provides a summary of key findings of the Civil Society Index Shortened Assessment Tool (CSI-SAT) project in Chile. It examines the state of Chilean civil society along four dimensions—structure, environment, values, and impact—highlighting the main weaknesses and strengths.

The Civil Society Diamond (figure 5.1) visually summarizes the assessment's findings in Chile. Civil society's structure is assessed as moderately strong, despite low levels of citizen participation and limited organizational resources. The operating environment for civil society is seen as rather conducive, due to a cooperative relationship with government and an enabling socioeconomic context. Civil society's

Figure 5.1 Civil Society Diamond for Chile

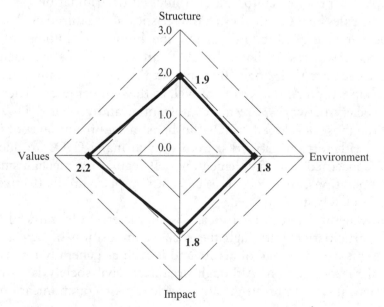

promotion of important values is significant, especially regarding poverty eradication and environmental sustainability. Its overall impact on politics and society is moderate, except in the areas of human rights advocacy, public education, and citizen empowerment, which are hallmarks of civil society's public activities.

Structure (1.9)

The structure dimension examines the makeup of civil society in terms of the main characteristics of individual citizen participation and associational life. The structure of Chilean civil society is moderately strong, with specific weaknesses in the limited extent of civic engagement and the insufficient financial resources for CSOs.

The participation of Chileans in civic activities, from membership in CSOs to occasional nonpartisan political actions, is quite low. For example, less than one-quarter of citizens have ever signed a petition, joined a demonstration, or participated in a boycott. Although data about CSO membership are sometimes contradictory, some opinion surveys show that less than half of the population belong to a CSO.

According to stakeholders involved in the CSI, CSOs operate throughout the country and reach the most isolated regions. In general, no social groups are significantly underrepresented or absent from CSOs' membership. Even disadvantaged ethnic minorities, such as the *Mapuche*, are effectively organized into associations and groups that promote cultural and ethnic self-determination.

The assessment of the key characteristics of organized civil society yields a mixed picture. In general, the human, technological, and financial resources available to CSOs are not seen as sufficient for them to achieve their goals. By contrast, the levels of communication and cooperation among CSOs, as well as the number and efficiency of civil society networks, are quite substantial and growing. However, only the most developed NGOs can boast a significant level of interaction with foreign networks. Even though many CSOs are increasingly concerned with implementing self-regulatory mechanisms for their operations, the procedures currently in place are ineffective and not adequately implemented.

In general, Chilean civil society is characterized by rather limited civic participation, although the social composition of civil society represents a wide range of actors and is seen as generally representative of the population. Although organized civil society is currently experiencing an improvement in the levels of communication and cooperation, the sector lacks effective self-regulation procedures and sustainable financial resources.

Environment (1.8)

The environment dimension considers political, legal, socioeconomic, and sociocultural contexts, as well as the relationships between civil society, the state, and the private sector. Although assessed as rather conducive, particularly with regard to political and socioeconomic factors, the environment in which civil society operates presents some obstacles with regard to the legal context and relations between civil society and the private sector.

Chilean civil society operates in a generally favorable political context, characterized by respect for the rule of law, as well as civil and political rights. The political system allows for a significant level of competition among a number of parties, although the number of citizens who do not vote has been growing because many people do not feel represented by the two main coalitions present in parliament, the *Concertación* (center-left) and the *Alianza* (right).

Overall, corruption levels are low and corrupt practices are generally stigmatized and persecuted, while civil liberties, information rights, and the freedom of the press are widely respected. However, the legal environment for civil society does not provide incentives for philanthropy, and tributary laws do not favor CSOs. At the same time, CSOs' proposals to improve the tax laws affecting civil society have not yet been taken up by government officials.

From a socioeconomic point of view, Chilean society has taken crucial steps forward since the Pinochet era. The poverty rate has dropped significantly from 45% in 1987 to less than 19% in 2004, although social inequalities and discrimination still exist. For example, the *Mapuche* communities that inhabit the southern part of the country have much higher rates of poverty and are subject to social discrimination, which has sparked frequent clashes with state authorities.

Relationships between civil society and the state have progressively improved over the past five years. This has allowed for the establishment of regular dialogue channels even though mutual suspicion is still present. The role of civil society has become increasingly important in the government's public discourse, especially after the new government took over in early 2006. The relationship between civil society and the private sector remains based on limited interaction and is generally marked by prejudice, since the Chilean private sector is characterized by strongly conservative views that render constructive dialogue and cooperation with actors outside of the business sector difficult.

The sociocultural context in Chile is particularly conservative, marked by low levels of interpersonal trust, with only 20% of citizens believing that other citizens can be trusted. Family structures remain the key affiliation for Chileans, and individualist attitudes are rather common, with negative consequences for civic engagement and collective solidarity.

Values (2.2)

The values dimension examines the extent to which civil society practices and promotes positive values. The values dimension received the highest score in the Chilean CSI assessment. Chilean CSOs practice and promote tolerance and nonviolence and have been playing a crucial role in promoting democracy, fighting poverty, and protecting the environment.

Chilean civil society's commitment to poverty eradication has been significant for decades. During the military dictatorship, when market reforms aimed at liberalization severely impacted workers and the poor, many CSOs became increasingly determined to address problems related to poverty and social marginalization. After the restoration of democracy in 1990, this commitment took different forms, especially at the political level, where CSOs became more involved in assisting the government in fighting poverty.

During the past few years, CSOs' actions to protect the environment have increased. Although most of the activities for environmental protection have been promoted by well-resourced NGOs, small groups of citizens have been particularly vocal, such as the cases of Celulosa Arauco and Pascua Lama in 2005. Moreover, environmental CSOs have steered the public debate on ecological issues and succeeded in influencing the government agenda. For example, during the 2005 presidential elections, both main candidates, Michelle Bachelet and Sebastián Piñera, gave detailed accounts of their environmental policies.

CSOs' activities to promote democracy played an important role during Chile's transition phase. In democratic Chile, the contribution of CSOs to democratic values has changed as a result of political normalization. In a context in which electoral democracy has been achieved, civil society's promotion of democratic practices, nonviolence, and tolerance now focuses more on the rights of marginalized groups. For example, women's groups are quite active on issues regarding equal opportunities for both genders, and indigenous associations lobby for the institutional recognition of ethnic-based rights and self-determination.

When it comes to the internal practice of values, such as democratic governance and transparency within CSOs, the picture is somewhat different. There are few mechanisms to ensure democratic and participatory decisionmaking within CSOs, and even if they exist the persistence of traditional approaches to leadership and authority provides little room for internal democracy. It is interesting that CSOs' financial transparency receives the lowest score in the CSI assessment.

The values most fervently promoted by Chilean CSOs are poverty eradication and environmental sustainability. In contrast, CSOs are still struggling to uphold internal democratic practices, especially financial transparency, as a crucial value to enhance the accountability and legitimacy of CSOs.

Impact (1.8)

The impact dimension assesses civil society's role in governance and society at large. The CSI finds the impact of civil society in Chile to be moderate. CSOs effectively respond to social interests, empower marginalized groups, meet social needs, and lobby for human rights protection, but they are largely absent from the national budgeting process and do not act as a watchdog of the corporate sector.

Chilean CSOs have been extremely vocal in demanding justice for the systematic violations of human rights committed during the Pinochet dictatorship. Many CSOs denounced these violations when the military junta was still in power and pushed for investigations during the transition period. Despite the onset of democracy, human rights abuses still occasionally occur, due to the persistence of certain authoritarian attitudes in public institutions, especially the defense and police forces.

In contrast, Chilean civil society fails to hold corporations accountable, mainly due to the conservative attitude of most local enterprises, which view civil society's role with suspicion. Civil society campaigns conducted to unveil the harmful behavior of corporations are mainly led by ecological groups and trade unions, and are only occasionally able to exert any significant impact on corporate policies.

Systematic information on the national budget is widely available in Chile, but the decisionmaking process is not completely transparent and is almost exclusively controlled by the government. When CSOs take part in consultations with government officials regarding budget issues, they are mainly expected to provide opinions on specific aspects and often lack the capacity to analyze the budget in its entirety.

Civil society has been very successful in informing and educating citizens, especially about issues concerning human rights, gender, and ethnic minorities, and also in empowering marginalized people, particularly indigenous communities, prisoners, and those living with HIV/AIDS. CSOs have been most successful in their work on women's empowerment. Not only was the position of women in society neglected during the military regime, but after the advent of democracy many obstacles remained, especially due to the remnants of a patriarchal culture. For example, divorce was only legalized in 2004. CSOs led by professional women are taking important steps in the struggle for women's rights, particularly in the areas of domestic violence, reproductive health, and equal opportunities in public institutions and policymaking. Additionally, the recent election of a woman as president marked a turning point in this process and established gender equality as one of the main goals of the new political era.

Although the Chilean state still features traditional centralist characteristics common to most Latin American countries, the *Concertación* governments managed to open up space for the inclusion of CSOs in various sectors of policymaking. CSOs are active in assisting marginalized groups and their impact on women's empowerment is significant; however, the rather conservative attitude of the private sector makes it difficult for CSOs to hold private corporations accountable.

Conclusion

The CSI assessment reveals that Chilean civil society is marked by rather low levels of citizen participation and operates within a sociocultural context of civic disengagement and mistrust. Nevertheless, the relationship between government and civil society has become more productive over the past few years. In comparison, much more remains to be done to improve the relationship between civil society and the private sector, which traditionally has been difficult because of the social tensions between both sets of actors.

Civil society has recently received a boost, appearing prominently among the main objectives of President Bachelet's tenure, which aims for closer cooperation between government and civil society and for the introduction of a number of reforms to modernize Chilean society at large, such as gender equality and social rights. This may be a chance for civil society to contribute toward social emancipation, which the military dictatorship seemed to have almost irreparably undermined.

CSI Report

Fundación Soles, *The Associational Reconstruction of a Nation: CIVICUS Civil Society Index Shortened Assessment Tool Report for Chile* (Santiago, Chile: Fundación Soles, 2006).

Notes

1. The CSI Shortened Assessment Tool was implemented in Chile by Fundación Soles over the course of 2006. This chapter presents the main findings of the CSI-SAT and is based on a comprehensive country report for Chile, which can be accessed on the CSI pages of the CIVICUS website at http://www.civicus.org.

Chapter 6

China[1]

The People's Republic of China is currently receiving significant international attention.[2] Widespread government reforms over the last twenty-five years have brought about explosive economic growth and a fundamental transformation of the Chinese social structure, which have also led to negative side effects, such as rapidly growing social inequalities and environmental degradation. In the context of a society that is becoming more diverse, the role of civil society as the sphere where different social interests can be negotiated is becoming increasingly important.

Table 6.1 Background Information for China

China	
Country size (square km)	9,572,900
Population (millions 2004)	1,296.200
Population under 15 years	22%
Urban population (2003)	38.6%
Seats in parliament held by women (2005)	20.2%
Language groups	Mandarin (official), Yue (Cantonese), Wu (Shanghaiese), Minbei (Fuzhou), Minnan (Hokkien-Taiwanese), Xiang, Gan, Hakka dialects, other minority languages
Ethnic groups	56 groups inciuding Han 92% and Zhuang, Manchu, Hui, Miao, Uygur, Yi, Tujia, Tong, Tibetan, Mongol and others
Religious groups	Officially Atheist, Buddhist, Taoist, Christian and Muslim
HDI score and ranking (2003)	0.755 (85th)
GDP per capita (US$ 2003)	$5,003
Unemployment rate (% of total labor force)	4%
Population living on less than US$2 a day (2001)	46.7%

The Communist Party has approached political reforms very cautiously and, due to the tradition of a strong state and given the party–state's tight control over society, the applicability of the civil society concept to China is a topic of intense debate.[3] Nevertheless, the concept and the empirical reality of Chinese civil society are receiving growing attention from the Chinese government, the international donor community, and researchers alike. Therefore, the Civil Society Index (CSI) assessment implemented by the NGO Research Centre at Tsinghua University came at a crucial time for Chinese civil society.

Historical Overview

Civil society's development in modern China began during the early twentieth century, late in the imperial era, when the ensuing modernization process led to the emergence of a diverse array of associational types, such as guilds, cooperatives, scientific associations, unions, and cultural groups. These developments drastically changed with the onset of socialist rule in 1949, when independent associations were either closed down or co-opted into the party–state structure in the form of mass organizations (MOs), such as women's, youth, and workers' organizations. In the 1960s the Cultural Revolution led to a further tightening of state control over associational life.

The implementation of economic and other reform policies by the ruling party, beginning in 1978, brought about fundamental changes, including a gradual and incremental process of opening public space for individual activities and social organizations. This reform was accelerated in the 1990s when the government's declared goal of "small government, big society" gave prominence to civil society, and new legislation on social organizations was passed.

Although economic growth continued to gather speed in the new millennium, tremendous social problems surfaced, such as socioeconomic inequalities, particularly between urban and rural areas; a lack of social safety nets for the unemployed, migrant workers, and other marginalized groups; the rise of HIV/AIDS; and environmental problems. In response, a small number of autonomous and mostly informal grassroots-oriented civil society associations arose to deal with these social concerns. At the same time, people's increased awareness of their rights and of existing injustices in society erupted in unplanned demonstrations and mass actions around the country. Between 1994 and 2004, government statistics noted a 700% increase in instances of social unrest. Correspondingly, international donors began to pay attention to the emerging social tensions and identified civil society as a potential partner in the delivery of their social programs. The Chinese government began to look into the division of labor between state, business, and civil society, with the likely consequence being a growing role for civil society organizations (CSOs) in social programs.

Civil society in contemporary China is multifaceted, ranging from government-controlled, government-organized nongovernment organizations (GONGOs) to a growing number of independent NGOs and informal grassroots initiatives. Recent estimates of the total number of registered CSOs, taken together with the number of unregistered CSOs and other informal social groups, go well into the millions.

The State of Civil Society in China

There are many different forms of CSOs in China. The majority are either registered as social organizations[4] or civilian nonprofit entities,[5] both of which are required to be affiliated with a government institution or to be noncommercial corporate entities, which do not have to meet the affiliation requirement. In addition, a growing number of unregistered organizations, mostly at the grassroots level, are utilizing the increasing opportunity for social initiatives in China. These CSOs are particularly active in community development, environmental protection, HIV/AIDS work, religious issues, trade, and culture. They also encompass village committees and independent workers' and peasants' associations.

The CSI examined the entire spectrum of formal and informal CSOs in China, although formal CSOs featured more strongly, due to the availability of information and access to their representatives. The CSI acknowledges that most Chinese CSOs are not formally independent of the state, but argues that they fulfill important civic functions of empowerment, interest representation, and advocacy. Due to their governance role in the state-party system, Chinese political parties were excluded from the definition of Chinese civil society.

This section summarizes the key findings of the CSI project in China. It examines the state of civil society in China along four dimensions—structure, environment, values, and impact—highlighting the main weaknesses and strengths.

As visually summarized by the Civil Society Diamond (figure 6.1), civil society in China has a rather weak structure, characterized by

Figure 6.1 Civil Society Diamond for China

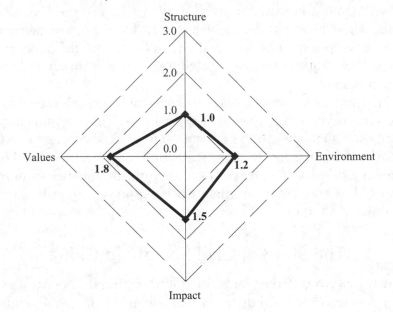

limited citizen participation in public life and poor organization. The general operating environment is rather disabling, particularly with regard to political and legal factors. A distinct strength of Chinese civil society is its values, especially the promotion of social principles such as poverty eradication and environmental protection. The internal practice within civil society and the external promotion of more political values, such as transparency and democracy, leaves much to be desired. Mirroring this division between social and political issues, civil society's impact is stronger in social areas, such as community empowerment and service provision, while its role in the political process remains extremely limited.

Structure (1.0)

The structure dimension examines the makeup of civil society in terms of the main characteristics of individual citizen participation and associational life. The structure of Chinese civil society is generally rather weak, characterized by low participation levels and a nascent organized civil society.

The CSI's population survey is one of the first empirical studies to examine the prevalence of various forms of citizen participation in China. It found that apart from informal volunteering for local neighborhood and community activities, forms of civic engagement are extremely limited. Membership in CSOs, aside from MOs, and non-partisan forms of political actions are almost absent in Chinese society. Practices of charitable giving are common in urban settings, where close to 70% of respondents gave to charity, individually or through their workplace, in the last year; charity is rare in rural areas, however, where only 25% of respondents participated in such an activity. This urban-rural gap is also apparent in the makeup of civil society participants. Poor and rural people are underrepresented among CSO members and there is an overrepresentation of registered CSOs in urban areas.

The last decade has witnessed a growth in registered and unregistered CSOs. This growth has mainly taken place in an uncoordinated manner and in the context of restrictive government regulations, which prohibit the formation of independent umbrella bodies. Thus, key structures, systems, and resources of an organized civil society are lacking in China. However, the first signs of a civil society infrastructure can be detected in the proliferation of civil society research and resource centers and information channels, the significant increase in international cooperation around civil society issues, and a diversification of funding sources for CSOs. The reliance on government support is becoming less pronounced as corporate funding, individual donations, membership fees, service fees, and grant support from foreign donors gain importance, although the average budget of Chinese CSOs remains small. In addition, due to legal restrictions, CSOs' proactive fundraising efforts are severely constrained. Linked to this tenuous financial base are inadequate human and material resources for most CSOs. Dedicated professional development courses for CSO leaders are still in infant stages and high salaries in the booming business sector make staff positions in CSOs financially unattractive.

Thus, although the number of CSOs is growing, both their social base and level of sectoral organization and infrastructure remain severely limited. Even though many of these factors are the result of a restrictive legal and political environment, more attention to issues of organizational development and sectoral infrastructure is likely to increase civil society's standing in society at large.

Environment (1.2)

The environment dimension considers political, legal, socioeconomic, and sociocultural contexts, as well as the relationships between civil society, the state, and the private sector. Chinese civil society operates in a rather disabling environment, where only the private sector's attitude and the state's effectiveness in fulfilling its main functions are somewhat conducive to its functioning.

The Communist Party of China controls all major aspects of political and social life. Basic political and civil rights, although partially existing on paper, in practice cannot be realized by citizens. State censorship and control over the media hampers freedom of information and the press, and the rule of law is only slowly gaining currency among public officials. In addition, although the Chinese state shows a remarkable level of effectiveness and enjoys widespread trust among Chinese people, corruption in the public sector is widespread and dissatisfaction with high-handed and unresponsive public officials, particularly in rural areas, is growing.

The state controls large parts of Chinese civil society. It is estimated that 4 out of 5 registered social organizations were set up by government and are generally fully financed by government. Thus, the boundaries between the state and civil society are often blurred. Existing registration provisions, particularly with regard to financial requirements, make it exceedingly difficult for independent organizations to register as social organizations and set up appropriate structures throughout the country. However, the system of government sponsorship also has certain advantages for registered CSOs, since they are located in close proximity to the center of power and have access to informal channels of advocacy within the party–state. Cooperation and dialogue between state and civil society follows an opportunistic pattern on the part of the state, which works with those CSOs that adhere to government policies but ignores the work of organizations that openly oppose its policies and seeks to obstruct outspoken advocacy NGOs. However, CSOs in the latter two groups, most of which are unregistered, are growing in quantity and vibrancy.

Relationships between civil society and the corporate sector are improving and expanding. On average, business donations make up approximately one-fourth of CSOs' income, and more than 9 out of 10 businesses make regular donations to charitable causes. Thus, given China's expanding business sector, corporate support might become a major resource for CSOs in the years to come.

Other important, though often overlooked, impediments to strengthening civil society are the prevailing sociocultural norms in Chinese society. Key indicators, such as interpersonal trust (particularly outside of the family), tolerance toward minorities, and public spiritedness, receive only moderate ratings. Therefore, although the restrictive character of the political and legal context seems to be the main hindrance to civil society's development, there are also other barriers, such as the limited stock of social capital, growing social inequalities, and increasing social tensions.

Values (1.8)

The values dimension examines the extent to which civil society practices and promotes positive values. The assessment of this dimension in China is modestly positive. A more in-depth analysis brings to light important variations in civil society's commitment to various norms and ideals.

Given its precarious character and difficult environment, it is not surprising that Chinese civil society is better at practicing values of transparency, tolerance, and nonviolence than at promoting them in society at large. For example, a large majority of NGOs publish annual financial reports, even though external auditors are involved in only 1 out of 8 of these reports.

There are clear differences in the scale of value promotion activities between social and political issues. Civil society's record is rather strong in promoting gender equity, environmental sustainability, and poverty eradication. However, civil society plays a limited role in promoting more sensitive political values, such as democracy, transparency, and tolerance. Civil society groups and activists that venture into political issues usually meet an uncompromising stance and a harsh response from the government.

Given the fast-paced economic development in China and its negative side effects on social cohesion and the environment, issues of social justice and environmental protection are high on civil society's agenda. For example, the Hope Project, which provides bursaries for poor children so they can attend school, is widely known and respected among the Chinese population. However, in relation to the escalating scale and intensity of social concerns, civil society's outreach to the population at large remains limited.

Impact (1.5)

The impact dimension assesses civil society's role in governance and society at large. The impact is assessed as moderate in China, and, mirroring the assessment of the values dimension, civil society's influence on social issues is stronger than on the political sphere.

Chinese CSOs actively work with marginalized groups, create livelihoods, and educate the public. The previously mentioned Hope Project was known to about two-thirds of those surveyed. In addition, 1 in 8 respondents remembered a CSO public education event in his or her community, for example an activity associated with direct community-level elections or HIV/AIDS education. However, given the state's dominant role in social service provision, civil society only plays a supplementary role, primarily focusing on servicing marginalized groups, such as the mentally handicapped, people living with HIV/AIDS, and migrant workers. Another indication of civil society's niche role is the 10 to 1 ratio by which Chinese people prefer state to civil society services.

The public not only prefers the state as a service provider, but it also has limited public trust in CSOs. Although many respondents were unaware of most CSO types, those who responded in the survey rated them as significantly less trustworthy than state institutions. This indicates a lack of awareness as well as significant doubts about these new forms of organizations, which likely reflects the legacy of a strong state in China.

Compared to its already limited role in society, civil society's impact on governance is even weaker. Given the Communist Party's claim of being the sole legitimate guarantor of social interests, space for other actors in policymaking is extremely limited. However, due to the diversification of interests and the adoption of more consultative approaches to policymaking, CSOs close to the government can make inputs at the technical level. It is important to recognize that confrontational advocacy approaches, pursued by NGOs in democratic societies, are not common in China. Environmental CSOs are a notable exception, where CSOs' public advocacy activities have found a strong public echo and have contributed to the government paying greater attention to environmental concerns. Generally speaking though, principles of participatory governance and state accountability are not entrenched in the public administration and the upper echelons of government. This severely constrains civil society's watchdog and policy roles.

Recommendations

In May 2006 a consultative meeting with stakeholders, including CSOs, grassroots organizations, and researchers, was held to present and discuss the CSI project findings in China. The following three key recommendations emerged:

- Civil society's structural foundation needs to be improved. Particular areas for improvement include stronger networking and cooperation, and stronger diversification of CSOs, in terms of fields and geographic reach.

- An enabling environment for CSOs needs to be created. This includes overhauling the registration framework and procedures, reforming existing tax laws, and abolishing severe restrictions on the establishment of networks and umbrella organizations.
- Civil society should increase its presence throughout society, particularly in the countryside, where partnerships with local authorities have already shown some positive results. Currently the concept and practice of civil society remains rooted in a rather small segment of the educated urban middle class.

Conclusion

China will likely approach a crucial crossroad in the next few years. The intensifying processes of economic development, social differentiation, and political emancipation will increase the diversity and strength of demands placed on the Chinese state. Although the 1990s mantra of "small government, big society" proved the government's awareness of the need for citizens to play a greater role in the country's development, current institutional arrangements continue to be a major hindrance.

Therefore, there is a distinct possibility of increased social conflict and unrest. However, the more desirable trajectory is a peaceful and stable transition toward a Chinese form of participatory, accountable, and equitable governance, led by the government. In both cases, civil society is likely to play a key role, either in the unorganized form of violent mass demonstrations and uprisings, or as a set of stable organizations, effectively addressing social concerns and channeling interests from society to the governance system. Civil society is currently too small and constrained to meaningfully play this role. However, a vibrant civil society is possible if the Chinese state recognizes the enormous potential of CSOs to be the glue that holds society together and provides them with increased space and autonomy. In such a scenario, a strong civil society would work in partnership with the state and corporate sector in the pursuit of equitable and sustainable development of China.

CSI Report

NGO Research Centre, *A Nascent Civil Society within a Changing Environment: CIVICUS Civil Society Index Report for China (Mainland)* (Beijing, China: NGO Research Centre at Tsinghua University, 2006).

Notes

1. The CSI assessment was implemented in China by the NGO Research Centre at Tsinghua University from 2003 to 2005. This chapter presents the main findings of the CSI and is based on a comprehensive country report for China, which can be accessed on the CSI pages at http://www.civicus.org.
2. Hereafter referred to as China.
3. See Kristina Gough, *Emerging Civil Society in China: An Overall Assessment of Conditions and Possibilities Available to Civil Society and Its Organizations to Act in China* (Stockholm, Sweden: SIDA, 2004); David Yang, "Civil Society as an Analytic Lens for Contemporary China," *China: An International Journal,* 2, no. 1 (2004):1–27. For the CIVICUS CSI, the civil society concept forms an analytical ideal-type, against which existing countries can be compared. Thus, although civil society in China is extremely limited and fledgling, the concept is a useful heuristic tool to analyze current social dynamics in the country.
4. In 2002, their number was 133,000.
5. In 2002, their number was 700,000.

Chapter 7

~~~

Croatia[1]

Since the turn of the millennium, Croatia has witnessed a period of stability and growth, which makes the country a likely candidate for accession to the European Union (EU). This period was accompanied by an improvement in the situation of civil society, as shown by comparing the CSI results from the 2001 pilot study with the 2005 findings.[2] The 2001 study highlighted poor cooperation between civil society organizations (CSOs) and the state and the private sector, lack of citizen engagement, a high concentration of urban CSOs, and lack of transparency as the main challenges facing civil society in Croatia. Civil society was viewed as lacking roots in local communities and had a reputation for speaking a "foreign language." Given the challenges revealed in the 2001 pilot phase report, the current assessment provides interesting insights about the extent to which problems identified in 2001 persist today and points out new issues affecting the development of Croatian civil society.

Table 7.1 Background Information for Croatia

Croatia	
Country size (square km)	56,538
Population (millions 2004)	4.4
Population under 15 years (2004)	15.8%
Urban population (2003)	59%
Seats in parliament held by women (2005)	21.7%
Language groups	Croatian (official), Serbian
Ethnic groups	Croats 78%, Serb 12%, Bosniak 1%, others 8%
Religious groups	Roman Catholic 88%, Orthodox 5%, other
HDI score and ranking (2003)	0.841(45th)
GDP per capita (US$ 2003)	$11,080
Unemployment rate (% of total labor force)	14.3%
Population living on less than US$2 a day (2001)	<2%

Historical Overview

At the turn of the nineteenth century, the emergence of modern Croatian civil society was strongly influenced by industrialization and the Catholic Church. Prominent industrialists established various types of foundations, and the church responded to the social welfare needs of the growing population.

Following World War II, the Socialist Republic of Yugoslavia severely restricted civil society, and organizations could exist only under the close control of the Communist Party. In the 1980s, the first independent Croatian CSOs emerged, focusing on environmental, political, and cultural activities. This rise of CSOs corresponded with the creation of new political parties, contributing to the breakdown of the socialist system and to Croatia's independence from Yugoslavia in 1991. However, after the fall of socialism, civil society continued to be impeded by an authoritarian government, the devastating effects of the homeland war, a refugee crisis, and an economic crisis. The state frequently used the media to accuse the largely donor-driven civil society sector of being foreign hirelings or spies, solely interested in protecting the rights and interests of Serbs.

In the late 1990s, following the war in the region, CSOs helped oust the authoritarian government and reduce presidential powers. By 2002, with the election of a new coalition government, state–civil society relations began to improve as dialogue and cooperation increased. In 2003 the old government returned to power, and its relationship with civil society again became partly conflict-ridden.

The State of Civil Society in Croatia

This section provides a summary of key findings of the CSI project in Croatia. It examines the state of Croatian civil society along four dimensions—structure, environment, values, and impact—highlighting the main weaknesses and strengths.

The Croatian Civil Society Diamond (figure 7.1) illustrates a well-balanced civil society sector at a medium stage of development. Civil society has a slightly strong structure, which is on an upward trend due to increasing civic engagement and stronger networking among organized civil society. CSOs are operating in a relatively enabling environment, which does not feature any severe impediment to the growth of civil society. The extent to which civil society practices and

Figure 7.1 Civil Society Diamond for Croatia

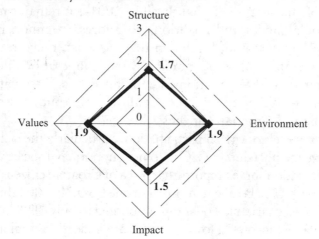

promotes positive values is relatively significant, although its impact on governance and society is somewhat limited. This is mainly due to its inadequate role in public policy processes.

Structure (1.7)

The structure dimension examines the makeup of civil society in terms of the main characteristics of individual citizen participation and associational life. The score for this dimension indicates a slightly strong structure. Although the sector's weak organization, poor networking, and limited citizen participation remain key challenges, compared to the 2001 assessment, relations among civil society actors have improved and citizen engagement in civil society has increased somewhat.

The assessment reveals that weak organization is a primary challenge for the sector's structure. In the regional stakeholder consultations, participants consistently cited the lack of networking among CSOs and mentioned the need for CSOs to recognize the importance of umbrella organizations. With respect to self-regulation within civil society, less than 20% of stakeholders confirmed the existence of effective and enforceable self-regulatory mechanisms, such as a code of conduct. In addition, a majority of stakeholders believe that the support infrastructure is inadequate and that there is a shortage of civil society support organizations. However, the establishment of the National Foundation for Civil Society Development in 2003 is an important step toward developing an adequate support infrastructure.

Ad hoc issue-based communication and cooperation among civil society actors has improved slightly since 2001 but remains moderate. Cross-sector alliances and coalitions to address common issues are not particularly common, but when they do exist, they are generally effective. Examples of good practices and cooperation include the GRAK campaign, the Coalition of Human Rights Associations, the Croatian Women's Network, the Coalition of Youth Associations, and the Union of Croatian Citizens Alliance.

Moderate levels of citizen participation, particularly the lack of widespread active membership in CSOs, do not support civil society's growth. The CSI population survey reports that 35% of Croatian citizens belong to a CSO and only 12% belong to more than one CSO.[3] In 2004 the financial value of citizens' charitable donations amounted to only 1.2% of the average individual net income. However, there are indications that a civic culture is slowly taking root in Croatia. According to the CSI population survey, since 1990 61.3% of Croatian citizens have signed a petition, and 2 out of 3 citizens donated to humanitarian causes in 2004. Likewise, the growth of volunteerism, and the public's increased interest in volunteering, will potentially invigorate civil society. The CSI's National Advisory Group (NAG) also pointed out that there is a slight increase in the emergence of civil society initiatives at the community level.

The concentration of CSOs in large cities and urban areas and the lack of representation of the rural population in the membership and leadership of CSOs remain key weaknesses of the sector. According to government statistics, 50.4% of registered associations are located in or near Croatia's four largest cities.[4] One regional stakeholder noted, "Civil society is concentrated in big towns, while small communities do not benefit. In Zagreb, civil society is well-developed; however, these activities have no impact on those of us outside of Zagreb."

To strengthen the sector's structure and sustainability, civil society needs to mobilize participation at the local level by taking advantage of Croatians' growing propensity to get involved in civic initiatives. Improving international, national, regional, and local networking should also deepen cooperation among CSOs, limit overlapping program activities, and encourage economies of scale to increase the size, strength, and vibrancy of civil society.

Environment (1.9)

The environment dimension considers political, legal, socioeconomic, and sociocultural contexts, as well as the relationships between civil society, the state, and the private sector. The CSI assessment reveals that Croatian civil society currently operates in a relatively favorable environment. Predominant strengths include the positive legal environment, the socioeconomic context, and the entrenchment of basic human rights and freedoms. Less favorable factors include the political context, the sociocultural context, and civil society's relations with the state and the private sector.

With respect to the political context, though generally favorable, the rule of law is undermined by a weak judicial system, which contributes to legal insecurity. Judicial independence and professionalism has been especially problematic in the Croatian war crimes trials. Similarly, from 2003 to 2004, public perceptions of corruption worsened, as the government was involved in numerous corruption scandals, which perpetuated high levels of mistrust toward state authorities and other public institutions.[5]

Low levels of interpersonal trust continue to challenge the development of a civic culture. The population survey reveals that only 30% of Croatians believe people can be trusted, though this is comparatively better than the 20% found in the *1999–2000 European Values Study*. With regard to public trust in CSOs, national television has a tendency to focus on scandals involving CSOs and presents civil society as an arena suffering from conflict, mistrust, and rivalry, which perpetuates public mistrust and impedes the work of CSOs.

The civil society–state and civil society–private sector relations are fluctuating. During the 1990s civil society–state relations were ridden with conflict, but they steadily improved after 2000 as government and CSO representatives established ad hoc consultative bodies to address issues such as child rights, minority rights, and gender equality. However, experts feel that these bodies created a facade of civil society involvement but failed to give civil society any real power or voice. After 2000 two important mechanisms that were designed to facilitate CSO-state cooperation began to prove effective: the Government Office for Cooperation with NGOs and the Council for Development of Civil Society. Both functioned as advisory bodies to the national government. Unfortunately, the current administration has not made full use of these institutions' potential, and cooperation between government and civil society has waned since the new government took power in 2004. Therefore, although relations have improved since the 1990s and mechanisms have been put in place to establish dialogue and rules of engagement, CSOs need to pressure the state to ensure that existing forms of state–civil society cooperation and dialogue continue to function.

Only recently has the private sector become interested in cooperating with civil society. Of stakeholders, 75.4% believe the private sector is indifferent to or suspicious of civil society. The corporate sector tends to consider CSOs as nothing more than beneficiaries of its support, and many CSOs see the corporate sector solely as donors. Corporate philanthropy remains rather low, with approximately 18% of CSOs' average income coming from corporate-sector funds, although small and medium businesses are increasingly interested in working with CSOs and have begun to make charitable donations.

Legal and socioeconomic factors are seen as widely supportive of civil society. A majority of stakeholders view CSO registration as quick, simple, and inexpensive, despite certain bureaucratic difficulties faced by smaller CSOs. Tax laws favorable to CSOs were enacted in the early 2000s. In April 2004, Amendments of the Value Added Tax (VAT) Law exempted humanitarian assistance, social welfare, health, education, culture, science, religion, and sports CSOs from paying VAT on goods and services when using foreign donations, but environmental protection, human rights, and democracy CSOs remain excluded from these benefits. Companies and citizens also receive tax incentives for donating to CSOs.

The socioeconomic context has substantially improved since the 1990s and is relatively enabling for civil society's development. Nonetheless, members of the NAG view the legacy of war and discrimination against ethnic minorities to be an ongoing challenge slowing down the formation of a new middle class and economic advancements in Croatia, with negative consequences for the growth of civil society in the country.

Values (1.9)

The values dimension examines the extent to which civil society practices and promotes positive values. In the case of Croatia, this yields a rather positive picture. The CSI findings reveal that civil society is dedicated to democracy, tolerance, nonviolence, gender equity, and environmental sustainability, but it is weak at practicing and promoting transparency and promoting the fight against poverty. Civil society also appears to be better at practicing these values internally than promoting them externally.

Given Croatia's recent history, democracy has been a key issue for civil society. To date, the majority of activities promoting democracy pertain to minority rights and the aftermath of the homeland war. Important civil society campaigns include GONG's role in the election process, the Croatian Helsinki Committee, the Legal Services Coalition's advocacy for the Freedom of Information Act, and the sixteen-day campaign against violence against women.

Another highlight is civil society's dedication to environmental protection. Since the 1980s, environmental CSOs have sensitized and mobilized the public around environmental issues and have effectively cooperated with business and government. Environmental CSOs are now regarded as important stakeholders, able to successfully advocate their interests, such as with the Druzba-Adria oil pipeline project.

In contrast, civil society is rather weak at practicing and promoting transparency. As in the CSI pilot study, financial transparency within CSOs is seen as problematic. Due to some CSOs' unscrupulous activities and the media's focus on scandals involving CSOs, the perceived level of corruption among CSOs is quite high. Establishing more effective transparency and accountability practices should therefore be a priority for civil society.

Furthermore, civil society's commitment to fight poverty is limited. Although this is a likely legacy of the socialist era, when the state was responsible for dealing with social issues, policymakers and CSOs need to develop strategies to effectively incorporate civil society into existing national poverty eradication plans. In general, civil society must begin to embrace and prioritize the fight against poverty.

In general, Croatian civil society's track record on values is divided. Although its efforts to promote poverty reduction and transparency are inadequate, its role in promoting environmental sustainability, democracy, and gender equality is widely recognized. The positive relationship established between environmental CSOs and the media could be a good model for CSOs working in other fields.

Impact (1.5)

The impact dimension assesses civil society's role in governance and society at large. This aspect of civil society receives the lowest dimension score, reflecting civil society's relatively limited impact on society. In general, Croatian civil society plays a rather significant role in empowering and meeting the needs of marginalized groups, but its influence on government policy and its role as a watchdog of the government and private sector are limited.

According to the CSI findings, civil society's advocacy and lobbying skills are inadequate to significantly impact policy and monitor state and corporate behavior. Although there are initial signs of some CSOs holding the state accountable, there is widespread reluctance among CSOs to bite the hand that feeds them, or to serve as a watch-dog of the private sector. Since 2004 the new government has limited its engagement with CSOs and civil society's potential contribution to policymaking. In addition, CSOs lack the capacity and experience to articulate their interests to government. Based on these findings, it is therefore proposed that CSOs should pool their skills and build networks among like-minded CSOs to develop the necessary advocacy skills and the capacity to effectively participate in the policy process.

Civil society's impact is also weakened by mistrust and its poor public image. Although CSOs enjoy more trust than most institutions, they are not widely trusted by citizens, state representatives, or the corporate sector. With the exception of the faith-based CSO Caritas, which has very positive ratings, citizens generally mistrust CSOs more than they trust them. Representatives of the state and media perceive CSOs as lacking professionalism, capacity, and efficiency. Due to this image of professional incompetence, CSOs' valuable ideas often do not make it onto the public agenda, and if they do they are quickly discredited.

It appears that space is opening up for CSOs to influence social and human rights issues. Although the state remains the dominant service provider, CSOs have been relatively successful in providing social welfare services and responding to the needs of marginalized communities and groups, such as the elderly, the poor, and the disabled. Particularly at the local level, CSOs have also been accepted as social partners by assisting victims of family violence and providing services absent from state programs. CSO activities have also contributed to the government's adoption of the National Strategy of Family Violence Protection. The strong track record of CSOs in working on social concerns places them in a good position to influence the development of social policy. However, the majority of CSOs play a reactive role, responding to existing social needs, rather than preventing the emergence of social problems by influencing key policies.

A key challenge to increasing the impact of Croatian civil society is to strengthen the trust and relations between Croatian citizens and civil society. This will likely increase citizen involvement, and therefore anchor civil society in local communities, ground its work in the needs of society, and encourage CSOs to take a more proactive approach to their work.

Recommendations

Participants at Croatia's CSI National Workshop and regional stake-holder consultations reflected on the CSI findings and put forward recommendations for the healthy growth of Croatian civil society. The following list includes the key recommendations for civil society, the state, and the corporate sector, the media, and foreign donors:

For civil society:

- Increase public trust in CSOs by preparing and adopting a code of ethics for CSOs and increasing mechanisms for transparency.
- Enhance networking and information exchange among CSOs.

For the state:

- Establish effective and transparent funding processes, including multi-year grant agreements and timely invitations for tenders and VAT exemption benefits for all CSOs buying goods and services with foreign donations.
- Institutionalize civil society–state communication and dialogue mechanisms.

For the corporate sector, the media, and foreign donors:

- The corporate sector should convene intersectoral discussions and activities.
- The media should improve its contribution to a civic culture by giving CSOs' activities and achievements more prominence.
- Foreign donors and stakeholders should improve their dialogue on program design, preparation, and implementation.

Conclusion

The health of Croatian civil society appears to be improving. The Croatian Civil Society Diamond indicates a rather well-balanced sector, of medium size. Although constraints and impediments remain, Croatian civil society is alive and active. At the community level, civic engagement is on the rise and CSOs are increasingly attracting citizens' support. Local entrepreneurs and local government are also becoming interested in cooperating with civil society initiatives. Thus, civil society is in the process of building trust and good relations with other stakeholders through new networks, which are initiated at the local level, but will, it is hoped, extend to the national level as well.

CSI Report

Gojko Bezovan, S. Zrinscak and M. Vugec, *Civil Society in Croatia— Gaining Trust and Establishing Partnerships with the State and Other Stakeholders: CIVICUS Civil Society Index Report for Croatia* (Zagreb, Croatia: Centre for Development of Non-Profit Organizations [CERANEO], 2005).

Notes

1. The CSI project was implemented in Croatia by the Centre for Development of Non-Profit Organizations (CERANEO) from September 2003 to May 2005. This chapter presents the main findings of the CSI and is based on a comprehensive country report for Croatia, which can be accessed on the CSI pages of the CIVICUS website at http://www.civicus.org.
2. Bezovan, Gojko, "Croatian Civil Society: On the Path to Becoming a Legitimate Public Actor," *CIVICUS World Alliance For Citizen Participation Paper Series* 1, no. 4 (July 2001).
3. Of these 35% belonging to a CSO, 16% belong to sports associations, 12.8% to trade or labor unions, 8.5% to the war veterans association, 7.8% to social welfare organizations, and 7.3% to faith-based organizations.
4. *Central Government Administration Office of the Republic of Croatia and Statistical Yearbook 2004* (2004):28.
5. According to Transparency International's 2005 Corruption Perception Index, Croatia ranked 70 out of 159 countries; in 2004 Croatia ranked 67 out of 146.

Chapter 8

⌒⌒

Cyprus[1]

The island of Cyprus, located in the Eastern Mediterranean, gained independence in 1960. Since 1974 it has been de facto divided into a southern and a northern part, separating the Greek and Turkish communities. Given civil society's potential role in fostering bi-communal cooperation, a coordinated assessment of the state of civil society in both parts of the island was deemed useful.

The CSI project was conducted separately in the two parts of the island by two independent Project Advisory Groups (PAGs). The CSI was the first coordinated study on civil society in the two communities and one of the few existing cooperative projects in which two major institutions from the northern and southern parts of Cyprus collaborated. The results highlighting the main findings of this study are presented in two separate sections.[2]

Southern Part of Cyprus

Historical Overview

In 1960 the island of Cyprus was granted independence from British colonial rule. Despite some instances of bi-communal cooperation, the island's anticolonial struggle failed to unite Greek and Turkish Cypriots into an all-encompassing social movement. During the 1960s and early 1970s, few social forces advocated notions of common Cypriot citizenship. Instead, from 1963 to 1974, political unrest and armed conflict persisted within the Greek Cypriot community and between Greek and Turkish Cypriots. This culminated in the de facto division of the island in 1974, after a coup staged by the Greek junta, with the help of radical nationalist groups, led to a military intervention by Turkey. Within the Greek Cypriot community, a minority challenged the

75

Table 8.1 Background Information for Southern Part of Cyprus

Cyprus (South)	
Size (square km)	9,250
Population	703,529
Population under 15 years	22%
Urban population	69%
Seats in parliament held by women	16.10%
Language groups	Greek, Turkish, and English
Ethnic groups	Greek 99.0%, Armenians 0.3%, Maronites 0.6%, Latin 0.04%, and Turkish Cypriots 0.06%
Religious groups	Orthodox 94.8%, Catholic 1.5%, Church of England 1%, Moslem 0.6%, Maronite 0.6%, Armenian 0.3%, atheist 0.2%, and other 1%
GDP per capita (CYP 2005)	9,142
Unemployment rate (%)	3.5%

legitimacy of the state and advocated for unification with Greece at all costs (known as *enosis*), while a majority maintained that although union with Greece was a worthwhile goal, the international circumstances were not ripe to pursue *enosis* at the time.

The impact of the political situation on Greek Cypriot civil society was immense. The public sphere, including civil society, was in a constant state of mobilization, and populist slogans and fanaticism prevailed. Public criticism of the state was limited: because the Republic of Cyprus was preoccupied with its survival, citizens were expected not to raise issues that were not deemed a national priority. Nevertheless, apolitical CSOs, such as professional associations, welfare organizations, and cultural and sports organizations continued to develop.

After the island's division in 1974, though the Republic of Cyprus's political system had many features found in modern democracies, notions of active citizenship remained weak, and civil society was limited to the trade union movement, social welfare organizations, and sports and recreational associations. There were relatively few human rights and advocacy groups, which tended to focus on supporting victims of the 1974 clashes. The omnipresence of the political in all spheres of Greek Cypriot social life characterized the public sphere in the southern part of Cyprus. Greek Cypriots regarded most issues as having a political cause and consequence, and expected politicians to deal with almost all issues affecting society. During this time, the state and political parties had pervasive influence over Cypriot society.

Since the mid-1990s, the focus of Greek Cypriot politics and the public discourse shifted toward the prospects and negotiations regarding EU membership, which was achieved in 2004. There has also been increased attention to overcome the division of the island in recent years. For example, a plan was launched by then United Nations Secretary General Kofi Annan and talks resumed between the Greek-Cypriot and Turkish-Cypriot communities regarding reunification of the island. So far, however, these attempts have failed to come to fruition.

The State of Civil Society in the Southern Part of Cyprus

This section provides a summary of key findings of the CSI project in the southern part of Cyprus. It examines the state of civil society along four dimensions—structure, environment, values, and impact—highlighting the main weaknesses and strengths.

The PAG opted to exclude political parties from the CSI's assessment. Due to their high degree of influence on many CSOs and the resulting erosion of CSOs' autonomy, the PAG believed that including political parties as part of civil society would create a distorted picture and reduce the analysis to a discussion of the pervasive role of political parties.

Figure 8.1 Civil Society Diamond for Southern Part of Cyprus

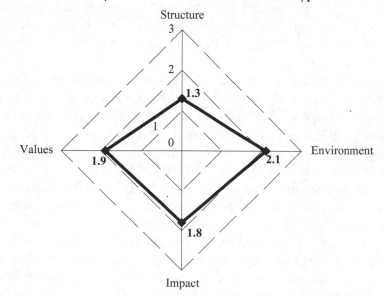

The Civil Society Diamond (figure 8.1) for the southern part of Cyprus visually summarizes the assessment's findings. The diamond reflects that civil society's structure is slightly weak, mostly due to low citizen participation, poor networking among civil society actors, a heavy concentration of CSOs in the two main cities, and the absence of significant social groups from CSOs' membership and leadership. The environment in which civil society operates is relatively conducive, but civil society suffers from a lack of institutionalized communication with the state as well as the private sector. Civil society's practice and promotion of positive values is rather strong, although there is a lack of emphasis on ethnic tolerance and transparency. Finally, civil society's impact on politics and society is moderate and impeded by the sector's weak influence on public policy.

Structure (1.3)

The structure dimension examines the makeup of civil society in terms of the main characteristics of individual citizen participation and associational life. In the southern part of Cyprus, the structure of civil society is the weakest dimension of the Civil Society Diamond.

Levels of citizen participation in public life are moderate. Although a large percentage of citizens claim to have donated to charity (87%) or participated in nonpartisan political action (59%), a minority of citizens report belonging to a CSO (43%). Nearly half of citizens volunteer at least once a year; however, the depth of volunteering is quite low, with more than half of respondents not having volunteered during the month prior to the study. Likewise, charitable donations by citizens only represent a rather small percentage (1.3%) of people's annual income.

The lack of depth in citizen participation can be seen in conjunction with a lack of diversity among the population involved in CSO activities. Foreign workers and ethnic and linguistic minorities tend to be mostly absent or excluded from CSOs, and other social groups, such as the poor and rural dwellers, are severely underrepresented in the membership and leadership of CSOs. The affluent, however, are very well represented. There is a geographical imbalance as well, with CSOs excessively concentrated in the capital of Nicosia and, to a lesser extent, in the second largest city, Limassol.

Civil society's weak structure is also due to the sector's poor level of organization. Few CSOs have international connections, and only a few umbrella bodies exist. During CSI consultations, it emerged that many CSOs are either unaware of the potential benefits of these structures or reluctant to join networks due to fear of losing their autonomy. In general, there is insufficient infrastructure to support CSOs, inadequate self-regulation, and limited communication between CSOs.

Structurally, the sector benefits from adequate human and technological resources. Over 70% of surveyed stakeholders claim that their CSOs have either adequate or rather adequate human and technological resources to achieve their objectives. Also, 60% of stakeholders report having adequate or rather adequate financial resources. At the same time, the PAG mentioned that the adequacy of resources varies from one CSO to another, depending on their affiliation. For example, professional associations, trade unions, and CSOs linked to political parties have more adequate financial resources than smaller organizations or advocacy CSOs.

As can be seen by the low overall score, structural shortcomings are the most substantial hindrance to the development of civil society in the southern part of Cyprus. Mobilizing citizens to participate in civil society and improving networking and communication between CSOs are important steps for strengthening the structural foundations of civil society.

Environment (2.1)

The environment dimension considers political, legal, socioeconomic, and sociocultural contexts, as well as the relationships between civil society, the state, and the private sector. Civil society in the southern part of Cyprus operates within a relatively enabling environment, where political rights and civil liberties are safeguarded and there is institutionalized political competition, a clear separation of powers, and a generally independent and respected judiciary. Civil society's environment is constrained by its problematic relations with the state and the private sector, as well as the prevailing political culture.

There is a shortage of established procedures and legal provisions for institutionalized dialogue between CSOs and the state, and regulations for state financing of CSOs. Where legal provisions and procedures for CSOs are in place, they are not necessarily enforced. Though there are few legal restrictions on CSOs' advocacy activities, relations between CSOs and the state are mostly determined by connections with particular political parties. Due to close relations and party funding of CSOs, political parties frequently attempt to promote their ideology or cause through the CSOs they support. Thus, in the southern part of Cyprus a political culture, characterized by clientelistic relationships, strongly shapes civil society and its role in politics.

With regard to civil society's relations with the private sector, the study reveals the private sector's negative attitude toward civil society, the limited extent of corporate philanthropy, and weak notions of corporate social responsibility (CSR). With the exception of the largest three banks—the Bank of Cyprus, the Popular Bank, and the Hellenic Bank—the vast majority of Greek Cypriot private companies do not have CSR policies in place.

Despite the weaknesses highlighted above, it is important to note that the environment is generally conducive and nonrestrictive for civil society activities. With a rather vibrant economy and effective institutional safeguards for basic freedoms and rights, the environment is relatively enabling for civil society, even though the political culture plays a major role in preventing civil society from becoming a more autonomous voice for citizens' concerns.

Values (1.9)

The values dimension examines the extent to which civil society practices and promotes positive values. Civil society's internal practice and external promotion of positive values is rather widespread in the southern part of Cyprus. Civil society is not very active in promoting transparency and tolerance; however, it plays a strong role in promoting nonviolence, gender equity, and environmental sustainability, though none of these activities enjoys broad-based, sustained support by citizens.

A majority of CSI stakeholder survey respondents report that civil society actions to promote government and corporate transparency are limited or insignificant, and no such actions were mentioned in the three newspapers monitored. A civil society active in promoting transparency presupposes a strong sense of citizenship, which remains underdeveloped in Cyprus. To understand the values of civil society in the areas currently under the control of the Republic of Cyprus, one needs to remember that citizens have not yet learned to act as members of a polity who have the right to know, be informed, and be respected by state agencies.

Civil society also plays a limited role in promoting tolerance, which should also be seen in the broader context of rather widespread intolerance among the Cypriot population. Civil society does not play an active role in cultivating tolerance and sensitivity toward less privileged groups. Participants at the CSI National Workshop highlighted a need for schools to educate students on tolerance. Civil society also needs to further entrench its own democratic practices, such as developing more inclusive procedures for including CSO members in decisionmaking processes and promoting these values within society at large.

A final weakness of civil society's values is its inactivity in the area of poverty eradication. The overall societal context has a bearing on civil society's record on this issue, since, according to CSI participants, Greek Cypriot society perceives itself as affluent and is characterized by blindness toward the *other*, such as the poor, immigrants, and the elderly.

Despite a poor record in promoting transparency, tolerance, and the fight against poverty, civil society is more sensitive and active in promoting gender equity, environmental sustainability, and nonviolence. The use of violence by civil society groups is occasional and isolated. Although women remain underrepresented in leadership positions, discrimination against women within Greek Cypriot civil society is not widespread.

Impact (1.8)

The impact dimension assesses civil society's role in governance and society at large. Overall, civil society has a moderate impact on Greek Cypriot politics and society. However, despite its mixed record, PAG members emphasized that efforts are under way for civil society to better respond to social needs and to influence public policy.

There are many areas where civil society's impact in the southern part of Cyprus remains limited, including involvement in the national budgetary process, empowering marginalized groups, building social capital, supporting livelihood creation activities, and lobbying for state service provisions. In particular, very little progress is discernible in empowering marginalized groups, such as foreign workers, immigrants, or the elderly. Also, civil society does not seem to make a significant contribution to increasing tolerance and trust within Greek Cypriot society.

The impact of civil society on social and human rights policy is modest, but noticeable. The PAG assesses the impact of civil society as moderate, which shows that steps are being taken to respond to social needs and influence public policy. Civil society is relatively prompt at responding to social interests, and many public education and information campaigns are considered successful. Thus, although Greek Cypriot civil society's impact is not strong, it is also not negligible.

Recommendations

Participants at the CSI National Workshop in September 2005 had an opportunity to reflect on the CSI assessment and put forward recommendations for the future development of Greek Cypriot civil society. The following is a list of the major recommendations:

- Improve civil society's level of organization: Develop cooperation and communication mechanisms within the sector and establish umbrella organizations, networks, and federations.
- Diversify funding sources: Given the sector's financial dependence on political parties and the state, efforts should be made to diversify funding sources, and the funding opportunities of EU membership should be utilized. This would improve the sector's autonomy and limit state and political party manipulation of the civil society agenda.
- Improve the democratic culture within society and civil society: CSOs need to improve internal governance processes and promote public campaigns that are in line with the sector's declared commitment to transparency, tolerance, and democratic practices. Civil society's role in promoting government and corporate accountability could be enhanced by cultivating a democratic ethos within civil society and society at large, through programs devoted to civic education and civil liberties. Civil society also needs to ensure that schools are characterized by tolerance and dialogue in a democratic and inclusive environment. Therefore, civil society should lobby for more efficient methods of educating students on civil rights.

Conclusion

For Intercollege, the CSI partner in the southern part of Cyprus, it was important to emphasize that CSI findings should not be seen as the definitive analysis on the state of civil society, but rather as a roadmap for Greek Cypriot civil society. Due to long-standing political tensions with regard to the island's political status, important norms such as active citizenship and social tolerance are in their infancy. It was repeatedly stated that it was crucial to understand the dominance of politics, in order to grasp the specific character of Greek Cypriot civil society. Additionally, the study emphasized the heterogeneous nature of civil society and stressed that the objectives, social composition, mode of conduct, impact, and available resources of CSOs vary. Nevertheless, the findings on civil society's structural weaknesses and relative lack of autonomy are applicable to most CSO types and should be addressed by all projects working to strengthen the sector.

Northern Part of Cyprus

Historical Overview

The role of civil society in the northern part of Cyprus is particularly unique since the territory is not recognized internationally as a sovereign state. The Turkish Republic of Northern Cyprus (TRNC) declared independence in 1983, but only Turkey has recognized it, which has limited civil society's ability to access many international legal and institutional resources.

Table 8.2 Background Information for Northern Part of Cyprus

Cyprus (North)	
Size (square km)	3,355
Population	215,790
Seats in parliament held by women	6%
Language groups	Turkish
Ethnic groups	Turkish 98%, Greek Cypriot 0.2%, Maronite 0.1%, other 0.9%
Religious groups	Muslim 92.2%, Orthodox 3%, atheist 0.2%
GDP per capita (US$)	$6,000
Unemployment rate	2.0%

An active Turkish Cypriot civil society predates the island's independence in 1960. Prior to independence, various clubs, foundations, and associations, such as the Kardeş Ocaği Club in Nicosia (Hearth of Brethen or Fraternity Home), played an important role in bestowing a sense of political community upon Turkish Cypriots. However, despite examples of bi-communal cooperation during the anticolonial struggle, a unified civil society did not emerge. Following the island's division in 1974, civil society developed independently on either side of the Green Line that separates the northern and the southern parts of the island.

Upon independence from the British colonial regime, the Republic of Cyprus was formed as a partnership between the Greek Cypriot and Turkish Cypriot communities, based on the principle of federalism. In the immediate postcolonial phase (1960–1963) civil society flourished in the new environment. Non-nationalist parties and the media demanded the legal protection of individual rights, rejected ethnocultural segregation, fought against the use of violence as a means of political action, and began to function independently of the respective community's political leadership. Overall, the dominant feature of civil society in the first years of independence was its opposition to nationalist policies of community leadership.

From 1963 to 1967, however, intercommunal fighting severely weakened civil society. Many organizations closed down or were subjected to political control as authorities penetrated almost all social activities in the country. Consequently, nationalist doctrines replaced the public good–oriented agenda and began to dominate the demands and actions of many CSOs.

After the division in 1974, a number of new autonomous organizations were established in the northern part of Cyprus. As society developed and modernized, so did civil society. By the 1990s the number of CSOs had grown substantially and become an important element of political opposition in the Turkish Cypriot community, as well as a provider of necessary services to the community. The 1990s witnessed the rise of CSOs committed to bi-communal activities, environmentalism, women's issues, and human rights. Despite the physical and de facto division of the island, civil society in both parts developed a common language in support of peace, bi-communal dialogue, and unification.

To date, the most significant civil society development has been its role in promoting the plan by then United Nations Secretary General Kofi Annan to settle the division of Cyprus with a referendum requiring acceptance by both sides of the island. In the northern part of Cyprus, the Turkish Cyprus Chamber of Commerce took the lead in forging the Common Vision of the Turkish Cypriot Civil Society, signed by ninety-one CSOs. It emphasized the urgency to solve the problem before the Republic of Cyprus acceded to the EU in 2002. Likewise, prior to the Common Vision document, the This Country Is Ours Platform, which called for self-governance of the Turkish Cypriots and demilitarization, garnered widespread support within society. These coalitions led Turkish Cypriots to demonstrate in favor of the Annan Plan. Today, in the aftermath of the disappointment with the failed Annan Plan, which was rejected by a majority of Greek Cypriots in April 2004, many stakeholders fear that CSOs will divide instead of coalesce, and civil society's common agenda will shift away from the EU-induced reforms toward a revival of nationalist politics in civil society and society at large.

State of Civil Society in the Northern Part of Cyprus[3]

This section provides a summary of key findings of the CSI project in the northern part of Cyprus. It examines the state of civil society along four dimensions—structure, environment, values, and impact— · highlighting the main weaknesses and strengths.

Given the dominant role of political parties in the northern part of Cyprus, the PAG excluded political parties from the study. The PAG also noted that in public and expert discourse, civil society usually refers to an association independent of the state that contributes to the development of civic values.

The Civil Society Diamond for the northern part of Cyprus visually summarizes the assessment's findings (figure 8.2). The size of the diamond reveals that civil society is relatively small and needs considerable growth to have a stronger presence within society. The structure of civil society requires the most improvement, particularly regarding levels of citizen participation and the level of organization within civil society. The environment is moderately conducive for civil society, but CSOs are constrained by a lack of autonomy from political forces. Civil society gains strength from its values, particularly its commitment to nonviolence. The overall impact of civil society on politics and society remains relatively limited, especially with regard to its influence on public policy and holding the state and the private sector accountable.

Figure 8.2 Civil Society Diamond for Northern Part of Cyprus

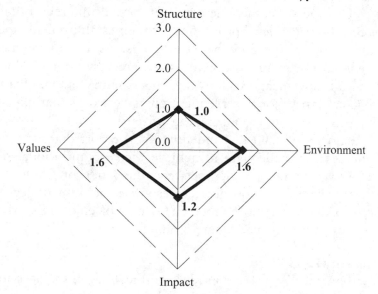

Structure (1.0)

The structure dimension examines the makeup of civil society in terms of the main characteristics of individual citizen participation and associational life. Apart from the mass demonstrations for and against the Annan Plan, the examination of civil society's structure · indicates that citizen participation and civil society's degree of organization remains weak. Although approximately half of Turkish Cypriots belong to a CSO, particularly trade unions and sports organizations, only a minority engages in volunteering, charitable giving, nonpartisan political action, and collective community action. The unprecedented degree of political action associated with the debate over the Annan Plan from 2002 to 2004 was clearly an exception to the usually low levels of citizen participation in the northern part of Cyprus. Another problem is the inadequate representation of significant social groups, such as minorities, the poor, and foreign workers, in civil society.

With regard to civil society's level of organization, there is a shortage of umbrella bodies and international linkages, and rivalries among CSOs prohibit greater cooperation. Sixty percent of stakeholders believe that communication among CSOs is limited or nonexistent. In part, this problem stems from CSOs with overlapping agendas competing for limited funding, and overly politicized CSOs that have leaders closely affiliated to politicians and uninterested in collaborating with other CSOs.

An impediment for the emergence of formal umbrella organizations is the absence of legal provisions for their establishment, and the political/ideological divisions between CSOs. Aside from numerous sports federations, umbrella organizations are very limited. Notably, ad hoc social movements, such as the This Country Is Ours Platform and the Common Vision deserve mention as networks that have been somewhat successful in mobilizing the citizenry.

The majority of CSO respondents (63%) report that their financial resources are inadequate to achieve their organizational objectives. However, funding varies between the kinds of CSOs. Trade unions, for example, enjoy greater resources because of legislated membership dues, but most other CSOs do not enjoy this privilege and are constrained by inadequate funding.

Environment (1.6)

The environment dimension considers political, legal, socioeconomic, and sociocultural contexts, as well as the relationships between civil society, the state, and the private sector. The CSI reveals that the environment is not as debilitating for civil society as is generally assumed. Despite the presence of tens of thousands of troops from Turkey, and a general dependence on Turkey, civil society in the northern part of Cyprus exists in an environment that is, for the most part, relatively free and enabling. Additionally, despite the fact that residents of the northern part of Cyprus have been isolated from the international community for more than forty years, the socioeconomic context is largely favorable for civil society. The population suffers more psychologically than from a lack of material well-being. The "Cyprus problem" and its ancillary effects, such as uncertainty about the future, affect people more heavily than the traditional conceptions of crisis, such as severe economic recession or civil war.

The CSI finds civil society's operating environment to be constrained by weak state–civil society relations, which impede the sector's autonomy. There remains a degree of state interference in civil society activities that prevents the independent development of the sector. The rule of law is marred by patronage. The state controls resources and implements policies without adequate transparency or accountability. Although generous transfer payments from Turkey have helped sustain the Turkish Cypriot community, they have also created dependency on Ankara and led to an unresponsive public administration in the northern part of Cyprus.

A lack of democratic values has curtailed the sector's autonomy, due to its affiliations and close relations with government and opposition political parties. CSOs that pursue more narrow agendas, related to the interests of their constituency, are more influential than those supporting general public interests, such as human rights organizations. In general, the government's cooptation of many CSOs stifles potential cooperation among civil society actors and dampens citizens' enthusiasm to participate in civil society. Although advocacy groups remain distant from the state apparatus, their critical position toward the government rarely translates into policy impact. In contrast, trade unions are embedded in the state, and public-sector trade unions are run by special laws, which entitle them to privileged status and economic benefits.

The legal environment affecting civil society is problematic, because most CSOs lack access to legal advice and are ill-informed of the rules, laws, and regulations affecting them. Civil society is not a partner in the governance system in the northern part of Cyprus and with an executive that is generally not responsive to civil society, state–civil society relations are not particularly favorable. Nonetheless, since socioeconomic and sociocultural factors are rather conducive, civil society's overall environment was assessed as slightly above average.

Values (1.6)

The values dimension examines the extent to which civil society practices and promotes positive values. The analysis of civil society's values demonstrates that civil society's practice of positive values is fairly strong; however, there is less promotion of these values in society at large. Although the values dimension is one of the sector's strongest dimensions, several weaknesses remain. According to stakeholders, these weaknesses are primarily related to shortcomings in CSOs' internal structure. For example, limited citizen participation in CSOs, combined with CSO leadership, which lacks long-term commitment to organizational objectives, undermines civil society's ability to promote important values to the community.

Tolerance and nonviolence appear to be deeply embedded values, and these are practiced within civil society. A majority of CSOs promote nonviolence and principles of inclusion within the Turkish Cypriot community. In the context of an ethnically divided Cyprus, the propagation of these values by civil society is critical to fostering peace and the betterment of society at large. Of course, given the heterogeneous nature of civil society, a few CSOs remain committed to a more exclusive concept of society based on ethnicity and consider violence a legitimate means.

Civil society is less active in propagating transparency, gender equity, democracy, and poverty alleviation. Sixty-one percent of stakeholders report that civil society activities are insignificant or limited in promoting poverty alleviation. Also, civil society does not actively promote transparency and democracy within society at large, since, for each of these two values, as many as two-thirds of stakeholders believe public campaigns, actions, and programs to promote these values are quite limited.

The discrepancy between the internal values and their external promotion highlights CSOs' strength in practicing values and their weakness in promoting these values within society. Overall, the values practiced by civil society in northern Cyprus bode well for the future, insofar as CSOs sustain democratic practices and norms of nonviolence and tolerance that could serve as a foundation to foster campaigns to promote empathy and inclusiveness. These values appear to be civil society's greatest asset, especially considering the need to build trust within the community as well as toward the Greek Cypriot community.

Impact (1.2)

The impact dimension assesses civil society's role in governance and society at large. The CSI findings reveal that Turkish Cypriot civil society's impact on politics and society is relatively limited. It is particularly weak in regard to influencing the state's budget and holding the state and private sector accountable. Although civil society is more adept at empowering citizens, its effectiveness is impeded by a public perception of lack of capacity and reliability.

Although civil society played an important role in galvanizing support for and against the Annan Plan, its impact in other areas remains quite weak. Given the northern part of Cyprus's dependency on Turkey, the government is less responsive and less able to respond to citizens' concerns than a fully autonomous state. With respect to civil society's ability to influence public policy, and the budgetary process in particular, stakeholders maintain that Turkey ultimately determines policy and, therefore, civil society is unable to meaningfully engage government on these issues.

The impact of advocacy groups is especially weak compared to trade unions and professional associations. These latter organizations have a narrower agenda and enjoy a privileged position with government, while advocacy groups remain marginalized and distant from government, since they seek to address broad social concerns. For example, although trade unions are actively engaged with government, they generally remain relegated to negotiating salaries and wages for public sector employees rather than influencing overall policy priorities.

Civil society is also weak at holding the state and the private sector accountable, and it is not effective as a watchdog or as a voice lobbying for the provision of essential services by the state. An overwhelming 98% of stakeholders believe that civil society plays an insignificant or somewhat insignificant role in holding private corporations accountable. Not only are the government and the private sector relatively averse to scrutiny, but CSOs lack the necessary skills to monitor the state and businesses. Furthermore, many CSOs are not autonomous from the government and political party interests.

The sector is most successful at empowering citizens through information campaigns, building capacity for collective action, and building social capital. For example, the teachers' union, Cyprus Turkish Primary School Teachers' Union (KTOS), requested a discussion on educational policies, and various CSOs called for a protest and cooperation against the growth in criminal activities in the community. However, civil society's overall impact on society is constrained by low public trust in CSOs, an adversarial relationship between rival CSO leaders, and an overall lack of professionalism within civil society. The poor public image of civil society perpetuates structural problems, such as low levels of public enthusiasm and interest in supporting or participating in civil society activities.

Recommendations

Participants of the CSI final workshop in September 2005 had an opportunity to reflect on the project's findings and offer recommendations for the development of Turkish Cypriot civil society. The following items are some of the key recommendations:

- Raise levels of professionalism and public trust: CSO leaders and members need to be educated on professional norms. Civil society should utilize the media and publicize CSO activities to improve the public's perception of civil society and stimulate citizen interest in becoming involved in civil society.
- Improve civil society–state relations: Civil society needs to continue to pressure the government to develop mechanisms for civil society to provide input into the public policy process. In the context of scarce funding, civil society should advocate to receive a share of government funds currently earmarked as political.
- Combat the politicization of civil society: Civil society needs to protect itself against its current politicization as a vehicle for personal and political career advancement. Attempts should be made to develop further links between international donors and CSOs. Greater transparency in government, in relations between government and CSOs, and within CSOs themselves might increase public trust in CSOs, improve relations among CSOs, and reduce the politicization of civil society.

Conclusion

The CSI findings reveal that structural shortcomings are a dominant obstacle for a stronger civil society in the northern part of Cyprus. Low levels of citizen participation, poor networking, and competition among civil society actors, as well as inadequate funding, characterize the sector's current situation. A recurring theme raised by CSI participants was civil society's lack of autonomy, which remains constrained by the political forces at play in Cyprus. Efforts proposed to increase the sector's self-regulation, transparency, and accountability might help depoliticize and professionalize the sector and improve its public image.

Island-Wide Conclusion and Recommendations

Given that the CSI assessment was carried out in parallel in both parts of the island, the Management Centre of the Mediterranean (MC-Med) in the northern part and Intercollege in the southern part decided to have an island-wide discussion of the CSI findings. In September 2005, following both mono-communal workshops, the groups convened to discuss island-wide issues.

Participants from across the island suggested five areas of focus to promote the development and healthy growth of civil society in Cyprus. First, there is a need for more capacity-building of CSO professionals. Second, participants identified the need for CSOs to collaborate by establishing networks and links both locally and internationally to consolidate their efforts. Third, more constructive relations need to be developed between civil society and the authorities. Fourth, participants highlighted the need to enhance public awareness of civil liberties and promote human rights education for the youth. Finally, participants noted the need to redress transparency and accountability issues within CSOs to strengthen civil society's credibility as well as its effectiveness.

It is hoped that by publishing this joint report on the state of civil society in Cyprus, civil society stakeholders and researchers will be able to utilize the findings to support and inform their work. The recommendations, which are based on the strengths and weaknesses of the respective civil societies, point toward a future path for developing a healthy and vibrant civil society on the island of Cyprus.

CSI Report

Efstathios Mavros, Monica Ioannidou, and Erol Kaymak, *An Assessment of Civil Society in Cyprus—A Map for the Future: CIVICUS Civil Society Index Report for Cyprus* (Cyprus: Management Centre for the Mediterranean [MC-Med] in collaboration with Intercollege, 2005).

Notes

1. The CSI assessment was implemented by Management Centre for the Mediterranean (MC-Med) in the northern part of Cyprus and Intercollege in the southern part from March to September 2005. This chapter presents the main findings of the CSI and is based on a comprehensive report, which can be accessed on the CSI pages of the CIVICUS website at http://www.civicus.org.
2. The southern part of Cyprus is controlled by the Republic of Cyprus and the northern part of Cyprus by the Turkish Republic of Northern Cyprus (TRNC). Reference made to the government, authorities, and institutions in the northern part of Cyprus does not imply recognition by the Greek Cypriots or the international community.
3. Although this section uses the terms "government" and "state" when referring to formal state and government institutions in the TRNC, the TRNC is currently recognized only by Turkey.

Chapter 9

~~

Czech Republic[1]

Since the end of the socialist regime more than fifteen years ago, the Czech Republic and its civil society have come a long way. The Civil Society Index (CSI) assessment finds a rather strong Czech civil society, which can draw on surprisingly high levels of civic engagement. Although civil society must confront a number of challenges, particularly financial sustainability and strengthening the sector's infrastructure, its positive environment and rather consolidated structure are likely to sustain the sector in the future.

Table 9.1 Background Information for the Czech Republic

Czech Republic	
Country size (square km)	78,864
Population (millions 2004)	10.2
Population under 15 years (2004)	15%
Urban population (2003)	74.3%
Seats in parliament held by women (2005)	17%
Language groups	Czech (official), German, Polish, Roma
Ethnic groups	Czech 90.4%, Moravian 3.7%, Slovak 1.9%, other 4%
Religious groups	Roman Catholic 27%, unaffiliated 59%, Protestant 5%, Orthodox 3%, other 3%
HDI score and ranking (2003)	0.874 (31st)
GDP per capita (US$ 2003)	$16,357
Unemployment rate (% of total labor force)	8.3%
Population living on less than US$2 a day (1996)	<2%

Historical Overview

The Czech Republic has a vibrant tradition of civil society dating back to the early nineteenth century, when citizens began to form various types of associations. However, forty years of Communist rule constituted a major rupture for civil society, since independent associations were not permitted. Consequently, Czech civil society plunged into obscurity. Nevertheless, during the Communist period civil society traditions were not completely buried, as evidenced by the Prague Spring in 1968, Charta 77,[2] and the many organizations that operated illegally throughout the 1970s. These traditions were revived in the 1980s, culminating in the Velvet Revolution of 1989, when citizen demonstrations led to the collapse of the Communist regime. These events, and similar events in neighboring countries, contributed to the concept of civil society gaining currency in the Czech Republic and throughout central and Eastern Europe.

In the wake of the Velvet Revolution, the number of civil society organizations (CSOs) substantially increased. New laws, such as the Act on the Right of Assembly, and an influx of foreign donors, enabled the proliferation of new CSOs. The new CSOs contrasted with old, Communist-regime CSOs, such as the Czech Women's Union. However, many old CSOs survived and sought to transform themselves under the new democratic dispensation.

During the 1990s, the Czech people's perception of civil society's role in society was strongly influenced by the polemic debate between two leading political personalities, President Vaclav Havel and Prime Minister Vaclav Klaus. This public debate centered on the question of the legitimacy of CSOs to protect public interests, provide social services, and influence public policy, without a mandate to do so through elections. To a certain extent, this debate on CSOs' role in the decisionmaking process continues in the Czech political sphere today.

Despite the rapid growth and diversification of Czech civil society in the 1990s, in recent years many foreign donor programs have closed down and moved east, focusing their support on other post-Communist countries. Czech CSOs are aware of the impact this decline in donor funding has on the sector's activities, and they understand the need to develop new sources of financing. At the same time, the Czech Republic's 2004 accession to the European Union (EU) has created new opportunities for funding to support Czech civil society.

The State of Civil Society in the Czech Republic

In Czech discourse, civil society usually refers to an association of people independent of the state and contributing to the development of positive civic values and social capital. In response to the country's EU accession and the drafting of a new Civil Code, which is refining the concept of CSOs under the law, new definitions of civil society are being discussed.

To operationalize the concept of civil society within the Czech context, Czech political parties are excluded from the definition because they are more closely linked with government than with their members and constituents. Similarly, cooperatives are excluded due to their history under socialism, which led them to assume purely economic roles. In addition, unlike the CSI definition of civil society, which includes informal forms of citizen participation and negative manifestations of civil society, in the Czech Republic's CSI assessment, informal groupings and negative aspects of civil society are only examined peripherally.

This section provides a summary of key findings of the CSI project in the Czech Republic. It examines the state of Czech civil society along four dimensions—structure, environment, values, and impact—highlighting the main weaknesses and strengths.

The Czech Civil Society Diamond visually summarizes the CSI findings and indicates a relatively balanced and developed civil society sector (see figure 9.1). The diamond depicts a civil society with a slightly strong structure, which boasts rather high levels of citizen involvement in various civic activities, but is constrained by a rather weak financial resource base and low levels of organization within formal civil society. Czech CSOs operate in a relatively enabling environment, where the political and legal context are particularly conducive. However, the legacy of Communism in the form of weak social trust and low levels of social tolerance limits civil society's growth potential. Except for internal transparency and accountability standards, civil society practices and promotes positive values to a significant extent and exerts moderate impact on politics and society.

Structure (1.7)

The structure dimension examines the makeup of civil society in terms of the main characteristics of individual citizen participation and associational life. The structure dimension receives the lowest score among the four dimensions. Notable features include civil society's relatively strong citizen base, especially compared to

Figure 9.1 Civil Society Diamond for the Czech Republic

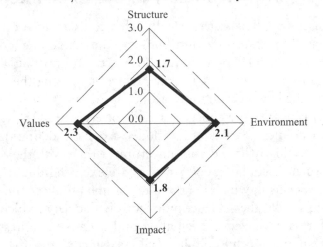

other post-Communist countries, and the moderately developed linkages and interactions between CSOs.

Despite the medium score, the structure of Czech civil society has many strengths, such as its diversity in organizational forms and mandates. Thousands of CSOs are working on a variety of issues and targeting a multitude of groups. Another strength is its human resource base, as demonstrated by the significant time volunteered by Czech citizens. Contrary to the prevalent assumption that citizens are detached from society due to the country's Communist legacy, levels of citizen participation are higher than expected. The CSI assessment finds that about 47% of Czech citizens donate to charity, and the same percent are members of a CSO. Forty-eight percent of Czechs have been involved in civic actions, such as writing a letter to a newspaper or participating in a demonstration, and about 57% of citizens participate in community activities. The relatively high levels of participation and civic involvement, supported by a favorable socioeconomic and political environment, have aided in successfully transforming the Czech Republic into a democratic society over the past fifteen years.

The weak relationships among civil society's actors are a primary area of concern for civil society's structure. Despite the presence of approximately eighty civil society umbrella organizations, only a few provide effective support to their member organizations or play a positive role in developing and monitoring codes of conduct and other joint efforts. Many umbrella organizations lack a representative membership base, but act as representatives of civil society when interacting with the government. This leads to a loss of credibility within the sector.

Another challenge to civil society's effective functioning is its financial base. Since most foreign donors are phasing out their support of Czech CSOs, it is not surprising that financial resources were identified as a pressing issue. More than 80% of consulted CSO representatives consider their organization's financial resources to be insufficient. At the same time, the Czech Republic's recent accession to the EU has opened up potential access to a variety of EU structural funds. Czech civil society needs to develop the capacity and the skills to tap into these resources, though the aim of these funds is to support the social welfare system, not to develop civil society. Human resources are also a concern. Although Czech civil society currently enjoys a sufficient human resource base, stakeholders fear that it is not sustainable since it is largely volunteer-based. In order to ensure the long-term sustainability and effectiveness of the sector, it is vital that a greater number of CSO professionals be trained in strategic planning, management, public relations, and fundraising.

For donors who have supported civil society infrastructure for the past fifteen years, the lack of cross-sectoral cooperation among Czech CSOs and their limited organizational resources might be somewhat disappointing. However, in the long run, the emerging citizen base is likely to provide both substantive human and financial resources for the civil society sector and be a driving force for generating stronger links among its various actors.

Environment (2.1)

The environment dimension considers political, legal, socioeconomic, and sociocultural contexts, as well as the relationships between civil society, the state, and the private sector. The overall environment for civil society in the Czech Republic is relatively enabling. Political and socioeconomic factors in particular are conducive to civil society activities. Over the past fifteen years, there have been positive developments in the regulatory and legal frameworks governing Czech civil society, and these developments are leading to increased collaboration between the state and civil society and a generally conducive political atmosphere.

In contrast, examining the sociocultural environment and collaboration efforts between civil society and the private sector reveals particular weaknesses in the environment within which civil society operates. The Communist legacy still influences social norms, such as trust, tolerance, and public spiritedness. Czech citizens rarely trust one another. Only 17% of Czechs believe that most people can be trusted, and despite a generally tolerant society, xenophobia and intolerance against minorities, such as the Roma, persist.

The relationship between civil society and the private sector is another weakness in civil society's external environment. The majority of stakeholders believe that the private sector is indifferent to civil society. This negative perception is substantiated by the fact that, although companies are establishing foundations as part of their corporate social responsibility (CSR) initiatives, collaboration between large companies and CSOs remains limited.

Over the past decade, the political and economic environments for Czech civil society have contributed to strengthening the sector. Advances were primarily made in the areas of CSO and tax legislation, and by developing mechanisms for dialogue between the state and civil society. However, to ensure the sustainability and future growth of civil society, CSOs must reach out to citizens and earn their trust. In addition, CSOs should increase their engagement with the private sector, which could become a vital funding source, particularly as foreign donors leave the country.

Values (2.3)

The values dimension examines the extent to which civil society practices and promotes positive values. The score for the values dimension reflects that, overall, Czech civil society practices and promotes positive values. The CSI analysis shows that values such as democracy, tolerance, nonviolence, gender equity, poverty eradication, and environmental protection are strongly entrenched in Czech civil society. In contrast, there is a lack of attention to internal transparency and accountability within the sector, which is a reflection of a society-wide problem of corrupt practices and informal relations.

The CSI identified environmental and social service organizations as flagship CSO types and examples of value-driven CSOs. For example, environmental organizations raised the profile of issues regarding environmental protection by increasing citizens' awareness. This resulted in uniquely high levels of public trust in ecological organizations, with 74% of citizens having confidence in the work of these kinds of organizations. Similarly, social service CSOs have raised awareness of, and concern for, socially marginalized groups. In addition, they have become important suppliers of social and health care services.

The level of financial transparency is problematic in Czech CSOs and requires considerable improvement. Examples of corruption within civil society were widely debated by the National Advisory Group (NAG), regional stakeholders, and national workshop participants. Civil society stakeholders felt that corruption mainly exists in the form of clientelism and abuse of power. However, given the generally high levels of corruption within society at large, one NAG member noted that "nothing entitles us to the opinion that civil society is any different from the rest of society."

Despite the presence of legal mechanisms to regulate financial matters in CSOs, financial transparency is also a concern within Czech civil society. Stakeholders believe that a primary cause of low financial transparency is the lack of financial skills and expertise within CSOs. In general, there is a need to improve transparency and accountability principles and mechanisms among CSOs. Greater attention to issues of transparency would likely increase citizens' trust and commitment to the civil society sector.

Impact (1.8)

The impact dimension assesses civil society's role in governance and society at large. The score for Czech civil society's impact reflects a relatively significant impact. In general, Czech CSOs are seen as fairly active and successful in their role as service providers and capacity-builders. However, civil society's public image is not pronouncedly better than that of the government (trust ratings of 40% and 37%, respectively).

Civil society plays an important role in influencing public policy and engaging with government on policy issues. The CSI findings identify two particularly important areas of CSO policy influence, namely environmental protection and social services. CSOs working on these issues have succeeded in placing their demands on the public agenda, as, for example, with the Social Services Act. In addition, trade unions and professional and economic associations are traditionally active and successful in influencing public policies at the national level. Civil society owes much of its success in influencing the policy agenda to the generally cooperative and amicable relations with the government.

Although Czech civil society is viewed as fairly effective in cooperating with the government, it is considered rather weak in monitoring the actions of the state and the private sector. This is particularly true today, as foreign donors leave civil society underresourced, placing its watchdog role under severe threat. Only ecological CSOs are currently visibly exerting an impact by monitoring the government. To a certain extent they are successful in holding the government and the private sector accountable for the environmental consequences of their policies and actions. Stakeholders suggested that other advocacy CSOs should learn from ecological CSOs, which are earning high levels of public trust by performing multiple functions, ranging from influencing public policy to acting as watchdogs and responding to social needs.

Recommendations

At the CSI National Workshop in October 2004 approximately fifty stakeholders engaged in a discussion of the findings and put forward recommendations for strengthening civil society.

Participants had one overarching recommendation for addressing many of the aforementioned weaknesses: to increase the credibility of civil society. To work toward this goal, stakeholders put forward the following specific recommendations:

- Establish effective communication channels and structures among CSOs.
- Improve CSOs' transparency by publicizing financial records and other organizational information.
- Strengthen enforceable checks and balances within civil society to increase public accountability.
- Strengthen the professionalism and professional skills of CSO staff and employees.
- Reform umbrella organizations to ensure that they are broadly representative of their constituents.

Other recommendations concerned the following areas:

- Establish equal partnerships among civil society, companies, and the public administration, including the EU.
- Explore opportunities to access EU structural funds to establish a global grant for the renewal and reinforcement of civil society for the period of 2007 to 2013, with a focus on capacity-building, growth, and greater independence of CSOs.
- Make the active involvement of CSOs in partnership with companies and public administration bodies a prerequisite for EU funding.
- Conduct a study on the success of ecological CSOs to provide other CSOs with the information, tools, and incentives for assuming a stronger role as public watchdogs.

Conclusion

Since the end of the Communist era, Czech civil society has developed quickly and is considerably stronger than is commonly perceived. To achieve long-term sustainability, Czech civil society must sustain the advances made during the phase of democratic transition.

The main challenges for the future of Czech civil society relate to issues of institutionalization and maturation. These include tackling poor management, improving inter-sectoral relations, gaining private sector support, assuming a watchdog role toward government and business, and achieving financial sustainability. Potential impediments to tackling these challenges lie in the Communist legacy of low levels of trust and public spiritedness, and high levels of corruption. Nevertheless, civil society has a number of strengths to draw upon, such as rather high levels of citizen participation, a positive values base, and a relatively enabling environment.

Through the CSI's participatory activities, the project created platforms for stakeholders to meet and reflect on the state of civil society. These activities have already yielded unintended results. One example is the relationship that developed between farmers' associations and environmental CSOs, which typically do not interact due to opposing interests. Preliminary findings also show that some regional governments have expressed interest in the CSI findings and have begun to engage more actively with regional CSOs. It is now up to the various stakeholders within civil society, the government, and other societal sectors to act upon the recommendations identified by the CSI in order to contribute to the further growth and sustainability of Czech civil society.

CSI Report

Tereza Vajdova, *An Assessment of Czech Civil Society in 2004—After Fifteen Years of Development: CIVICUS Civil Society Index Report for the Czech Republic* (Prague, Czech Republic: Civil Society Development Foundation [NROS], 2005).

Notes

1. The CSI assessment was implemented in the Czech Republic by the Civil Society Development Foundation (NROS) from December 2003 to November 2004. This chapter presents the main findings of the CSI and is based on a comprehensive country report for the Czech Republic, which can be accessed on the CSI pages of the CIVICUS website at http://www.civicus.org.
2. Charta 77 was an informal initiative by prominent Czech and Slovak citizens that criticized the Communist government's human rights violations.

Chapter 10

Ecuador[1]

As in other countries in Latin America, civil society in Ecuador is extremely vocal in advocating for the rights of indigenous people and marginalized groups. Popular mobilizations have frequently led to the collapse of governments or brought the country to a temporary standstill, reinforcing the volatile nature of the country's sociopolitical dynamics. It remains an open question whether civil society is able to change its dominant mode of engagement from a generally divisive approach to a more constructive approach, which would allow for civic mobilization as well as foster democratic stability.

Table 10.1 Background Information for Ecuador

Ecuador	
Country size (square km)	269,178
Population (millions 2004)	13
Population under 15 years (2004)	32.8%
Urban population (2003)	61.8%
Seats in parliament held by women (2005)	16%
Language groups	Spanish (official), Amerindian languages (especially Quechua)
Ethnic groups	Mestizo 65%, Amerindian 25%, Spanish and others 7%, black 3%
Religious groups	Roman Catholic 95%, other 5%
HDI score and ranking (2003)	0.759 (82nd)
GDP per capita (US$ 2003)	$3,641
Unemployment rate (% of total labor force)	11.4%
Population living on less than US$2 a day (1998)	37.2%

Historical Overview

The development of contemporary civil society in Ecuador is a rather recent phenomenon, dating back to the early 1900s. Previously, isolated forms of charitable activities and volunteerism existed, particularly at the local level, such as the Charity Committee of the Guayaquil Region, which was founded in 1887. The first half of the twentieth century was characterized by economic instability and the emergence of *campesino* (peasant) movements and trade unions. During the 1960s and 1970s, Ecuador saw a further growth of social movements, especially those that represented the demands of indigenous groups in the Amazon and the Highlands.

Since the late 1970s, new forms of civic participation have come to the fore. Rapid urbanization brought about by the oil boom strengthened the role of the middle class, while the indigenous movement acquired further popularity and support, and managed to establish a common platform for the various indigenous groups present in the country. During the 1970s CSOs and political parties developed independently of each other and grew highly suspicious of one another. Some social movements and CSOs participated in attempted coups or devised programs to establish direct democracy; however, these were hijacked by military leaders or *caudillos* for personal goals.

In the 1980s different indigenous groups began gravitating toward a single organization operating at the national level, the Confederation of Indigenous Nationalities in Ecuador (CONAIE), which is the most important social movement in the country today. In 1996 CONAIE, together with other social movements, gave birth to a political party, *Pachakutik*, which has established itself as an important political force.

In the 1990s the political climate in Ecuador became increasingly confrontational. The country went through a phase of economic recession culminating in the 1999 to 2000 financial crisis. During the same period, because of rampant corruption and deterioration of the rule of law, public institutions began to lose credibility. Dissatisfaction increased rapidly among the population, and growing mistrust in public institutions paved the way for social and political conflicts, especially between the indigenous movement and charismatic leaders with authoritarian agendas. For example, indigenous movements were the vanguard of protests and street demonstrations against governmental policies in the 1990s and played a crucial role in the downfall of presidents Abdalá Bucaram in 1997 and Jamil Mahuad in 2000. In 2005 many civil society actors were involved in a series of demonstrations that contributed to ousting President Lucio Gutierrez.

The State of Civil Society in Ecuador

This section provides a summary of key findings of the CSI project in Ecuador. It examines the state of Ecuadorian civil society along four dimensions—structure, environment, values, and impact—highlighting the main weaknesses and strengths.

Overall, Ecuadorian civil society is divided between a strong, well-organized indigenous movement and a variety of other CSOs and social movements with different agendas. At times, these forces cooperate with one another; however, usually they remain issue-specific and pursue different goals. As the Civil Society Diamond suggests (figure 10.1), Ecuadorian civil society has a slightly weak structure, mainly because of poor infrastructure and scarce resources, and operates in a slightly disabling environment due to mistrust in public institutions and widespread corruption. Civil society practices and promotes progressive values to a limited extent and exerts only moderate impact on policy and society.

Figure 10.1 Civil Society Diamond for Ecuador

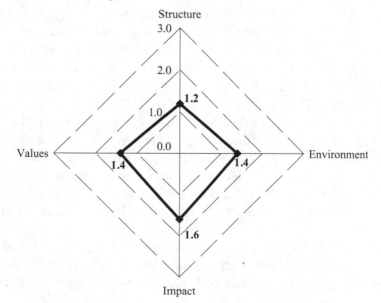

Structure (1.2)

The structure dimension examines the makeup of civil society in terms of the main characteristics of individual citizen participation and associational life. The structure of civil society in Ecuador is characterized by poor inter-sectoral communication among CSOs. Moreover, CSOs' financial resources are rather limited, particularly beyond a small group of urban-based professional NGOs. Marginalized groups remain underrepresented in civil society, with the exception of CSOs specifically concerned with the rights of women, children, and indigenous groups.

Ecuadorian civil society is characterized by rather low levels of citizen participation. According to the CSI population survey, 28% of citizens have participated in nonpartisan political actions and 32% in community activities. Membership rates in CSOs are estimated at 30%, with faith-based associations, mutual savings associations, and other forms of community groups having the highest membership rates. There are also compulsory forms of membership. For example, to practice a particular profession it is necessary to be a member of the respective professional association, and sometimes trade union membership is mandatory.

Apart from indigenous organizations and some traditional forms of community groups, CSOs are typically concentrated in major cities, and the presence of CSOs in rural areas is quite limited. Although the increase in representation of indigenous groups in civil society is noteworthy, this is mainly due to the prominence of the indigenous movement within Ecuadorian civil society and the formation of single-issue CSOs that focus specifically on minorities. In general, there are considerable barriers to equitable membership and leadership representation of other marginalized groups, especially women, the poor, and homosexuals.

The organizational development of CSOs is rather low throughout the country. This is further aggravated by the low number and limited effectiveness of existing support organizations. According to CSI stakeholders, one of the most significant obstacles to effective communication and the creation of alliances and networks among CSOs is the lack of mutual trust within civil society and society at large.

Although Ecuadorian civil society has traditionally received significant funding from international aid agencies, in the past few years the resources gathered at the local level have increased significantly through local donations and membership fees. CSI stakeholders saw this as an important step toward building an internally driven and sustainable civil society. However, the overall level of financial resources for the sector remains one of the most significant challenges for its sustainability. A few CSOs, based in large cities, control most of the available resources, and the majority of CSOs, especially those that operate at the grassroots level, lack funding and access to adequate human and technological resources.

The CSI assessment in Ecuador depicts a weakly organized civil society, surviving on limited financial resources. Civic engagement, apart from the vibrant indigenous movement, is rather limited and tends to be biased against marginalized groups, such as women, the poor, and sexual minorities.

Environment (1.4)

The environment dimension considers political, legal, socioeconomic, and sociocultural contexts, as well as the relationships between civil society, the state, and the private sector. The environment within which Ecuadorian civil society operates is slightly disabling, particularly due to ineffective state structures and high levels of corruption in the public sector and in society at large. Although the socioeconomic context has been improving over the last few years, a high poverty rate (37%) and pervasive social inequality (Gini-coefficient of 0.43) indicate the fundamental social development needs of the country.

The low level of interpersonal trust, with only 17% of respondents saying that most people can be trusted, undermines public spiritedness and fuels suspicion toward public authorities. State institutions are widely seen as ineffective and unaccountable, and skepticism about the honesty and accountability of social actors, including CSOs, is growing as well.

The perception of an ineffective state is based on its limited ability to provide basic services, uphold the rule of law, and fight corruption. Seventy percent of Ecuadorians believe bribing in the public sector is common, and Ecuador is ranked 117th in Transparency International's 2005 Corruption Perception Index. Due to a weak party system, institutional channels of communication between state representatives and citizens are virtually nonexistent. As a consequence, personal links between policymakers and citizens become the only communication channel, which contributes to the fragmentation of demands and gives way to clientelistic dynamics and corrupt practices.

Although there are a number of signs that governmental authorities are gradually changing their suspicious attitudes toward CSOs, a tendency exists among state actors to exert control over CSOs and co-opt them into a corporatist or even clientelistic relationship. This is despite the fact that only a minor portion of CSOs' financial resources come from the state. The relationship between civil society and the private sector is distant and marked by overall indifference. Although steps have been taken toward building a culture of corporate social responsibility (CSR), the CSI analysis reveals that civil society is not yet a significant partner for the private sector.

Values (1.3)

The values dimension examines the extent to which civil society practices and promotes positive values. The score for this dimension indicates a somewhat weak value basis for Ecuadorian civil society. The most significant weakness is related to the poor attention paid to internal democratic practices and transparency; in addition, the promotion of gender equity and tolerance is still in the initial stage. A strength in this dimension is civil society's forthright efforts in the fight against poverty and environmental degradation.

Civil society organizations' internal decisionmaking processes are often centralized in the hands of charismatic leaders. Marginalized groups do not have significant access to leadership positions. Efforts to ensure CSOs' financial transparency are still in their infancy, and self-regulation mechanisms are not yet in place. Initial steps have been taken to make CSOs more accountable to the public, but very little has been achieved in practice. The stakeholders interviewed for the CSI agree that, although there is a common willingness among Ecuadorian CSOs to promote transparency and democratic accountability for the whole sector, the lack of coordination prevents these intentions from translating into practice.

In the context of an intolerant and rather violent society, civil society's record of tolerant and nonviolent behavior is not particularly strong. The study notes the marginalization and latent discrimination against homosexuals, and, to a lesser extent, against women within civil society. There are also certain groups within civil society, such as some indigenous groups, that resort to violent means, such as kidnappings or sabotage, to pursue their goals. More worrisome is the fact that according to CSI stakeholders, these actions are rarely denounced by civil society at large.

In Ecuador, many CSOs are committed to fighting poverty and are supported by international donors that see poverty eradication as a priority area for development. Some of the key examples of CSOs' role in poverty eradication are the Plan Esperanza (Plan Hope), led by the Episcopal Conference of Ecuador, and a number of programs aimed at eradicating child poverty, such as Nuestros Niños (Our Children).

Given the country's large biodiversity, the field of environmental sustainability is another area of strong civil society activity. A large number of CSOs have developed working relationships with local government institutions to advise policymakers and implement common initiatives to protect the environment. CSOs also conduct educational campaigns on environmental issues, such as the socioeconomic impact of the unsustainable exploitation of natural resources.

According to the CSI assessment, the values practiced and promoted by civil society mirror the weaknesses of the operating environment. It seems that Ecuadorian civil society is vulnerable to the same forms of discrimination, corruption, and lack of transparency that are prevalent in the political, social, and economic life of the country. The lack of attention paid to internal democracy and transparency is particularly worrisome, as it undermines the credibility of civil society as a promoter of progressive values.

Impact (1.6)

The impact dimension assesses civil society's role in governance and society at large. The CSI assessment reveals that Ecuadorian civil society has been very active in the political realm. However, most of its efforts have been aimed at contesting the existing political power structure rather than affecting specific policies. Overall, civil society's impact is only moderate, and its capacity to directly assist the poor or direct the attention of government to their needs is particularly weak.

According to CSI stakeholders, Ecuadorian CSOs show a rather high level of activism in the political realm. However, the concrete results achieved by CSOs have fallen short of expectations, since the intensity of activism does not seem to be a factor for successfully influencing policymaking. For example, this is the case with social and human rights policies. Since the 1990s, CSOs' activism around these issues has been growing, particularly due to the efforts of organizations representing women and indigenous groups, but the impact on the policy level has remained modest. Not surprisingly, the contribution of CSOs to the national budget is limited, as the policymaking process involves only a few actors and is centralized in the hands of the government bureaucracy.

The lobbying activities of CSOs are directed more toward the state than the private sector. The stakeholders involved in the CSI assessment highlighted that Ecuadorian CSOs have not been able to exploit the opportunities provided by the fledgling notion of CSR.

In the context of widespread citizen disillusionment with public institutions, CSOs represent an alternative source of support. Therefore most CSOs enjoy a much higher level of public trust than state institutions and the private sector. This is particularly true of faith-based organizations, community associations, and foundations working on social issues. However, "politically oriented" organizations such as trade unions and professional associations have low levels of public trust, which are comparable to those of private enterprises and government.

Although the indigenous movement is active in most areas of the country and other CSOs are assisting marginalized groups, civil society's impact on the lives of the poor and disadvantaged remains fragmented. According to CSI participants, this fragmentation is partly due to the lack of systematic cooperation among CSOs working with marginalized groups, which has led to duplication of efforts. Moreover, the ineffectiveness of state institutions as a partner or funder undermines the potential gains of civil society's strong commitment in this area.

Ecuadorian civil society, through its activism and mobilization, has carved out a relevant space within the political realm. However, this has not resulted in a strong impact on public policy and government or corporate accountability. Against the background of a state that is highly ineffective in tackling social concerns, civil society's substantive impact on the lives of the poor and marginalized is impeded by CSOs' fragmented efforts and lack of coordination.

Conclusion

Ecuadorian civil society operates in a volatile environment with uncertain prospects. Despite the growing number of CSOs and the considerable power wielded by the indigenous movement, civil society has not been able to develop institutionalized mechanisms of interaction with the state or the private sector. The inherent weaknesses of Ecuadorian public institutions hamper the development of a constructive relationship between the state and CSOs. Also, Ecuadorian civil society has not been united in calling for the introduction of participatory governance mechanisms, which could more effectively and constructively channel popular demands into the political system and contribute to strengthening civil society's credibility.

It appears that the future of civil society in Ecuador is strongly dependent on CSOs' capacity to build mutual trust within the sector and society at large. In turn, this might help civil society to influence political processes more effectively and contribute toward the moral regeneration of the Ecuadorian political system.

CSI Report

Fernando Bustamante, Lucía Durán and Ana Cristina Andreetti, *Civil Society in Ecuador—Towards an Effective Civil Society Beyond Its Limitations: CIVICUS Civil Society Index Report for Ecuador* (Quito, Ecuador: Fundación Esquel, 2006).

Notes

1. The CSI assessment was implemented in Ecuador by Fundación Esquel from mid-2005 to early 2006. This chapter presents the main findings of the CSI and is based on a comprehensive country report for Ecuador, which can be accessed on the CSI pages of the CIVICUS website at http://www.civicus.org.

Chapter 11

Egypt[1]

Over the last half a century, Egyptian civil society has developed under the close supervision of an overbearing state. Civil society has remained weak, and its public role has been largely confined to service delivery and development work. However, as the CSI study indicates, recent political changes point to an easing of political repression in the country, which could mean stronger momentum for citizen-based advocacy and campaigning.

Table 11.1 Background Information for Egypt

Egypt	
Country size (square km)	997,740
Population (millions 2004)	72.6
Population under 15 years (2004)	33.9%
Urban population (2003)	34.3%
Seats in parliament held by women (2005)	2.9%
Language groups	Arabic (official), English, and French
Ethnic groups	Egyptian Arab 99%, others 1%
Religious groups	Muslim (mostly Sunni) 94%, Coptic and other Christian 6%
HDI score and ranking (2003)	0.659 (119th)
GDP per capita (US$ 2003)	$3,950
Unemployment rate (% of total labor force)	11%
Population living on less than US$2 a day (1999–2000)	43.9%

Historical Overview

Civic engagement has existed in Egypt since the beginnings of Islam and Christianity, which promoted values such as charitable giving, social justice, and tolerance. The history of contemporary Egyptian civil society dates back to 1821, when the first NGO, the Hellenic Philanthropic Association, was established to cater to the Greek expatriate community. Additional associations were established in the late 1850s by Egyptians who had studied abroad and returned home to promote national development through voluntary organizations.

The modern history of Egyptian .CSOs is closely aligned with Egypt's political history and can be conceptualized in three phases. The pre-1952 revolution era, during British colonialism (1870s–1952), can be described as the liberal phase, which saw the proliferation of a diverse range of CSOs, particularly in the 1920s and 1930s. In 1939 the Ministry of Social Affairs (MOSA) was founded, which oversaw CSOs' operations in Egypt.

Following the July 1952 revolution, Egyptian civil society entered its second phase. The monarchy was abolished, land reform laws were established, and political parties dissolved. The new government sought to either restrict existing CSOs through a set of laws, such as Law 91 of 1959 and Law 62 of 1964, which brought unions under heavy government control, or to co-opt them through the establishment of community development associations, which worked closely with the government in implementing its national development agenda.

The third phase, the post-Nasserist era, began in the 1970s, against the backdrop of President Sadat's embrace of an open market system, known as *infitah*. Under pressure for political liberalization, the government introduced modest political reforms, such as allowing the existence of political parties, granting amnesty to some political prisoners, and allowing some groups that were repressed under the previous regime to reemerge, such as Islamic movements. Despite this political opening, only business associations flourished during this time, since their mandates coincided with Sadat's open-door economic policy.

President Mubarak's accession to power in 1982 did not significantly change the state's attitude toward civil society. However, CSO activities expanded, particularly in the 1990s, which saw Egypt hosting the United Nations International Conference on Population and Development. This increase in civic activity was particularly noticeable among development-oriented NGOs, and it coincided with an increased donor interest in NGOs working on the ground, and in areas such as women's rights, sustainable human development, environmental protection, and children's rights. In terms of the legal environment, after extensive lobbying by CSOs, Law 32 of 1964 was finally replaced by a less restrictive law in 2002. Since then, the political environment for civil society has continued to improve, albeit at an incremental pace.

The State of Civil Society in Egypt

The CSI assessment in Egypt adopted the definition of civil society proposed by CIVICUS, despite difficulty distinguishing an arena that is separate from the family, state, and market in the Egyptian context, due to the existence of kinship-based associations and NGOs that are run by civil servants. However, the Egyptian CSI team wanted to be as inclusive as possible, and consequently opted to move beyond assessing only NGOs registered with MOSA, ultimately including a wide array of CSO types and unorganized forms of civil society. The assessment also included extremely progressive organizations, as well as conservative organizations, such as various social movements, traditional religious associations, and mosque- and church-based CSOs. Political parties, however, were excluded, primarily because they are conspicuously partisan, seek to acquire political power, and are historically considered a force independent of civil society.

This section provides a summary of key findings of the CSI project in Egypt. It examines the state of Egyptian civil society along four dimensions—structure, environment, values, and impact—highlighting the main weaknesses and strengths.

The Egyptian Civil Society Diamond visually depicts a relatively underdeveloped civil society (figure 11.1). The graph shows a civil society with a relatively weak structure characterized by limited citizen participation and limited resources. Its environment is assessed as quite disabling, particularly with regard to the restrictive political context. Civil society exhibits rather insignificant impact on government and society, and it is limited in its efforts to promote positive values among the public, despite a more favorable internal practice of these values within civil society.

Structure (1.2)

The structure dimension examines the makeup of civil society in terms of the main characteristics of individual citizen participation and associational life. The score for Egypt reflects a relatively weak structure, due to low levels of civic engagement. However, the structure of organized civil

Figure 11.1 Civil Society Diamond for Egypt

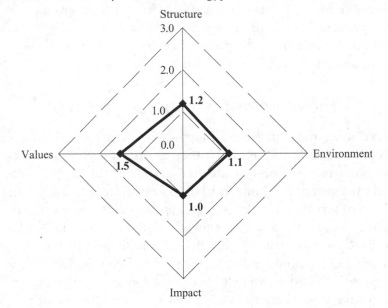

society is somewhat stronger, though limited organizational resources and weak intrasectoral coordination hamper civil society's development.

Individual participation in formal and informal civil society is weak. Only a minority of Egyptian citizens participates in nonpartisan political action or collective community activities. Due to political restrictions, in the context of the emergency law, which has been in place since 1981, citizens generally do not engage in civic activism, such as demonstrations or strikes. However, Egyptians are more inclined to undertake less confrontational forms of citizen action such as signing petitions (20%) and joining boycotts (37%). Egyptians also participate in civil society through charitable giving, which is primarily driven by religious motives and is extremely common, but rarely goes toward the work of formal CSOs. Citizen participation in organized CSOs, through membership and volunteering, is insignificant. Only a small minority of citizens (3.5%) is a formal member of a CSO, although volunteering in CSOs is slightly more common (6.4%).

When assessing the structure of organized civil society, one finds a large number of CSOs registered under MOSA, although many of these CSOs are inactive or only registered on paper. In addition, membership and leadership of active CSOs remains confined to a specific subset of the Egyptian population. Leadership tends to be dominated by older men distinguished by their relatively high socioeconomic status, and certain groups, such as women, the poor, and rural dwellers, are under-represented among CSOs' membership.

The level of Egyptian civil society's organization has shown significant improvement over the past few years, especially due to donor programs focused on building civil society's infrastructure. One of the main strengths of Egyptian civil society is its adoption of self-regulation rules, which, according to the CSI findings, are not a consequence of strict government laws, but are self-imposed by civil society. Despite the presence of a few civil society umbrella bodies, stakeholders believe the existing networks are effective, but that these bodies need to be more proactive in communicating with their members. This is in line with the overall assessment of communication among CSOs, which showed a need for increased communication, particularly across sectors.

Stakeholders identified government funding, membership fees, and donations as the main sources of funding for CSOs. However, according to an organizational survey conducted by the Center for Development Studies (CDS) in 2005, 63% of respondents indicated that a severe shortage of financial resources is a major obstacle to the implementation of their organization's activities. Donor funding goes primarily to a subset of CSOs working in the areas of development and human rights, a fact that the state and other critics of civil society have used to propagate the idea that these organizations are agents of external forces.

As the analysis of civil society's structure shows, a key priority for CSOs should be building a stronger membership base by increasing awareness of their activities among the public. This will help CSOs tap into citizens charitable giving, which may secure a more stable funding basis for CSOs.

Environment (1.1)

The environment dimension considers political, legal, socioeconomic, and sociocultural contexts, as well as the relationships between civil society, the state, and the private sector. The assessment reveals that the environment for Egyptian civil society is relatively disabling, constrained by socioeconomic problems, political repression, and weak sociocultural norms.

Egypt is characterized by rather low levels of socioeconomic development, with over 40% of the population living on less than $2 a day. Social inequality is on the increase, and with over 40% of the population illiterate, the general socioeconomic situation is not conducive for CSOs.

Another external factor that significantly impacts civil society's work is the political context, which, despite recent changes in the political climate, can be characterized as generally restrictive. For the past twenty-five years, Egyptians have been governed under an emergency law that suspends citizens' basic freedoms and rights. For example, citizens are occasionally held in detention without trial for an unspecified duration of time, and journalists are subject to arrests and closure of newspapers. Also, the government has not succeeded in increasing its level of effectiveness or curbing corruption in the public sector. This is mainly attributed to the poor skills of public officials and the low wages they receive.

The state–civil society relationship mirrors that of the relationship between the state and society at large, since the state seeks to control and confine independent citizen action. Legal regulations, such as the 2002 NGO law, do not enable the work of CSOs, and the application of these regulations is used selectively against specific types of CSOs, such as human rights and religious-based organizations. Civil servants are given immense power when it comes to interpreting the law, which has resulted in rejection of requests for registration by human rights CSOs on numerous occasions. Although there is no direct legislation restricting CSO advocacy activities, general CSO laws and the emergency law can be interpreted in such a way as to allow for the restriction of advocacy efforts.

Given the overall environment of control and mistrust, it is not surprising that Egyptian citizens have low levels of trust and public spiritedness. The restrictive political environment and the poor socioeconomic context have resulted in Egyptians looking out for their own individual interests, and to a certain extent this climate has eroded a sense of collectiveness and a strong social base that civil society could thrive on. However, the slight opening in the political system over the past few years and the emergence of some strong social movements, such as *Kefaya*,[2] which challenge the state and society's apathy, provide hope that these values might be regenerated in society.

Values (1.5)

The values dimension examines the extent to which civil society practices and promotes positive values. This dimension scored highest in Egypt, mainly due to civil society's propensity to practice core values, such as tolerance, democracy, and gender equity, internally. However, the promotion of these values in society at large is generally limited.

Specific provisions of the law and organizational values support Egyptian CSOs' adherence to principles of democracy. For example, Law 84 of 2002 specifies that CSOs must hold democratic elections for their boards. Other values, such as nonviolence, tolerance, and poverty eradication, are deeply rooted in Egyptian civil society, and are most noticeably practiced through charitable CSOs. These CSOs provide services to those most in need and raise awareness around issues such as interreligious tolerance. One of the most notable examples is the Coptic Evangelical Organization for Social Services (CEOSS) Forum for Intercultural Dialogue (FID).

With regard to the promotion of positive values in society at large, civil society fares better on rallying support for apolitical values than it does for politically sensitive values. For example, civil society actively promotes nonviolence, gender equity, and environmental sustainability, which are not seen as confrontational toward the state. However, CSOs do not actively promote more political values, such as democracy, tolerance, or transparency, even though they are increasingly embraced and advocated for by certain parts of the citizenry. Given the current period of political transitioning in Egypt, there is an increased space for civil society to play a stronger role in sensitizing the population to these political norms and principles.

Impact (1.0)

The impact dimension assesses civil society's role in governance and society at large. Civil society's impact on politics and society stands out as the weakest dimension of the assessment. Civil society's track record in policy influence and monitoring is particularly weak.

The Egyptian state remains the main social service provider for the poor. However, in the wake of open-door economic policies in the 1970s and structural adjustment policies in the 1990s, civil society has increasingly played an active role in supporting government efforts to address the needs of those most affected by these policies. Civil society, in particular religious-based CSOs, has been successful in reaching out to remote communities and marginalized groups, such as youth, women, and the poor, by providing them with much-needed services, such as day-care centers and microfinance schemes.

Civil society's impact on influencing public policy, holding the state and the private sector accountable, and lobbying the state for service provision is very limited. This is due to two factors: the first is civil society's perception of its role as being mainly that of a service provider. The second factor is the restrictive political environment and adversarial relationship between the state and advocacy CSOs. Despite civil society's persistent weakness in influencing public policy around social issues, there is some improvement when it comes to human rights issues, where CSOs put issues, such as the torture of prisoners, on the agenda and forced the government to acknowledge their demands.

In general, the CSI assessment reveals that civil society is able to directly impact people's lives by providing welfare services, but it has almost no role in influencing government policy and acting as a watchdog. The limited impact of Egyptian civil society should not be interpreted as a limited presence. Instead, it should be analyzed in relation to the other dimensions. Improvements in civil society's structure, environment, and values are necessary to improve the overall impact of Egyptian civil society and to strengthen the health, vibrancy, and sustainability of the sector. First and foremost, civil society must recognize the importance of diversifying its activities and strengthening its advocacy role in society in order to have a greater impact. The current political reforms could provide a crucial window of opportunity.

Recommendations

The recommendations presented in this section are based on the challenges and opportunities facing civil society in Egypt as gleaned from the CSI assessment. They are based on the reflections of stakeholders, such as civil society practitioners, government, media, and private sector representatives, as well as academics who were consulted in regional meetings and at the CSI National Workshop. The following are the most crucial recommendations:

- Further research on civil society in Egypt: There are gaps in the existing knowledge on civil society, which could be filled by drawing on universities, research institutes, and CSOs' own documentation.
- Increase citizen participation through better utilization of charitable giving: Egyptians make regular charitable contributions, based on their religious conviction. CSOs should tap into this substantive resource in order to develop a stronger human and financial support base for their activities. Civil society must raise awareness among citizens about the benefits of utilizing civil society as an arena for citizen participation, social solidarity, and support for the country's development.

- Promote stronger coordination among CSOs: CSOs and government should work together to reform existing unions and federations. Cases of cross-sector networking and cooperation should be publicized for civil society to learn from.
- A greater role for CSOs in public policy: There should be increased awareness in civil society about the importance of policy interventions in bringing about social change. The state should be encouraged to become more open to a greater role for civil society in policy formulation.

Conclusion

The CSI assessment for Egypt suggests that civil society is still in an embryonic stage and requires substantial growth in all four dimensions. Despite the long history of civil society, the diversity of CSOs, and traditional values of charity and solidarity in Egyptian society, civil society has not harnessed these positive assets and traditions and used them to strengthen its presence.

Given the lessening of political restrictions in late 2005, it is now time for civil society to push for substantial changes in the environment within which it operates. For civil society to fully capitalize on this transitional period, it must first change its role from one solely focused on service delivery to one that includes advocacy as a key tool for bringing about positive social change.

CSI Report

Centre for Development Services, *An Overview of Civil Society in Egypt: Civil Society Index Report for the Arab Republic of Egypt* (Cairo, Egypt: Centre for Development Services, 2005).

Notes

1. The CSI assessment was implemented in Egypt by the Centre for Development Services (CDS) from October 2003 to December 2005. This chapter presents the main findings of the CSI and is based on a comprehensive country report for Egypt, which can be accessed on the CSI pages of the CIVICUS website at http://www.civicus.org.
2. *Kefaya,* an Arabic word meaning "enough," is the slogan and informal name for the nonpartisan Egyptian Movement for Change, which incorporates several parties from different political currents: leftist, Islamic, pan-Arab, and liberal, in addition to intellectuals, journalists, students, and

more than 300 public figures. At the heart of the Movement for Change is an opposition to the nomination of President Hosni Mubarak for a fifth term, or as is suggested by its name *Kefaya*, "Enough of 24 years of presidency." The movement also calls upon the government to introduce a series of measures aimed at political reform, including the termination of the Emergency Law, the formation of a transitional government, and the drafting of a new constitution by a national assembly.

Chapter 12

~~~

Fiji[1]

While in May 2006 the first multiparty, multiracial government coalition was formed in Fiji, the following coup against the government in December 2006 has again highlighted the troubled political situation in the country. The CSI study shows that a number of institutional constraints impede the country's ability to move toward a model of democratic and accountable governance and people-centered development. While civil society has long been a key player in providing welfare services and fighting poverty, its roles as a policy advocate and watchdog of the state are somewhat underdeveloped. The CSI study points out a number of internal and external obstacles to achieving a greater role for civil society in Fiji's governance system.

Table 12.1 Background Information for Fiji

Fiji	
Country size (square km)	3,000,000*
Population (millions 2003)	0.8
Population under 15 years (2003)	32.3%
Urban population (2003)	51.7%
Seats in parliament held by women (2005)	8.5%
Language groups	English (official), Fijian, Hindustani
Ethnic groups	Fijian 51%, Indian 44%, other 5%
Religious groups	Christian 52%, Hindu 38%, Muslim 8%, other 2%
HDI score and ranking (2003)	0.752 (92nd)
GDP per capita (US$ 2003)	$5,830

*The archipelago is spread over this area including islands and islets.

Historical Overview

Located in the South Pacific, Fiji has a long history of community and associational life. The traditional unit of the *vanua,* in which members work together for the advancement of their community or settlement, comprised extended families and traditional clan groups for the indigenous Fijian population.

Modern forms of civil society emerged as a result of British colonialism (1874–1970) and Christian missionary activities. Charitable organizations in social welfare, education, health, and other social fields were set up. The British also brought indentured laborers from India to work in agriculture. They soon became the second largest ethnic group in the country and set up their own religious and welfare associations. Thus, associational life in Fiji generally reflected the diversity and structure of society at large.

In 1970 Fiji became an independent nation, and the state began to take over some welfare functions from CSOs, while others, such as education, remained largely run by CSOs. The 1970s and 1980s saw a surfacing of new concerns and causes for collective action around human rights, the environment, and gender issues. A strong environmental movement emerged in response to widespread testing of nuclear weapons in the Pacific Ocean by Western countries, and the issue of nuclear testing also carried strong connotations of political autonomy, international relations, and peace. This led to the politicization of formerly apolitical segments of Fijian civil society, such as Christian-based organizations.

The late 1980s through the 1990s was a period of turmoil in Fiji. Racial tensions between the indigenous population and the Indo-Fijians intensified. Indigenous Fijians were in charge of government and the military, and Indo-Fijians controlled much of the country's economy. In addition, corruption in the public sector was thriving, which led to the formation of a trade union–based Labor Party. Labor won the elections in 1987, and for the first time the government was dominated by Indo-Fijians; however, it was soon overthrown by the military. Between 1987 and 2000 there were alternating periods of democratic governments and military coups. In the aftermath of the various military coups, communal violence against Indo-Fijians' homes and businesses ensued.

During this same period, the government implemented structural adjustment policies imposed by international institutions. This led to a decreased role for the public sector in welfare and increased pressure

Figure 12.1 Civil Society Diamond for Fiji

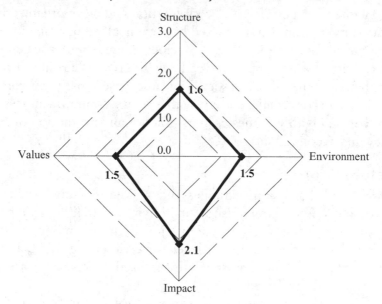

on civil society to intervene. As a consequence, professional NGOs increased significantly in number and activities, even though their financial and material resources and organizational capacities remained rather limited.

At the time of implementing the CSI, Fiji was still recovering from the 2000 coup, though the newly formed multiparty government promised to lead the country into a period of relative peace and prosperity. Just before this book went to print, however, another military coup ended the period of constitutional government yet again proving the highly volatile political situation in the country.

The State of Civil Society in Fiji

This section provides a summary of key findings of the CSI project in Fiji. It examines the state of Fijian civil society along four dimensions—structure, environment, values, and impact—highlighting the main weaknesses and strengths.

The Civil Society Diamond (figure 12.1) visually summarizes the assessment's findings in Fiji and depicts medium-level assessments for all dimensions. An interesting exception is the impact dimension, which is evaluated as rather strong, particularly with regard to civil society's social roles. However, its political functions are less developed. Civil society's structure emerged as twofold: high levels of civic engagement coexist with rather poor levels of coordination and weak organizational capacities. Its environment is marked by certain, albeit not fundamental, constraints in the political, legal, socioeconomic, and sociocultural spheres, most of which are, however, likely to grow as a result of recent political developments. Civil society's value base closely mirrors the prevalent norms of broader society, with a strong commitment to social values, coupled with weaknesses in its practice and promotion of transparency and accountability.

Structure (1.6)

The structure dimension examines the makeup of civil society in terms of the main characteristics of individual citizen participation and associational life. Civil society in Fiji is built on a moderate structural foundation; there are high levels of civic engagement, but the key institutions and mechanisms of organized civil society are only moderately well developed.

In Fiji, citizen involvement in various forms of civic activities is widespread. According to the CSI population survey, more than four out of five Fijians regularly give to charity, two-thirds are involved in volunteer work, and 57% recently participated in either a community meeting or a collective community activity. Sixty-eight percent of respondents report being a member of a CSO, with religious organizations (41%) being by far the most popular CSO type, followed by trade unions (12%), educational associations (10%), and sports groups (9%).

Fijian civil society strongly resembles the social composition of society, with strong ethnic, religious, and traditional forms of association. In addition, certain social groups, particularly rural people, the poor, and individuals with lower levels of education, are highly underrepresented. Thus, the civic sector has a strong, urban middle-class bias, which is especially pronounced in CSO leadership roles, where women are also underrepresented. Given the country's geographical characteristics, the logistical and financial implications for involving rural island communities in national-level civil society activities remain a considerable challenge.

While the size of organized civil society in Fiji has grown significantly over the past few decades, its infrastructure and level of organization is lagging behind. There are few resource centers for CSOs and international linkages, particularly beyond the Pacific region, remain weak, with the exception of local chapters of international NGOs

(INGOs). Efforts to establish a countrywide code of conduct have begun, but lack compliance mechanisms. However, a rather large number of umbrella bodies exist for specific civil society subsectors, such as social services, women, trade unions, human rights, and Christian-based organizations. These bodies are seen as largely effective in their coordinating role, though less successful in providing technical assistance to their members. CSOs' cooperation across these subsectors is rare, even though there is a growing need for multisector dialogue, given the challenges of good governance, HIV/AIDS, and poverty. CSI stakeholders mentioned examples of cross-sectoral cooperation during times of natural disasters, which are rather frequent in Fiji.

A slight majority of surveyed CSO respondents consider their organizations' financial resources to be rather or fully adequate. A similar picture emerges with regard to human and technical resources. One cause of this positive assessment of financial resources could be the diverse funding sources, which include membership fees, individual donations, foreign donations, and limited government and private sector funding. However, CSI stakeholders pointed toward further capacity-building needs with regard to the effective management of resources, combined with general training on good governance and organizational management, which are areas where Fijian CSOs remain rather weak.

Environment (1.5)

The environment dimension considers political, legal, socioeconomic, and sociocultural contexts, as well as the relationships between civil society, the state, and the private sector. Fijian civil society operates in an environment characterized by a mix of moderately enabling and disabling factors. The CSI assessment highlights civil society's weak sociocultural foundation as the most worrisome aspect of its external environment.

The socioeconomic environment presents formidable challenges for the country. Growing poverty, unemployment, and crime—as well as severe social inequalities—are the primary challenges to social development. Areas of progress include widespread literacy (92%), a growing communication infrastructure, and a substantial period of intercommunal peace.

Fiji's political context has been volatile. While the election of a multiparty, multiracial government in 2006 and increased adherence to principles of press freedom and civil liberties were signs of stabilization, the December 2006 coup d'etat has highlighted the instability of the country's governance system. Other institutional components, such as the complex electoral law, ineffectiveness of the public sector (especially in the areas of law enforcement, correctional services, and public welfare in rural areas), and widespread corruption remain barriers to democratic governance. It therefore comes as no surprise that, according to the CSI population survey, a majority of respondents had little trust in central government.

The issue of lack of trust permeates society and, given its multiracial and diverse religious makeup, presents major challenges for the development of a strong civil society. Only one out of five Fijians generally trusts fellow citizens, and social tolerance is low, particularly with regard to homosexuals, people living with HIV/AIDS, and people from a different race. In addition, the fact that almost half of respondents regard avoiding paying for public transport as at least sometimes justifiable attests to the rather low levels of public spiritedness.

Civil society's relations with the state present a two-sided image. While civil society's major role in providing services to the population is fully acknowledged and supported by the state, its advocacy activities often trigger hostile responses from government. Examples are the persecution of union leaders, the refusal to permit protest marches and demonstrations, the withholding of foreign donor funding (which is often channeled via government), and the occasional deregistration of critical CSOs. In 2005 the then prime minister questioned the legitimacy and mandate of advocacy NGOs, which he considered to be covert political parties.[2]

The potential to manipulate the existing legal framework for NGOs, which dates back to colonial times, has led to calls for legal reform—including the expansion of tax benefits for philanthropic giving, which has not yet been implemented. The Fiji Law Reform Commission (FLRC) is currently reviewing the Charitable Trusts Act and the Registration of Religious Bodies Act. The FLRC expects to report to Parliament in mid-2007.

Dialogue between CSOs and the state exists but is mainly confined to professional associations, trade unions, and some NGO networks. Advocacy CSOs, which criticize government policies, are excluded from dialogue with the state. Government funding mechanisms to CSOs exist in various ministries, but, according to the CSI stakeholder survey, constitute only 8% of overall funding. Similarly, corporate sector funding is negligible, constituting only 3% of the overall funding received by CSOs surveyed in the CSI stakeholder survey. However, there seems to be significant potential for growth, since a majority of respondents consider the private sector to be generally supportive of civil society and large companies, such as Vodafone, are increasingly engaging in philanthropic activities.

Values (1.5)

The values dimension examines the extent to which civil society practices and promotes positive values. In Fiji, it yields a somewhat positive assessment, although a number of value gaps were identified in the CSI assessment, such as a lack of CSO accountability and widespread intolerance in civil society (and in society as a whole).

Promoting key social issues such as poverty eradication, environmental protection, and gender equity in society at large are hallmarks of Fijian civil society's values. CSOs are widely recognized as experts and stakeholders in these fields, and media coverage, particularly of environmental campaigns, is widespread.

Given the deep social divisions in Fijian society, tolerance and peace are key values for achieving social inclusion and social development. Civil society is both part of the problem and part of the solution. Being the arena where social conflicts are negotiated, civil society is not immune from intolerant and violent behavior, and a significant minority of CSI stakeholders recognizes the occasional, if not regular, use of violence by civil society groups. The vast majority of civil society denounces these actions, and a number of CSOs, particularly faith-based organizations and women's groups, actively promote a culture of peace and nonviolence in the country. However, civil society activities to promote tolerance were less frequent and of limited visibility.

Participants at CSI consultative meetings identified civil society's transparency and accountability as key weaknesses among the values practiced by Fijian CSOs. Also, the level of perceived corruption within CSOs is rather high; 84% of CSI stakeholders agree that corruption occurs in civil society, with half considering it to be frequent or even very frequent. In the stakeholder meetings, participants identified the misuse of channels of influence for one's own gain as a common practice. This is seen as a likely consequence of the fierce competition for limited donor resources, rather than corruption per se. Financial transparency is also not viewed as widely practiced within the sector, and there is a lack of internal accountability mechanisms. Civil society is considered rather inactive in demanding accountability of the state and private sector, with some notable exceptions, such as Transparency International Fiji. Thus, the issue of creating a culture of accountability, within civil society and society at large, emerged as a key concern.

Impact (2.1)

The impact dimension assesses civil society's role in governance and society at large. Somewhat surprisingly, this dimension received the highest score of the four dimensions, indicating a particularly strong role for CSOs in society, although their role in governance is somewhat less pronounced.

Civil society plays a leading role in providing services, particularly to marginalized groups. As many as three out of four respondents to the population survey could recall a civil society activity aimed at empowering poor people in their community. Assistance to marginalized groups, such as the elderly, street children, and prison inmates, is an area of particular success. In addition, CSOs are active in a range of areas of citizen empowerment, such as microfinance, capacity building for community-management committees, and income-generation for women. As highlighted in the CSI assessment, due to the isolated nature of island communities and the limited presence of the state in remote areas, these activities are typically initiated by local citizens who decide to collectively address a common concern.

Reflecting the quality of CSOs' service provision, 69% of respondents to the CSI population survey feel civil society is providing better services than the state, while only 25% feel otherwise. This positive image of civil society is also reflected in the public-trust ratings. Religious organizations (89%) and NGOs (87%) have the highest trust ratings, while most state institutions, such as the justice system, military, police, and government, score 50% or lower trust ratings.

Civil society's presence in society through various activities—such as empowerment activities and service provision—is noteworthy; however, its track record in the political sphere is somewhat more limited. While CSOs are rather active in seeking to influence and monitor policies, their limited technical capacity is a key obstacle to their impact. Policy issues, such as school education fees, drug abuse prevention, and public water supply, are areas where civil society has had significant success. In contrast, its influence on the national budgeting process is more limited; though, for the first time, in early 2006, the then government extended an invitation to a small number of CSOs to discuss the budget.

Recommendations

The study's findings were discussed at several meetings, including the Fiji Council for Social Services annual meeting, where a large number of specific recommendations were made. The following are some of the key recommendations:

- Professionalize CSO volunteering schemes to attract young people to participate in civil society.
- Strengthen civil society's level of organization by supporting existing networks and encouraging the establishment of informal networks and resource centers outside of the capital city.
- Strengthen individual CSO and sector-wide accountability and governance by promoting the existing code of conduct, running leadership courses on issues such as organizational democracy and financial transparency, and involving religious organizations in these debates.
- Augment civil society's work in addressing social exclusion, poverty, intolerance, and reconciliation by setting up a truth and reconciliation commission to address crimes committed in past coups.
- Strengthen civil society's advocacy and policy-monitoring capacity.

Conclusion

The structure, values, and activities of civil society in Fiji closely mirror the key features of Fijian society as a whole. The importance of traditional life, family, religion, and ethnicity are expressed in the various forms of civic life in the country. However, civil society is also a key actor in building the Fijian nation, working toward reconciliation, respecting human rights, and promoting intercultural dialogue and exchange.

In recent years, civil society's work has been severely impeded by the country's political dynamics, which fueled ethnic tensions and strife. Even though the multiparty government formed in May 2006 was ousted by a military coup at the end of the year, it seems that ethnic tensions, which often accompany Fijian coups, are not on the increase. While civil society's external environment is therefore likely to remain volatile, the CSI also highlights a number of internal weaknesses, such as poor accountability, poor advocacy skills, and a rather limited infrastructure. These need to be addressed for civil society to make full use of emerging opportunities.

CSI Report

Fiji Council for Social Services, *Building Civil Society's Capacity and Accountability for Participatory Governance in Fiji: CIVICUS Civil Society Index Report for Fiji* (Suva, Fiji: FCOSS, 2006).

Notes

1. The CSI assessment was implemented in Fiji by the Fiji Council for Social Services (FCOSS) over the course of 2004 and 2005. This chapter presents the main findings of the CSI and is based on a comprehensive country report for Fiji, which can be accessed on the CSI pages of the CIVICUS website at http://www.civicus.org.
2. See http://www.un-ngls.org/cso/cso7/fiji.htm, accessed September 25, 2006.

Chapter 13

Georgia[1]

Over the past few years Georgia has undergone significant changes that have had significant implications on civil society. The consequences of the Rose Revolution have been somewhat mixed and generally less positive than anticipated. Thus, an assessment of the current state of Georgian civil society was deemed a useful undertaking by the Centre for Training and Consultancy (CTC). Due to resource and time constraints, CTC implemented the Civil Society Index Shortened Assessment Tool (CSI-SAT), which relies on available secondary data only.

Table 13.1 Background Information for Georgia

Georgia	
Country size (square km)	69,700
Population (millions 2004)	4.5
Population under 15 years (2004)	19.5%
Urban population (2003)	52%
Seats in parliament held by women (2005)	9.4%
Language groups	Georgian (official), Russian, Armenian, Azeri
Ethnic groups	Georgian 83.8%, Azeri 6.5%, Armenian 5.7%, Russian 1.5%, other 2.5%
Religious groups	Orthodox Christian 83.9%, Muslim 9.9%, Armenian-Gregorian 3.9%, Catholic 0.8%, other 0.8%, none 0.7%
HDI score and ranking (2003)	0.732 (100th)
GDP per capita (US$ 2003)	$2,588
Unemployment rate (% of total labor force)	11.5%
Population living on less than US$2 a day (2003)	25.3%

Historical Overview

The development of civil society in contemporary Georgia can be traced back to the mid-nineteenth century, when young students and professionals brought liberal ideas to Georgia from their studies abroad and founded several cultural and educational organizations. After a brief period of independence (1918–1921), which was supported by a thriving civil society, the invasion of Georgia by Soviet Russia led to the country's inclusion in the Soviet Union and the suppression of independent civic activity for the next half-century.

In the 1970s a small dissident movement emerged that gained traction in the 1980s under Gorbachev's *perestroika* and *glasnost* policies. As in many other Communist countries, the environmental movement was the first to challenge the state and stage successful public demonstrations. This laid the ground for subsequent social and political protests. In the late 1980s, uncivil forms of citizen action emerged, such as the *Mkhedroni,* a movement based on a criminal network, which appealed to Georgians' nationalist sentiments.

Once Georgia gained independence in 1992, foreign donors set up aid programs to develop a vibrant Georgian civil society. Consequently, a new type of civil society organization (CSO), the NGO, entered the scene. During the 1990s, a diverse and professional NGO sector emerged in Georgia. However, it faced problems of overreliance on foreign funding and, consequently, weak legitimacy and grounding in Georgian society. NGOs were often perceived as grant-guzzlers, wasting aid money—and generally promoting Western interests and values.

At the turn of the century, CSOs operated in a gradually worsening political context. President Shevardnadze's government was widely perceived as incompetent, corrupt, and meddling with political and civil rights. When a strong political opposition emerged, many CSOs, which had previously steered clear of politics, became involved in political issues, such as election monitoring and voter education. More significantly, in response to the November 2003 rigged parliamentary elections, Georgian citizens mobilized and organized themselves in protest rallies. These led to President Shevardnadze's resignation and the installation of a new government under Mikhail Saakashvili. These events were known internationally as the Rose Revolution.

After the Rose Revolution, civil society was presented with the challenge of how to relate to the new government, particularly since

Figure 13.1 Civil Society Diamond for Georgia

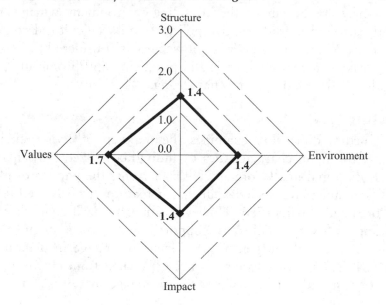

many CSOs were now seen by the public as closely aligned with the new regime. While many civil society leaders joined the government, others remained in civil society. However, those who remained in the civic sector began to face funding challenges, as many foreign donors shifted their priorities from supporting NGOs' watchdog function to supporting less traditional functions of civil society, such as capacity building and providing technical assistance to the new government. Additionally, due to strong public support, the new government did not feel the need to consult with civil society, and civil society's overall impact declined. The situation worsened once the government began to implement policies that were seen by many as violating democratic norms. The Georgian CSI-SAT assessment was conducted within this dynamic and open-ended context.

The State of Civil Society in Georgia

This section provides a summary of key findings of the CSI-SAT project in Georgia. It examines the state of Georgian civil society along four dimensions—structure, environment, values, and impact—highlighting the main weaknesses and strengths.

The Civil Society Diamond (figure 13.1) visually summarizes the assessment's findings in Georgia. The diamond is relatively small, primarily due to a somewhat weak structure of civil society. Civil society operates in a rather disabling environment, which is particularly affected by the negative political and sociocultural context. Civil society's impact on politics and society is considered to be relatively weak, while its track record in practicing and promoting positive values is assessed as somewhat strong.

Structure (1.4)

The structure dimension examines the makeup of civil society in terms of the main characteristics of individual citizen participation and associational life. Georgian civil society fits the pattern of many post-Communist civil societies, in that it features a fairly well-developed organized civil society. However, this organized civil society is operating on a very small social support base. What is unique about Georgia is the high propensity of citizens to engage in demonstrations, strikes, and other forms of once-off civic action. However, this does not translate into a willingness to engage in CSOs' long-term activities.

Although rather small in size, many key features of an organized civil society are present in Georgia, such as the availability of adequate human resources and organizational infrastructure, the existence of support organizations, accountability mechanisms, and well-developed communication and cooperation among CSOs. Additionally, financial resources are available, but these are drawn almost exclusively from foreign donors, which mainly work with CSOs based in the capital, Tbilisi. The center-periphery gap in financial resources is also mirrored in other structural indicators, such as the limited linkages with international networks and the uneven distribution of CSOs throughout the country. While Tbilisi is home to only 25% of the population, it hosts 60% of all registered associations and foundations.

Citizen participation in CSOs remains extremely limited, apart from a small group of mainly young professionals based in the capital. A 2002 survey found only 5.8% of Georgians to be involved in a CSO. Additionally, the practice of involving volunteers is less common among Georgian CSOs than would be expected. Twenty-five percent of Tbilisi-based CSOs and 14% of those based outside of Tbilisi do not work with volunteers. There are few membership-based CSOs in the country, and political parties, trade unions, and other civic associations remain weak. However, the Orthodox Church is a powerful institution in the country, but civic groups connected with the church are not integrated within wider civil society.

Civic activism is far from absent in Georgia. As epitomized by the Rose Revolution, spontaneous and unorganized forms of citizen participation, such as public demonstrations or strikes, remain common and popular among citizens. Attending a protest rally is seen as a more preferred form of influencing the government by Georgians (57.3%) than attending a meeting with government representatives (44.8%) or appealing to local authorities (36.2%). However, it is problematic for the strength of civil society that this widespread protest behavior is not accompanied by participation in more long-term constructive forms of activism, such as the advocacy work undertaken by CSOs.

The legacy of Communism, including the lack of experience of democratic governance, low levels of social capital, the predominance of informal networks, and widespread economically motivated emigration, presents major challenges for the development of a civic culture in Georgia. However, it appears that over the past few years there has been an improvement in the quality and quantity of civic engagement in civil society activities. This gives hope for the development of a more robust structure for Georgian civil society in the years to come.

Environment (1.4)

The environment dimension considers political, legal, socioeconomic, and sociocultural contexts, as well as the relationships between civil society, the state, and the private sector. Georgian civil society operates in a rather disabling environment, as indicated by this dimension's low score. While factors affecting civil society directly, such as registration and taxation laws, are regarded as rather conducive, the more systemic political and sociocultural trends present significant barriers to civil society's effective functioning.

Georgia's political system can be described as a weak democracy with strong authoritarian tendencies. While basic political and civil rights are guaranteed in the constitution, the actual political situation in Georgia features a variety of problematic areas, such as a weak political opposition, poorly entrenched rule of law, abuses against civil liberties (such as torture and frequent intimidation of the few independent media outlets), and widespread corruption.

Despite certain improvements, the state's capacity to govern remains extremely limited. This is visible in the decrepit state of public infrastructure. However, while the government has not resolved the status of its two breakaway territories, the self-proclaimed republics of

Abkhazia and South Ossetia, major progress has been made in curtailing violent conflicts in Abkhazia. Apart from the potential eruption of ethnic conflicts within the country, the status of religious and other minorities is another key issue of concern. There is widespread social intolerance of these groups, particularly Jehovah's Witnesses, Baptists, and homosexuals.

Despite these challenges, civil society enjoys considerable space and a rather enabling legislative environment. Freedom of association is ensured and operationalized effectively in registration laws and procedures, and most CSOs can operate independent of the government. A new tax code encourages corporate giving to charitable causes, and CSOs are not taxed on grant income, even though claiming back value added tax (VAT), to which CSOs are entitled, is difficult in practice. When examining whether positive relations exist between civil society and government, it is apparent that dialogue is limited to CSOs that are close to the government, and independent advocacy NGOs are increasingly discouraged. Primarily due to the predominance of an informal economy, relations between the business sector and civil society are weak, and engagement is sporadic. A survey of business representatives reveals that only 17% of respondents provide financial support to CSOs. Similarly, another survey found that only 9% of CSOs receive financial support from the Georgian corporate sector.

The development of a more enabling environment for civil society is strongly dependent on the overall progress of the country, particularly its political system. If the Georgian state decides to fully embrace the basic tenets of democracy, such as political competition, accountability, and an independent civil society, and proves to be capable of increasing its effectiveness as a provider of basic services and ensuring law and order, civil society is likely to flourish. However, based on the current political climate, such a scenario is far from certain.

Values (1.7)

The values dimension examines the extent to which civil society practices and promotes positive values. Civil society's performance in practicing and promoting key positive values emerges as the strongest dimension of the assessment.

An interesting discrepancy emerges when comparing CSOs' internal practice of key values with their external promotion activities. While the latter is generally a strong point for civil society, the former is rather weak. In other words, Georgian CSOs often do not practice what they preach. The levels of internal democracy in CSOs are very weak, due to weak membership structures, ineffective governance systems, and dominating leaders. Additionally, even though recent years have witnessed improvements in democratic practices driven by foreign donors, CSOs still lack adequate accountability and transparency mechanisms. For example, while the share of CSOs that make their annual reports publicly available has more than doubled between 2002 and 2005, it remains below 30%.

The promotion of key liberal values—such as democracy, human rights, tolerance, and nonviolence—is the hallmark of a core group of Georgian NGOs. However, as the example of widespread religious intolerance shows, these values often do not permeate into wider society, and this core group of NGOs, despite their strong public visibility, remains somewhat isolated from society at large.

Civil society pays little attention to political issues that are not regarded as priority areas, such as gender equity and environmental protection. The most striking omissions relate to the values of social justice and poverty eradication, which clearly present serious problems for the country, since almost every fourth Georgian lives in conditions of extreme poverty. However, fighting poverty is not an area of focus for Georgian civil society's activities. Due to the Communist legacy, which cemented the predominant role of the state in all aspects of society, social services are viewed by civil society as an issue that should be addressed in the context of broader economic and democratic reforms by the state.

Because of the influential role of foreign donors and the isolated nature of civil society, there appears to be a gap between the priorities of most CSOs and those of Georgian citizens, which has important bearings for civil society's public role and standing. If this agenda gap remains unaddressed by civil society, the goal of increased civic engagement in civil society's activities is likely to remain elusive.

Impact (1.4)

The impact dimension assesses civil society's role in governance and society at large. The impact of Georgian civil society peaked during the Rose Revolution, when civil society was active in providing crucial independent monitoring of the elections, mobilizing citizens, and influencing the course of public discussions and subsequent reforms. Since then, because of the developments described above, civil society's impact has declined. However, the impact dimension's score still indicates a civil society that wields some influence, particularly as a watchdog of the country's democratic governance processes.

The assessment shows that civil society exerts its strongest impact on political issues such as human rights, democracy, and accountability. However, due to the migration of key civil society leaders into government—which depleted civil society of key personnel and skills—and an increasingly negative government attitude toward civil society's advocacy, its influence on public policies remains limited. As a result of an increasingly uncooperative government, civil society is more influential as a watchdog than as a partner of government, since the government leaves enough space for external criticism.

Similarly, in their interactions with the population, CSOs focus on political issues such as human rights and civic education. Their involvement in crucial social and economic issues such as social service provision, livelihood creation, and social inclusion is limited, again showing their strongly liberal tendency. However, this disregard of social issues by CSOs cements the disconnect between them and the Georgian people. It is likely that the limited presence of CSOs in these areas where the Georgian population requires most assistance is a major impediment for stronger and more positive relations between citizens and their civil society.

Conclusion

The CSI-SAT assessment of Georgian civil society presents a rather coherent picture of its current state. Small in size, Georgian civil society is rather well developed and institutionally connected, but it is generally isolated from society, the private sector, and government. Civil society is dependent on foreign donors and their funding sources. These features determine civil society's priorities in terms of its values, namely a liberal democratic agenda without sufficient attention to poverty and social exclusion. They also determine civil society's areas of impact, namely government accountability, civic education, and generation of social capital at the expense of social and economic concerns and needs.

Georgian civil society needs to break out of its own comfort zone and engage with wider society, ideally on issues important to Georgian citizens, such as social protection and fighting unemployment. Only then will civil society be able to build sustainable bonds with the citizenry, which is a prerequisite for progress toward the development of a responsive sector strongly rooted in society and wielding considerable power in Georgian public life.

CSI Report

Paata Gurgendize, *An Assessment of Georgian Civil Society 2006—Strong Commitment to Democratic Values in a Challenging Environment: CIVICUS Civil Society Index Shortened Assessment Tool Report for Georgia* (Tbilisi, Georgia: Centre for Training and Consultancy, 2006).

Notes

1. The CSI Shortened Assessment Tool was implemented in Georgia by the Centre for Training and Consultancy over the course of 2005. This chapter presents the main findings of the CSI-SAT and is based on a comprehensive country report for Georgia, which can be accessed on the CSI pages of the CIVICUS website at http://www.civicus.org.

Chapter 14

❦❦

Germany[1]

Since the turn of the millennium, Germany has witnessed a noticeable increase in public interest in civil society, civic engagement, and volunteerism. Thus, the implementation of the Civil Society Index (CSI) project by the German partner-organization Maecenata Institute for Philanthropy and Civil Society was embedded in a larger debate about civil society in contemporary German society and sought to contribute to this debate by obtaining data to compare German civil society with countries around the world. Since civil society issues in Germany are rather well researched, the Maecenata Institute decided to rely on available secondary data and a media analysis of civil society issues.

Table 14.1 Background Information for Germany

Germany	
Country size (square km)	356,973
Population (millions 2004)	82.5
Population under 15 years (2004)	14.6%
Urban population (2003)	88.1%
Seats in parliament held by women (2005)	32.8%
Language groups	German (official), Turkish, Italian, English, Danish, Dutch, Slavic
Ethnic groups	German 92%, Turkish 2%, other 6%
Religious groups	Protestant 34%, Roman Catholic 34%, Muslim 4%, unaffiliated or other 28%
HDI score and ranking (2003)	0.930 (20th)
GDP per capita (US$ 2003)	$27,756
Unemployment rate (% of total labor force)	9.8%

143

Historical Overview

The history of voluntary associations in Germany is closely connected to the processes of industrialization and state modernization, and also to the emergence of a bourgeoisie in the nineteenth century. The middle class, in particular, was left politically powerless in an authoritarian state and turned to voluntary associations to express its interests and needs. In the last quarter of the century, the growing mobilization of the working class led to the emergence of a wide range of workers' associations, including unions and various cultural and social organizations. In general, civic life was deeply divided by sociocultural milieus, mainly between Protestants, Catholics, nationalists, and social-democratic workers. The Weimar Republic (1918–1933) was characterized by the emergence of the welfare state, weak political institutions, and an intensification of divisions among these sociocultural groups, which increasingly turned into violent clashes between their respective organizations. Between 1933 and 1945, the totalitarian Nazi regime did not allow for independent citizen associations.

After 1945, citizens of the German Democratic Republic (GDR) continued to be denied freedom of assembly and association, and only state-sanctioned associations were permitted. In West Germany, associational life grew in the postwar period, developing in close cooperation with the state. As a consequence of government's adherence to the subsidiarity principle, welfare organizations became deeply embedded in the public welfare system and were responsible for delivering a substantive portion of state services.[2] The 1970s witnessed the emergence of public good–oriented associations in the form of social movements, self-help groups, and local citizen initiatives, particularly around environmental issues.

The most recent hallmark for German civil society was the reunification in 1990. The immense citizen mobilization that led to the overthrow of the GDR's socialist regime quickly diminished, but it lives on in a host of small local initiatives. The mid-1990s saw a transfer of West Germany's deeply entrenched associational system to the East. Due to a period of economic stagnation and demographic changes since the turn of the millennium, the German welfare state, including its major social welfare organizations, is increasingly seen as being in need of a major overhaul. In the context of the declining room for the state to maneuver, increased civic engagement and a stronger role for civil society are seen as potential remedies for Germany's current crisis. Thus, the implementation of the CSI came at a crucial point in time, when the division of labor between citizens, the market, and the state was a topic of intense public debate.

The State of Civil Society in Germany

This section provides a summary of key findings of the CSI project in Germany. It examines the state of German civil society along four dimensions—structure, environment, values, and impact—highlighting the main weaknesses and strengths.

A unique feature of the German CSI implementation was the indicator scoring process, which was undertaken by two separate National Advisory Groups (NAGs) to detect potential biases or impacts of group dynamics. However, in general, the scores of both NAGs strongly resembled each other. The averaged scores for both groups are presented here.

The German Civil Society Diamond (figure 14.1) depicts a rather well-developed and healthy sector. The lower score for structure stands out, indicating relatively weak levels of citizen participation and an only moderately developed sector-wide infrastructure. Nonetheless, German civil society is operating in an enabling environment, where only corporate philanthropy has significant room for improvement. Civil society's value base is rather strong, with mobilization around environmental issues being a hallmark of civic activism in the country. The high score for civil society's impact on governance and development is also noteworthy and clearly a result of the close relations between many voluntary associations and the German state.

Figure 14.1 Civil Society Diamond for Germany

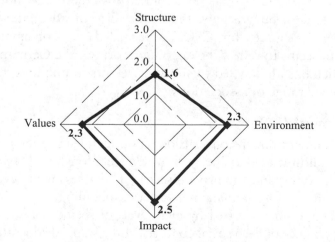

Structure (1.6)

The structure dimension examines the makeup of civil society in terms of the main characteristics of participation and associational life. The structure dimension received the lowest score of the four dimensions. Most notably, it reflects low levels of citizen participation outside of associations, rather weak international links, and certain financial and human-resource vulnerabilities within the sector.

Germany boasts a diverse range of civil society organizations (CSOs), which can be divided into two distinct areas: the heavily state-financed social welfare sector and the diverse sector of cultural, advocacy, environment, sports, and other types of associations. This second type is far less dependent on public sector funding.

The level of associational membership in Germany is reasonably high, with roughly every second German being a member of an association. However, other forms of civic involvement are not very widespread. For example, only 5% of the population is involved in collective community activities. In examining the participation rates of different social groups, one notices a clear correlation between socioeconomic factors and levels of involvement, which is not unique to Germany. There are also pronounced regional differences. The population in West Germany exhibits a higher level of civic engagement and a larger number of associations than people living in the former GDR territory.

Compared to the moderate levels of civic engagement, the structural characteristics of German civil society receive more positive assessments, with high scores for levels of interorganizational cooperation and organization, as exemplified by the large number of umbrella bodies. Surprisingly, the availability of adequate financial and human resources for CSOs is regarded as problematic. This assessment seems to reflect the ongoing reform of the German welfare state, which has already led to substantive cuts in public sector funding to a wide range of associations.

Environment (2.3)

The environment dimension considers political, legal, socioeconomic, and sociocultural contexts as well as the relationships between civil society, the state, and the private sector. The assessment reveals that the environment for German civil society is enabling.

Germany is characterized by high levels of socioeconomic development, the absence of deep social conflicts, and a stable democratic system of government, where civil and political rights are widely safeguarded.

Despite the need for reform, the state effectively provides services and fully upholds the rule of law. Civil society's legal environment is seen as favorable, although civic and advocacy-oriented associations do not receive the same levels of tax benefits as public good-oriented organizations. The relationship between civil society and the state is assessed as overwhelmingly positive, with a host of cooperative structures and mechanisms in place. However, the strong financial dependency on the state, with close to two-thirds of civil society's operations being funded by the state, is seen as having negative implications for the autonomy and long-term sustainability of the sector.

With regard to the level of public spiritedness among Germans, the CSI detects some room for improvement. For example, only one-third of Germans feel that paying taxes is a contribution toward the public good. Another moderate weakness is corporate philanthropy, which is neither seen as comprehensive nor as being able to constitute a reliable source of income for CSOs.

Values (2.3)

The values dimension examines the extent to which civil society practices and promotes positive values. The assessment finds that German civil society practices and promotes these values to a relatively significant extent.

German CSOs are at the forefront of promoting important values, such as environmental sustainability, poverty eradication, democracy, nonviolence, and tolerance. However, the strong role of CSOs in promoting tolerance contrasts with the growth of intolerant forces within German civil society, such as the neo-Nazi movement. Civil society's activities to promote environmental sustainability receive the highest score within the values dimension. Originally rooted in a vibrant sociocultural milieu, the environmental movement has lost some of its mobilizing power but remains a prominent component of Germany's civil society.

Certain weak areas also exist in civil society's values. CSOs' level of financial transparency is assessed as very weak, and only minor attempts within civil society exist to strengthen CSOs' accountability and transparency. The low score for internal transparency goes hand in hand with a rather negative assessment of civil society's activities to promote the value of transparency within society. Despite a number of positive examples, civil society is not generally seen as a driving force in this field. Another value with a mixed assessment is gender equity. Civil society's internal practices to promote gender equity within associations and in broader society are seen as only moderate.

Impact (2.5)

The impact dimension assesses civil society's role in governance and society at large. German civil society's impact on politics, society, and the economy stands out as the strongest dimension. Only civil society's impact on the national budgeting process receives a lower-than-average assessment.

The dual character of German civil society—of publicly funded welfare associations on the one hand and independent advocacy organizations on the other—also shapes civil society's role and impact on society. Social welfare organizations, due to their integral role in the German welfare state, are the main social service providers. However, a large number of mostly local citizen initiatives actively empower citizens by running public education campaigns, advocating for marginalized groups, and building citizens' capacity to act collectively. One example is the recent growth of community foundations.

Because of the long-standing close relationships between key interest groups, important civil society umbrella bodies, and Germany's main political parties, civil society's impact on policymaking is assessed as substantive. However, civil society's role seems to be confined to specific policies. The evaluation of civil society's impact on the overall national budgeting process, as the government's key financial policy decision, is rather low, since no CSO or coalition of CSOs, which are monitoring, analyzing, or advocating around the budgeting process could be identified.

The analysis of civil society's impact shows that, even though service provision is often described as the main role of German civil society, civil society's role in stimulating public participation, integrating social concerns into the public sphere, and advocating for social interests is almost as pronounced as its widely recognized contribution to social welfare.

Conclusion

The German CSI was implemented at a time of profound change, reform, and upheaval in Germany's entrenched social market economy. The state has initiated several reform programs aimed at shedding certain state social welfare and health responsibilities. A more proactive role for citizens in the welfare state is promoted through the concept of an activating state, in which civil society is often assigned a key organizing function. While the CSI findings paint a picture of a rather strong civil society with a particularly strong impact—operating in a strong environment—they also point toward certain weaknesses relevant to the debate about the future of the German welfare state. Civil society's capacity appears to be already at its limits, since the level of CSOs' financial and human resources are inadequate to effectively fulfill their missions. Civil society's main funder, the German state, is unlikely to make additional funds available; in fact, public sector funding is decreasing. At the same time, the business sector, which could provide much-needed financial support, is not seen as embracing a closer relationship with civil society.

Last, civil society itself is not free from internal weaknesses. The rather high level of associational membership aside, other indicators of individual civic engagement, such as collective community action and nonpartisan political action, point toward a moderately active citizenry. The CSI also finds room for improving CSOs' internal transparency and accountability. Problems of accountability are closely linked to the overall level of public trust in civil society and consequently to any potential increase in public financial support to CSOs, which could be an additional source of income for the sector.

In the discussions about the German welfare system and civil society's role in it, it is important not to lose sight of the range of other equally—if not *more*—important roles German CSOs are successfully performing, such as informing, educating, and mobilizing citizens; advocating on behalf of marginalized groups; and promoting positive social values and the public good. Different from the third sector discourse, the civil society concept highlights these democratic functions, which are at the core of the CSI's assessment in Germany. Thus, the CSI's contribution to the debate about the future of German civil society is to raise awareness about CSOs' various activities and roles, which, taken together, are key in sustaining a vibrant public life and in strengthening the democratic system of governance in the country.

CSI Report

Sabine Reimer, *Civil Society—A New Solution Beyond State and Market?: CIVICUS Civil Society Index Report for Germany* (Berlin, Germany: Maecenata Institute, 2005).

Notes

1. The CSI assessment was implemented in Germany by the Maecenata Institute for Philanthropy and Civil Society from 2003 to 2005. This chapter presents the main findings of the CSI and is based on a comprehensive country report for Germany, which can be accessed on the CSI pages at http://www.civicus.org.
2. Rooted in social philosophy of modern Catholicism, the subsidiarity principle proposes that the institution most local and most directly linked to citizens should provide social services. In general, voluntary organizations fulfill this requirement better than state agencies.

Chapter 15

Ghana[1]

In 1957 Ghana became the first British colony in sub-Saharan Africa to gain independence. In 1992 it was one of the first African countries to reintroduce multiparty democracy after several decades of single party and military dictatorships, which had swept most of the continent. Although the advent of democracy allowed civil society to thrive, the new democratic dispensation has yet to produce the reforms that many civil society activists were expecting. In addition, civil society in Ghana is currently struggling with crucial internal challenges of representation, accountability, and organization.

Table 15.1 Background Information for Ghana

Ghana	
Country size (square km)	238,533
Population (millions 2004)	21.7
Population under 15 years (2004)	39.5%
Urban population (2003)	45.4%
Seats in parliament held by women (2005)	10.9%
Language groups	English (official), about 75 African languages including Akan, Moshi-Dagomba, Ewe, and Ga
Ethnic groups	Akan 44%, Moshi-Dagomba 16%, Ewe 13%, Ga 8%, Gurma 3%, Yoruba 1%, other 15%
Religious groups	Christian 63%, Muslim 16%, indigenous beliefs 21%
HDI score and ranking (2003)	0.520 (138th)
GDP per capita (US$ 2003)	$2,238
Unemployment rate (% of total labor force)	8.2%
Population living on less than US$2 a day (1998-1999)	78.5%

151

Historical Overview

A wide range of civil society organizations (CSOs) developed in Ghana as early as the late 1700s, when the country was still known as the Gold Coast. The first associations and groups comprised broad membership, including traditional leaders, elders, peasants, indigenous cocoa producers, and youth.

The interwar period (1918–1939) saw an increase in civil society's vibrancy, particularly due to the process of urbanization and recurrent mobilizations against British colonial rule. The constitutional reforms of the 1940s gradually moved the country toward self-government. The reforms enabled local elites to obtain a share in government, but created divisions among various civil society groups, some of which sided with the Convention People's Party (CPP), led by Kwame Nkrumah, while others aligned against the CPP.

After independence in 1957, Nkrumah's government co-opted most CSOs and introduced a series of measures aimed at constraining civil society, including the Trade Union Act, which made strikes illegal. The ousting of the CPP government in 1966 was followed by a series of military coups. During this period, student organizations, trade unions, and the press were coerced into obedience, but developmental NGOs were permitted to operate as long as they did not venture into the political sphere. In 1976 the Union government was introduced as a political arrangement. Under the Union government the police, the military, and major social groups, such as business associations and unions, shared power on a nonpartisan basis.

In 1983, ahead of most African countries, Ghana began to pursue an economic recovery program based on the principles of structural adjustment. Ghana's last military regime, the Provisional National Defence Council (PNDC) (1981–1992), led by Jerry Rawlings, introduced reforms under the sponsorship of the World Bank and International Monetary Fund. The introduction of these reforms brought hardships to Ghanaian citizens. Public sector workers were laid off, and the state drastically reduced its range of services. Toward the end of the 1980s, a growing number of CSOs, spearheaded by trade unions and professional associations, became increasingly vocal against the Rawlings government and significantly contributed to the process of installing and developing a democratic system in 1992.

After the National Democratic Congress (NDC) government's two terms under Rawlings in the 1990s, the New Patriotic Party's (NPP) won the 2000 elections. This marked the first time in Ghana's history

Figure 15.1 Civil Society Index Diamond for Ghana

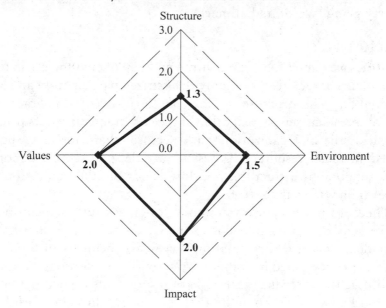

that power was peacefully handed over from one regime to the other and was a landmark victory for democracy in Ghana. Although the NPP enjoyed widespread support from civil society before the elections, this cordial relationship changed somewhat in the following years. Civil society and the state clashed over differing views on important development issues, such as water privatization, basic services, and the government's use of foreign funds to promote development.

The State of Civil Society in Ghana

This section provides a summary of key findings of the CSI project in Ghana. It examines the state of Ghanaian civil society along four dimensions—structure, environment, values, and impact—highlighting the main weaknesses and strengths.

The Civil Society Diamond (figure 15.1) visually summarizes the assessment's findings in Ghana. Ghanaian civil society exhibits a slightly weak structure, particularly with regard to the composition and resources of organized civil society, but levels of individual civic engagement are rather high. Civil society operates in a somewhat disabling environment, marred by significant socioeconomic problems and a rather weak and unaccountable state. However, civil society's impact on society is relatively significant, as is its practice and promotion of positive values, with democracy and the fight against poverty being two of its hallmarks.

Structure (1.3)

The structure dimension examines the makeup of civil society in terms of the main characteristics of individual citizen participation and associational life. The structure of Ghanaian civil society is characterized by widespread citizen participation at the community level. Its primary weaknesses lie in organizational and sectoral characteristics, such as limited financial resources, CSOs' strong dependence on donors, a weak support infrastructure, and low levels of communication and cooperation within the sector.

The CSI finds a significant amount of citizen involvement in civil society activities in Ghana. For example, slightly more than half of respondents to the CSI population survey are members of CSOs and 80% have participated in community activities or meetings. Additionally, during the preceding year 57% of respondents carried out volunteer work for their communities, primarily through faith-based associations.

The CSI finds that most professional CSOs in Ghana are based in urban areas, and the best-equipped CSOs operate in the main cities. CSOs tend to gravitate to urban settlements to access basic facilities, such as electricity and telephone lines. Civil society's social composition is also skewed, with women and especially the rural population being underrepresented in the membership of most CSOs and almost completely excluded from leadership roles.

Organized civil society is rather poorly structured. There is a lack of support infrastructure for civil society. Only a minority of CSOs belongs to an umbrella organization, and the overall level of coordination among CSOs is considered particularly weak. CSI stakeholders highlighted that the adage "united we stand, divided we fall" has not taken root in Ghanaian civil society and needs to be addressed as a key priority for the sector.

The CSI also highlights the low levels of local financial and technological resources available to Ghanaian CSOs. As a consequence, the civil society sector is marked by significant dependence on foreign donors. Interestingly, this general lack of technological and financial resources does not seem to affect CSOs' human resources, which are seen as an asset of Ghanaian civil society, particularly in the form of a strong volunteer base.

In general, the structure of Ghanaian civil society can be described as twofold: it has strong levels of civic engagement and rather weak levels of organization and coordination.

Environment (1.5)

The environment dimension considers political, legal, socioeconomic, and sociocultural contexts, as well as the relationships between civil society, the state, and the private sector. The environment within which Ghanaian CSOs operate is somewhat disabling, mainly due to widespread poverty and illiteracy, socioeconomic problems such as lack of basic services, and corruption in public institutions.

Ghanaians enjoy a wide range of political rights, with no noticeable restrictions on people's right to vote and run for office. Although the government generally upholds freedom of the press, the CSI registers some instances of state control, such as the government using libel legislation to harass the media. In some cases, journalists who were investigating corruption regarding the president and his family were harassed by the police. In terms of CSOs' legal environment, the CSI stakeholders agree that the registration procedures for CSOs are undermined by inconsistencies that make the whole process cumbersome and time-consuming. In the early 2000s a proposal for a new legal framework was developed through a widely consultative process, but because of insufficient advocacy on behalf of civil society and an indifferent government, it has not moved forward since.

Despite the fact that Ghana has been one of the most stable countries on the continent, macro indicators in Ghana point to a rather difficult socioeconomic situation. Surveys indicate that basic necessities, such as food and medical care, are not available to all Ghanaians. For example, 40% of citizens report having gone without food at least once. Poverty and illiteracy are still widespread, especially in rural communities, which creates a further divide between urban and rural populations.

Civil Society Index stakeholders maintain that both the state and the private sector do not understand or appreciate the contributions civil society can make toward social and economic development. The relationship between CSOs and government has evolved from limited interaction and friction during the early days of democracy to increased engagement over the past decade, which was partially triggered by the insistence of international actors such as the World Bank. Although by law CSOs enjoy autonomy, certain threats by state authorities still undermine this autonomy. For example, government officials have threatened NGOs that point out growing social problems, such as child trafficking. A fairly large number (44%) of surveyed stakeholders feel the state sometimes interferes with CSOs.

Finally, the relationship between CSOs and private business is generally marked by indifference. The large majority (71%) of CSI stakeholders see the private sector as indifferent or suspicious of civil society. In their view, in spite of significant efforts made by the government to boost economic growth, the private sector remains relatively underdeveloped, which limits the support it can offer to civil society.

Values (2.0)

The values dimension examines the extent to which civil society practices and promotes positive values. In Ghana the score for this dimension is quite high, though certain challenges remain, such as limited practice of transparency and gender equity.

Democracy is rather deeply entrenched in Ghanaian civil society. Decisionmaking processes in Ghanaian CSOs are characterized by a significant level of democratic participation and contribution from members. The stakeholders interviewed for the CSI assessment maintain that members have a substantial influence on their CSOs' agenda, although they admit that internal democratic practices are much less common for the selection of CSOs' leaders.

Civil society's activities to eradicate poverty in Ghana enjoy broad-based support and are carried out throughout the country. Local NGOs have joined forces with international organizations on issues such as fair trade and have conducted campaigns to support local peasants and their products. In some cases, CSOs' activities complement government's policies aimed at reducing poverty, and many CSOs are quite active in the most poverty-stricken areas of the country.

Regarding nonviolence, stakeholders involved in the CSI feel that violent actions, such as damage to property or people, are relatively frequent within civil society, especially among the youth leagues of the main political parties. In December 2005 some members of the opposition NDC claimed that intra-party rivals physically attacked them. However, most CSOs are quick to denounce violent acts.

In contrast to positive assessments for democracy and poverty eradication, values of gender equity and transparency are scarcely practiced by Ghanaian CSOs. Many organizations do not have internal policies on gender equity, even though they implement numerous activities to promote gender equity in society. At the same time, financial information pertaining to CSOs' donations and investments are rarely made public. Such a lack of transparency further strengthens the perception that CSOs, particularly NGOs, are rich. Due to excessive spending on hotels, meals, transport allowances, and per diems, many local communities see CSOs as moneymaking entities. This phenomenon negatively affects the impact of CSOs' activities and the extent of community involvement in CSOs.

Although the assessment of the values dimension receives the highest score, CSI stakeholders admit that the sector is seriously challenged by its limited transparency and accountability. According to some, the lack of a regulatory framework for CSOs' conduct is not conducive to the healthy growth of the sector. According to the researchers who implemented the CSI in Ghana, this laissez faire regulatory attitude leaves room for unscrupulous people to establish NGOs with questionable agendas, which discredit the reputation of the whole sector.

Impact (2.0)

The impact dimension assesses civil society's role in governance and society at large. The CSI findings show that civil society in Ghana contributes significantly toward empowering women and providing basic services to local communities, whereas its role in policy and as a watchdog of the state and the private sector is limited.

Civil society in Ghana has significantly contributed to the economic and social empowerment of women. Moreover, CSOs successfully provide rural communities with basic services, such as education, water, and health care, particularly in the fight against the guinea worm infection. An overwhelming majority (80%) of survey respondents consider CSOs to be more effective than the state in assisting marginalized groups, such as women, children, and the disabled.

As in other African countries included in the CSI assessment, Ghanaian civil society is particularly active and successful in providing a range of services to marginalized groups, but not as successful in influencing policies. In spite of the formally conducive political environment created by the 1992 constitution, CSOs' active policy engagement is limited. The advent of democratic government created new channels for CSOs to influence policy, particularly through mechanisms such as advocacy campaigns and parliamentary lobbying. However, confrontational strategies remain prevalent. For example, trade unions have little influence on national budget policies and have resorted almost exclusively to strikes and demonstrations to pursue their agendas, with limited results.

Nevertheless, the CSI noted some signs of success in specific policy sectors. For example, in 2004, a coalition of CSOs strongly opposed a water privatization program implemented by government and endorsed by the World Bank, and the group succeeded in modifying the state's agenda on this issue. Similarly, in 2005, human rights NGOs formed a coalition to educate citizens about domestic violence and organized seminars and marches that eventually led to parliament considering a bill that was proposed by the organizations themselves. There are also instances of evidence-based and technical advocacy work by CSOs—for example, around the national budget—that are not found in many other countries of the global South and indicate the advanced level of advocacy skills of Ghanaian CSOs.

Civil society is not generally successful in holding private corporations accountable, although exceptions exist. The CSI registered some cases of environmental organizations holding foreign corporations accountable, especially in the mining sector, and advocating for the rights of local communities and villages affected by the extraction of natural resources.

In short, the overall impact of Ghanaian civil society is quite significant, especially in the field of service provision and empowerment, whereas policy influence is gradually expanding in spite of recurrent frictions between CSOs and government regarding pro-poor policies.

Recommendations

The CSI National Workshop was held in April 2006, with more than 140 representatives from civil society, government, academia, business, the donor community, and the media. A set of recommendations was identified, based on the CSI study's findings. The following are the key recommendations:

- Capacity building and infrastructure: CSOs should improve their financial management and reporting, strengthen the role of umbrella organizations, and improve networking and information exchange among CSOs and other sectors, such as the media.
- Clarify registration and reporting procedures: The CSO registration and reporting process should be decentralized and simplified.
- Resource mobilization: Ghanaian CSOs should adopt innovative methods of fundraising and resource mobilization to supplement their traditional sources of income.

- Self-regulation: Civil society should self-regulate and develop a code of conduct that clearly spells out methods of sanctioning CSOs that do not comply. This will enhance their image and credibility and prevent the public from lumping together good and bad CSOs.
- Advocacy and policy impact: CSOs should improve their capacity to make use of existing institutional channels to influence policy-making and hold government accountable. A stronger commitment to advocacy could help CSOs convince government that its involvement is crucial to ensure equitable development. Civil society should also be more proactive and use its networks to engage in the policymaking process, instead of waiting to be consulted.

Conclusion

In 2000 Ghana saw the first peaceful handover of power in the country's history. Although this was a promising sign for democratic consolidation, the government of John Kufuor has been slow in implementing pro-poor reforms, defying the expectations of many civil society groups. However, for civil society to become more powerful vis-à-vis the government and act as a true voice of the poor, CSOs must improve their internal transparency and accountability to overcome the public perception that they are elitist organizations primarily interested in private financial gains rather than in actual social development and furthering the interests of the people.

CSI Report

A. Darkwa, N. Amponsah and E. Gyampoh, *Civil Society in a Changing Ghana—An Assessment of the Current State of Civil Society in Ghana: CIVICUS Civil Society Index Report for Ghana* (Accra, Ghana: GAPVOD, 2006).

Notes

1. The CSI assessment was implemented in Ghana by the Ghana Association of Private Voluntary Organizations in Development (GAPVOD) from January to November 2005. This chapter presents the main findings of the CSI and is based on a comprehensive country report for Ghana, which can be accessed on the CSI pages of the CIVICUS website at http://www.civicus.org.

Chapter 16

Greece[1]

Civil society has historically been a marginal feature in Greek society, which has been dominated by the state, political parties, the Greek Christian Orthodox Church, and the family. Given these hierarchical tendencies, today's civil society in Greece is struggling to enhance its role in society and governance, as the results of the Civil Society Index-Shortened Assessment Tool (CSI-SAT) confirm.

Table 16.1 Background Information for Greece

Greece	
Country size (square km)	131,957
Population (millions 2004)	11.1
Population under 15 years (2004)	14.4%
Urban population (2003)	60.9%
Seats in parliament held by women (2005)	14%
Language groups	Greek (official), English, French
Ethnicity groups	Greek 98%, other 2%
Religious groups	Greek Orthodox 98% (official), Muslim 1%, other 1%
HDI score and ranking (2003)	0.912 (24th)
GDP per capita (US$ 2003)	$19,954
Unemployment rate (% of total labor force)	10.2%

Historical Overview

The modern form of Greek civil society has its origins in the early nineteenth century, when civil society played an active role during the Greek War of Independence against the Ottoman Empire (1821–1827). Throughout the nineteenth century, nationalist, philanthropic,

161

education, and faith-based CSOs participated in the drive to expand the modern Greek state.

The democratic development of the country was interrupted by World War II and the Greek Civil War (1946–1949), as well as by a series of subsequent military interventions into Greek politics, which led to the breakdown of democracy in 1967 and the subsequent military dictatorship. Following the civil war, CSOs were largely controlled by the Greek state, which was led by the conservative political elite. During the military dictatorship (1967–1974), leftist political parties and left-wing organizations of civil society were closely monitored by the state, and their operations were restricted. Although many left-wing activists, politicians, intellectuals, and students were arrested, tortured, or murdered, some sought refuge in other countries and others continued their resistance underground.

Today, Greek civil society has achieved a considerable level of development, given the transition to democracy in 1974 and the previously restrictive environment. Greece's accession to the European Union (EU) in 1981 marked a significant milestone. Various EU policy frameworks provide opportunities for stronger civil society engagement and influence, such as policies relating to anticorruption, the environment, and corporate social responsibility (CSR). However, a more widespread proliferation of CSOs did not occur until the 1990s.

Despite its growth over the last thirty years, Greek civil society is less well-developed than civil society in other Western European countries, since its development was hampered by two sets of factors. First, economic and political instability impeded the development of social capital, particularly trust within society. Throughout much of the twentieth century, foreign interventions, periods of civil war, an influx of refugees and immigrants, and dictatorship characterized Greek society and political culture. Second, most Greek CSOs have been heavily dependent on key state institutions. This dependency was part of a system of patronage and nepotism, which lowered the state's credibility and accountability in the eyes of Greek citizens. As a result, widespread mistrust was nurtured among the citizenry, which impaired the ability and willingness of citizens to engage in collective action for the public good.

Thus, the state, church, political parties, and the family remain the most influential institutions in Greek society. Within the sphere of civil society, traditional organizations lacking a strong focus on public interests, such as trade unions, professional associations, and sporting and recreational associations, continue to have the widest membership.

The State of Civil Society in Greece

Civil society is a widely used term in public and expert discourse in Greece. The CSI study focused on formal organizations, but included certain forms of informal activities, such as small groups working on local community issues and networks of people exchanging messages over the internet or cell phones. It excluded political parties and the Greek Orthodox Church, given their institutional stature and particular relationship with society and state.

This section provides a summary of key findings of the CSI project in Greece. It examines the state of Greek civil society along four dimensions—structure, environment, values, and impact—highlighting the main weaknesses and strengths.

The Civil Society Diamond for Greece (figure 16.1) is a visual representation of the assessment's findings. The diamond depicts a relatively unbalanced and underdeveloped sector. Civil society has a particularly weak structure, with low levels of citizen engagement in civic activities. Similarly, the analysis of civil society's impact reveals a weak record of service delivery, advocacy, and policy activities. In contrast, the sector's operating environment is relatively enabling and its value base is rather strong, despite deficiencies in the practice of gender equity and transparency among CSOs.

Figure 16.1 Civil Society Diamond for Greece

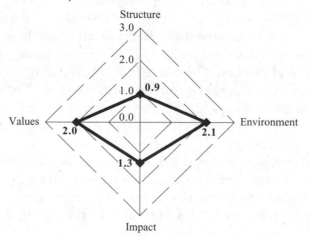

Structure (0.9)

The structure dimension examines the makeup of civil society in terms of the main characteristics of individual citizen participation and associational life. The structure of Greek civil society is relatively weak, receiving the lowest assessment among the four dimensions. Citizen involvement in CSOs is quite low, CSOs do not mirror the different social groups in Greek society, and substantial funding constraints inhibit the sector's development. Together these weaknesses result in a poorly structured sector, although ad hoc or issue-based cooperation among CSOs is quite common.

With the family being the cornerstone of Greek social life, few citizens participate in organized associational life. Only 8% of the population is a member of a CSO and charitable giving is similarly limited, with only 9% of citizens donating to charity on a regular basis. The emerging picture is one of a relatively small civil society where citizens are rather disengaged and apathetic toward organizational life.

The social composition of Greek civil society is not representative of the overall population. Unlike in other Western European countries, young people and the elderly remain underrepresented. Furthermore, CSOs are unevenly distributed across the country and rather concentrated in urban areas, where more favorable socioeconomic conditions make it easier to participate in an organization. The dominant actors in Greek civil society are trade unions, sports organizations, professional associations, and employee organizations. Public interest organizations, such as NGOs or social movements, are less prevalent. The Greek Orthodox Church is a powerful institution in society, and faith-based organizations, controlled by the church, provide many social services to the population.

Civil society suffers from inadequate resources and low levels of organization and professionalism. Expenditures tend to exceed average revenues by 10%, and half of CSOs' expenditures go to operational costs and salaries. There is a lack of diverse funding sources, with one-third of all revenue coming from the state. The absence of effective umbrella bodies and limited international linkages for the majority of CSOs hinders the development of a strong civil society infrastructure in Greece.

On a more positive side, the findings indicate that citizens' mobilization and engagement dramatically increases during periods of crisis or in response to particular events. Many citizens mobilized to oppose the Iraq War in 2003 and to help victims of the earthquakes in northeastern Turkey and in Western Athens in mid-1999. Likewise, volunteering and community service surged during the Olympic Games in Athens in 2004. Although there is no civil society arena, where a common agenda can be formed, there are specific issue-areas where CSOs and citizens become engaged, such as poverty eradication, environmental concerns, anti-trafficking issues, and minority rights issues.

As this evidence indicates, Greek civil society is characterized by a lack of civic engagement and issue-based outbursts of cooperation and volunteerism, rather than sustained and well-organized, cross-sectoral collaboration.

Environment (2.1)

The environment dimension considers political, legal, socioeconomic, and sociocultural contexts, as well as the relationships between civil society, the state, and the private sector. Overall, the environment is relatively enabling for civil society's activities. The sector's ineffective relationship with the state and the private sector, as well as the low levels of social capital in society, are the most limiting factors.

There are no major legal factors inhibiting the growth of civil society. The 1975 Constitution fully guarantees basic rights and freedoms, and the state respects freedom of speech and association. CSO registration procedures are relatively simple and inexpensive, and other legal provisions, such as tax laws, are viewed as enabling, although fiscal incentives for giving could be improved. However, the key features of Greek politics pose certain challenges for an independent civil society. The system of government is highly centralized and dominated by party politics, which also permeate civil society. State funding to CSOs is discriminatory, at times clientelistic, and largely determined by which party is in power. In addition, corruption within the public sector is rather widespread. Outside of labor relations and dialogue with trade unions, there is very little state–civil society dialogue. However, some initiatives to improve state–civil society relations are taking place. For example, in September 2005, the Economic and Social Council of Greece issued a proposal called *opinion,* which acknowledges the importance of NGOs and calls for actions to include organized civil society in the government's official consultation processes.

Over the last three to five years, civil society and private sector relations have improved somewhat, but they remain underdeveloped.

In general, corporate support for a broad range of CSOs is limited. The concept of sponsorship gained ground during the 2004 Olympic Games, and, similarly, practices of CSR increased in response to pressures from the EU. However, these practices remain minimal, and most private funding and CSR initiatives focus on CSOs working in the fields of sports, environment, and children's issues, whereas more political causes are rarely supported by businesses.

The sociocultural basis for a strong civil society is not in place. Against the backdrop of the legacy of authoritarian political regimes and the strong role of the family, widespread mistrust prevails in society. Only 18% of Greeks agreed that most people can be trusted.[2] In addition, society's overall level of tolerance is low, and problems of xenophobia toward minority groups persist, particularly toward foreigners, homosexuals, and people of a different ethnicity.

Aside from needing to develop more cooperative relations and institutionalize channels for dialogue with the state, civil society's main challenge is to stimulate social capital in a society where the concept of engaging in public life remains rather unpopular.

Values (2.0)

The values dimension examines the extent to which civil society practices and promotes positive values. Greek civil society is relatively strong in promoting key values such as democracy, poverty eradication, nonviolence, and environmental sustainability. However, civil society less actively practices and promotes gender equity, accountability, and transparency within CSOs and in society at large.

Greek civil society is a leading force in advancing important social norms and principles. For example, a large number of CSOs are active in promoting democracy, such as the Citizens' Union PAREMVASSI, which advocates for civil society, citizen rights, and participatory democracy in the country. In response to rising poverty and, particularly, homelessness, certain CSOs focus their work on affected families and children, such as the Greek branch of SOS Children's Village. Although a significant number of civil society activities propagate environmental sustainability, there is less broad-based support or public visibility of these efforts than in other Western European countries.

Transparency and corruption are a concern within civil society, and a problem for Greek society as a whole. Transparency International categorized Greece as one of the most corrupt countries in Western Europe. In its 2005 Corruption Perception Index, Greece ranked 47th globally. Also, only a small proportion of CSOs publish their financial statements. Given the lack of transparency in CSOs, perceived corruption levels in Greece, and civil society's limited actions to promote these values, civil society needs to improve its own accountability mechanisms and strengthen actions to advance transparency within civil society, as well as for the government and private sector.

Although government and civil society discourse supports gender equity, the programs and policies to operationalize the principle of gender equity within civil society and in society at large are inadequate. Women are underrepresented in leadership roles within civil society, and do not feature widely in most areas of political, social, and economic life. To improve women's status in society, the project's Stakeholder Assessment Group highlighted the need for civil society to increase its actions to promote gender equity, in collaboration with the state and the private sector.

Impact (1.3)

The impact dimension assesses civil society's role in governance and society at large. In Greek politics and society, civil society's role is somewhat limited. Civil society does not have much impact in service delivery, in citizen empowerment and advocacy, or as a watchdog of the state. In contrast, civil society is fairly good at taking up and responding to social concerns.

The study reveals that parts of civil society are swift at responding to social, political, and economic concerns affecting the public. In particular, special interest groups have a record of responding quickly to developments that may affect their constituents. For example, in the last few years trade unions quickly mobilized to protect employment and monitor working conditions, pensions, and salary levels, particularly in large state-run companies and in the banking and transportation sectors. Strikes in the public sector are relatively frequent, and public sector trade unions have successfully resisted reforms in labor relations and the social security system. Public trust in trade unions is rather high (57%), at a similar level to the parliament, police, and media, and significantly higher than the umbrella body for Greek industries, which received the lowest rating (33%).

Civil society plays a limited role in service delivery, which continues to be dominated by government and church institutions. Generally, Greek CSOs do not have the resources to meet societal needs, and most Greek citizens' believe that the state should be responsible for providing welfare services. Only recently have some CSOs begun to engage more extensively in service delivery, such as providing legal services to refugees through the Greek Council for Refugees.

As a watchdog of the state, civil society's activities are mainly related to human rights, environmental protection, and consumer rights, but their overall impact remains limited. Civil society's lobbying activities are few and involve more widespread issue-based mobilizations, such as large-scale protests, or focus on international issues, such as peace and globalization.

Conclusion

For the first time, a comprehensive and participatory assessment on the state of Greek civil society was carried out through the CSI-SAT project. As the findings reveal, civil society has a weak structure and a limited impact on society at large, but exists in a relatively enabling environment and espouses rather positive values. The sector has grown in recent years, partly due to the crisis of traditional institutions, such as the inability of political parties to meet major societal needs, and partly due to the influence of EU membership, which has led to increased funding and requirements for civil society's participation in public issues.

A shortage of institutionalized channels for coordinated action within the civil society sector, the highly centralized state, and generally low public support for civil society impede civil society's further growth and stronger influence in society. Therefore, developing Greek civil society requires increased public support and civic engagement, particularly among young people and marginalized groups. Civil society also needs to strengthen its engagement with the state and the private sector, both as partners and as potential funders of its work.

CSI Report

Dimitri A. Sotiropoulos and Evika Karamagioli, *Greek Civil Society—The Long Road to Maturity: CIVICUS Civil Society Index Shortened Assessment Tool Report for Greece* (Athens, Greece: Access2democracy, 2006).

Notes

1. The CSI Shortened Assessment Tool was implemented in Greece by Access2democracy from April 2005 to June 2006. This chapter presents the main findings of the CSI-SAT and is based on a comprehensive country report for Greece, which can be accessed on the CSI pages of the CIVICUS website at http://www.civicus.org.
2. This is based on the 2004 Eurobarometer Study and contrasts with 33%, the average trust level of all European countries.

Chapter 17

Guatemala[1]

After decades of authoritarian rule and the worst genocide in Latin America's recent history, Guatemala's peace accords of 1996 signaled the advent of democracy and peace in the country. This event constituted the birth of the current civil society in the country, spearheaded by human rights groups, indigenous associations, and development NGOs.

Table 17.1 Background Information for Guatemala

Guatemala	
Country size (square km)	108,889
Population (millions 2004)	12.3
Population under 15 years (2004)	43.5%
Urban population (2003)	46.3%
Seats in parliament held by women (2005)	8.2%
Language groups	Spanish (official), more than 20 Amerindian languages (including Quiche, Cakchiquel, Kekchi, Mam, Garifuna, and Xinca)
Ethnic groups	Mestizo 55%, Amerindian 43%, other 2%
Religious groups	Mostly Roman Catholic, some Protestant and indigenous Mayan beliefs
HDI score and ranking (2003)	0.663 (117th)
GDP per capita (US$ 2003)	$4,148
Unemployment rate (total% of total labor force)	2.8%
Population living on less than US$2 a day (2002)	31.9%

Historical Overview

Guatemala's colonial era was marked by the systematic repression and exclusion of its indigenous people. This process was epitomized by the concentration of land ownership in a few hands, those of the colonizers, who dominated all aspects of political, cultural, and social life.

The strong control over Guatemala exerted by big farmers, especially those involved in the production of coffee, received a blow in 1944, when the October revolutionaries led a revolt against the state and began the "ten years of spring," a decade marked by freedom of speech, high levels of political and civic activism, and progressive policies that promoted land redistribution and other social issues.

In 1954 the American government initiated a campaign against the democratically elected government that culminated in a coup d'etat and the installation of a military regime. The US intervention, the first of a long series of interventions in Latin America, gave way to a series of military juntas and three decades of civil war, which resulted in the death of an estimated 200,000 civilians, mainly of Mayan origin. The long civil war led to widespread physical and human destruction, as well as wide-scale social fragmentation in Guatemala.

According to the UN-sponsored Truth Commission, government forces and paramilitaries were responsible for over 90% of the human rights violations during the war. During the first ten years, the victims of the state-sponsored terror were primarily students, workers, professionals, and opposition figures, but in the last years thousands of mostly rural Mayan farmers and noncombatants were targeted. More than 450 Mayan villages were destroyed and over one million people became refugees, in what is generally considered the worst ethnic cleansing in modern Latin American history. During this phase, due to the widespread terror permeating the country, civil society was almost nonexistent in Guatemala. The few social movements that did exist were deeply intertwined with the leftist guerrilla movements.

The bloody civil war ended in 1996 when the UN negotiated a peace accord between the guerrilla forces and the government of President Álvaro Arzú. Civil society played a significant role in this process, through the Assembly of Civil Society. A new phase began in which civil society organizations (CSOs) could carve out an independent space, separate from the state, political parties, and armed movements. Nevertheless, the contemporary Guatemalan sociocultural environment remains deeply affected by the prolonged atmosphere of conflict.

Figure 17.1 Civil Society Diamond for Guatemala

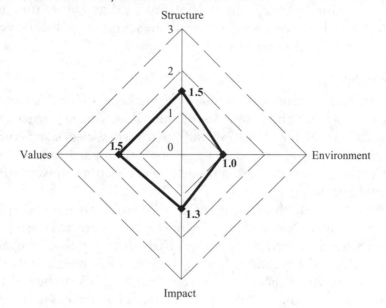

The State of Civil Society in Guatemala

The 1996 peace agreements significantly contributed to shaping civil society in Guatemala. During the negotiations, various civil society actors, from leftist social movements to indigenous groups and human rights defenders, were given a chance to have a voice in the peace process and demand justice for the numerous acts of violence committed during the civil war. For the first time in Guatemala, civil society discourse was used in this context and challenged the traditional ideological polarization of the Guatemalan political context, providing a common identity for many organizations that opposed the military and the guerrilla movements.

This section provides a summary of key findings of the CSI project in Guatemala. It examines the state of Guatemalan civil society along four dimensions—structure, environment, values, and impact—highlighting the main weaknesses and strengths.

As visually summarized by the Civil Society Diamond (figure 17.1), the structure of civil society in Guatemala is of moderate strength, characterized by strong civic engagement, but a rather poorly organized civic sector. Civil society's operating environment is rather disabling since the legacies of social alienation, socioeconomic disparities, political violence, corruption, and elite politics still dominate the country. Guatemalan CSOs promote positive values to a moderate extent, with the exception of democratic values, where they are a leading force, but civil society's overall impact on the political system and society at large remains relatively limited.

Structure (1.5)

The structure dimension examines the makeup of civil society in terms of the main characteristics of individual citizen participation and associational life. The CSI finds that civil society's structure is characterized by widespread and growing citizen participation, especially at the grassroots level, although civil society's infrastructure is rather underdeveloped.

The main strength of Guatemalan civil society is the widespread practice of citizen participation. Mobilizations and demonstrations are rather frequent, and many citizens participate in public campaigns around issues of education, health, and the implementation of the peace agreements. Although a quarter of respondents to the CSI population survey claim to have participated in nonpartisan political actions at least once in their life before the peace agreement, the percentage of those participating in a similar action after 1996 rises to 62%. In the past few years, various sectors of civil society, such as women's associations, indigenous groups, and peasant organizations, have held a number of demonstrations around issues such as concessions to foreign corporations to exploit minerals and oil, land redistribution, and the delivery of basic services.

In general, local committees and community associations are the most common spaces for civic engagement at the grassroots level. Citizen involvement, especially in local-level organizations, is particularly widespread. Three-quarters of respondents to the population survey have volunteered in their community during the previous twelve months.

The weaknesses of civil society's structure relate to its social and geographical composition and the generally low level of organization in the sector. Most CSOs (83%) are concentrated in urban areas, such as Quetzaltenango, Chimaltenango, and Alta Verapaz. The CSI also found that social groups, such as the poor, youth, and the elderly are almost absent in the membership and leadership of CSOs, while women and indigenous groups are somewhat underrepresented.

Civil society's poor level of organization is another concern, since the current formations of civil society are relatively recent and an adequate support infrastructure, which is crucial to strengthening civil society, is lacking. Nevertheless, umbrella organizations and federations are gradually emerging in the country. Examples of effective networks are the Movimiento Indígena, Campesino, Sindical y Popular; the Coordination of NGOs and Cooperatives; Coordination of Indigenous and Peasant Organizations; the Frente del Polochic, which unites peasant organizations waging territorial disputes in the Polochic river area; and social movements opposing the Free Trade Agreement of the Americas. The CSI found a lack of collaboration within the civil society sector, with CSOs rarely sharing expertise and struggling to speak with one voice. According to CSI stakeholders, although self-regulation mechanisms are encouraged by the current legislation, only a minority of CSOs has these mechanisms in place and they are seldom put into practice.

Finally, it must be noted that most professional Guatemalan CSOs depend on international aid, whereas most cooperatives and local groups manage to carry out their activities through local fundraising and community donations. Although most CSI stakeholders assess their organizations as having adequate financial resources, there are many small organizations that struggle to raise enough funds to run their activities.

Environment (1.0)

The environment dimension considers political, legal, socioeconomic, and sociocultural contexts, as well as the relationships between civil society, the state, and the private sector. Guatemalan civil society operates in a rather disabling environment, where widespread and rising poverty, social alienation, and a weakly entrenched rule of law present the most important barriers to its effective functioning.

Although the democratic regime, established in 1996, protects and promotes human rights and basic freedoms, Guatemalan society lacks a democratic culture and most of the principles enshrined in the Constitution struggle to permeate society. Corruption is widespread and the rule of law is rather weak. Crime is on the rise and clandestine paramilitary groups still play a relevant role in society. For example the 2003 presidential elections were marred by a general atmosphere of intimidation and violence.

The Guatemalan sociocultural environment is characterized by suspicion, racist attitudes, and social fragmentation among the different communities. Exclusion and discrimination between different ethnic groups and against marginalized people, such as women and the poor, are frequent. According to the population survey, 77% of respondents do not trust fellow citizens, and a large majority of respondents show a high level of mistrust of the police and military, both of which are widely associated with the long history of violations that security forces were responsible for during the authoritarian regime.

Poverty is widespread, affecting about one-third of the population. Extreme poverty is also on the rise (from 16% in 2000 to 21% in 2003), which reveals the disastrous consequences of successive governments disregarding the living conditions of indigenous and rural communities.

Despite the difficult sociocultural and socioeconomic contexts, the democratization process that began in 1996 significantly improved the overall environment for civil society, especially since it ensured freedom of association and freedom of the press. By contrast, labor rights are underdeveloped and few workers are unionized, while abuse is rampant, especially in the *maquilas,* the small businesses that produce goods at a low cost for multinational corporations.

The specific laws regulating civil society were seen by CSI participants as particularly conducive, such as the provision of tax exemptions for CSOs and incentives for philanthropy and charitable donations. CSI stakeholders maintained that although Guatemalan CSOs participate in various forums to strengthen dialogue with government, their recommendations are rarely integrated into legislation. Stakeholders also agreed that the contribution of the private sector to civil society's development is virtually nonexistent.

In general, the CSI analysis found that although democratic provisions are in place and a number of important rights are enshrined in the Constitution, civil society in Guatemala still operates in what CSI participants called a "state of fear," generated by the atrocities of the civil war.

Values (1.5)

The values dimension examines the extent to which civil society practices and promotes positive values. According to the CSI assessment, Guatemalan civil society practices and promotes positive values to a moderate extent, with special attention being paid to democratic values and nonviolence, which are crucial in a country that was ravaged by violence and authoritarian rule.

During the Guatemalan peace process, indigenous groups, social movements, and human rights NGOs played an important role in influencing the agenda and negotiating agreements between the parties. Currently, many CSOs promote democratic practices and a human rights culture in local communities. Most of these activities target groups such as women and youth, and promote grassroots participation in local policymaking and a human rights culture.

Guatemalan CSOs also have programs that promote democracy at the national level and carry out campaigns to inform the population, monitor elections, and educate citizens and policymakers on the implications of the peace accords. CSOs conduct activities aimed at ensuring government's transparency, which was highlighted by the CSI media review as a key intervention by Guatemalan civil society. For example, since 2002, a number of CSOs have contributed to the work of the National Commission for Transparency and Against Corruption, which focused specifically on fighting corruption in public institutions. CSOs can draw on significant foreign aid to address this issue.

The rather strong internal practice of democratic governance is also noteworthy, as underlined by the participants in the CSI, who maintained that most CSOs elect their leaders through general assemblies and members generally wield significant influence on their organizations' decisionmaking.

Although Guatemalan CSOs are rather active in promoting transparency in public institutions and society at large, the CSI found CSOs to be less committed to demanding transparency from the private sector or ensuring transparency within their own organizations. According to CSI stakeholders, instances of corruption in CSOs are rather frequent and, although CSOs usually publicize their financial records, they rarely disseminate this information beyond their direct stakeholders. A similar disconnect was found between the practice and promotion of gender equity. Although many CSOs promote gender equity in society at large, due to the principles of the new democratic system, only a minority of organizations have established gender equity practices for themselves.

Finally, Guatemalan CSOs actively promote environmental sustainability and the fight against poverty. CSOs have conducted campaigns against multinational corporations' exploitation of natural resources, such as oil and minerals. Through direct assistance to the poor and campaigns to influence local government policies, CSOs are active in the fight against poverty. They also receive significant support from international aid agencies that view poverty eradication as a priority in Guatemala.

Impact (1.3)

The impact dimension assesses civil society's role in governance and society at large. In Guatemala, civil society is assessed as having a somewhat limited impact, particularly in the realm of policy formulation, monitoring, and public accountability.

Guatemalan civil society is rather active in providing services to the population and meeting societal needs. For example, CSOs are quite successful in empowering women and rural communities, usually through activities aimed at generating income and supporting livelihoods. According to the CSI population survey, 76% of respondents claimed that CSOs provide better services to the population than the state. The CSI also reveals that Guatemalan citizens consider CSOs, except political parties, to be much more trustworthy than public institutions. The lowest levels of trust were recorded for the police and military, mainly due to the mistrust of security forces resulting from decades of human rights violations.

Although many CSO activities focus on opening spaces for dialogue and cooperation with government, those that exist are rarely afforded any concrete power and mainly play a consultative role. Nevertheless, in the fields of human rights and social policy, Guatemalan civil society has enjoyed varying degrees of success. With regard to discrimination and racism, civil society lobbied for the state to establish the Commission on Racism and Discrimination Against Indigenous People (CODISRA). However, when it was established, CODISRA received only limited resources, in spite of the crucial role it is expected to play. Civil society has also influenced the government's social policies—for example in the area of housing—although CSOs' lack of expertise limits their potential contribution to the policymaking process.

International donors have invested significant resources to support state–civil society dialogue, which is in keeping with the principles of the peace accord. However, Guatemalan civil society struggles to monitor policies or hold the state accountable. Civil society's achievements are hampered by the lack of information available to CSOs and the limited responsiveness of government to civil society's demands. The lack of collaboration among civil society actors further diminishes its impact on government accountability, as CSOs rarely share expertise and struggle to speak with one voice. Civil society has even less impact on monitoring private corporations. CSI stakeholders admit that most CSOs do not view holding the private sector accountable as a key responsibility, nor have donors identified it as a priority.

The analysis of the impact dimension points out that Guatemalan civil society is more successful in providing services to the population and empowering citizens than it is in affecting policymaking and holding government and corporations accountable. Since civil society's involvement in policy only began in 1996, it is understandable that CSOs still lack the expertise to influence the policymaking process, even though this is a priority area for international donors. It appears that this lack of expertise has provided government with a justification to only concede a consultative role to CSOs in most areas of policymaking.

Conclusion

Guatemalan civil society in its current form is a by-product of the post–civil war peace process in Guatemala. Within the context of a young, liberal democracy and a society that is still affected by decades of atrocities and genocide, CSOs continue to play a significant role in service delivery and citizens' empowerment, and have increasingly distanced themselves from political parties.

Policy influence is still limited, and CSI stakeholders maintain that civil society should develop a stronger working relationship with government in order to more effectively participate in political processes. However, since the existing mechanisms for dialogue have not always led to actual voice and impact, CSI participants agree that civil society should not refrain from using public campaigns and demonstrations as additional means to influence the democratic process in Guatemala.

CSI Report

Institute of Cultural Affairs Guatemala, *CIVICUS Civil Society Index Report for Guatemala* (Guatemala: Institute of Cultural Affairs Guatemala, 2006).

Notes

1. The CSI assessment was implemented in Guatemala by the Institute of Cultural Affairs Guatemala from mid-2003 until October 2006. This chapter presents the main findings of the CSI and is based on a comprehensive country report for Guatemala, which can be accessed on the CSI pages of the CIVICUS website at http://www.civicus.org.

Chapter 18

Honduras[1]

Honduras is one of the poorest countries in Latin America. The devastating effects of Hurricane Mitch in 1998 aggravated the social problems in the country, but also led to the strengthening of civil society and its role in post-disaster reconstruction. Since then, civil society has struggled to establish an effective relationship with a rather unresponsive government and private sector to tackle the challenges facing the country.

Table 18.1 Background Information for Honduras

Honduras	
Country size (square km)	43,277
Population (millions 2004)	7
Population under 15 years (2004)	39.7%
Urban population (2003)	45.6%
Seats in parliament held by women (2005)	5.5%
Language groups	Spanish (official), Garifuna, Amerindian dialects
Ethnic groups	Mestizo 90%, Amerindian 7%, black 2%, white 1%
Religious groups	Roman Catholic 97%, Protestant 3%
HDI score and ranking (2003)	0.667 (116th)
GDP per capita (US$ 2003)	$2,265
Unemployment rate (% of total labor force)	5.1%
Population living on less than US$2 a day (1999)	44%

Historical Overview

Honduras has traditionally been among those Latin American countries that are characterized by a particularly diverse civil society. The emergence of civil society organizations (CSOs), such as trade unions, associations of workers in the banana industry, organizations related to the Catholic Church, women's organizations, and business associations, dates back to the middle of the twentieth century.

In October 1955, one year after a general strike by banana workers on the north coast, young reformists staged a coup that installed a provisional junta. Various military governments ruled the country in the decades to follow, and during General Osvaldo Arellano's tenure, the tensions with neighboring El Salvador exploded in the so-called Football War of 1969, when Honduras was invaded by El Salvador.

During the years following the return to civilian rule in 1981, civil society groups became increasingly active, especially trade unions and *campesino* (peasant) movements. Although Honduras was spared the violence and conflicts that ravaged other Latin American countries, military forces retained significant influence and waged a series of campaigns against social movements, particularly those inspired by leftist ideals. During the 1980s, US influence over the country grew exponentially, and Honduras became home to a significant US military presence, which used the country as a base to support the Contras' insurrection against the Sandinistas in Nicaragua. During this period, a severe socioeconomic recession stimulated a gradual growth of NGOs concerned with service delivery.

At the end of the Cold War, an easing of regional tensions and a strengthening of civilian control over the military meant that the political environment in Honduras became more conducive for civil society. As a consequence, the 1990s saw an increase in peasant movements, trade unions, environmental organizations, women's groups, business associations, and developmental NGOs. On October 20, 1998, Honduras was devastated by Hurricane Mitch. The catastrophe triggered a wave of national and international solidarity, fueling the growth of NGOs focused on humanitarian assistance and social reconstruction.

The disaster caused by Hurricane Mitch marked the beginning of a new era for civil society. Although CSOs that were established in the aftermath of the hurricane were able to build coalitions and improve cooperation among themselves, a gap remains between most of the new organizations and the CSOs that already existed.

The State of Civil Society in Honduras

This section provides a summary of key findings of the CSI project in Honduras. It examines the state of civil society in Honduras along four dimensions—structure, environment, values, and impact—highlighting the main weaknesses and strengths.

As visually summarized by the Civil Society Diamond (figure 18.1), the structure of civil society in Honduras is somewhat limited in strength. Civil society boasts strong networks, but it is weakened by CSOs' limited resources. It operates in a rather disabling environment, affected by widespread corruption, poverty, and a difficult relationship between civil society and the state and the private sector. Civil society's promotion and practice of key social values, such as poverty eradication, is significant, but the lack of transparency and internal democracy are major weaknesses of Honduran CSOs. According to the CSI assessment, civil society exerts considerable impact on society, especially in terms of citizens' empowerment; however, its success in influencing policy is rather modest.

Structure (1.3)

The structure dimension examines the makeup of civil society in terms of the main characteristics of individual citizen participation and associational life. In Honduras, the CSI study found a medium-sized civil society in which many CSOs are constrained by a lack of financial and human resources.

Figure 18.1 Civil Society Diamond for Honduras

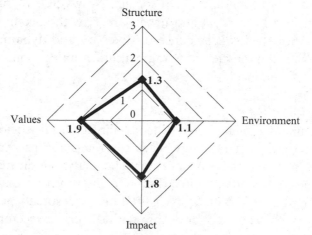

Honduran civil society is characterized by rather significant citizen participation. For example, a large number of respondents to the CSI population survey are members of at least one CSO (75%), especially religious organizations and social cooperatives, or regularly engage in volunteer work (40%). Charitable donations are rather common, with 63% of respondents claiming to donate to charity, even though donations amount to a minimal percentage of the average income (0.4%).

Civil society stakeholders believe that resources are inadequate for the goals that nonmembership CSOs set for themselves. For example, the CSI finds that in the Valle district, although the overall volume of financial resources for CSOs is significant, a small minority of CSOs control 63% of all resources. This uneven distribution of financial resources also affects CSOs' human resources, with, on average, only 10% of CSOs' personnel receiving a salary. However, since professional associations and trade unions receive most of their financial resources from members, these groups are financially more sustainable.

In contrast, the extensive links and relations among civil society actors are a particular strength of Honduran civil society, especially for CSOs that operate at the national level. Various networks and federations bring together CSOs, as is the case with the main trade unions and peasant movements. In the past few years, a number of coalitions and alliances have proliferated around specific issues, such as the *Bloque Popolar,* which spearheads the opposition to the Free Trade Agreement of the Americas, and the Civic Movement for Democracy, which focuses on the electoral process.

Given the inherent diversity of CSOs, it is difficult to draw a comprehensive map of Honduran civil society. New CSOs regularly come into existence in both rural and urban areas, with specific goals and agendas. Although this is evidence of diversity and dynamism, it can easily lead to redundancies and fragmentation unless communication is improved at the local level.

Environment (1.1)

The environment dimension considers political, legal, socioeconomic, and sociocultural contexts, as well as the relationships between civil society, the state, and the private sector. The analysis indicates that civil society in Honduras operates in a disabling environment, mainly due to the difficult political context, a weak state, widespread poverty, and civil society's problematic relationship with the private sector.

Honduras is one of the poorest countries in Latin America, and poverty has increased since the natural disaster in 1998. Currently, 40% of citizens live on less than US$2 per day, and as a consequence migration has increased over the last years. In addition, the country has witnessed a strong rise in HIV/AIDS infection rates and an increase in violence, particularly against women and girls.

Relationships between civil society and the state are riddled with problems. According to CSI stakeholders, there are regular attempts by the state to control or co-opt CSOs. This is particularly problematic since the state is a significant source of income for at least one-fifth of CSOs. Although the right of association is protected by the Constitution, in practice, CSOs run significant risks when challenging strong interest groups or political leaders, as demonstrated by the assassinations of ecologist Carlos Reyes in 2003 and indigenous leader Elpidio Martínez in 2004. Trade unions are subject to significant repression, and workers are often threatened, especially in the *maquilas,* the small local firms that are subcontracted by multinationals to produce commodities at low cost. The highly bureaucratic procedures governing the registration of CSOs severely curtail their effectiveness, as epitomized by the obstacles posed to the legal recognition of CSOs representing homosexual, lesbian, and transgender citizens, which was finally granted in 2004.

The Honduran state is struggling to uphold the rule of law and carry out its basic functions. Gang violence has become pervasive, corruption in the public and private sectors is widespread, and the justice system is rather ineffective in its efforts to prosecute perpetrators. In 2003, parliament condoned agrarian enterprises that bribed top politicians, and there have been cases highlighted by the press of Honduran politicians connected with gangs involved in drug trafficking.

Interestingly, the overall sociocultural conditions appear to be relatively conducive for civil society. In spite of high levels of corruption and public dishonesty, one-third of respondents to the CSI population survey trust fellow citizens. The same survey also found the general level of tolerance in society to be comparatively high.

The CSI found that the private sector is viewed as either indifferent or hostile toward CSOs. Although chambers of commerce have developed some corporate social responsibility (CSR) initiatives, few CSOs are involved in these programs. In general, CSO representatives see themselves as being at odds with the private sector and, although business organizations are by definition members of civil society, the team that implemented the CSI in Honduras noted a clear rift between these associations and other CSOs.

Values (1.9)

The values dimension examines the extent to which civil society practices and promotes positive values. Civil society's rather strong value base seems to be its hallmark in Honduras, given that the score for this dimension is the highest among the four dimensions of the diamond. Among a set of key values, poverty eradication is the one that CSOs promote most wholeheartedly.

Tolerance, nonviolence, and environmental sustainability are values that civil society actively practices and promotes. However, values such as gender equity, internal democracy, and CSOs' financial transparency are not regarded as pivotal values for civil society. Most CSOs are reluctant to publicize their financial records and, more importantly, the sources of funding they use to carry out their activities. CSI stakeholders maintain that the poor practice of financial transparency is mainly due to the lack of education of CSOs' staff and CSO leaders' general defensiveness. CSO leaders tend to regard this type of information as confidential, and are only willing to share it with other CSOs or international donors. In contrast, CSOs' promotion of transparency in public institutions and the private sector is noteworthy and includes high-profile campaigns to promote transparency with regard to the debt cancellation and privatization policies.

The strongest value for Honduran civil society is poverty eradication. A large number of organizations carry out numerous programs aimed at eradicating poverty, and they regularly collaborate with government at different levels. For example, at the regional level, many CSOs have been directly involved in the formulation of the Poverty Reduction Strategy, and twelve CSOs are represented in the national Consultative Council. There are also organizations, such as the Honduran Social Forum for the External Debt (FOSDEH), that monitor debt cancellation policies and procedures, and a number of CSOs, particularly within the peasant and labor movements, that conduct research on the effects of free trade agreements on poverty and unemployment.

Recently, many CSOs have become increasingly involved in promoting democracy, public participation, and nonviolence in society at large. During the November 2005 elections, networks of CSOs, such as the Civic Movement for Democracy, carried out various programs of voter education and election monitoring and organized public forums.

The CSI assessment noted that civil society practices and promotes most of the values included in the assessment and does so to a significant extent. Although the practice of transparency and internal democracy remain the most crucial weaknesses for Honduran CSOs, civil society plays a key role in fighting poverty, both directly through their programs/activities and indirectly by lobbying the state to improve services or to introduce policies that favor the poorest segment of the population.

Impact (1.8)

The impact dimension assesses civil society's role in governance and society at large. The impact of Honduran civil society on governance is moderate and is reflected in civil society's limited success in holding the state and especially the private sector accountable; its impact on society, however, is relatively significant.

Honduran CSOs exert the most significant impact in responding to social interests, empowering citizens, and directly meeting pressing social needs, especially the needs of the most marginalized groups. In general, the mass media identifies priority social issues. However, there have been many occasions when CSOs managed to steer public attention to specific social problems and issues, such as fuel hikes (transporters' unions), droughts (peasant organizations), water provision (community-based groups), minimum wage (labor movements), and land issues (peasant and indigenous movements). The strong presence of CSOs in society is supported by society's rather strong trust in CSOs. Although half of respondents trust CSOs, religious organizations are the most trusted (88%), followed by NGOs (53%), trade unions (35%), and the *Bloque Popolar* (30%).

The 1992 United Nations Earth Summit gave way to a new phase of ecological awareness. Since then, several environmental groups have educated citizens on the protection of the environment and food security. More recently, there has been a growth in organizations active in protecting consumers and fighting against child labor.

In contrast to its strong social role, the impact of Honduran civil society on policy processes and governance is rather limited. Although CSOs are active in various areas, the government is rarely open to listening or taking into account civil society's input. Nevertheless, there are some signs of encouragement. For example, the Human Rights Committee and the Committee of the Relatives of Detainees and the Disappeared in Honduras successfully lobbied for investigations into the murders and disappearances of trade unionists, students, and other activists that were perpetrated by military forces in the 1980s. Some occasional impact has also been made by CSOs representing workers or peasants, and the CSOs involved in the Consultative Council on Poverty Reduction Strategy have been advocating for utilizing the cancellation of foreign debt for specific pro-poor policies.

Honduran CSOs actively seek to influence anticorruption policies and conduct initiatives to monitor electoral processes, but the actual impact is minimal. Although some CSOs specialize in monitoring the national budget process, they rarely influence the drafting or implementation process in a significant way. CSOs have perhaps been most successful at the local level, where they have been more effective in influencing budget allocations, and some municipalities have adopted participatory budget mechanisms.

Similarly, a number of CSOs are active in holding the state accountable through public campaigns or legal initiatives, although their actual influence is moderate. Civil society is least successful in holding private corporations accountable. Although the media review conducted for the CSI shows that trade unions and a few NGOs are quite vocal against abuse at the workplace or harmful business practices, especially by transnational corporations, their actual impact remains very limited. The reality in Honduras is that most private corporations are not open to scrutiny by external actors, and civil society has not embraced the cause of corporate accountability as a key mission.

Recommendations

Approximately eighty representatives of civil society, government, academia, political parties, the media, and the private sector participated in the CSI National Workshop on May 26, 2006. Workshop participants discussed the CSI findings and identified recommendations for strengthening civil society. The following list presents some of the key recommendations:

- Encourage charitable giving: CSOs need to encourage more significant levels of charitable giving by Hondurans, to help address their financial sustainability concerns.
- Improve internal democracy and transparency: This will help CSOs gain trust and increase their credibility vis-à-vis the state, which is affected by corrupt practices at all levels.
- Increase dialogue among CSOs: Dialogue among CSOs should be strengthened, especially between older CSOs and post–Hurricane

Mitch organizations. Dialogue should also be encouraged between civil society, the state, and the private sector. An improved relationship with the private sector is crucial in a country where hostility and indifference between CSOs and corporations is quite widespread.

Conclusion

Honduras is one of the poorest countries in Latin America. Since the disaster brought about by Hurricane Mitch in 1998, civil society's work in addressing crucial social concerns, such as poverty and people's empowerment, has become stronger and increasingly visible. Although civil society's operating environment remains problematic, mainly due to challenging relationships with the state and the private sector, CSOs have managed to influence a number of policies, primarily at the local level, and have built effective networks and alliances to reach their goals.

CSI Report

Centro Hondureño de Promoción para el Desarrollo Comunitario (CEHPRODEC), *From Consultation to Participation: CIVICUS Civil Society Index Report for Honduras* (Honduras: CEHPRODEC, 2006).

Notes

1. The CSI assessment was implemented in Honduras by the Centro Hondureño de Promoción para el Desarrollo Comunitario (CEHPRODEC) from November 2004 to March 2006. This chapter presents the main findings of the CSI and is based on a comprehensive report for Honduras, which can be assessed on the CSI pages of the CIVICUS website at http://www.civicus.org.

Chapter 19

❦

Hong Kong[1]

Hong Kong's civil society currently finds itself in an environment where its basic freedoms and rights are protected, but full democracy remains a distant possibility. Civil society organizations (CSOs) in Hong Kong have historically focused on their role as state-funded welfare providers; however, they are becoming increasingly active in advocacy and citizen mobilization. Unfortunately, the Civil Society Index (CSI) assessment predicts that internal and external weaknesses will make it extremely challenging for civil society to play a significantly stronger role in the years to come.

Table 19.1 Background Information for Hong Kong

Hong Kong	
Size (square km)	1,092
Population (millions 2004)	6.9
Population under 15 years (2004)	14.8%
Urban population (2003)	100%
Language groups	Chinese (Cantonese), English (both official)
Ethnic groups	Chinese 95%, other 5%
Religious groups	eclectic mixture of local religions 90%, Christian 10%
HDI score and ranking (2003)	0.916 (22nd)
GDP per capita (US$ 2003)	$27,179
Unemployment rate (% of total labor force)	7.9%

Historical Overview

Since British colonial rule was established in 1842, civil society has played a significant role in developing the Hong Kong community. Through the activities of guilds, welfare organizations, religious organizations, and neighborhood associations, CSOs swiftly became the main welfare provider for the population. Supported by wealthy businessmen and foreign missionaries, the task of welfare provision was mainly left to CSOs. In fact, the government regarded CSOs as key partners in service provision, in which the government provided the funding and CSOs provided the services to the community.

In the 1970s, rapid urbanization and industrialization, and the subsequent growth in government revenues, led to greater government involvement in the social sphere. Unfortunately, this increased involvement was accompanied by the deterioration of state–civil society relations. During this period, social activism was very much alive, and residents became increasingly conscious of social and environmental issues. This stimulated the development of new types of CSOs. Although most of these groups viewed their role as educators and service providers, many were also vocal in advocacy and people's empowerment.

The December 19, 1984, Joint Declaration between the People's Republic of China (PRC) and the United Kingdom declared that Hong Kong would be reunified with the PRC on July 1, 1997, and signaled the beginning of a period of political transition. This transition coincided with the Asian economic crisis (1998–2000). Faced with decreased revenues, the government was forced to reduce its funding of civil society and for social service provision in general.

Despite the Chinese government resuming sovereignty, Hong Kong retained its own legal system, which, however, lacks full democratic rights for its citizens. The issue of universal suffrage therefore remains one of the foremost items on Hong Kong's public agenda. Since Hong Kong's reunion with the PRC, concerns have also been raised over the regression in the protection of civil liberties. In 2003 proposed changes to Article 23 of the Basic Law were seen as severely curtailing key human rights. These proposed changes caused alarm among the population and international human rights NGOs alike. The popular discontent culminated in a protest by a half-million people on July 1, 2003, causing the government to delay the implementation of this controversial law, and, ultimately, to cancel the legislation altogether for the time being. However, the damage to the image of Hong Kong as a free society was already done.

Figure 19.1 Civil Society Diamond for Hong Kong

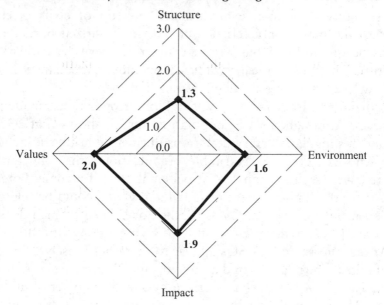

The State of Civil Society in Hong Kong

In Hong Kong, the term "civil society organization" has only recently begun to find its way into public discourse. In the past. CSOs were synonymous with volumtary associations, while the term NGO gained currency in the 1960s and 1970s.

This section provides a summary of key findings of the CSI project in Hong Kong. It examines the state of civil society in Hong Kong along four dimensions—structure, environment, values, and impact—highlighting the main weaknesses and strengths.

The Hong Kong Civil Society Diamond (figure 19.1) visually summarizes the CSI findings and indicates that civil society is operating in a slightly disabling environment, characterized by limited dialogue with, and, in many cases, financial dependency on, the government. Civil society's structure is relatively weak, characterized by low levels of citizen participation and a loosely organized civic sector. Civil society's promotion and practice of positive values, and its impact on politics and society are assessed as relatively significant, particularly with regard to civil society's ability to shape the public agenda, respond to societal needs, and provide services to the population.

Structure (1.3)

The structure dimension examines the makeup of civil society in terms of the main characteristics of individual citizen participation and associational life. Hong Kong's civil society reveals a rather weak structure. The most critical weaknesses include inadequate resources and low levels of citizen participation in civil society.

A major challenge facing CSOs in Hong Kong is their inadequate resources. Although the CSI population survey shows that 93% of respondents made monetary donations during the last year, including 63% who had given to charitable organizations, the total amount donated averages less than 1% of personal annual income. Potential reasons for the limited extent of individual giving could be related to the dependency of welfare CSOs on the government, which does not encourage CSOs to develop a culture of giving among citizens.

At the sectoral level, CSOs appear to be rather loosely connected, with limited interrelations and a limited support infrastructure for the sector. The sector is also characterized by a small number of umbrella bodies. The few umbrella bodies that do exist are effective and sizable, and they play a relatively significant role in civil society's activities. The fact that CSOs largely work individually can also be attributed to the funding situation, since CSOs often compete for a restricted pool of resources.

Although cooperation between CSOs from different sectors is found to be increasing, it often remains ad hoc and rather unstructured. The CSI assessment identifies several recently formed alliances and over 180 events involving cooperation among different CSOs. The Citizen Envisioning @ Harbour is one of the most vocal alliances. Its mission is to promote sustainable development and involve civil society in the development of the city's harbor.

Self-regulation within CSOs is particularly strong among welfare, education, and professional CSOs, as many have a code of conduct within their respective sector. At the same time, these organizations only represent a portion of all CSOs, and evidence indicates that smaller CSOs in Hong Kong are less involved in these efforts, and that, where self-regulation mechanisms exist, they are only loosely enforced.

Despite major challenges embedded in civil society's structural dimension, the CSI found some signs of progress, such as the increased number of partnerships between CSOs. As a consequence of Hong Kong society maturing and the strengthening of a local identity, civic participation in civil society is also expected to increase.

Environment (1.6)

The environment dimension considers political, legal, socioeconomic, and sociocultural contexts, as well as the relationships between civil society, the state, and the private sector. The findings indicate that the environment for civil society in Hong Kong is slightly disabling, due to such factors as a problematic sociocultural context, lack of enforcement of certain political rights, and rather weak dialogue and cooperation between civil society and both the government and the private sector.

The lack of full democracy in Hong Kong remains the most significant restriction on people's political rights. The Chief Executive, as the head of government, is elected by an 800-member Election Committee, which is not popularly elected and whose membership is largely confined to the local elites and business tycoons. Hence, the issue of universal suffrage remains one of the foremost items on Hong Kong's public agenda and has mobilized civil society and citizens in a number of large-scale political marches.

The CSI assessment reveals that civil society's relations with the government and with the private sector are far from ideal. The CSO survey, conducted by the CSI, finds a distrustful relationship between the government and civil society. Two-thirds of respondents deemed dialogue between the government and civil society to be nonexistent or limited. Despite the fact that commercial businesses are a significant part of Hong Kong society, the connections between civil society and the business sector are surprisingly weak. Respondents estimated that a mere 5.3% of CSOs' total income comes from the business sector, which is much lower than the income from individual donations (35.6%), membership fees (20.4%), the government (14.5%), service charge or sales (13.0%), and overseas donations (7.2%). Moreover, another study estimates that 70% of 346 nonprofit social service organizations' income comes from the government, which accounts for 2.4% of the total public expenditure, or 0.5% of the GDP.

Despite problematic relations between the government and civil society, the citizens of Hong Kong enjoy a relatively high degree of civil liberties, both in law and in practice. For example, Falun Gong, a religious sect outlawed by an anti-cult law in China in 1999, continues to operate freely in Hong Kong. However, concerns have been expressed over the regression in the protection of civil liberties since the 1997 handover to the PRC, particularly with regard to access to information, freedom of assembly, self-censorship of some media, and the independence of the judiciary.

Civil society enjoys a relatively favorable legal environment, with an open climate for advocacy activities. Notable examples include the Hong Kong Human Rights Commission and Hong Kong Human Rights Monitor, which promote and protect human rights. Other enabling factors include favorable tax laws for CSOs and low levels of corruption among state authorities. In summary, civil society's operating environment in Hong Kong features both disabling and enabling conditions.

Values (2.0)

The values dimension examines the extent to which civil society practices and promotes positive values. The score for this dimension indicates that Hong Kong civil society's efforts to practice and promote positive values are relatively significant. Among the seven values making up this dimension, nonviolence is widely practiced and upheld, as are, to a somewhat lesser extent, the values of tolerance, democracy, poverty eradication, gender equity, and environmental sustainability.

Hong Kong's civil society is rather active in promoting democracy and mainly focuses on the issue of universal suffrage. Many activities have been organized to promote democracy, such as marches, petitions, and public forums. On December 4, 2005, it was reported that between 80,000 and 100,000 individuals marched in the name of democracy, calling for universal suffrage.

In recent years, CSOs have individually and collectively striven for environmental sustainability. There have been successful calls from CSOs for more environmentally sustainable practices, such as simple packaging, using recycled materials, reducing plastic bags, and adjusting the temperature in air-conditioned places. The CSO survey also shows that 70% of respondents could recall at least one public civil society event focusing on environmental protection in the last year.

The findings also demonstrate that Hong Kong's civil society is relatively strong in promoting tolerance and nonviolence, and that the role of explicitly racist, discriminatory, or intolerant groups is insignificant. Since Hong Kong is a nonviolent society, the use of violence as a means of conflict resolution is rather rare and, consequently, activities to promote a nonviolent society are also limited.

Although the CSI findings indicate that civil society in Hong Kong is strongly value-driven, it also reveals that CSOs do not always practice what they preach, and internal democratic practices and financial transparency still need to be addressed. The large number of CSOs that refrain from disclosing their full financial statements to the general public was raised as a concern by CSI participants. Regarding democratic practices within CSOs, only one-third of the respondents in the CSO survey reported that their leaders were elected by members. This reveals that CSOs in Hong Kong have a long way to go in adhering to their own values, particularly concerning internal practices of democracy and accountability.

Impact (1.9)

The impact dimension assesses civil society's role in governance and society at large. The CSI assessment reveals that Hong Kong's civil society has a rather strong impact on society, most significantly in its social service provision role, particularly with regard to marginalized groups. However, its role in the territory's governance processes is more limited.

Hong Kong's CSOs have a long history of service provision, as many started as charitable organizations or mutual aid groups. Although this tradition continues today, many CSOs have recently taken on new roles, particularly with regard to shaping the public agenda and challenging public policy. Even though institutionalized channels of communication between government and CSOs are weak, if not absent, CSOs' efforts to monitor the government significantly contribute to upholding civil rights and freedoms in society, and to ensuring that government is responsive to societal needs and demands. In contrast, the CSI reveals that only limited and ineffective efforts have been made by civil society to hold private corporations accountable.

Civil society's ability to influence public policy has been successful in specific areas, such as human rights policies, but more limited in areas of social policy and the budget process. On July 1, 2003, to channel citizens' dissatisfaction with antiterrorism legislation seen as posing serious threats to civil liberties, civil society brought together over a half-million people to protest. This mobilization caused the government to delay the implementation of the law, and, ultimately, to withdraw it altogether for the time being.

The CSI indicates that Hong Kong's civil society seems to have broken out of its traditional confines of social service and has increased its advocacy activities in order to respond to growing concerns in the fields of democracy and other areas of public policy. However, the level of civil society's advocacy success remains very uneven across policy issues.

Recommendations

On April 29, 2006, over sixty civil society actors participated in the CSI Workshop in Hong Kong. After a lively debate, the following five key recommendations were put forward:

- Break many CSOs' dependency on government funding by seeking increased support from private foundations and by establishing mechanisms to help solicit donations from the general public.
- Create a common platform for civil society to share information, pool resources, devise a division of labor, and put pressure on the government and other relevant institutions.
- Increase involvement in CSOs. CSO leaders should be equipped with basic organizational management skills that will allow them to retain and motivate individuals to become involved in civil society. CSOs must become more sensitive to the abilities, interests, and needs of volunteers and also improve their own legitimacy and transparency, particularly with regard to internal democratic practices.
- Strengthen civil society's advocacy power by strengthening its research capacities, engaging stakeholders in dialogue, and forming alliances.
- Strengthen civic education, in order to instill the value of volunteering and social responsibility. For example, students should be encouraged to do volunteer work.

Conclusion

Hong Kong's civil society can be described as loosely organized and rather vibrant. It is loose because of the low level of infrastructure and poor communication among CSOs. Civil society is vibrant because it actively, and often successfully, strives to respond to social needs, empower minority groups, and protect people's rights. Also, although CSOs have historically focused on their role as state-funded welfare providers, they are becoming increasingly active in advocacy and citizen mobilization.

Overall, the CSI assessment depicts a somewhat positive situation for civil society in Hong Kong today. However, the CSI study concludes that a number of formidable challenges, including limited civic engagement, lack of accountability within CSOs, a weakly organized sector, and a problematic legal and political environment, are likely to constrain the future growth of civil society in Hong Kong.

CSI Report

Hong Kong Council of Social Service, *CIVICUS Civil Society Index Report for Hong Kong* (Hong Kong: Hong Kong Council of Social Service, in collaboration with the University of Hong Kong, the Hong Kong Polytechnic University, and the Chinese University of Hong Kong, 2006).

Notes

1. The CSI assessment was implemented in Hong Kong by the Hong Kong Council of Social Service in collaboration with scholars from three local universities (the University of Hong Kong, the Hong Kong Polytechnic University, and the Chinese University of Hong Kong) from 2004 to 2005. This chapter presents the main findings of the CSI and is based on a comprehensive report for Hong Kong, which can be accessed at the CSI pages of the CIVICUS website at http://www.civicus.org.

Chapter 20

Indonesia[1]

Democracy returned to Indonesia almost ten years ago. During this time, major progress has been made toward developing a culture of human rights and active citizenship, and civil society has flourished at an unprecedented level. However, as the Civil Society Index (CSI) assessment indicates, significant internal constraints seem to be preventing it from increasing its role in governance and development.

Table 20.1 Background Information for Indonesia

Indonesia	
Country size (square km)	1,978,700
Population (millions 2004)	217.6
Population under 15 years (2004)	28.6%
Urban population (2003)	45.5%
Seats in parliament held by women (2005)	11.3%
Language groups	Bahasa Indonesia (official, modified form of Malay), English, Dutch, Javanese, and other local dialects
Ethnic groups	Javanese 45%, Sundanese 14%, Madurese 8%, coastal Malays 8%, other 25%
Religious groups	Muslim 88%, Protestant 5%, Roman Catholic 3%, Hindu 2%, Buddhist 1%, other 1%
HDI score and ranking (2003)	0.697 (110th)
GDP per capita (US$ 2003)	$3,361
Unemployment rate (% of total labor force)	9.9%
Population living on less than US$2 a day (2002)	52.4% (2002)

Historical Overview

The beginnings of nontraditional forms of associations in Indonesia are closely related to the country's quest for independence from Dutch colonial rule. The liberalization of Dutch colonial policies in the early twentieth century gave the Indonesian population greater space for autonomous organizing. This led to the emergence of a wide range of community-based organizations, which, despite working in different fields, were united behind the common goal of achieving independence, which was gained in 1945. Two socioreligious organizations, Nahdlatul Ulama (NU) and Muhammadiyah, that emerged during this time to work on education, health, and other development issues still have particularly significant followings and influence in the country today.

In the early years of independence, Indonesia was deeply politicized and polarized between different political and ideological groups, mainly Nationalists, Communists, Modern Muslims, and Orthodox Muslims. These groups permeated society and mobilized supporters through a wide range of associations, from the community to the national level, and thus intensified the levels of social and political conflict. The six years of "Guided Democracy" under President Sukarno (1959–1965) saw a curtailment of the democratic procedures intended to keep sociopolitical conflicts at bay and, eventually, gave way to three decades of military-backed authoritarian rule under President Suharto (1966–1998).

Under Suharto's New Order regime, which sought to install a strong corporatist state, there was initially little room for associational life. Civil liberties were abolished, and most existing organizations were integrated into corporatist arrangements with the state. For example, only one trade union, one journalist association, and one peasant organization was allowed to exist and these were tightly controlled by the state. Semiautonomous organizations, such as NU and Muhammadiyah, were allowed to continue operating, as long as they did not challenge the state. By the 1970s, as elsewhere in the global South, development NGOs focusing on specific and largely apolitical community development issues emerged in Indonesia. They were seen as complementing the role of the state.

By the 1980s civil society's discourse became pronouncedly more political, advocating for people-centered development and raising concerns about environmental degradation and other problems associated with the country's rapid industrialization. In the 1990s, while the regime was increasingly losing its legitimacy and its grip on society, radical leftist student associations and social movements gained strength, and human rights and democracy issues, as well as increasingly confrontational strategies, became part of civil society's agenda. The term "civil society" became the rallying cry of the pro-democracy movement. In 1997 the effects of the Asian financial crisis hit Indonesia hard, and students and the urban poor mounted spontaneous, and sometimes violent, demonstrations against the Suharto regime, which culminated in the fall of Suharto in May 1998.

The ensuing democratic transition led to a series of political and legal reforms, reinstating basic civil and political rights. However, authoritarian personnel of the New Order remained in the public service and practices such as military violence, secrecy, and corruption hampered the reform process. CSOs lacked a coherent agenda, a strong level of organization, and sufficient institutional resources. They were confronted with difficult decisions on whether to align themselves to a political party, how to build their capacity to engage in policy advocacy, and how to respond to the ensuing separatist violence in several parts of the vast archipelago.

In recent years, the country has been successfully moving toward a democratic system, with free and fair elections and a change in government in 2004. Although the number of NGOs, labor unions, and independent mass media organizations continues to grow, questions about CSOs' legitimacy, governance, and accountability have emerged. The devastation caused by the Indian Ocean Tsunami in late 2004 led many CSOs to temporarily abandon their organizational core mandate and focus on working with the government on relief and reconstruction efforts. Interestingly, this may have opened up new avenues for effective cooperation between CSOs and the government.

The State of Civil Society in Indonesia

Indonesian civil society is extremely diverse and ranges from informal community-based groups to professional NGOs. Since most of informal civil society's work takes place at the local level, it was only peripherally addressed by the CSI study, which largely focused on the activities of NGOs and other formal civil society entities.

This section provides a summary of key findings of the CSI project in Indonesia. It examines the state of Indonesian civil society along four dimensions—structure, environment, values, and impact—highlighting the main weaknesses and strengths.

Figure 20.1 Civil Society Diamond for Indonesia

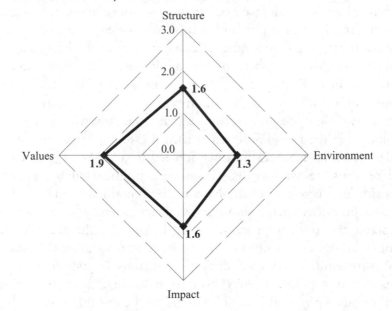

The Civil Society Diamond (figure 20.1) depicts a medium-sized civil society which has undergone a period of rapid growth. Indonesian civil society operates in a somewhat disabling environment, where a particularly negative socioeconomic context and the legacy of a weak centralist state impede civil society's development. It exerts a moderately strong impact on politics and society and is seen as actively promoting positive values, although the practice of certain values, such as transparency and gender equity within CSOs, remains problematic.

Structure (1.6)

The structure dimension examines the makeup of civil society in terms of the main characteristics of individual citizen participation and associational life. Indonesian civil society has a moderately strong structure, with high levels of civic engagement and strong relations among organized civil society. Its key weaknesses are the lack of adequate financial resources, the urban middle-class bias of professional CSOs, and a rather weak support infrastructure.

Various forms of civic engagement, particularly charitable giving, volunteering, and engagement in community activities, are extremely common among the population and are predominantly expressed through community-based channels. For example, 57% of Indonesians belong to a CSO. Groups with the highest membership are local groups, such as neighborhood associations (17%), women's groups (17%), religious organizations (16%), and cooperatives (15%), rather than modern organizations, such as NGOs (2.5%), trade unions (2%), and professional organizations (3%). Religious-based charity (*zakat*) is the dominant form of charity in Indonesia, mostly given directly to the needy, although charitable giving to nonreligious CSOs is also relatively high and growing.

The social composition of organized civil society is inclined toward the urban middle class and biased against marginalized groups, such as the poor, ethnic minorities, religious minorities, and rural people. Various studies highlight the decisively urban nature of NGOs, which are particularly concentrated on the island of Java. It is estimated that 70% of NGOs carry out their work in urban areas.

Civil society networks are proliferating, though mainly at the national level and in large cities. The lack of penetration of these networks in remote provinces and at the local level is noted in the CSI stakeholder survey, even though recent examples of country-wide networks exist. The existing networks are assessed as moderately effective, particularly in advocating for their constituents' needs, but successful policy influence remains rare, due to lack of advocacy skills and difficult relations with the government.

A code of ethics for CSOs was drawn up in 2002 to respond to growing public doubts about civil society's accountability, but it is not widely promoted and compliance is not monitored effectively. Other indicators of civil society's infrastructure, such as the existence of support organizations and strong international linkages, are also rather limited in Indonesia.

The major structural challenge for civil society is organizational, particularly financial sustainability. In general, non–membership-based CSOs, particularly professional advocacy NGOs, are heavily dependent on foreign funding, and contributions from the government and the private sector remain minimal. Dependency on foreign donors makes much of the Indonesian NGO sector highly vulnerable to shifting agendas or a complete pull-out by donors. In contrast, membership-based organizations, such as large socioreligious organizations, are largely financially self-sustainable, through local donations, government grants, or service charges. These examples might provide useful lessons for other CSOs on how to achieve financial sustainability.

Environment (1.3)

The environment dimension considers political, legal, socioeconomic, and sociocultural contexts, as well as the relationships between civil society, the state, and the private sector. Indonesian civil society operates in a somewhat disabling environment, characterized by weak governance structures, a lingering socioeconomic crisis, gaps in the legal framework, and largely suspicious relations between civil society and both the state and the private sector.

The economic crisis of 1997 exacerbated an already difficult socioeconomic context. A majority of Indonesians was still living on less than US$2 a day, and the country was burdened with severe socioeconomic inequities and high levels of foreign debt. In 2004 the country was hit hard by the Indian Ocean Tsunami, which claimed an estimated 125,000 lives. In addition, Indonesia experienced a number of ethnic- and/or religious-based conflicts, showing that it is built on a somewhat fragile sociocultural foundation. Although interpersonal trust is rather high, with close to 50% of Indonesians trusting fellow citizens, social tolerance is rather low, particularly toward homosexuals, people living with HIV/AIDS, and, to a lesser extent, people from a different religion, race, or nationality. Thus, CSOs operate in a rather resource-poor context, but are called upon to attend to the many pressing needs of a largely poor population and to mediate in a range of social conflicts.

Since the demise of authoritarian rule in 1998, Indonesia's political system has made significant progress. Political and civil rights are largely respected, although the police and military often act in a disproportionately heavy-handed way when dealing with public demonstrations. However, despite legal improvements and an ambitious administrative decentralization program, the country's governance is riddled with problems that limit the state's overall effectiveness. Public services, such as education, are often dysfunctional. There is widespread corruption in the public and the private sectors, and a weak entrenchment of the rule of law, with particular problems in the judiciary and police forces.

The legal environment for civil society contains a mix of conducive and less conducive regulations. Although there are no legal restrictions on CSOs' advocacy activities, the tax laws do not provide significant incentives for philanthropy or substantive exemptions for nonprofit organizations or foundations. Most CSOs register as a foundation, which requires approval from the Minister of Justice, thus subjecting them to the inefficient and often corrupt government bureaucracy.

Overall, while the state generally respects civil society's autonomy, it does not seek extensive dialogue with it, although some positive examples can be found at the local level. CSOs are in part to blame, since their advocacy strategies are often confrontational. Similarly, a majority of stakeholders surveyed regard the private sector as indifferent to civil society. However, signs of change are apparent, as corporate social responsibility (CSR) practices and community development programs gain ground within the business sector. Still, it will take time for the private and civil society sectors' attitudes to change, since they are based on a legacy of intense conflict around sustainable development and environmental protection issues.

Values (1.9)

The values dimension examines the extent to which civil society practices and promotes positive values. Indonesian CSOs are at the forefront of promoting key values, such as democracy, transparency, tolerance, gender equity, poverty eradication, and environmental sustainability. However, they are significantly less committed to practicing these values internally, particularly transparency and accountability.

Over the past few years, issues of internal democracy and accountability have received significant attention from Indonesian CSOs. A number of studies have confirmed that mechanisms for organizational accountability are not strongly developed among NGOs. For example, in more than one-third of the organizations surveyed, the positions of Chair of the Board and Executive Director are occupied by the same person. Likewise, the level of perceived corruption within the sector is high, with more than half of CSI stakeholder survey respondents regarding it as occurring often or very often. Financial transparency is also not widely practiced among NGOs. A recent study found that only 17% of surveyed organizations make their annual reports publicly available.

While internal standards and practices of transparency and accountability are highly problematic, Indonesian CSOs are nevertheless leaders in promoting the transparency of the government and, to a lesser extent, the private sector. The media review found that more than 9 out of 10 media articles dealing with civil society and transparency were related to promoting rather than practicing transparency. It is estimated that as many as fifty CSOs focus on this field, and a network exists to coordinate the activities of anticorruption NGOs.

Tolerance and nonviolent conflict resolution are important issues for a country as diverse and volatile as Indonesia. The large majority of CSOs practice these values within their organizations; however, there are instances of violent behavior by radical groups. Civil society is also rather active in promoting social tolerance and peace, particularly in regions where violent conflicts among ethnic or religious minorities are taking place.

Two hallmarks of civil society's agenda are gender equity and environmental sustainability, which have been actively promoted by a large range of CSOs since the 1980s. Wahana Lingkungan Hidup Indonesia (WALHI) is the most prominent environmental NGO network, and a coalition of women's NGOs has been successfully lobbying for the introduction of a range of gender policies. Yet, as with transparency, CSOs' internal record on these issues is far weaker than the standards they set for the government and society at large.

Impact (1.6)

The impact dimension assesses civil society's role in governance and society at large. In general, the CSI assessment found moderate levels of activity and impact in Indonesia on influencing policy, holding government and the private sector accountable, responding to social concerns, empowering people, and meeting societal needs.

A set of case studies on civil society's policy influence shows a large range of advocacy issues being addressed by civil society, with moderate levels of success. Lack of technical skills, insufficient networking, and problematic relations with the government are cited as key obstacles. However, successful examples include domestic violence legislation, the establishment of the constitutional court, and the increase in the state's annual education budget.

Civil society is rather active in a range of social issues, as witnessed by the rather high percentages of CSI population survey respondents who recalled civil society activities to empower citizens. For example, of survey respondents, 64% remembered a public education campaign; 40% remembered CSO programs to build community capacities, and 48% and 20%, respectively, remembered CSO projects to empower poor people and women. In addition, a large range of developmental programs are implemented by CSOs throughout the country. Despite these indications of substantive civil society activity, CSI stakeholders felt that its overall role remains rather limited. This assessment owes much to the large size of the country, NGOs' difficulty reaching a majority of the population, significant resource constraints, and the fact that professional NGOs are often out of touch with the needs of the people. In addition, the more than thirty years of a bureaucratic-developmental state model left its mark on society. Correspondingly, with a high ratio of 7 to 1, Indonesians think the state provides better services than CSOs, and the public trust ratings of government institutions are twice as high as those of NGOs and labor unions. A notable exception is socioreligious organizations, such as NU and Muhammadiyah, which receive the highest trust rating of all institutions in the country and can count on a joint membership of approximately 70 million Indonesians and a nationwide presence.

Recommendations

The CSI findings were discussed at a National Workshop in June 2006, which brought together approximately eighty participants from seventeen of the thirty-three provinces, representing CSOs, government, academia, media, and the donor community. A large number of suggestions for strengthening civil society were put forward. The following key recommendations capture the critical challenges facing Indonesian civil society.

- Diversify the resource base: NGOs need to increase their domestic resource base through income-generation activities, membership fees, and other local fundraising activities. Funds should also be sought from the government and the private sector, but the utmost care should be taken not to endanger the independence of CSOs.
- Strengthen CSOs' accountability: Civil society's work needs to better reflect the needs of the people, through stronger citizen participation in CSOs' program design and implementation, and a stronger reliance on needs assessments. A joint code of ethics should be developed, and donors should be encouraged to provide funds for the improvement of CSOs' accounting and financial reporting systems.

Conclusion

In Indonesia, the number of CSOs has been expanding in the new democratic dispensation, from the local to the national level, and in diverse forms, such as NGOs, trade unions, social movements, and community-based groups. Yet, after a period of rushed growth, questions about the sustainability of this growth are being raised. As is often the case with rapid growth, not enough attention was paid by civil society stakeholders to generating sustainable structural foundations, accountability mechanisms, and support structures.

Thus, Indonesian civil society faces a formidable accountability challenge. Also, as foreign donors are likely to move elsewhere, financial sustainability, particularly of NGOs, will emerge as a key concern.

To address accountability and financial sustainability, Indonesian civil society needs to strengthen its relations with the public, the government, and the private sector. After a decade of CSOs regarding themselves as the country's vanguards of democratization and social emancipation, a stronger outreach to the population is required. However, given the country's formidable socioeconomic challenges—particularly pervasive poverty—building a domestic support base will likely be a long-term goal.

CSI Report

Rustam Ibrahim, *Indonesian Civil Society 2006—A Long Journey to a Civil Society: CIVICUS Civil Society Index Report for the Republic of Indonesia* (Jakarta, Indonesia: YAPPIKA, 2006).

Notes

1. The CSI assessment was implemented in Indonesia by YAPPIKA from 2003 to 2006. This chapter presents the main findings of the CSI and is based on a comprehensive country report for Indonesia, which can be accessed on the CSI pages of the CIVICUS website at http://www.civicus.org.

Chapter 21

❦

Italy[1]

Italian civil society is built on a long tradition of civic activism. Recently, international campaigns and a growing number of individuals involved in volunteer work have given new momentum to civic activism, although most citizens remain reluctant to participate in nonpartisan political actions and community activities. In 2001 direct civic engagement was enshrined in the Constitution as a guiding principle for public policymaking.

Table 21.1 Background Information for Italy

Italy	
Country size (square km)	301,000
Population (millions 2004)	57.6
Population under 15 years (% 2004)	14.1%
Urban population (% of total 2003)	67.4%
Seats in parliament held by women (% of total 2005)	11.5%
Language groups	Italian (official), German, French, Slovene, and Albanian
Ethnic groups	Mostly Italian (official), German, French, Slovene, and Albanian
Religious groups	Predominantly Roman Catholic
HDI score and ranking (2003)	0.934 (18th)
GDP per capita (US$ 2003)	$27,119
Unemployment rate (% of total labor force)	8%

Historical Overview

It is difficult to establish the exact origins of civil society in Italy, as many forms of civic participation can be traced back to different historical eras. Nevertheless, the current character of Italian civil society was significantly shaped by the political developments that occurred in the nineteenth century when modern political parties, trade unions, cooperatives, and mutual benefit societies, which were linked to the workers' movement and the Catholic Church, emerged during the process of nation building.

From 1922 to 1943, the Fascist regime severely restricted fundamental freedoms and political rights and persecuted civil society organizations (CSOs). Although many groups and associations were forced to close down, the regime promoted a corporatist arrangement, which co-opted professional, business, and employee associations and was epitomized by the institution of the Camera dei Fasci e delle Corporazioni, a governmental body that supervised the activities of CSOs.

When democracy was reinstated after World War II, political parties with strong links to associations and trade unions became the backbone of the new republic. A new wave of CSOs emerged in the 1970s, when many new citizens' organizations and initiatives arose in response to political violence between right- and left-wing terrorist groups and the state. The main feature of these new associations was their strong autonomy from political parties and public institutions. This signified a new propensity of citizens to directly contribute to the public interest. Most of these organizations were oriented toward advocacy, service delivery, and empowering people and communities. This new wave, common to most developed countries, was caused by two major factors: the decrease in state expenditure, especially within the welfare system, and the decline of public trust in public institutions.

In terms of the legal relationship between civil society and the state, a recent turning point was the 2001 reform of the Italian Constitution. The engagement of citizens in public affairs, beyond basic freedoms of association, was enshrined in the new Constitution as a pillar of democratic governance in the country, and the concept of horizontal subsidiarity, in terms of cooperation and support between the state and citizens' organizations, became a guiding principle of policymaking.

The State of Civil Society in Italy

This section provides a summary of key findings of the CSI project in Italy. It examines the state of Italian civil society along four dimensions—structure, environment, values, and impact—highlighting the main weaknesses and strengths.

The Civil Society Diamond visually summarizes the assessment's (figure 21.1) findings in Italy. The diamond indicates a medium-sized structure, weakened by poor communication and interaction among CSOs as well as by decreasing civic participation in many traditional organizations such as trade unions and political parties. The environment in which civil society operates is rather conducive, but it has been negatively influenced by corruption and mistrust in public institutions. Civil society practices and promotes many progressive values, with the exception of gender equity, which is seen by local stakeholders as not sufficiently embraced. Civil society's overall impact is significant, particularly in its relation to society at large rather than in its role in the political realm.

Figure 21.1 Civil Society Diamond for Italy

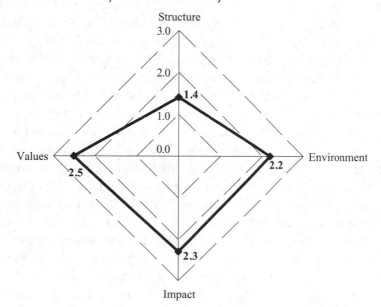

Structure (1.4)

The structure dimension examines the makeup of civil society in terms of the main characteristics of individual citizen participation and associational life. A minority of Italians participated in nonpartisan political actions, belonged to a CSO, or participated in a collective community action during the past year. Nevertheless, there are significant examples of citizen involvement, such as the large number of participants in the Rome march against the Iraq War in 2003 and the growing phenomenon of citizens volunteering for civil defense, a nationwide institution made up of volunteers who respond to various emergencies, such as natural disasters.

There are both positive and negative trends in civil society's structure. Some positive trends are the growing number of people that donate to charity, although donations are on average less than 1% of personal income, and the meaningful participation of volunteers in the sector, where more than three million people devote significant time to volunteer work. In contrast, while women make up about half of the people working in the voluntary sector, they only hold one-third of leadership roles, mainly in women's organizations.

In general, CSOs exist throughout the country and reach isolated regions. However, the concentration of organizations in northern and central Italy is higher than in the south (44 CSOs/10,000 inhabitants in the north, 42 CSOs/10,000 in the central regions, and 29 CSOs/10,000 in the south). Italy has long been characterized by a significant difference in socioeconomic development between the north and the south. However, it appears that this gap is gradually closing and that CSOs operating in the south are growing in number and attracting increased citizen support.

Communication and cooperation among civil society actors is rather limited, especially among small organizations. Even though umbrella organizations can draw on significant membership, cooperation among civil society groups is not as common as one would expect. A number of cross-sectoral alliances and coalitions exist and show varying degrees of effectiveness; however, they are often ad hoc and issue specific. Only a limited number of CSOs have strong international linkages, though networking within European Union (EU) countries is rapidly growing.

The structure of Italian civil society is the weakest of the four dimensions, mainly due to limited citizen participation and a lack of regular communication and cooperation between different types of CSOs. However, both of these weaknesses are showing signs of improvement.

Environment (2.2)

The environment dimension considers political, legal, socioeconomic, and sociocultural contexts as well as the relationships between civil society, the state, and the private sector. Italian CSOs operate in a relatively safe and favorable legal and socioeconomic environment, although the socioeconomic situation has gradually worsened due to reforms aimed at decreasing public expenditure on social welfare.

Political rights and civil liberties are generally respected, though some important aspects of the rule of law are occasionally violated. For instance, press freedoms are restricted by the concentration of media ownership in a few hands. The bulk of the media is controlled by the former prime minister and leader of the opposition bloc. According to Freedom House, in 2005, Italy ranked seventy-ninth in terms of freedom of the press, much lower than Mauritius, Botswana, and Papua New Guinea.

The CSO registration process is sufficiently simple and quick, and CSOs' autonomy and freedom in criticizing government is guaranteed. Also, supportive fiscal legislation for CSOs and tax benefits for donors are in place. For example, individuals and companies can deduct donations from their taxable income. The public sector remains the main financial resource for CSOs, providing 70.5% of the funds for healthcare organizations and 59% for social cooperatives. Private companies show a growing interest in CSOs, both in terms of dialogue and financial support. About 70% of Italian private companies make donations, and a number of them have corporate social responsibility (CSR) policies in place.

As for weaknesses in civil society's environment, Italian society is affected by a substantial level of mistrust and perceived corruption in the public sector. In 2005 Transparency International ranked Italy fortieth on the Corruption Perception Index. Public-spiritedness is particularly low among citizens, and violations of the law, although typically minor, are extremely frequent. In addition, organized crime still poses obstacles to the growth of civil society, especially in the south.

Public institutions have different attitudes toward civil society, with local government showing a stronger inclination to establish regular dialogue with CSOs than the national government. Some attempts have been made by government to control certain CSOs, for instance through regulations that infringe upon the privacy of sensitive information collected by CSOs.

What emerges from the CSI assessment is that the environment within which Italian CSOs operate is rather conducive. Key problems lie in the unclear relations between civil society and the state and low levels of public-spiritedness and trust in society at large.

Values (2.5)

The values dimension examines the extent to which civil society practices and promotes positive values. It is the strongest dimension of the Civil Society Diamond for Italy. Values such as democracy, tolerance, and nonviolence are widely practiced by civil society actors, and issues of environmental protection and the fight against poverty are regularly highlighted in CSOs' work.

In terms of daily practice, Italian civil society is a driving force in the promotion of democracy and tolerance at all levels. Violent groups are an isolated minority and are largely stigmatized. Most CSOs play a significant role in fighting discrimination against immigrants, people living with HIV/AIDS, the mentally ill, homosexuals, the disabled, and others.

Civil society also plays a leading role in poverty alleviation. For example, Caritas, the most prominent Catholic network working on poverty relief, is supported by about 200,000 volunteers, who provide assistance to people in need through the network's 2,000 centers, which include soup kitchens, shelters, and social canteens.

The protection of the environment has become increasingly prominent in the activities of Italian civil society. The main environmental groups, such as Legambiente, have hundreds of thousands of members who regularly conduct campaigns to educate citizens on environmental issues and monitor government policies and private corporations.

Civil society is active in promoting transparency in the public and private sectors. A number of consumer organizations, such as the National Council of Consumers and Users, have proliferated in the past few years, with the aim of monitoring public and private enterprises. In several cases, they have actively supported judicial investigations into fraud committed by large corporations and banks, at the expense of investors and consumers, such as the case against the multinational company Parmalat. Despite a significant commitment to promoting transparency in society at large (spearheaded by local organizations such as Libera) CSOs' internal practice of financial transparency is insufficient, according to members of the project's National Advisory Group (NAG).

It seems that Italian civil society has not wholeheartedly embraced gender equity. Practices of gender equity within CSOs are much less developed than any other value espoused by civil society. Although some women's networks are vocal and some CSOs' activities promote gender equity in society at large, the scant information available on current gender equity practices within CSOs is an indication that gender issues are not a key priority for CSOs' internal governance.

Overall, the values dimension is the strongest dimension in the CSI Diamond. This confirms that Italian CSOs are committed to promoting and practicing a range of important values, with the exception of gender equity and adherence to transparency and accountability within their organizations.

Impact (2.3)

The impact dimension assesses civil society's role in governance and society at large. Civil society's impact on Italian society is significant. CSOs exert most of their social impact when they conduct activities aimed at protecting rights, delivering services, meeting people's needs, and informing and empowering citizens. Additionally, some CSOs show a rather strong capacity to hold the state and private sector accountable.

Many CSOs successfully inform and educate citizens and support people's initiatives to self-organize. For example, the number of television ads that mentioned CSO campaigns grew from 11,015 to 23,276 between 1999 and 2003. Additionally, fair-trade initiatives have grown considerably, and consumer groups have helped thousands of users deal with skyrocketing costs for phone service and other utilities and have provided legal assistance to shareholders impacted by the fraudulent behavior of large companies and financial institutions.

A significant number of CSOs are active in empowering marginalized groups, such as prisoners, drug addicts, and immigrants, and in building social capital and supporting livelihoods. In this regard, there are several well-entrenched networks of social cooperatives and local associations whose goal is to facilitate productive activities at the local level. All of this is reflected in citizens' high level of trust in certain types of CSOs. Voluntary organizations are the most trusted entities in Italy (86%), with higher levels of trust than the most commonly trusted actors, such as the president (79%) and the special police forces (73%). Trade unions (20%) and political parties (9%) remain the least trusted actors.

CSOs' impact is also significant when it comes to holding the state accountable and monitoring government policies. In social policy discussions, despite a number of anti-union labor reforms introduced during the past few years, trade unions still have a say when it comes to policymaking. For example, they are regular partners of government and business in tripartite consultations. In 2001, during the reform of the Italian Constitution, new policy-making provisions were introduced, such as the principle of horizontal subsidiarity, which underlines the importance of mutual cooperation between civil society actors and public institutions. This was due in large part to CSOs' recognition of and subsequent advocacy for the constitutional value of citizens' engagement in public interest activities. In other policy areas, CSOs' activities enjoy varying degrees of success. For example, while CSOs significantly contributed to the adoption of new laws on sexual crimes in 1996, their capacity to influence the national budget remains limited. Trade unions and business organizations influence the Italian national budget the most, along with some coalitions and movements such as Sbilanciamoci and Cittadinanzattiva, as well as some consumers' associations operating at the national level.

It can be argued that CSOs, especially during the past three decades, have deeply influenced public life in Italy. This has occurred at all levels, from the national to the local and in political as well as social spheres. In many cases, CSOs have successfully addressed problems of public interest, particularly those that were not sufficiently addressed or not tackled at all by state institutions.

Recommendations

The following recommendations were made during the CSI National Workshop, held in Rome on May 24, 2006, where the results of the CSI assessment were discussed among a wide range of stakeholders, including academics, representatives of the private sector, civil society, the media, and EU institutions:

- Encourage new forms of civic participation, different from those practiced in traditional organizations, to attract the attention of those who do not participate in public life, especially the youth.
- Strengthen the capacity of CSOs to represent, and be led by, women and emerging marginalized groups, particularly immigrants.

- Strengthen CSOs' accountability by developing a code of conduct and charter to monitor CSOs' work on policy issues.
- Increase information, communication, and cooperation among CSOs, and combat attitudes that favor isolation, by strengthening umbrella organizations and using information technologies more effectively.

Conclusion

Since the 1970s, Italy has been experiencing a decrease in the credibility of the political system and a shift in forms of citizen participation. Against this backdrop, civil society has faced challenges and opportunities. On the one hand, traditional organizations, such as political parties and trade unions, have lost membership even though they remain the most influential actors in influencing policymaking. On the other hand, CSOs' activism in new voluntary organizations has grown as has the number of citizens who do volunteer work.

Against this background of changing forms of activism, CSOs should strive to identify common goals and strengthen structures that contribute to better cooperation within the sector, such as umbrella organizations, networks, and coalitions. This would help overcome the paradox of Italian civil society: the inverse relation between the high levels of public trust in most voluntary organizations and their relatively limited role and power in policymaking.

CSI Report

Giovanni Moro and Ilaria Vannini, *Italian Civil Society—Facing New Challenges: CIVICUS Civil Society Index Report for Italy* (Rome, Italy: FONDACA, 2006).

Notes

1. The CSI assessment was implemented in Italy by Cittadinanzattiva (Active Citizenship) and FONDACA from early 2003 to June 2006. This chapter presents the main findings of the CSI and is based on a comprehensive country report for Italy, which can be accessed on the CSI pages of the CIVICUS website at http://www.civicus.org.

Chapter 22

～～

Lebanon[1]

Lebanon has a vibrant and diverse civil society, one of the largest per capita in the Arab region, with more than 5,000 organizations working on a wide range of issues in various fields. The political environment, characterized by a confessionally based political system, a weak state, and a history of civil war, is the most relevant factor determining civil society's path of development.

The Civil Society Index (CSI) assessment was conducted during a time of intense citizen mobilization demanding better governance of the country and was completed prior to the devastating war between Israel and the Hezbollah militia in 2006. While civil society's current focus is on providing relief and assistance to the victims of the war, the advances made toward a more democratic system of governance in Lebanon in the past years are likely to strengthen civil society in the midterm future.

Table 22.1 Background Information for Lebanon

Lebanon	
Country size (square km)	10,230
Population (millions 2004)	3.5
Population under 15 years (2004)	29.1%
Urban population (2003)	87.5%
Seats in parliament held by women (2005)	2.3%
Language groups	Arabic (official), French, English, and Armenian
Ethnic groups	Arab 95%, Armenian 4%, other 1%
Religious groups	Muslim 60%, Christian 39%, other %
HDI score and ranking (2003)	0.759 (81st)
GDP per capita (US$ 2003)	$5,074

Historical Development

The multiconfessional nature of Lebanon has played a significant role in the development of its civil society. The population of Lebanon is composed of more than fifteen ethnic groups and religions, including Muslim Shiites and Sunnis, Druze, Christian Maronite Catholics, Greek Orthodox, and Armenian Apostolic.

In general, the history of civil society in twentieth century Lebanon can be roughly divided into five phases. The first phase (1900 to 1930s) was marked by legislation aimed at regulating the increasing number of civil society organizations (CSOs), which were established at the turn of the century. At the time, most CSOs had a religious base and catered to the needs of their communities. On the other hand, nonreligious CSOs also emerged in the forms of professional associations, labor unions, political parties, and service delivery CSOs dealing with the aftermath of World War I.

The second phase (1940s and 1950s) witnessed Lebanese independence. Civil society consolidated, and sectarian associations, welfare associations, and women's, workers' and youth movements grew in response to rapid urbanization.

The third phase of development occurred roughly between 1960 and the outbreak of war in 1975. During this period, the establishment of nonsectarian associations adopting nonconfessional and nonpolitical agendas was most dynamic.

The fourth phase began with the eruption of the civil war (1975 to 1990), which paralyzed the Lebanese state. Thus, civil society became more active in the social sphere to compensate for the absence of a strong government, but it did so in the presence of influential militias from the various sectarian groups. While civil society focused on emergency relief and welfare activities, few CSOs demanded an end to the devastating civil war.

The fifth phase of development extends from the end of the war in 1990 to the present. After the war ended, civil society, like the rest of the country, faced new challenges amid a tense political situation, a deteriorating economy, a shattered society, displaced families, and a weak state. Civil society was called on to respond to huge needs with limited resources, but CSOs generally perceived their role as complementary to that of the government. During this phase, structured and long-term civil society advocacy coalitions and networks also emerged throughout the country.

In the past few years, Lebanese society has experienced positive and negative changes. The assassination of former prime minister Rafik Al Hariri, the eruption of the citizen-led "upheaval for independence," and the Syrian withdrawal from Lebanon promised changes in all spheres and levels of society. Based on the outburst of citizen participation immediately after Hariri's assassination, civil society began to mobilize citizens and organize their participation in a more structured way. However, the devastating war between Israel and Hezbollah in 2006 destroyed much of the hope and enthusiasm from the previous year and forced civil society to refocus on emergency relief and humanitarian aid. Thus, today Lebanon is facing serious challenges to its goal of becoming a stable and peaceful country run by accountable governance institutions.

The State of Civil Society in Lebanon

The concept of civil society—in Arabic, *Al Mojtamaa Al Madani*—is familiar and widely used in Lebanon. However, defining what civil society encompasses in Lebanon is tricky, since there are different perceptions of civil society's roles and actors. In an effort to be inclusive in the assessment of civil society, the Lebanese CSI team adopted CIVICUS's broad definition of civil society and focused on both organized and informal civil society. However, due to methodological reasons (such as the unavailability and inaccessibility of data as well as country-specific factors), political parties, labor unions, and cooperatives were excluded from the list of CSOs covered in this study.

This section provides a summary of key findings of the CSI project in Lebanon. It examines the state of Lebanese civil society along four dimensions—structure, environment, values, and impact—highlighting the main weaknesses and strengths.

The Lebanese Civil Society Diamond (figure 22.1) depicts a civil society of moderate size with relatively balanced dimensions. Civil society's structure is of limited strength, featuring moderate levels of civic engagement and a rather poorly resourced and structured civic sector. The weakest component is civil society's environment, which is characterized by political instability, a weak state and rule of law, socioeconomic problems, and a sectarian social structure. Conversely, civil society's values receive the highest score of the four dimensions; however, certain problematic areas are apparent, particularly CSOs' limited practice of democracy and transparency. Due to its weak influence on public policy and limited watchdog role, Lebanese civil society's impact on politics is relatively limited, but its role in providing services to the population is significant.

Figure 22.1 Civil Society Diamond for Lebanon

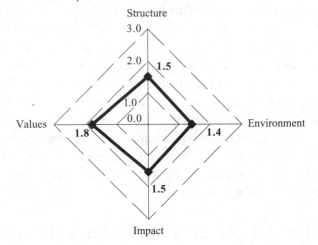

Structure (1.5)

The structure dimension examines the makeup of civil society in terms of the main characteristics of individual citizen participation and associational life. The structure of Lebanese civil society is of moderate strength.

In general, Lebanese citizens show rather strong levels of engagement in various forms of civic activities. However, the question is whether the massive citizen mobilization after the assassination of Hariri, which was particularly strong among the youth, was an exception or the beginning of a new era of active citizenship. Slightly more than one-third (36%) of respondents to the CSI population survey are members of at least one CSO, with NGOs or civic groups (14.8%) and professional associations (8.0%) being the most popular forms. Charitable giving (71% of Lebanese do give regularly) and volunteering (57% engage in some form of volunteer work) are even more widespread. In general, the social composition of CSOs mirrors the country's social structure, in particular with regard to its confessional characteristics.

Civil society's infrastructure remains rather weak. A majority of stakeholders agreed that support infrastructure (such as resource centers, information services, and technical assistance programs) is limited and that very few institutions to support civil society exist. Civil society is also not very active in self-regulation. Certain efforts to establish collective codes of conduct exist, but CSI stakeholders have yet to see their impact.

Though the extent of communication among civil society actors remains limited, cooperation through alliances or joint campaigns is quite common. However, these alliances are typically issue based rather than cross sectoral and more common at the local level than at the national. In general, the competitive dynamic among CSOs hampers efforts to establish sustainable communication and collaboration. This is exacerbated by limited internal human, financial, and technological resources. The financial sustainability of Lebanese civil society is a key challenge for civil society, particularly given the heavy reliance of professional urban NGOs on foreign funding and the absence of financial resources for most small CSOs.

Environment (1.4)

The environment dimension considers political, legal, socioeconomic, and sociocultural contexts as well as the relationships between civil society, the state, and the private sector. Lebanese civil society operates in a slightly disabling environment, due in large part to the political instability and weakness of its governance system.

The Lebanese political system is an intricate system of confessional-based power divisions among the eighteen recognized sectarian communities. This system encourages clientelistic networks and patronage between people of a particular confession, their organizations, and political representatives. There is a devastatingly low level of confidence in the rule of law, with frequently reported—and sometimes uncondemned—violations of the law by citizens and the state. Despite the Constitution's emphasis on citizens' political and civil rights, the government has a rather poor human rights record due to violations such as warrantless arrests, ill treatment of detainees, and banning of demonstrations.

As a result of more than fifteen years of civil war and military occupation, the state's capacity to govern is extremely limited and corruption is widespread. In light of the country's history of a weak polity and divided society, it is not surprising that the existing sociocultural norms are not conducive to civil society's growth. The results of a community survey reveal that 86% do not trust fellow citizens and nearly half of them have serious reservations toward certain groups, such as foreign workers and people living with HIV/AIDS.

Civil society–state relationships are complex and range from interference to support. Interestingly, in mid-2004, the NGO Resource and Support Unit (run jointly by the United Nations Development Programme [UNDP] and the Ministry of Social Affairs) was established to build the capacity and provide resources to the NGO sector. Also, CSOs are free, in principle, to criticize the government and its policies. However, the government, particularly through the Ministry of the Interior, exerts strong control over civil society by using its discretion in approving organizational by-laws, dissolving CSOs that are deemed to do political work, and delaying funds or excluding certain CSOs from bilateral projects. While registration procedures are generally simple and conducive, they are also open to interpretation and, therefore, misuse by the public authority. The same situation of unclear, outdated, and inconsistent laws applies to tax issues. However, a 2006 memo by the Minister of the Interior assures the consistent application of the legislation and promises an end to restrictive government practices.

Civil society's relationship with the private sector can be described as unproductive. Businesses are largely seen as indifferent toward civil society, providing on average only 10% of CSOs' income and rarely engaging in civil society activities through business associations.

The CSI assessment highlights the overarching problem of a weak state apparatus and clientelistic networks, which, together, obstruct socioeconomic progress and political reform. Assisting in the building of an effective and accountable governance system in Lebanon should therefore be one of civil society's key priorities.

Values (1.8)

The values dimension examines the extent to which civil society practices and promotes positive values. Due to Lebanese civil society's rather strong efforts to practice and promote important values such as tolerance, nonviolence, gender equity, poverty eradication, and environmental sustainability, this dimension receives the highest rating of the four dimensions examined. However, the assessment also detects crucial weaknesses, particularly in the internal practice of key values such as democracy and transparency within CSOs.

Due to the multiconfessional character of the country, issues of tolerance and nonviolence are particularly important in Lebanon. While there are political and religious fundamentalist groups within Lebanese civil society, their intolerant or violent behavior is usually strongly denounced by civil society at large. In the aftermath of the civil war, efforts to promote sectarian tolerance emerged, such as the Permanent Committee for Islamic-Christian Dialogue. Also, recent years have seen a growth of secular initiatives around social tolerance issues such as civil marriage, women's rights, and homosexuality. A similar level of activism is detected in the promotion of nonviolence and peace, ranging from projects on nonviolent conflict resolution to domestic violence and youth-focused initiatives.

In response to the state's inability to provide relief and welfare services during the civil war, civil society has begun to address poverty and welfare issues as a priority concern. More than half of registered NGOs are working in this field, particularly in health care and education. However, reflecting the country's overall socioeconomic crisis and civil society's limited resources and weak voice in economic policy, civil society's role in addressing poverty received a rather negative assessment.

Women's issues historically feature rather strongly on civil society's agenda. For example, the Lebanese Council for Women is more than fifty years old and comprises around 170 member organizations. Recent campaigns have focused on domestic violence and the large number of discriminatory laws, such as the social security laws, nationality laws, and penal laws. Discriminatory practices present within the patriarchal society also extend to certain parts of civil society. Women are excluded from certain organizations (mainly religious organizations), and the quota of women with leadership roles in professional associations is marginal.

Internal democracy and transparency within CSOs, in the form of holding elections, involving members in decisionmaking, and publishing financial reports, are not widespread, and many CSOs are family-based or one-person NGOs. In addition, 43% of surveyed stakeholders report that corruption, such as mismanagement of funds and unprofessional behavior, occurs frequently within civil society. While the actual extent of corrupt practices remains unclear, the public's negative image of civil society must be addressed.

The assessment of civil society's values finds a rather strong rift between the active role civil society is playing in promoting key values in society and its rather weak record of practicing many of these values internally, particularly internal democracy and transparency. In the long run, this discrepancy is likely to limit civil society's ability to mobilize citizens around the very issues on which it advocates.

Impact (1.5)

The impact dimension assesses civil society's role in governance and society at large. Reflecting its historical focus on assisting Lebanese people in the context of a weak state, Lebanese civil society has a strong impact on empowering and serving people but is rather weak in influencing and monitoring the government and its policies.

In examining civil society's impact, it is apparent that CSOs are quite effective at meeting societal needs and empowering citizens. CSOs have a strong track record in building infrastructure in rural areas; providing schooling, housing, and health services; and initiating microcredit and other income-generating programs. The ratio of citizens who believe that CSOs are more helpful in providing services than government agencies is extraordinarily high (10 to 1). Also, public trust in NGOs (39%) and religious institutions (55%) is comparatively higher than in key political institutions, such as political parties (9%) and the government (9%).

Compared to its strong permeation in society, civil society's influence on public policy and efforts to hold the state and private sector accountable are limited. While civil society, particularly professional associations, religious associations, and, increasingly, NGO networks, are beginning to voice their views on specific policies, advocacy work does not have a long tradition in Lebanon. This is not surprising, given the historically unresponsive and weak government. A stakeholder consultation revealed the lack of a concerted and organized effort to put pressure on government during the national budget process. This also applies to most other policy areas and civil society's watchdog role toward the state. Thus, 80% of surveyed stakeholders are dissatisfied with civil society's performance in this regard, and an even higher percentage feels that its activities in monitoring the private sector are weak.

Recommendations

The CSI project held a National Workshop with representatives from civil society, government, and other sectors to build on the CSI assessment and identify specific recommendations for strengthening the capacity and role of the sector. The following are key recommendations raised during the CSI National Workshop:

- Public image: CSOs should reach out to the population, particularly the youth. This requires creativity as well as stronger internal accountability and democracy. A civil society ombudsman position should also be created to deal with complaints against CSOs. Better relations with the media would also help strengthen public trust and involvement in civil society activities.
- Coordination: CSOs should emphasize cooperation, networking, and partnerships to overcome the sector's fragmented and uncoordinated character and strengthen their voice and role in the country's governance and developmental processes.

Conclusion

The composition and roles of Lebanese civil society reflect the overall social and political structures and processes in this complex country. Lebanese civil society is crucial in the lives of its citizenry. While it is often structured along sectarian lines, it plays a quasi-state role by providing essential services to the population. It is difficult for Lebanese civil society to break away from its traditional focus on social welfare and engage with a political system based on patronage and an unresponsive and fragile state that was further weakened by the 2006 war between Israel and the Hezbollah militia. Yet, there are also positive signs. One significant example was the successful mobilization of millions of Lebanese, especially youth, following the assassination of former prime minister Rafik Al Hariri, which shook the country's protracted political system. A crucial issue for the future of Lebanese civil society is the extent to which major civil society actors will be willing and able to move beyond their sectarian confines, embrace internal organizational democracy and accountability, and reach out to the young generation, which is fervently pushing for political reforms.

CSI Report

Assi Abou Khaldoun, *Lebanese Civil Society—A Long History of Achievements Facing Decisive Challenges Ahead of an Uncertain Future: CIVICUS Civil Society Index Report for Lebanon* (Beirut, Lebanon: International Management and Training Institute, 2006).

Notes

1. The CSI assessment was implemented in Lebanon by the International Management and Training Institute from June 2003 to December 2005. This chapter presents the main findings of the CSI and is based on a comprehensive country report for Lebanon, which can be accessed on the CSI pages of the CIVICUS website at http://www.civicus.org.

Chapter 23

✦✦

Macedonia[1]

After fifteen years of an independent Macedonia, the country and its civil society are nearing the end of the transition period. While significant progress has been made, the Civil Society Index (CSI) study found a number of key challenges for the sustainability of civil society. Most notably, Macedonia's accession to the European Union (EU) is expected to lead to a departure of foreign donors, which will make civil society financially vulnerable. Establishing stronger roots in the citizenry and better relations to other sectors are key tasks for Macedonian civil society in the years to come.

Table 23.1 Background Information for Macedonia

Macedonia	
Country size (square km)	25,713
Population (millions 2004)	2.0
Population under 15 years (2004)	20.1%
Urban population (2003)	59.6%
Seats in parliament held by women (2005)	19.2%
Language groups	Macedonian (official), Albanian, Turkish, Roman, and Serbian
Ethnic groups	Macedonian 67%, Albanian 23%, Turkish 4%, Roma 2%, Serb 2%, other 2%
Religious groups	Macedonian Orthodox 32%, Muslim 17%, other and unspecified 51%
HDI score and ranking	0.797 (59th)
GDP per capita (US$ 2003)	$6,794
Unemployment rate (% of total labor force)	36.7%
Population living on less than US$2 a day (2003)	<2%

Historical Overview

In Macedonia, civil society began to play an important role in public life during the national renaissance period of the late nineteenth and early twentieth centuries. The Internal Macedonian Revolutionary Organization (VMRO) was a pivotal organization in the independence movement at the turn of the century, and charity organizations, as well as literary and cultural circles, were also active before World War II.

After the war, Macedonia became a constituent republic within the Socialist Federal Republic of Yugoslavia. Due to its underdeveloped state, with a largely rural population (70%) and high levels of illiteracy, the integration of Macedonia within Yugoslavia triggered important economic, social, and cultural developments as well as the emergence of many cultural, athletic, and professional organizations. However, during the socialist period (1945–1990), the Yugoslavian state and the ruling Communist Party dominated public life and controlled all civic organizations. During this period, churches and religious organizations, in particular, were strongly suppressed.

Following the collapse of Yugoslavia in December 1991, Macedonia became the only former Yugoslav Republic to gain independence without a war. Beginning during the final phase of the Yugoslavian Republic, and intensifying during the 1990s, a new wave of civic organizations emerged in Macedonia, including environmental organizations in the 1980s, humanitarian organizations (in response to the economic and refugee crisis from the former Yugoslavia) in the early 1990s, and human rights organizations in the mid-1990s. Also during this period, foreign donors entered Macedonia and infused new ideas and resources into civil society.

As elsewhere in the Balkans, the experience of war was a defining feature of Macedonian civil society. The long history of unrest includes the Balkan Wars of 1912–1913, World Wars I and II, and the overarching threat of war in the 1990s. These events, along with conflicts in neighboring Croatia (1992–1995), Bosnia-Herzegovina (1992–1995), and Kosovo (1999), all served to entrench Macedonian civil society's strong commitment to peace. In particular, the humanitarian consequences of the 1999 Kosovo crisis shaped civil society's agenda. In 2001, in response to armed conflict within Macedonia, civil society insisted on a peaceful and nonviolent resolution to the conflict.

In the new millennium, state–civil society relations underwent some changes. Initially, civil society was often attacked as a fifth column representing foreign interests. Since 2001 and 2002, the government has become more open to recognizing and accepting CSOs' role. For example, it established a Unit for Cooperation with CSOs, and there have been increased attempts at cooperation between Ministries and CSOs. In 2005 Macedonia became a candidate for EU membership, which will likely provide opportunities and challenges for civil society. Civil society will have an important role to play in mediating the integration of a traditional, multicultural Balkan society into postmodern Europe. Civic organizations will be expected to be advocates of crucial values such as participatory democracy, inclusion, equality, transparency, and accountability. However, this stance might clash with the country's legacies of authoritarian governance, exclusion, and corruption. Moreover, European integration will shift the priorities of foreign donors to other countries, and civil society will have to find new ways to secure its financial sustainability.

The State of Civil Society in Macedonia

In Macedonia, there is no common understanding of the concept of civil society. Unlike other countries in the region, where the term was rediscovered by neoliberal forces, the reemergence of the concept in Macedonia in the early 1990s stemmed from reformed Communists and politically leftist forces, which used it to counter the ideas of the Macedonian ethno-nationalist elites. The 1998 Law on Citizen Associations and Foundations defines and regulates two types of organizations, associations and foundations, based on values, interests, and activities that are positive, nonpartisan, not for profit, and not for business. This normative and value-driven definition of CSO types, which withholds registration for organizations espousing racial discrimination, intolerance, or violence, was broadly used as a basis for the CSI assessment.

This section provides a summary of key findings of the CSI project in Macedonia. It examines the state of Macedonian civil society along four dimensions—structure, environment, values, and impact—highlighting the main weaknesses and strengths (figure 23.1).

The Civil Society Diamond for Macedonia reflects a value-driven civil society that is moderately well-developed. The structure is average, constrained by limited civic engagement, but stronger in terms of a rather well-developed civil society sector. Due to a dominant state, deep public mistrust, and the absence of a supportive legal framework, the operating environment for civil society is assessed as slightly disabling. The promotion and practice of positive values, particularly

Figure 23.1 Civil Society Diamond for Macedonia

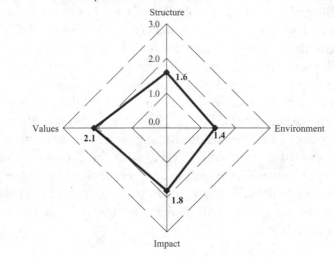

gender equity and nonviolence, is a key strength of civil society. Finally, civil society has only a moderate effect on policy. However, it does demonstrate a favorable record of empowering citizens, particularly women and marginalized groups.

Structure (1.5)

The structure dimension examines the makeup of civil society in terms of the main characteristics of individual citizen participation and associational life. The structure is characterized by rather weak levels of citizen participation on the one hand and extensive communication and cooperation among CSOs on the other.

Citizen's participation in the public sphere has increased significantly since the pre-1991 period. According to the CSI population survey, 52% of citizens have signed a petition (compared to 9% before 1991) and 45% have taken part in a protest or demonstration (compared to 14% before 1991). However, the survey reveals that only 23% of the population is a member of a CSO, which increases to 34% when pensioners' associations are included. In addition, the share of the population that volunteers for CSOs is also rather limited, even though many CSOs rely on volunteers as a key human resource.

The social composition of civil society continues to be skewed, with the poor, rural dwellers, and ethnic minorities (particularly ethnic Albanians) being underrepresented. Most CSOs tend to be ethnically homogenous in composition and concentrated in urban areas. For example, only 6.3% of registered organizations are based in a village. These rather low and skewed levels of civic engagement in civil society lead to what stakeholders refer to as a minority effect, where civil society lacks a wider constituency base and is unable to reach out to society at large.

In contrast, civil society's level of organization in Macedonia is strong. There is adequate support infrastructure and a significant level of networking among associations and within umbrella structures, of which there are approximately 200 in the country. They are particularly prevalent in the various subsectors and have contributed significantly to the consolidation of these sectors. There are also examples of cross-sectoral alliances and coalitions of CSOs, such as the Civic Platform of Macedonia.[2] Other ad hoc coalitions have formed in reaction to particular issues, such as the Enough Is Enough coalition, which responded to dissatisfaction with the government during the 2001 to 2002 crisis.

Many CSOs are in an unsustainable financial situation. A particular problem is the lack of diversified finances and an overreliance on foreign funding, while local financing and charity donations play a minor role. For example, 91% of stakeholders claim they received less than 20% of their budget from individual donations. Since the next few years will be marked by a withdrawal of many foreign donors, civil society is likely to see its financial situation deteriorate. Civil society must therefore begin to devise new funding strategies to attract local funding and motivate philanthropic donations.

Environment (1.4)

The environment dimension considers political, legal, socioeconomic, and sociocultural contexts as well as the relationships between civil society, the state, and the private sector. Civil society operates in a slightly disabling environment, which is marred by low levels of trust within society, limited state support, an unfavorable tax system for CSOs, and mutually indifferent relations between civil society and the private sector.

The Macedonian state has made substantive progress in the protection of basic rights and freedoms and in reducing corruption in recent years. However, the political context remains characterized by a weak entrenchment of the rule of law and a highly centralized state apparatus. Structural weaknesses in the implementation of laws and the functioning of the courts, and corruption, particularly in the judiciary, negatively affect the political environment. In addition, in 2001 the country faced an interethnic crisis, leading to six months of armed conflict, which was, however, brought to a successful close by the Ohrid Framework Agreement.[3]

Macedonia's socioeconomic conditions have been strained by other regional events. These include the effects of the Greek embargo on the country, the United Nations (UN) sanctions against the Federal Republic of Yugoslavia, and the large number of refugees in Macedonia from the war in Bosnia and Herzegovina and the Kosovo crisis. Macedonia also has a particularly high unemployment rate (37%).

Civil society's operating environment is further affected by extremely low levels of both interpersonal trust and social tolerance. The CSI population survey indicates that only 6% of citizens believe others can be trusted. Intolerance between different ethnic groups, such as Macedonians, Albanians, and Turks, while decreasing, is still rather prevalent. A quarter of population survey respondents did not want a member of another ethnic community as a neighbor.

In terms of state–civil society relations, dialogue is improving and four out of five stakeholders feel CSOs are, by and large, autonomous from the state. However, these positive trends are not accompanied by increased financial support by the state. Only a few CSOs, such as unions of associations of people with disabilities, sports organizations, and the Trade Union of Macedonia, receive significant state funding, and the allocation of funds lacks transparency. On the whole, the legal provisions pertaining to CSOs are rather conducive, although existing laws do not provide significant exemptions for CSOs or incentives for individual and corporate donations. This further exacerbates civil society's economic woes.

Relations with the private sector are not conducive to civil society's development. There is virtually no dialogue between the sectors, no corporate social responsibility (CSR), and no financial support from the business community. In a 2001 survey, almost half of surveyed business representatives reported being unaware of the importance of civil society and having no information about its activities.

Macedonian civil society operates in a somewhat problematic environment. While the conditions for civil society's work are not openly hostile, civil society cannot draw on any group of actors, institutions, or norms that would support its work. Therefore, civil society occupies a rather marginalized position among the social forces in the country.

Values (2.1)

The values dimension examines the extent to which civil society practices and promotes positive values. Its strong value base is a key asset for Macedonian civil society. The strongest values are nonviolence, gender equity, and environmental sustainability, while the practice and promotion of transparency were identified as problematic areas.

The strong commitment to gender equity is a legacy of Macedonia's socialist past, and socialist women's organizations adapted well to the new democratic context. Women's CSOs constitute 15% of all CSOs in the country, and both genders tend to be equally represented within civil society membership and leadership.

Within Macedonian civil society, there is widespread consensus about the use of nonviolent means to express an organization's position. Overall, nonviolence is a cornerstone value for civil society, and 91% of stakeholders believe civil society plays a significant role in the peaceful resolution of conflicts.

Transparency, however, is civil society's Achilles heel. CSOs have a poor record of making their own financial accounts available to the public, due to a lack of emphasis on internal transparency and insufficient financial management and reporting skills. Similarly, there is a shortage of activities encouraging transparency in society, and 68% of stakeholders were unable to recall a CSO activity dedicated to promoting government transparency.

Though poverty eradication is a declared value of Macedonian civil society, the CSI found that it is not a priority area for CSOs' work. The few activities in this area focus particularly on the Roma people and treat symptoms rather than root causes. There are a variety of reasons for civil society's modest record in promoting the fight against poverty, most notably the legacy of socialism and the state's responsibility for social welfare. In addition, since civil society is primarily an urban middle-class phenomenon, its ability to listen and learn from those who are directly affected by poverty is limited. This is further supported by the CSI finding that the most positive examples of poverty alleviation initiatives come from CSOs based in the marginalized community of the Roma people.

Impact (1.8)

The impact dimension assesses civil society's role in governance and society at large. Overall, Macedonian civil society exerts a moderate level of impact. Citizen empowerment activities are a key achievement while its limited role in public policy and governance processes is a particular weak point.

Many civil society activities are targeted at empowering social groups such as women, disabled people, youth, and pensioners. In

2003 40% of Macedonian CSOs were running initiatives targeting marginalized groups. The establishment of the Inter-party Parliamentary Lobby Group for people with disabilities and the Macedonian Women's Lobby (MZL) are results of these efforts. MZL successfully increased the presence of women in public life and has helped raise the number of women in parliament from 4.2% in 1990 to 17.5% in 2002. Other civil society empowerment activities focus on pensioners, farmers, the unemployed, homosexuals, and the Roma community.

Informing and educating citizens is another area where civil society has been very active and successful. Over 60% of stakeholders claim that civil society is active in this area, and 95% assess the activities as either somewhat successful or very successful. Activities often combine informing citizens (through media campaigns, information phone lines, or information offices) and lobbying for public services. Well-known information campaigns in 2004 included Don't Look Away for breast cancer and Nobody Is Perfect for people with disabilities. Civil society also actively promotes microfinance and runs business and professional training courses in an effort to support and create livelihoods in the context of widespread unemployment.

In terms of impacting public policy, civil society has the most influence on social policies related to women, the disabled, and pensioners. Success with more political initiatives, such as access to information and influencing the national budget, remains low. In addition, civil society's role as watchdog of the state is underdeveloped and largely limited to human rights issues. Here, civil society's attempts to secure funding and develop positive relations with the state and private sector may weaken its commitment to holding these actors accountable.

Thus, while civil society's social contributions are significant, its policy and watchdog roles are considerably less developed.

Recommendations

During the CSI National Workshop in Skopje in July 2005, participants from civil society, the government, and the media developed the following recommendations, based on civil society's strengths and weaknesses:

- Embrace the fight against poverty: Apart from its social, humanitarian and charity work, civil society should strive to become an advocate against poverty.

- Improve transparency and democracy: Civil society needs to cultivate public trust and strengthen its transparency by increasing
members and constituencies' participation in organizational
decisionmaking processes. Civil society also needs to strengthen
internal governance practices, such as codes of ethics and professional standards, and adhere to legal and statutory obligations.
- Strengthen public trust in civil society: Civil society should publicize its successes and achievements, demonstrate its responsiveness
to society's needs (particularly in regard to unemployment, poverty, and corruption), and augment its activities related to these
areas.
- Diversify civil society constituencies: Civil society should
strengthen the participation of rural people, the poor, and ethnic
communities in its work. Its active involvement in the decentralization process will help increase civil society's outreach to these
communities.

Conclusion

A commitment to nonviolence, peace, tolerance, and environmental
sustainability are cornerstones of Macedonian civil society. In the
context of several problematic legacies of the socialist past, the Balkan wars, and the 2001 violent conflict within Macedonia, civil society has contributed considerably to instilling these positive values in
society. With the stabilization of the country and the ensuing process
of EU accession, the country's priorities are likely to shift toward
more technical and political issues of good governance and socioeconomic policy. The CSI assessment reveals certain weaknesses (such as
a lack of relevant skills, knowledge, and public support) of civil society in these areas. To play a more significant role in the country's governance and development processes—and to counter the significant
drop in funding due to the departure of foreign donors—CSOs need
to engage the communities and citizens they work with as primary
stakeholders of their activities.

CSI Report

Macedonian Center for International Cooperation (MCIC), *An
Assessment of Macedonian Civil Society—Fifteen Years of Transition,
A Country Moving Towards Citizen Participation: CIVICUS Civil
Society Index Report for the Republic of Macedonia* (Skopje,
Macedonia: MCIC, 2005).

Notes

1. The CSI assessment was implemented in Macedonia by the Macedonian Center for International Cooperation (MCIC) from February 2004 to July 2005. This chapter presents the main findings of the CSI and is based on a comprehensive country report for Macedonia, which can be accessed on the CSI pages of the CIVICUS website at http://www.civicus.org.
2. The Civic Platform includes twenty-nine organizations from various civil society subsectors and provides an open space for democratic debate, free exchange of ideas, and cooperation of CSOs dedicated to building civil society.
3. The Framework Agreement is the political solution signed by top political leaders and guaranteed by the president and international community. The agreement aims to preserve democracy, develop civil society, and work toward a multicultural society with equitable inclusion of all ethnic communities.

Chapter 24

~~

Mongolia[1]

Locked between the two giants, China and Russia, Mongolia rarely receives international attention. As such, the CSI study is the first attempt to gauge the state of civil society in the country and present it to an international audience. As the CSI indicates, Mongolia's recent history and current conditions include both advances and challenges for civil society's development in a postsocialist developing country.

Table 24.1 Background Information for Mongolia

Mongolia	
Country size (square km)	1,565,000
Population (millions 2004)	2.5
Population under 15 years (2004)	31.3%
Urban population (2003)	56.8%
Seats in parliament held by women (2005)	6.7%
Language groups	Khalkha Mongol, Turkic, and Russian
Ethnic groups	Mongol 85%, Turkic 7%, Tungusic 5%
Religious groups	Tibetan/Buddhist/Lamaist 50%, none 40%, others 10%
HDI score and ranking (2003)	0.679 (114th)
GDP per capita (US$ 2003)	$1,850
Unemployment rate (% of total labor force)	14.2%
Population living on less than US$2 a day (1998)	74.9%

Historical Overview

After seventy years of authoritarian socialist rule, in 1989 Mongolia embarked on a dual transition to a liberal democracy and a market-based economy. Following a successful democratic transition phase, Mongolia's democratic consolidation has been seriously challenged by the lack of government accountability, widespread corruption, a weak multiparty system, and low levels of civic engagement. Socioeconomic factors such as persistently high poverty and unemployment rates, widespread alcoholism, violence, an increased gap between urban and rural development, and a massive migration into urban areas have posed further obstacles to Mongolia's democratization.

Historical forms of collective action in Mongolia can be found in the mass resistance led by feudal lords to overthrow the Manchu yoke in the eighteenth century. After the introduction of socialist rule in 1921, a dense network of hierarchically structured mass organizations (MOs)—such as the Mongolian Women's Federation, the Mongolian Union of Young Revolutionaries, the youth wing of the ruling Mongolian People's Revolutionary Party (MPRP), and trade unions—emerged, operating under the control of the party-state.

The emergence of prodemocracy movements in the late 1980s mobilized citizens to demand democratic reforms and opened political space for the establishment of opposition political parties and NGOs. Supported by foreign donor organizations, NGOs quickly became major actors in civil society, addressing a broad range of issues, including human rights, women's rights, economic development, and democratic reforms. Meanwhile, the socialist MOs, or inheritor organizations, sought to transform themselves to fit the country's new democratic agenda, but largely retained their close ties with state bodies through their connections with the former Communist Party, which continued to dominate party politics. As a result, inheritor organizations maintained their monopoly in several subsectors of civil society, such as trade unions and pensioners' organizations.

In the new millennium, widespread social discontent over the lack of improvement of living conditions, increased crime, and increased corruption among public officials was channeled into the formation of a number of mass movements, which mounted public protests. The activities of these movements grew stronger following the 2004 parliamentary elections, which ended the MPRP's near-monopoly of political power by more evenly distributing the seats between the MPRP and other parties. This significantly helped expand the political space for independent citizen action.

The State of Civil Society in Mongolia

The broad scope and heterogeneity of Mongolian civil society has often been obscured by an application of the term NGOs to both independent and quasi-governmental organizations and the interchangeable use of NGOs with the term "civil society." In the CSI assessment, the National Advisory Group (NAG) decided to use CIVICUS's broad definition of civil society to better account for the diversity of Mongolian civil society. Thus, the assessment encompasses NGOs, MOs, mass movements, trade unions, chambers of commerce, savings and credit cooperatives, political parties, religious organizations, apartment owners' unions, nonprofit media, and informal self-help health and leisure groups.

This section provides a summary of key findings of the CSI project in Mongolia. It examines the state of Mongolian civil society along four dimensions—structure, environment, values, and impact—highlighting the main weaknesses and strengths.

The overall state of Mongolian civil society is visually depicted in the Civil Society Diamond (figure 24.1). Mongolian civil society is of a relatively small size. Its structure is relatively weak, primarily due to CSOs' poor institutional capacities, even though levels of civic engagement and joint activities of CSOs are on the rise. Civil society's operating environment is rather disabling to independent citizen action, primarily because it is marked by state domination of the

Figure 24.1 Civil Society Diamond for Mongolia

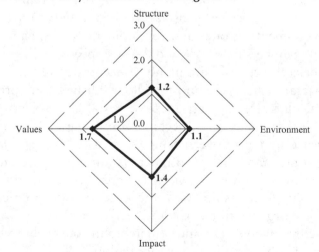

social and economic spheres. Civil society is rather active in promoting a set of key values, but there are problems in the practice of some of these values within the sector. Civil society's overall impact is somewhat limited. However, there are examples of significant influence on human rights and public awareness-raising.

Structure (1.2)

The structure dimension examines the makeup of civil society in terms of the main characteristics of individual citizen participation and associational life. Despite increased grassroots mobilization in the post-Communist period and positive trends with regard to strengthened inter- and intrasectoral cooperation among CSOs, civil society's development is impeded by low citizen participation, unequal geographic distribution of CSOs strongly biased toward the capital city, partisan polarization among CSOs, and lack of financial resources.

Though the overall level of citizen participation and formal memberships in CSOs outside of political parties remains rather low, there are signs of increasing grassroots mobilization and a growth in CSO membership. For example, there were massive public protests and demonstrations following the 2004 parliamentary elections that demanded government accountability and social equity as well as the reopening of political space. This led CSI participants to emphasize the increased mobilization of citizens in recent years. Overall, just less than half of the adult population is a member of at least one CSO. While 41.2% of citizens belong to a political party, the most popular types of membership in nonparty CSOs are trade unions (14.1%), professional associations (6.2%), credit and savings associations (5.4%), community organizations (4.8%) and women's organizations (4.4%). Other types of CSOs, such as environmental groups and development NGOs, have extremely low levels of membership (0.2% and 0.4% respectively).

Civil society's activities are highly concentrated in the capital city of Ulaanbaatar, where the most well-established and professional CSOs, particularly NGOs, are located. Rural civil society is poorly developed, lacks financial and technical resources, and is vulnerable to interference by local government. Rural dwellers, especially herders, poor people, and ethnic and religious minorities, are underrepresented in CSOs, although women figure prominently in CSO leadership and membership, with the exception of political parties and religious organizations. Civil society provides an avenue for women's active involvement and leadership in society, but women are largely excluded from political decisionmaking roles.

There are positive trends of strengthened inter- and intrasectoral cooperation among CSOs, but the effectiveness and legitimacy of umbrella organizations remain contentious, due in part to the predominance of insufficiently reformed inheritor organizations. Though these organizations are officially nonpartisan, functionally they often serve party interests and contribute to partisan polarization, animosity, and distrust among civil society actors. In fact, the prevalence of partisanship was found to be a key obstacle to stronger coordination and cooperation within the sector.

CSOs differ widely in their institutional capacities. Only 13% of surveyed stakeholders judge CSOs' financial capacity to be sufficient. While inheritor CSOs benefit from better access to state resources and are generally financially secure, new CSOs, particularly independent advocacy NGOs, are almost exclusively dependent on foreign funding and rarely financially sustainable. Similarly, rural CSOs suffer from a perpetual lack of resources.

There has been some improvement in recent years in civil society's structural foundation. However, the CSI findings highlight the importance of strengthening nonpartisan civic and political activism and reducing partisan polarization within civil society so that it might play a stronger role in public affairs.

Environment (1.1)

The environment dimension considers political, legal, socioeconomic, and sociocultural contexts as well as the relationships between civil society, the state, and the private sector. In spite of the existence of formally democratic institutions and the rule of law, domination of society by the state, excessive centralization of state power, and widespread corruption in government are serious obstacles to civil society's effective functioning.

The Mongolian state does not officially recognize that the country is in deep social, political, and economic crisis. Frequent violations of human rights, poor adherence to laws, deep distortions in the national economy (as evidenced by excessive foreign debt), widespread poverty and unemployment, a considerable urban-rural development gap, and significant social problems such as alcoholism and crime are major barriers to the development of civil society. Given these pervasive social and political problems and the legacy of seventy years of socialist rule, it is not surprising that the CSI reveals rather low levels of interpersonal trust and public-spiritedness in Mongolia. Only one out of five Mongolians state that other people can generally be trusted.

Although some advances have been made, the CSI findings indicate that state–civil society relations and private sector–civil society relations require significant improvement. Eighty-five percent of surveyed stakeholders believe that CSOs are not free from government interference and cite examples such as cumbersome CSO registration procedures, restrictions on public protests, and intimidation, interrogation, and undue surveillance of CSOs operating at the local level. Similarly, dialogue between civil society and the state is poorly institutionalized and generally limited. The state rarely provides financial support to CSOs, and where it does, it tends to favor a small range of social service delivery CSOs and inheritor organizations. Buddhist organizations also occupy an advantaged position vis-à-vis the state, due to the close relationship between top religious leaders and top government officials.

The private sector's attitude toward civil society is also uneven, depending on the type of CSO, and indifferent when looking at the sector as a whole. The private sector generally tends to support CSOs operating in the realms of arts and culture, sports and recreation, and charitable and religious affairs, whereas politically oriented organizations, such as human rights, women's rights, environmental, and anti-corruption CSOs (except for mass movements), tend to rely almost exclusively on foreign donors. Corporate philanthropy is limited and corporate social responsibility (CSR) is a nascent concept in Mongolia, with over 80% of stakeholders judging CSR to be limited.

Values (1.7)

The values dimension examines the extent to which civil society practices and promotes positive values. Comparatively speaking, its value base is the greatest strength of Mongolian civil society, even though CSOs often do not practice the values they promote in society.

Civil society organizations, particularly NGOs and social movements, demonstrate a significant commitment to promoting democracy, government accountability, gender equity, poverty alleviation, and environmental protection. A number of new issue-oriented independent NGOs and political opposition parties have contributed to liberalizing, diversifying, and decentralizing the public sphere through public education, policy advocacy, and oversight activities to promote a democratic society. Democracy promotion activities are a key example of civil society's role in advancing positive values in society. Though largely confined to urban areas, frequently cited CSO activities include long-standing programs on nonpartisan voter education, the Political Education Academy's national democracy training for government officials, civic education programs of the Citizens' Education Center and the Democracy Education Center (DEMO), and Globe International's advocacy for the Law on the Right to Information.

Despite the active promotion of positive values, the CSI study indicates that some CSOs fail to consistently apply the principles of democracy, accountability, and financial transparency to their internal practices. However, at the CSI National Workshop, many participants resisted accusations of high levels of corruption among CSOs, but they agreed that corruption is particularly problematic in political parties, apartment owners' unions, some inheritor organizations, and business and religious organizations.

Potential worrisome trends are the escalation of violence, increasing xenophobia in civil society, and the continuing partisan polarization of civil society. First, there has been an escalation of conflict between rural communities desperately trying to protect their livelihoods from mining and construction companies that are destroying their environment. Second, there is some evidence of the intensification of nationalist (particularly anti-Chinese) sentiments and a growing influence of xenophobic movements. Third, civil society remains plagued by partisan polarization within the sector, which perpetuates intolerance and prevents constructive communication and cooperation between citizens and CSOs as well as within the sector. In order to strengthen the principles of nonviolence and tolerance in Mongolian civil society, and to avoid blaming specific groups in response to adverse political, economic, and social conditions in the country, these issues must be addressed

Overall, civil society's values, especially its commitment to the promotion of democracy and human rights, are an important source of optimism for the future strengthening of Mongolian civil society and its contribution to the cultivation of a democratic society.

Impact (1.4)

The impact dimension assesses civil society's role in governance and society at large. While there are a number of civil society success stories in the fields of gender equity, human rights, and democracy promotion, the overall impact of Mongolian civil society is rather limited.

As evidenced in the values dimension, civil society is a leading force in promoting citizen rights and democracy in the country. These are also the areas where civil society shows a strong impact. For example, women's organizations successfully advocated for the Law against Domestic Violence in 2004, and CSOs ran numerous civic education and democracy promotion campaigns. The concept of CSR is nascent in Mongolia, but there have been significant efforts to raise public awareness about the economic and social rights of citizens, including the right to be protected from the destructive effects of mining and construction companies.

However, these awareness-raising activities and pockets of issue-specific impact do not translate into an overall stronger role for civil society in the governance processes. Civil society has almost no impact on holding the state and private sector accountable or in influencing the national budgeting process. While combating corruption and increasing government accountability is a key concern for civil society, the government has little political will to respond to civil society's demands and take decisive measures.

Civil society's work in empowering women has had a relatively significant impact. CSOs have enjoyed considerable success in improving the legal framework for the protection of women's rights and equipping women with knowledge of their rights. Numerous projects, such as health education, skills training, microcredit, and literacy training, have improved women's income, employment opportunities, and ability to protect their rights in the judicial system. More broadly, civil society is active in service delivery to marginalized citizens, such as free legal aid, psychological counseling, services for abused women and children, and informal education for poor children. However, since they are usually undertaken on a project-specific basis, service delivery activities tend to be largely focused on urban areas and remain limited in scope. The dominant role of the state in social services is visible by the fact that twice as many respondents to the population survey regard the state as better at providing services than CSOs. Similarly, public trust ratings for most CSO types are around 30%, while public institutions reach 50–60%. This further attests to CSOs' limited social reach.

The impact of civil society in Mongolia is still confined to specific issues, such as democracy and human rights, and specific target groups, such as women. Weak organizational capacity, poor coordination among CSOs, and problematic relations with the state are likely to impede CSOs from scaling-up their social and political impact.

Recommendations

As a result of regional stakeholder consultations and national consultations, CSI participants developed recommendations and a strategic plan of action, with concrete actions for civil society to undertake. The following are key recommendations:

- Establish an effective civil society justice system, beginning with the development of ethical self-regulatory mechanisms for CSOs.
- Develop a national civil society network of information and communication, with an emphasis on *aimag*[2] to *aimag* information-sharing and regular distribution of information from Ulaanbaatar to the *aimags*.
- Build CSOs' monitoring, research, and analytical skills, to increase their ability to hold the state and private corporations accountable.
- Promote the institutional and financial capacity of CSOs, particularly in rural areas, and strengthen institutional relations between local legislatures and CSOs.
- Conduct further CSI exercises at the *aimag* level, to better understand local situations and to strengthen rural civil society by enhancing local stakeholders' analytical capacity, collective action, and networking.

Conclusion

The CSI assessment brought to light the heterogeneous and vibrant character of Mongolia's civil society as well as its generally small and underdeveloped nature. Mongolia is dominated by an overbearing state that maintains close ties to big business and exerts considerable control over the public sphere via the state-friendly media. Although the majority of CSOs are poorly organized, insufficiently resourced, and relegated to a rather marginalized role, a fair number of CSOs have influenced specific aspects of Mongolia's development and democratization processes.

The CSI assessment process proved to be an important tool in identifying the strengths and weaknesses of civil society, in fostering a higher degree of integration and mutual trust among a diverse set of civil society actors, and in contributing to the development of a common strategic vision for strengthening civil society, particularly outside the urban centers. By identifying areas requiring improvement, it is hoped that the CSI assessment will serve as a springboard for empowering civil society and strengthening its ability to contribute to the development of a democratic and prosperous Mongolian society.

CSI Report
Center for Citizens' Alliance, *State of Civil Society in Mongolia: Civil Society Index Report for Mongolia* (Ulaanbaatar, Mongolia: Center for Citizens' Alliance, 2005).

Notes

1. The CSI assessment was implemented in Mongolia by the Center for Citizens' Alliance (CCA) over the course of 2004 and 2005 as part of a broader long-term effort to institutionalize a democracy watch system in Mongolia. The chapter presents the main findings of the CSI and is based on a comprehensive country report for Mongolia, which can be accessed on the CSI pages of the CIVICUS website at http://www.civicus.org.
2. Aimag is an administrative unit, such as province or state. Mongolia is administratively divided into twenty-one aimags. Aimags are further divided into soums and soums into baghs.

Chapter 25

$\sim\!\!\bullet\!\!\sim$

Montenegro[1]

In May 2006, as a result of a popular referendum, Montenegro became an independent country. Unfortunately, the political situation remains quite polarized, which weakens the legitimacy and power of the state. In this context, Montenegrin civil society, which is highly dependent on foreign donors, plays a rather marginalized role in society. However, civil society actors are increasingly recognizing the need to reach out to government, the private sector, and the citizenry at large to build stronger relationships to sustain the work of civil society in the future.

Table 25.1 Background Information for Montenegro

Montenegro	
Country size (square km)	13,812
Population	620,145
Seats in parliament held by women	10.67%
Language groups	Serbian
Ethnic groups	Montenegrin 43.16%, Serb 31.99%, Albanian 5.03%, Bosnians 7.77%, Croats 1.10%
Religious groups	Orthodox 72.74%, Muslim 17.74%, Roman Catholic 3.54%, atheists and those without statement on religious belief 3.21%
GDP per capita (US$ 2005, est.)	$3,800
Unemployment rate	14.67%

Historical Overview

Civil society's recent development is closely linked to the political changes that Montenegro has undergone over the past century. Amid these political shifts, notions of statehood and identity have played a central role.

The history of civil society in Montenegro dates back to the sixteenth century, when the royal family began to engage in philanthropic activities. The first institutionalized forms of civil society emerged in the late 1900s, such as voluntary fire fighters associations, which were first founded in Kotor in 1867. During the short reign of the parliamentary monarchy, from 1905 to 1915, a large number of associations emerged, mainly in the form of trade unions, workers' associations, and cultural societies.

When the Communist regime took power in 1945, all associations working in the fields of recreation, culture, and sports, as well as all professional associations, were closed down and integrated into the state-controlled system. After some time, however, new associations were allowed to form as long as they did not challenge the regime's ideology and were apolitical in nature.

Like the rest of Communist Europe, between 1989 and 1990 Yugoslavia underwent a shift from a one-party Communist system to a multiparty system and opened up space for independent citizen associations. However, full democracy did not materialize, and the 1990s were marked by several violent wars related to the ensuing break-up of the former Yugoslavia. During this time, a sizable number of associations and individuals resisted the war, nationalism, xenophobia, and hate speech, and condemned the political and military actions of the Yugoslav authorities under President Milosevic.

From the early 1990s until May 2006, Montenegro's statehood remained unresolved, as Montenegro, together with Serbia, constituted the remainder of the Former Republic of Yugoslavia. The question of whether to remain linked to Serbia or become an independent country burdened civil society and society as a whole. During this period the country was divided into pro-Milosevic and anti-Milosevic camps. Most CSOs gave their support to the struggle of Montenegrin authorities against Milosevic, and continued to support ambitions for independence.

In the run-up to the referendum for independence on May 21, 2006, the two political camps—the pro- and anti-independence movements—registered as NGOs, which were immediately dissolved after the referendum took place. The majority (55.5%) of citizens voted for independence. The Parliament of Montenegro adopted a

Declaration of Independence on July 3, 2006, and the Republic of Montenegro was admitted as a member of the United Nations on June 28, 2006. However, as the split vote on the referendum indicates, Montenegro remains a deeply divided country politically, which presents a number of problems for the development of a healthy civil society.

The State of Civil Society in Montenegro

Civil society is not a common term in Montenegro. In 1999 the Law on NGOs introduced the concept of NGOs, which includes two organizational forms: nongovernmental associations and nongovernmental foundations. The NGO sector is the driving force of Montenegrin civil society, while other forms of civil society, such as faith-based organizations or trade unions are rather weak.

This section provides a summary of key findings of the Civil Society Index Shortened Assessment Tool (CSI-SAT) project in Montenegro. It examines the state of Montenegrin civil society along four dimensions—structure, environment, values, and impact—highlighting the main weaknesses and strengths.

The Civil Society Diamond for Montenegro (figure 25.1) visually summarizes the assessment's findings. The diamond indicates that Montenegrin civil society is relatively underdeveloped. It has a rather weak structure, due to limited citizen participation and a resource-poor civil society sector, which is still in the early stages of development. Civil society operates in a slightly disabling environment, in which

Figure 25.1 Civil Society Diamond for Montenegro

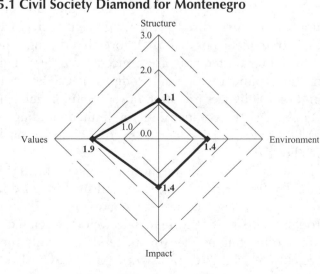

the political context constrains civil society's ability to maneuver. Accordingly, civil society's impact, particularly on governance processes, is rather limited. The strength of civil society lies in a set of progressive values, which it adheres to internally and promotes within society at large, with the notable exceptions of transparency and poverty eradication.

Structure (1.1)

The structure dimension examines the makeup of civil society in terms of the main characteristics of individual citizen participation and associational life. Montenegrin civil society's structure is rather limited, with key weaknesses in the areas of citizen participation and financial resources.

The level of citizen participation in Montenegrin society is low. Due to the strong family ethics upheld within Montenegrin society, citizens are more inclined to engage with their families than become involved in the public sphere. According to the 2000 World Value Survey (WVS), only 28.9% of Montenegrin citizens have engaged in some form of nonpartisan political action, such as demonstrations or signing a petition. The percentage of citizens that are a member of a CSO is moderate. According to the Stakeholder Assessment Group (SAG), not more than 30% of the adult population is a member of a CSO, while according to the WVS 18% of the population volunteer in CSOs.

Institutionalized civil society is growing quickly in Montenegro, with an average of forty new CSOs registering every month, although a significant share of them are letterbox NGOs, which do not run any activities. Support infrastructure to strengthen civil society exists and is growing as a consequence of dedicated foreign aid programs. However, most CSOs in Montenegro are concentrated in urban areas, especially in and around the capital, Podgorica. CSOs are not well connected, and their alliances are often unsuccessful in achieving their proclaimed goals. Due to competition for limited funding and personal clashes between CSOs' leaders, effective cooperation between CSOs remains limited.

Financial sustainability is among the key problems facing civil society's structure. The majority of CSOs depend on foreign donors for their survival, since foreign donations make up 73.7% of CSOs' income. Through their significant financial support, foreign donors, as well as the state, often pursue their own agenda and only fund CSOs that they have close working relations with. Most CSOs also function under difficult working conditions, due to lack of basic infrastructure, such as computers and office facilities. On the other hand, NGOs can draw on a growing cadre of qualified personnel, even though the number of full-time staff in most NGOs remains limited.

The CSI assessment shows that due to the long and protracted transition to democracy and an independent Montenegrin state, civil society is still in the early stages of development. The main challenge will be to develop a civil society that is sustained by Montenegrin citizens rather than foreign donors.

Environment (1.4)

The environment dimension considers political, legal, socioeconomic, and sociocultural contexts, as well as the relationships between civil society, the state, and the private sector. The findings reveal that the operating environment for civil society is slightly disabling, primarily due to a weak state, negative sociocultural norms, and limited relations between civil society and other sectors.

Montenegro's current environment reflects the political and sociocultural legacies of the socialist period. The political system remains highly centralized, and national government is unwilling to share its power, since, despite passing a set of laws on local self-governance, none of the laws have been properly implemented. The state's effectiveness is also limited, and many citizens feel that government lacks administrative capacities and transparent processes, and that it is pursuing a highly partisan agenda. The level of perceived corruption in the public sector is also substantive, with a score of 5.25[2] by Freedom House, citing the government's approach to the 2003 "trafficking affair" as an illustrative example.[3]

The sociocultural context is characterized by low levels of trust, tolerance, and public spiritedness among citizens. According to the WVS 2000, two-thirds of Montenegrins feel they need to be careful when dealing with other people. Levels of tolerance in society are especially low toward marginalized social groups, such as alcoholics, the mentally disabled, drug addicts, homosexuals, and people living with HIV/AIDS.

Despite the fact that the registration process for CSOs is considered simple, quick, inexpensive, and consistently applied, it is abused by businesses, such as restaurants that register as CSOs to benefit from tax breaks. The exploitation of this legal loophole negatively influences the otherwise rather positive public perception of civil society, which is based on the important work undertaken by real CSOs. Recently, the

NGO Legislative Framework Reform program began addressing these issues, with the assistance of the European Center for Non-profit Law.

The nature and quality of the relationship between CSOs and the state is wrought with a mutual lack of trust. The state regards civil society mainly as a necessary evil and often seeks to undermine the work and reputation of critical CSOs. Consequently, dialogue between the state and civil society and financial support from the government to CSOs are relatively limited. Government funding for CSOs mainly exists in the form of grants. Unfortunately there is no coherent strategy for distributing the funds, and there have been accusations of grant mismanagement by the government, which was accused of allocating grants to inactive or unreliable CSOs and of focusing solely on CSOs supportive of its policies.

Montenegrin civil society operates in a political environment that is characterized by high levels of corruption and strong political influence over the governance system. Citizens do not trust the government or one another, and an atmosphere of general mistrust permeates society. The relationship between the state and civil society requires further development, especially in the context of Montenegro's recent independence.

Values (1.9)

The values dimension examines the extent to which civil society practices and promotes positive values. In Montenegro, values scored the highest among the four dimensions, reflecting a civil society that is relatively active in practicing and promoting a core set of positive values.

Montenegrin civil society has been particularly active in undertaking numerous initiatives to promote democracy, tolerance, nonviolence, and peace, as well as gender equality. For example, a significant number of NGOs work on projects promoting the concept and practice of democracy through civic education.[4] Yet there are also examples of NGOs following the divisive and authoritarian value patterns of political parties, thereby tainting the public image of the entire civic sector.

Financial transparency is a major challenge for Montenegrin civil society. According to the United States Agency for International Development's (USAID's) 2005 NGO Sustainability Index, a small group of specialized NGOs have well-developed financial systems in place, and only this minority sends annual financial reports to the tax authorities, even though the law obliges all NGOs to do so. On some occasions CSOs have been accused of corrupt practices, especially around issues of mismanagement of funds or conflict of interest. As a result, in recent years some CSOs have actively worked to increase the transparency of CSOs. For example, the national NGO strategy for 2006 includes the goal of developing a code of conduct for CSOs.

It is also worth noting that CSOs are not seen as significant actors in fighting poverty. In part, this is due to the legacy of a strong public administration that has kept poverty eradication within the mandate of government. A significant exception was the participatory process around the government's Poverty Reduction Strategy Paper in 2004, which involved more than sixty CSOs and more than 6000 citizens.

Civil society organizations have a successful track record in promoting and protecting the environment. An example of civil society's active role in ecological issues is the campaign for saving the river Tara, which is protected by UNESCO. It was supposed to be flooded, based on an international cross-border cooperation treaty, to establish a hydro-power plant. Due to efforts of environmental CSOs, government backed out of completing the project.

Impact (1.4)

The impact dimension assesses civil society's role in governance and society at large. The findings reveal that Montenegrin civil society has a somewhat limited impact, and is generally more active in service delivery than in influencing public policy.

Given the politically charged environment and limited CSO advocacy skills, only a group of powerful Podgorica-based NGOs play a strong advocacy role. Nevertheless, civil society's actual impact on public policies is limited, especially on politically sensitive issues, such as the national budget process, where CSOs are completely excluded because neither the government nor parliament openly discusses the budget before it is passed. However, in recent years some NGOs have managed to build closer relations with certain policymakers and have provided input on issues such as the role of NGOs in the EU integration process and the right of citizens to coexist in ethnically mixed municipalities. In general though, civil society's limited knowledge, advocacy skills, and social base, as well as an uncooperative government, prevent a stronger role for civil society in the country's governance.

Civil society's role in society is more pronounced. Civil society actors are capable of recognizing key social problems and devising actions aimed at solving them, even though the number of initiatives remains rather small. CSOs are especially active in areas such as informing and educating citizens. For example, the NGO network "Action" is a successful campaign that educates citizens about necessary reforms for a democratic society. When it comes to direct service provision, particularly to marginalized groups, civil society has begun to provide a number of services that the state has neglected. For example, CSOs offer shelter to victims of domestic violence or sex trafficking, day care for disabled children, additional or preparatory education for Roma children, and legal counseling for victims of violence.

CSOs are also seen as doing their job rather well. According to a public opinion poll conducted in 2005, citizens rank NGOs as the third most efficient institutions, after schools and hospitals, while government, parliament, and political parties were rated significantly worse. However, this does not necessarily translate into substantial trust in NGOs, since a recent poll conducted by the Center for Development of NGOs shows that only 37% of the public have a high level of trust for NGOs.

Civil society is regarded as rather successful in meeting the needs of the population. Still its influence on policy processes is clearly constrained by the politicized and centralized nature of Montenegrin politics and civil society's limited capacity, skills, and public support.

Conclusion

Civil society in Montenegro has weak roots. Half a century of Communism and the subsequent decade of authoritarian government and violent conflicts are having long-term effects on the prospects for a vibrant civil society. Active citizen engagement in civil society is not customary for most citizens, as they consider the state to be the sole agent responsible for providing solutions to the country's problems. At this stage, the main challenges stirring the political debate pertain to matters of identity, such as statehood status, nation, language, and church, which leave little room for core issues of civil society, such as social development and human rights.

Therefore, civil society remains a rather marginalized force in Montenegrin society, with the state, the private sector, and the media paying little attention to its activities. As a consequence, many of the recommendations emerging from the CSI assessment focus on building stronger relationships between civil society and other sectors, particularly the state, which is likely to increasingly turn to civil society as a requirement of the pre-accession negotiations with the EU.

CSI Report

Center for Development of Non-Governmental Organizations (CRNVO), *An Assessment of Montenegrin Civil Society 2006—Weak Tradition, Uncertain Future: CIVICUS Civil Society Index Shortened Assessment Tool Report for Montenegro* (Podgorica, Montenegro: CRNVO, 2006).

Notes

1. The CSI Shortened Assessment Tool was implemented in Montenegro by the Center for Development of Non-Governmental Organizations (CRNVO) from September 2005 to September 2006. This chapter presents the main findings of the CSI-SAT and is based on a comprehensive country report for Montenegro, which can be accessed on the CSI pages of the CIVICUS website at http://www.civicus.org.
2. Scale from 1 (low corruption) to 7 (high corruption).
3. The trafficking affair began in late 2002. It refers to a Moldavian girl who was trafficked into Montenegro as a sex slave. The case gained special public attention because of the alleged involvement of high government officials. Unfortunately, it never went to court since the victim went to a third country. The report depicts the misconduct in the handling of the case. The case is often raised in political debates, and it is argued that the officials who opened the case, including the Minister of Interior and National Coordinator for Trafficking, were dismissed as a result.
4. The Centre for Civic Education has developed several month-long programs, such as the Democracy School, Human Rights and Minority Rights School, and Young Leadership School.

Chapter 26

~~◆~~

Nepal[1]

Nepalese civil society has been strongly influenced by the extremely volatile political situation of recent years. After years of unstable multiparty governments and in response to a violent insurgency by Maoist groups, King Gyanendra took direct power in 2005 and declared a state of emergency. Basic rights and freedoms were curtailed, and civil society activities were severely restricted. In April 2006 a people's uprising toppled the king, and a democratic government was restored. The Civil Society Index (CSI) project was implemented during these political upheavals, making it challenging to capture the implications of these immediate and ongoing changes. It is already clear that political space has reopened, but the extent to which the democratic advances will be sustainable remains to be seen.

Table 26.1 Background Information for Nepal

Nepal	
Size (square km)	147,181
Population (millions 2004)	26.6
Population under 15 years (2004)	39.5%
Urban population (2003)	15%
Seats in parliament held by women (2005)	5.9%
Language groups	Nepali (official) with about 30 dialects and 12 other languages
Ethnic groups	Newar, Indian, Gurung, Magar, Tamang, Rai, Limba, Sherpa, Tharu
Religious groups	Hindu 81% (official), Buddhist 11%, Muslim 4%, other 4%
HDI score and ranking (2003)	0.526 (136th)
GDP per capita (US$ 2003)	$1,420
Population living on less than US$2 a day (2003–2004)	68.5%

259

Historical Overview

Civil society in Nepal has a long history that dates back to the ancient *Vedic* age around 2000 BC. Civic life grew during the *Vedic* age, when *dharma* (institutional duties and roles), *shastras* (moral and legal treatises), and *shastartha* (philosophical discourses) shaped the behavior of subjects and monarchs. During this ancient period, Nepal had traditional indigenous organizations, such as *Gurukul* (voluntary residential schools), *Guthi* (trusts), and *Parma* (voluntary contributions and exchange of labor). The history of civil society in Nepal is also closely related to its ethnic composition and caste system, comprising more than sixty ethnic and caste groups.

In 1769 King Prithvi Narayan Shah unified the Himalayan land of Nepal. From 1775 to 1951 the political climate was characterized by confrontation between the royal family and other noble families. The accession of the Rana regime (1846–1951) resulted in a state that was captive to familial loyalty and aristocracy, thus preventing democratic ideas from entering society. The Ranas lost their external support when the British withdrew from India in 1947. They were overthrown in 1951, and the incoming democratic government introduced basic freedoms and rights for citizens. Establishing democracy proved difficult, and tensions between the monarchy and administration prevailed. The Nepali Congress (NC) won Nepal's first election in 1959, but King Mahendra dissolved parliament and banned political parties in 1960; this led to thirty years of authoritarian rule under the Panchayat regime (1959–1990), which suspended basic rights and curtailed civil society activities.

In 1990 a broad coalition of citizen groups, backed by the major political parties, campaigned for basic political reforms. The movement led to strikes and protests across the country, and in November 1990 a new constitution was developed that provided for a constitutional monarchy and a multiparty parliamentary political system. The restoration of democracy in 1990 also made active civil society building possible, particularly through donor-funded programs. Consequently, the number of development and community-based NGOs grew exponentially, and these organizations began to perform important roles in education, health, community development, networking, organizing public discourse, human rights advocacy, and providing relief to those in need.

However, the 1990s were a period of political instability, characterized by fragile government coalitions, frequent changes in government, and the widespread use of patronage and corrupt practices among the political elite. Civil society was not able to provide effective checks against the deteriorating governance situation, with urban NGOs either disinterested or co-opted by government and rural civil society too weak to make its voice heard. Instead, the situation turned violent. In 1997 the Maoists declared a people's war against the government, which had almost completely retreated from rural areas, leaving the population without essential services. In 1999 the war intensified, culminating in November 2001 when a state of emergency was declared to combat the Maoist insurgency.[2]

In February 2005 the king seized all executive powers and again declared a state of emergency. However, civil society protested the restrictions placed on its activities, and antigovernment protests became commonplace in Kathmandu. In April 2006 the monarchy was reduced to a ceremonial role, the Nepali army was brought under civilian control, the Maoist movement was included in the interim government, and work began on drafting an interim constitution. The main parties in the conflict held talks regarding Constituent Assembly elections. The government also reiterated the important role of CSOs in the nation's development, which suggests that the environment for civil society in Nepal might become increasingly conducive.

The State of Civil Society in Nepal

This section provides a summary of key findings of the CSI project in Nepal. It examines the state of Nepalese civil society along four dimensions—structure, environment, values, and impact—highlighting the main weaknesses and strengths.

The Civil Society Diamond (figure 26.1) for Nepal reflects a moderately developed civil society. Civil society's structure is medium sized and it benefits from widespread citizen engagement, though it requires a more organized civil society to facilitate its growth. Until the recent political changes, the environment in Nepal was rather unconducive for civil society's activities, and its impact remained limited.

Structure (1.7)

The structure dimension examines the makeup of civil society in terms of the main characteristics of individual citizen participation and associational life. Nepalese civil society exhibits a medium-sized structure, driven by widespread citizen participation. In contrast, the social composition of organized civil society, its level of organization, and its resources remain problematic and require further development.

Figure 26.1 Civil Society Diamond for Nepal

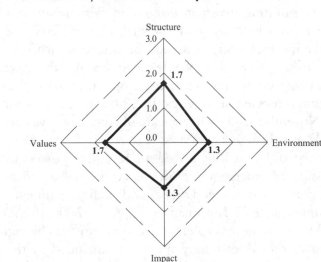

Nepalese civil society exhibits a high level of individual citizen participation in various civic activities. The CSI population survey reveals that 79% of citizens took part in a nonpartisan political action, such as signing a petition or attending a demonstration. Of survey respondents, 55% were members of a CSO, particularly a local-level organization, such as a farmers' association, death rites society, or village committee. Nepalese society, particularly rural communities, is also committed to assisting those in need. According to the survey, 93% of people take part in voluntary work at least once a year, and 86% have taken part in some form of collective community action within the last year. Volunteering in Nepal mainly takes place through mutual aid and self-help activities, various services for the poor, and participation in self-governance mechanisms. It is commonly said that Nepalese people are materially poor but rich in spirit, stemming back to the ancient period.

There are many types of CSOs, active in many sectors and covering a variety of issues, but civil society's social composition is unbalanced, since certain social groups, such as women, the poor, and ethnic minorities, are underrepresented in formal CSOs. In addition, the presence of organized civil society is largely restricted to major towns and urban areas.

With regard to civil society's level of organization, a number of areas require significant development. Communication and cooperation between civil society actors is somewhat limited, but steadily increasing. Some umbrella organizations or federation bodies connect

CSOs, such as the NGO Federation, an umbrella body of more than 2,200 NGOs, and the Nepal Civil Society Forum; however, most stakeholders believe that only a minority of CSOs belong to such groups. There are also examples of cross-sectoral alliances such as the Professional Alliance for Peace and Democracy (PAPAD) and broad-based coalitions pressing for a return to democracy during the 2005 to 2006 crisis. However, since the return to democracy, civil society has remained fragmented and politicized, which might weaken its potential role in the period of democratic transition.

Other areas of weakness include self-regulation mechanisms, such as codes of conduct, which are in a nascent stage of development, support infrastructure, funding, and international linkages. Strengthening civil society's infrastructure in terms of support organizations, resource centers, and networks has received little donor attention and is therefore highly underdeveloped. Unlike local charity-based organizations, many Nepalese CSOs rely on foreign-donor funding, and the sector's financial resources are rather inadequate. Anecdotal evidence suggests that some CSOs do not even have office space to hold meetings with members. Also, the proportion of Nepalese CSOs with international linkages remains negligible, and civil society's participation in international events is nominal.

Environment (1.3)

The environment dimension considers political, legal, socioeconomic, and sociocultural contexts, as well as the relationships between civil society, the state, and the private sector. The findings reveal a relatively disabling operating environment; however, given the recent volatile political situation, the environment is best viewed as being in a state of flux.

When the CSI assessment was conducted, from 2004 to 2005, a major disabling factor was the political context. Political rights and civil liberties were systematically violated, and outspoken CSOs were routinely threatened. The conflict between the government and the Maoists plunged the country into chaos, and the regime lost control over half of its territory. With the Maoists controlling the rural areas, CSOs' work in the countryside was hampered by the violent conflict and political instability. As the conflict intensified, citizens' basic freedoms were suspended, and in April 2005 the government banned any assembly of more than five people. In October 2005 a media order prohibited criticism of the government, and in November a code of conduct was adopted to regulate and restrict the autonomy of NGOs. On both sides of the conflict, summary executions, torture, forced disappearances, unlawful killings, and other human rights abuses proliferated. Following a three-week-long demonstration in April 2006, the regime was ousted and parliament was reinstated. Subsequently, many restrictions against civil society were lifted, and basic rights and freedoms for citizens were reinstated.

Socioeconomic conditions in Nepal are another challenge for civil society. Aside from the adverse economic effects of the recent conflict, Nepal is one of the poorest countries in the world. It ranks 136th in the 2005 Human Development Index. Poverty is widespread, with 32% of the population living below the national poverty line and 82.5% surviving on less than US$2 a day. In addition, the overall infrastructure of the country is rather poor. These socioeconomic challenges make CSOs development work both important and difficult.

Despite the harsh political and economic environment, people have not lost their trust or their sense of public spiritedness, which enables citizens and associations to operate in such a difficult moment of history. Thus, sociocultural norms in Nepal are quite conducive for civil society. This is indicated by the fact that 4 out of 5 respondents to the CSI population survey trust their fellow citizens. Nepalese people also generally feel an obligation to disadvantaged communities, and Hindu-Buddhist religious people believe that unless one fulfills public duties one cannot achieve spiritual emancipation.

In the current period of transition, the government has demonstrated its willingness to dialogue with civil society. The private sector is becoming increasingly engaged with civil society and is becoming more involved in civil society activities. Of stakeholders, 67% report the private sector attitude to be supportive or favorable for civil society. Corporate social responsibility (CSR) and corporate volunteering are drawing more attention in Nepal and many businesses are participating in community activities.

Given the recent rapid political changes in Nepal, it is difficult to fully capture the implications of the new political environment for civil society. Nonetheless, the government's reversal of key political restrictions and its commitment to ensuring a prominent role for civil society in the future of Nepal has reopened the space for civil society. In addition, prevailing sociocultural norms and increased business sector support are likely to nurture the development of civil society.

Values (1.7)

The values dimension examines the extent to which civil society practices and promotes positive values. The findings reflect a somewhat positive value base. Civil society is especially dedicated to democracy, tolerance, nonviolence, and environmental sustainability, while the practice of key values such as democracy and transparency within CSOs leaves much to be desired.

Civil society played a catalytic role in the restoration of democracy and peace in Nepal. The majority of stakeholders could recall campaigns and programs to promote democracy, such as the activities of Pro-Public, a leading Nepalese NGO dedicated to raising public awareness on democracy and curbing corruption. More broadly, civil society activists pioneered and mobilized the 2005 to 2006 movement for democracy and encouraged democratic forces within the government to dialogue with the Maoists.

Civil society organizations also play a role in promoting tolerance and have organized various programs related to mediation, conflict resolution, and peacebuilding among social groups. While the majority of CSOs uses nonviolent means, some groups, such as the Maoists, resort to violence to express their interests. Until their unilateral ceasefire in September 2005, Maoist groups regularly used blockades and violence directed at key businesses, and committed human rights abuses against civilians. Nonetheless, when viewing civil society as a whole, violence tends to be isolated and occasional, and broadly denounced by civil society at large.

Nepal has a rich biological and cultural diversity, making tourism a key asset in the country's economic development. A number of CSOs and conservation groups focus on increasing environmental awareness and conservation practices. Recently, a number of advocacy groups began raising awareness about urban pollution from vehicle and new industry emissions.

Different from its active role in promoting key values in society, civil society's internal norms and processes are rather weak. There are frequent accusations of feudalist governance structures, corruption, and limited internal democracy within CSOs. Civil society actors also identify transparency as a problem, with 93% of stakeholders reporting that CSOs do not make their financial information publicly available. Improving mechanisms for internal democracy, accountability, and transparency are therefore key challenges for many Nepalese CSOs.

Impact (1.3)

The impact dimension assesses civil society's role in governance and society at large. In a country with a long history of autocratic rule, it is not surprising that civil society's influence on governance processes is limited. However, civil society plays a leading role in empowering citizens, particularly marginalized groups.

Civil society's greatest impact on Nepalese governance concerns its participation in restoring parliament in 2006. It has become clear, however, that this did not lead to a return to a stable form of governance. The uncertain period of transition, with frequent battles for power among key political actors, is likely to continue. This will impact civil society's role, which has not come together under a common agenda and remains fragmented and highly politicized.

However, civil society is active in public education, supporting livelihoods and empowering marginalized citizens, such as minorities and women. Also, many CSOs, with the support of international donors, have spearheaded activities to improve the socioeconomic condition of the *dalit*[3] people.

Some stakeholders describe citizens' increasing awareness of human rights as a silent revolution in Nepal. Women activists and organizations are educating women on self-determination, the right to inherit property, and reproductive health rights, as well as raising awareness on specific issues, such as child labor, HIV/AIDS, bonded labor, prostitution, and human trafficking. These various CSO programs to educate citizens on their rights and provide basic skills development are stimulating grassroots social and political changes across the country.

The CSI findings indicate that civil society's overall impact is somewhat limited. While it plays a strong role in empowering marginalized groups, civil society struggles to find a voice in the country's current politicized and volatile governance situation.

Recommendations

During the CSI National Workshop in Kathmandu in May 2006, participants from civil society, the government, and the media gathered to develop recommendations based on civil society's strengths and weaknesses. Five key recommendations are listed below:

- Civil society should reach out to marginalized social groups and communities. This will enable CSOs to become people-centered, rights-based, demand-driven, and change-oriented organizations.
- CSOs should improve their internal governance and transparency to increase legitimacy, public support, and participation.

- CSOs should lobby for increased government support and government should establish mechanisms to work with CSOs.
- CSOs should improve communication and cooperation among themselves. CSOs need to minimize overlapping efforts and share information to increase their impact.
- INGOs in Nepal should work through local partners, and international donors should focus on capacity building for local and national NGOs.

Conclusion

Nepalese civil society has been strongly influenced by the highly volatile political context of recent years. Yet, despite severe government restrictions and the conflict that destabilized the country, Nepalese citizens demonstrated their commitment to a free and democratic society. Widespread citizen participation in the democracy movement contributed to the reinstatement of democracy in Nepal. However, given the uncertain outcomes of the transition and the highly politicized atmosphere, the impact of the people's democratic movement will only be realized as democracy consolidates and social forces begin to work together for the betterment of society. The challenge for civil society is to find its own role, outside of the control of major political forces, to voice the concerns and needs of the many marginalized groups in the country.

CSI Report

Dev Raj Dahal and Tatwa P. Timsina, *Civil Society in Nepal—Searching for a Viable Role: CIVICUS Civil Society Index Report for Nepal* (Kathmandu, Nepal: Institute of Cultural Affairs, 2006).

Notes

1. The CSI assessment was implemented in Nepal by the Institute of Cultural Affairs Nepal from November 2004 to May 2006. This chapter presents the main findings of the CSI and is based on a comprehensive report for Nepal, which can be accessed on the CSI pages of the CIVICUS website at http://www.civicus.org.
2. The Communist Party of Nepal/Maoist (CPN-M or Maoists) is an insurgent group that aims to end the constitutional monarchy and the feudal structure that persists in many parts of Nepal.
3. A dalit is a person whose ancestors were of the caste once called "the untouchables," who performed duties that were important to the well-being of society, but menial in nature.

Chapter 27

The Netherlands[1]

The image of the Netherlands as a stable, tolerant, liberal, and quiet country has recently been challenged by several violent crimes related to fundamental Islam, which led to a heated public debate about the country's approach to immigration and integration. As the Civil Society Index Shortened Assessment Tool (CSI-SAT) study shows, Dutch civil society, which historically played a strong role in mediating social tensions and conflicts, is currently struggling to find answers to this crucial new challenge for Dutch society.

Table 27.1 Background Information for the Netherlands

The Netherlands	
Country size (square km)	41,864
Population (millions 2004)	16.3
Population under 15 years (2004)	18.3%
Urban population (2003)	65.8%
Seats in parliament held by women (2005)	36.7%
Language groups	Dutch (official), Frisian, and Flemish
Ethnic groups	Dutch 83%
Religious groups	Roman Catholic 31%, Protestant 21%, Muslim 4%
HDI score and ranking (2003)	0.943 (12th)
GDP per capita (US$ 2003)	$29,371
Unemployment rate (% of total labor force)	4.3%

Historical Overview

The roots of Dutch civil society date to the Middle Ages, when people living in the Low Countries practiced joint water management to deal with the perils of living close to the sea. Until the end of the nineteenth century, it was primarily the churches and the bourgeoisie that drove the expansion of associational life. This shifted significantly at the turn of the twentieth century, when the state assumed a stronger role and the processes of industrialization, modernization, and emancipation led to the emergence of three distinct social blocs, or pillars—Catholic, Protestant, and Socialist—that were in sharp conflict with each other. The Dutch system of *Verzuiling* (pillarization) sought to address these tensions by organizing all aspects of social and civic life along these pillars. For example, a specific political party, trade union, and broadcasting organization existed for each pillar. Also, community life and the welfare system were divided into associations separated by the three pillars, and the leaders of the pillars negotiated the necessary compromises in various consensus-oriented institutions.

In addition, based on the principle of subsidiarity[2] and in the context of a divided society, the Dutch state relied heavily on welfare organizations associated with each respective pillar in the provision of a wide range of social services to the population. This created one of the largest nonprofit sectors in the world.[3] While secularization and modernization processes in the 1970s led to a depillarization of Dutch society, the prominent role of nonprofit organizations in the field of social services remains a significant feature of Dutch civil society today. However, in recent years an opening up of the traditional welfare system has increased competition among nonprofits and service providers from the private sector.

Patterns of associational participation in the Netherlands, similar to elsewhere in modern Western societies, have undergone significant change during the last three decades. Membership rates in the traditional pillarized forms of association (political parties, churches, and trade unions) have decreased, and new forms of association, such as public benefit-oriented and recreational organizations, have attracted growing membership. More recently, new forms of civic engagement that are not bound to formal organizations, such as looser networks and internet discussion groups, are gaining ground and have contributed to further transforming the landscape of Dutch civil society.

Figure 27.1 Civil Society Diamond for the Netherlands

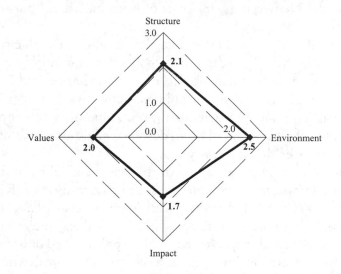

The State of Civil Society in the Netherlands

Whereas the Dutch CSI team sought to adhere to the broad and encompassing definition of civil society proposed by CIVICUS, the fact that existing studies mainly focus on formal organizations resulted in an underrepresentation of informal forms of associational life in the study. In addition, political parties and chambers of commerce were excluded from the definition because they were viewed as belonging to the public and private sectors, respectively.

This section provides a summary of key findings of the Civil Society Index (CSI) project in the Netherlands. It examines the state of Dutch civil society along four dimensions—structure, environment, values, and impact—highlighting the main weaknesses and strengths.

The Civil Society Diamond (figure 27.1) visually summarizes the assessment's findings in the Netherlands. It depicts a rather strong civil society with a fairly well-developed structure that operates in an enabling environment. Although civil society's values are assessed as rather strong, civil society's impact on society at large is rather disappointing, particularly because of its somewhat limited role in assisting marginalized groups in society and its limited impact on public policy.

Structure (2.1)

The structure dimension examines the makeup of civil society in terms of the main characteristics of individual citizen participation and associational life. The CSI assessment found a rather strong civil society in the Netherlands, in terms of both individual participation and organized civil society.

In general, the levels of civic engagement among Dutch citizens are high, with the notable exception of collective community activities. More than 4 out of 5 Dutch citizens donate to charity, and 3 out of 5 engage in nonpartisan forms of political action, such as signing petitions or participating in a demonstration. A majority of people are a member of at least one association, despite a slight downturn in membership rates over the past few years.

Given the current debate about the porous social fabric of the Netherlands, it is important to examine the social composition of civil society organizations (CSOs). Individuals with lower levels of education, the unemployed, single people, older people, homemakers, and urban dwellers are somewhat underrepresented. A more pronounced underrepresentation is found among immigrants, especially Muslims, who have a participation rate 24% lower than the national average. Although there are no hard data on the representation of these groups in CSO leadership positions, the CSI assessment group believes bias against the groups mentioned above is likely to be even more pronounced at these levels.

The key features of organized civil society in the Netherlands indicate the presence of a robust civic sector. Civil society organizations are present throughout the country, rely on a relatively strong system of support centers, and are fairly well-organized in various umbrella bodies and networks, which increasingly span different subsectors of the civic sector. There are extraordinarily strong linkages between Dutch civil society and international networks, which reflect the historical, geographical, and ideological position of the Netherlands, rendering the country particularly open and vulnerable to global processes. In addition, CSOs generally do not suffer from any serious financial, human, or technological resource problems. However, whereas many organizations once relied quite heavily on public funding, the government's move toward cutting funding to nonprofits and increasingly introducing more competition into its financial allocation procedures has shaken up the comfortable funding arrangements of many organizations.

Thus, whereas the general picture depicts a rather strong Dutch civil society, in terms of both levels of civic engagement and levels of funding, there exist some worrisome trends that may indicate a weakening of civil society's robust structure.

Environment (2.5)

The environment dimension considers political, legal, socioeconomic, and sociocultural contexts, as well as the relationships among civil society, the state, and the private sector. Dutch civil society operates in an enabling environment, characterized by favorable legal and socioeconomic conditions. However, civil society's relationships with the state—and particularly with the private sector—leave some room for improvement.

The Netherlands is an established liberal democracy where the rule of law and basic freedoms and rights are protected and upheld. In addition, political party competition is vibrant and follows democratic procedures. The Dutch state is largely able to fulfill its given functions, even though there are mounting criticisms of its lack of efficacy and efficiency. However, as a consequence of the government's measures in relation to the war on terror, certain political rights and civil liberties are increasingly being infringed upon, particularly those of Muslim organizations.

The specific legal provisions for CSOs' registration, allowable advocacy activities, and tax regulations were evaluated as supporting the functioning of CSOs. The state has a generally favorable attitude toward civil society, signified by conducive de jure provisions of the legal framework. It is interesting to note that the de facto relationship among the sectors has recently witnessed some negative trends. The widely recognized and far-reaching consultation mechanisms between the state and politically active civil society have been cut back and are being replaced by more informal contacts. In addition, state funding of nonprofits is decreasing, and the autonomy of certain critical CSOs has come under attack by the government. Examples of such assault include the heated debate with the Minister of Integration and Immigration regarding the treatment of immigrants, and incidents related to the Minister for Development Cooperation regarding the autonomy of NGOs, which receive state funding. Thus, the political space available for civil society is decreasing.

Similarly, the relationship between civil society and the private sector is far from ideal, although the CSI study noticed an upward trend. While principles and practices of corporate social responsibility (CSR) are on the increase among Dutch businesses, to some extent they remain lip service rather than sincere commitment to society at large. In addition, the extent of corporate philanthropy is limited, and private philanthropy— which combines donations from individuals, businesses, and foundations—makes up less than 3% of the overall funding of the sector.[4] Corporate philanthropy focuses on the apolitical fields of sports and recreation (37%) and culture (23%), while international development and environmental protection receive only a minimal contribution (2%).

Despite these somewhat negative trends, which cause concern for the continued safeguarding of civil liberties, Dutch civil society continues to exist and function in a conducive environment.

Values (2.0)

The values dimension examines the extent to which civil society practices and promotes positive values. The CSI assessment finds the values base for Dutch civil society to be quite strong. However, over the past few years, insecurities have surfaced, connected to debates over the social integration of minorities and immigrants.

Civil society's commitment to transparency and nonviolence is particularly strong. Dutch CSOs are regarded as exemplary in practicing these values internally and are rather active in promoting them throughout society. However, incidents of violence by extremist groups are on the rise, often targeting religious buildings. Other values, such as gender equity, are fairly well-entrenched in civil society. This is indicated by the fact that 41% of all voluntary leadership positions are occupied by women. Historically, Dutch CSOs have also been active in promoting democracy and environmental principles, and in the fight against poverty.

In the context of the current public debate about social tolerance and diversity, civil society receives a rather low score. Given the current prominence of these issues, there are too few civil society campaigns dedicated to the promotion of social tolerance and respect for diversity. Thus, it appears that although Dutch civil society is strongly committed to its traditional core values of gender equity, democracy, environmental protection, and social justice, it is responding with difficulty to the emerging challenge of how to promote a tolerant and diverse society in the Netherlands.

Impact (1.7)

The impact dimension assesses civil society's role in governance and society at large. It represents the lowest score among the four dimensions of Dutch civil society. Here, civil society's modest influence on the policy process and its limited role in assisting marginalized groups in society stand out as weak points.

Given the tradition of a consultative style of decisionmaking, in which key CSOs had ample access to government consultative bodies, it is somewhat surprising that civil society's policy impact is limited. The assessment indicates that the current government regards the old model of consultative policymaking as outdated, and—compared to other social forces, particularly the business sector—CSOs now yield less influence in Dutch politics.

Overall, the CSI paints a picture of a moderately influential civil society, rather engaged as a watchdog of government and the private sector, which works with the Dutch population through public education and the provision of social services. Consequently, public trust in CSOs is high, with 77% of citizens showing confidence in voluntary associations, 72% in trade unions, and 46% in church institutions. Interestingly, because survey results show significantly higher interpersonal trust levels for CSO members (61.3%) than for nonmembers (41.4%), CSOs seem to play a positive role in building social capital in society.

A key weakness, identified by the CSI assessment group, is civil society's limited role in empowering marginalized groups. The insufficient integration of immigrants and the growing intolerance in Dutch society stand out as a sore thumb, and are seen as inadequately addressed by Dutch civil society.

Conclusion

Dutch civil society is generally regarded as one of the world's most vibrant and sustainable civic sectors. This view is largely corroborated by the CSI assessment, which found a rather active and well-organized civil society operating in an enabling environment. However, the study also identified a number of negative trends, particularly with regard to civil society's limited role in maintaining social cohesion (especially in light of growing social tensions and the state's shift toward a less accommodating style of interaction with CSOs). The hope is that the CSI process of joint assessment and reflection will help civil society stakeholders address these emerging challenges.

CSI Report

De Nieuwe Dialoog, *CIVICUS Civil Society Index Report for the Netherlands* (Netherlands: De Nieuwe Dialoog, 2006).

Notes

1. The CSI Shortened Assessment Tool was implemented in the Netherlands by De Nieuwe Dialoog from January to June 2006. This chapter presents the main findings of the CSI-SAT and is based on a comprehensive country report for the Netherlands, which can be accessed on the CSI pages of the CIVICUS website at http://www.civicus.org.

2. Rooted in the social philosophy of modern Catholicism, the subsidiarity principle proposes that the institution that is the most local and the most directly linked to citizens should provide social services, and that voluntary organizations fulfill this requirement better than state agencies.

3. A. Burger et al., "Netherlands," in *Global Civil Society: Dimensions of the Nonprofit Sector*, eds. Lester Salamon et al. (Baltimore, MD: The Johns Hopkins Comparative Nonprofit Sector Project, 1999): 145–61.

4. Ibid.

Chapter 28

~~~~~

Northern Ireland[1]

Northern Ireland and its civil society have been marred by more than thirty years of conflict. The Civil Society Index (CSI) assessment was conducted at a time when the nation might be able to leave this history of conflict behind. The CSI assessment marks the first comprehensive study of civil society in Northern Ireland, and indicates the potential role for civil society as a vanguard of cross-community engagement and cooperation.

Table 28.1 Background Information for Northern Ireland

Northern Ireland	
Size (square km)	13,576
Population (millions 2005)	1,724,408
Population under 15 years (2005)	355,074
Urban population (% of total 2003)	65.1%
Seats in parliament held by women (2005)	11.1%
Language group	English
Ethnic groups	Caucasian 99.1%, Chinese 0.2%, Other 0.7%
Religious groups	Protestant and other Christian 53.1%, Roman Catholic 43.7%, Other 3.2%
HDI score and ranking (2003)	0.930 (13th)*
GDP per capita (US$ 2003)	$29,000
Unemployment rate (% of total labor force)	4.60%

*UK score

Historical Overview

The administrative entity of Northern Ireland did not exist until the Government of Ireland Act of 1920. Prior to 1920, Northern Ireland, like the rest of Ireland, existed as part of the United Kingdom (UK). While Northern Irish civil society shared many characteristics that defined the development of civil society in the United Kingdom, it also had unique features, such as the significant role in public life played by churches and faith-based organizations.

Two distinct groups have significantly shaped society in Northern Ireland: (1) the Roman Catholic Irish and (2) the immigrant Protestant English and Scots. Civil society was (and to some degree still is) organized along these sectarian lines. Prior to the 1960s, two separate systems of social volunteerism provided services to those in need. Since the mid-1960s, divisions and inequities came to the fore, the civil rights movement gained currency, and sectarian violence ensued. The violence would simmer and erupt from time to time during the next thirty years. By 2000, more than 3,600 people had been killed and 36,000 injured as a result of the conflict.

During the 1970s, when violence peaked, strong vocal community groups emerged throughout the country. The rapid growth of community action during this period was a direct response to the urgency of need and the partial breakdown in the statutory provision of health, education, and housing services. Formal government policies regarding civil society organizations (CSOs) were also introduced in the 1970s.

In 1998 the Good Friday Agreement was adopted. This momentous event was followed by the establishment of the New Northern Ireland Assembly, the end of direct rule from Westminster, and the creation of a Civic Forum that acts as a consultative mechanism between civil society and the government on social, economic, and cultural matters. During this period, with the support of European Union (EU) structural funds, the voluntary and community sector grew rapidly in Northern Ireland. A range of partnership programs and consultative bodies institutionalized dialogue and cooperation with the government, and firmly entrenched the role of civil society in community development.

Since October 14, 2002, the suspension of devolved powers and an absence of local political control have somewhat weakened civil society's influence on government. However, a range of policy documents emanating from Westminster in relation to civil society regeneration and its activities will have significant impact on the sector's growth.

Civil society played an important role in filling the democratic deficit during the years of civil unrest in Northern Ireland. When the government was unable to provide social services (or considered unacceptable), voluntary and community organizations delivered services to communities and those in need, albeit within two parallel systems of voluntary social welfare: Catholic and Protestant. In recent years, government and EU resources have poured into the community to improve sectarian relations between Catholics and Protestants. However, divisions between the communities persist, with greater residential segregation and a growing sense of alienation within the Protestant community. The legacy of conflict still casts its shadow, and many remain reluctant to become involved in collective cross-community action in Northern Ireland.

The State of Civil Society in Northern Ireland

This section provides a summary of key findings of the Civil Society Index (CSI) project in Northern Ireland. It examines the state of civil society in Northern Ireland along four dimensions—structure, environment, values, and impact—highlighting the main weaknesses and strengths. To operationalize the concept of civil society, the National Advisory Group (NAG) adopted CIVICUS's broad and inclusive definition of civil society, including positive and negative and peaceful and violent forces that may advance or obstruct social progress.

Northern Ireland's Diamond (figure 28.1) visually summarizes the assessment's findings. The diamond is well-developed and balanced in its four dimensions. Civil society's structure is relatively strong, but it is impeded by limited cross-community citizen participation. The environment is enabling for civil society, and is supported by a positive political, socioeconomic, and legal context and by strong state–civil society relations. Civil society practices and promotes positive values to a relatively significant extent, but efforts to promote internal transparency within civil society are limited. The impact of civil society is relatively significant, although it needs to be improved with regard to public policy and its activities in holding both the state and the private sector accountable.

Structure (1.8)

The structure dimension examines the makeup of civil society in terms of the main characteristics of individual citizen participation and associational life. The structure of civil society in Northern Ireland

Figure 28.1 Civil Society Diamond for Northern Ireland

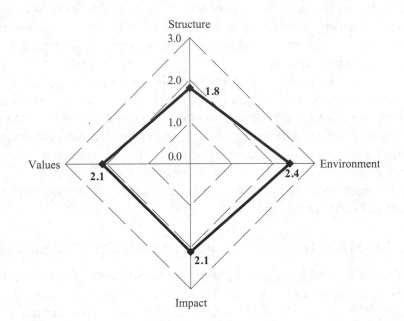

benefits from a culture of giving, in terms of both time and money. CSOs are widely distributed throughout Northern Ireland, a significant proportion of the population participates in civil society, and resources are adequate for the sector's activities. However, self-regulation and poor cooperation among civil society actors are distinct weaknesses of the sector's structure.

Civil society has a solid foundation of volunteer activity and charitable giving. The proportion of citizens who give to charity is higher in Northern Ireland than in the rest of the UK. According to a 2004 survey conducted by the Northern Ireland Council for Voluntary Action (NICVA), 94% of citizens donated to charity in the previous month. Charitable donations tend to be part of a "small change culture," in which small amounts are given regularly to collectors on the street or through door-to-door solicitation. Approximately 60% of the population engages in formal or informal volunteering, and 61% of citizens belong to at least one CSO. Membership of religious or faith-based organizations and sports organizations is also much higher in Northern Ireland than in the rest of the UK, while trade union involvement is much lower.

Self-regulation within CSOs is moderate. Only 40% of representatives believe the sector is well regulated. In the absence of a regulatory framework, and aside from legal requirements emanating from government and donor agencies, there is no pressure or incentive for CSOs to self-regulate. As a result, the majority of stakeholders emphasize the need for self-regulation and legal provisions that are more binding, e.g. through the establishment of a UK-type Charity Commission to increase CSOs' accountability and transparency.

Civil society's structure is also weakened by a shortage of collective cross-community cooperation. Conflict between Catholic and Protestant communities impedes a sense of connectivity and collaboration in Northern Irish civil society. However, there have been recent examples of cross-community support for public issues, such as campaigns against the war in Iraq.

Environment (2.4)

The environment dimension considers political, legal, socioeconomic, and sociocultural contexts, as well as the relationships among civil society, the state, and the private sector. The external environment in Northern Ireland is very conducive to civil society's growth and development. Civil society enjoys a largely supportive political, socioeconomic, and legal context, and particularly favorable relations with the state. Civil society's operating environment could be further improved by cultivating better relations with the private sector, by developing higher levels of trust and tolerance within society, and by stimulating increased corporate philanthropy.

Citizens enjoy a wide range of civil and political rights, and the rule of law is generally upheld, although there are instances of vigilante policing. Legally, there are no official constraints inhibiting civil society from criticizing the government. A wide range of tax incentives exist to encourage individuals and businesses to make charitable donations. CSOs register either as a company limited by guarantee or as an unincorporated association. The majority of CSOs register as unincorporated associations. There is no standardized registration process. Instead groups apply for charitable status with the Inland Revenue, which is inexpensive and straightforward. However, it is recognized that the current level of regulation could invite abuse, and that civil society is fortunate that it has not suffered any major scandals.

As regards relations with the state, CSOs operate freely and are subject only to reasonable oversight. However, CSO stakeholders did voice concerns that the government's increased funding of CSO service delivery may constrain the ability of these organizations to criticize government. Nevertheless, there are well-supported institutionalized structures for dialogue between the state and CSOs, such as the Joint

Government, Voluntary, and Community Sector Forum. A wide range of government funding and grant programs are available to CSOs, and government is the largest source of income for voluntary and community organizations, contributing 37.4% of the sector's income in Northern Ireland, compared to 29% in the rest of the United Kingdom.

The primary weakness of civil society's environment is its relationship with the private sector and corporate philanthropy. The level of corporate support to civil society in Northern Ireland is far less than in the rest of the United Kingdom, although corporate giving is expanding. Nonetheless, research indicates that the notion of corporate social responsibility (CSR) remains poorly developed and less entrenched in Northern Ireland than in the rest of the United Kingdom.

In addition to weak relations with the private sector, civil society is impeded by low levels of trust and tolerance. Figures collected in 1999 indicated that 39.5% of the Northern Irish population believed people could be trusted, which disguises a society with high levels of mistrust between the Catholic and Protestant communities. These figures show that a significant proportion of people feel trustful on an abstract level, although the situation appears very different when it comes to day-to-day living, which is still characterized by intercommunity fear and mistrust. There are ongoing sectarian attacks, divisions in local communities, and growing alienation felt in the Protestant community. In addition, the incarceration of asylum seekers and increased incidence of attacks and discrimination against ethnic minorities reveal a lack of tolerance toward perceived outsiders.

Values (2.1)

The values dimension examines the extent to which civil society practices and promotes positive values. The CSI finds that Northern Irish civil society practices and promotes positive values to a relatively significant extent, even though there are some areas of concern, such as the limited practice and promotion of democracy and transparency by CSOs.

With little regulatory pressure on civil society, CSOs are left to self-regulate their internal practices. There is hope that changes in the regulatory framework will improve public monitoring and further develop the democratic practices within civil society. With regard to civil society's transparency, corruption is considered to be fairly rare, although a recent report by the Independent Monitoring Commission claimed that community organizations are often used as fronts for various paramilitary groups. However, no publicly established evidence supports these claims. In addition, CSOs' financial transparency could be improved. For example, CSOs registered as limited companies are legally required to make their accounts publicly available, but CSOs registered as unincorporated associations are bound by no such legal requirements.

The picture remains mixed on the sensitive issues of nonviolence and tolerance. Many CSOs have adopted policies designed to prevent racist and discriminatory language and to encourage peace among communities. However, some CSOs—in particular, paramilitary groups and supporters of the Catholic-Nationalist and Protestant-Loyalist communities—are intolerant of other sections of society. Of these, the majority are observing a ceasefire and some are disarming, although others remain actively engaged in violent attacks on members of the opposite community. It can be generally stated that some members of community and voluntary organizations and of some political parties have been involved in violence, although these activities are widely denounced and not endorsed by civil society at large.

Despite these incidents of intolerance and isolated violence, civil society's role in promoting tolerance and nonviolence in society is substantive, with almost every tenth CSO focusing its efforts on cross-community cooperation and tolerance. Prominent organizations such as the Irish Network for Nonviolent Action, Training, and Education, actively promote nonviolence, and the trade unions are working to deter violent attacks on their members working at community level.

Northern Irish civil society has a particularly strong commitment to overcoming poverty. Civil society's activities in this field enjoy broad-based support and strong public visibility. Key players are the Northern Ireland Anti-Poverty Network (a virtual network with more than 300 members) and the Society of St. Vincent de Paul, whose nationwide branches have helped to alleviate poverty for the past 150 years.

Impact (2.1)

The impact dimension assesses civil society's role in governance and society at large. Although civil society's impact on society is rather significant, particularly with regard to empowering communities and marginalized groups, it has a somewhat poor record in influencing politics.

With respect to influencing public policy, the political circumstances in Northern Ireland are unique because of the absence of democratic government. Civil society's influence on the national budget, for example, is restricted to the local level. Although anti-poverty organizations and trade unions attempt to influence the budget, their work tends to focus on specific issue areas and does not have much impact.

Many organizations function as watchdogs of the state, but only 6% of stakeholders feel that their efforts are successful. This may indicate a fear of biting the hand that feeds, because government is the single largest donor to Northern Irish CSOs. All CSOs working to hold the private sector accountable are part of wider UK-based efforts, which often fail to progress far in Northern Ireland. For example, a boycott of Shell fuel in the rest of the United Kingdom did not transfer to Northern Ireland, despite widespread public support. This may be partly because of the relatively small private sector in Northern Ireland, an economy that is dominated by its public sector, and partly because the majority of companies in Northern Ireland are UK firms that have headquarters in other parts of the United Kingdom.

In the context of a historically weak state, civil society has the most significant impact in empowering citizens and meeting social needs. For example, dozens of housing associations provide affordable rental housing to more than 20,000 households. Likewise, CSOs provide services such as health and social care, guidance and training, to 90,000 families (almost one-third of the entire population). Northern Irish CSOs are most active in assisting marginalized groups such as ethnic minorities, the unemployed, and victims of domestic violence, and have gained a public image as effective lobbyists and first-line providers of services for these groups. This is due to the fact that CSOs focus more on the empowerment and participation of the target groups than do the state providers. However, it has to be noted that they receive substantial government funding for carrying out these social service activities.

Because of their strong penetration in society, voluntary and community organizations are among the most trusted institutions in Northern Ireland. Their ratings are twice as high as those of the central government, local government, or political parties, and are higher than the ratings for similar organizations in the rest of the United Kingdom.

Although civil society's social impact is assessed as relatively strong, given the level of resources, skills, and conducive operating environment in Northern Ireland, CSI stakeholders feel that civil society's impact should be greater.

Recommendations

The state of civil society in Northern Ireland was the focus of the Northern Ireland Council for Voluntary Action at its annual conference in Belfast on December 2, 2005. During the forum, participants from CSOs, the government, and academia reflected on the CSI results for Northern Ireland. Key recommendations include the following:

- Promote the concept of civil society: The assessment process reveals an underlying lack of knowledge and acceptance of civil society as a tool to bring various types of organizations together.
- Practice and promote transparency: The introduction of a Charity Commission will likely be an important opportunity to mount a campaign focused on such CSO practices as transparency and accountability.
- Cultivate a relationship between civil society and the private sector: Civil society needs to develop positive relations with the private sector to secure funding and promote a better understanding of the benefits of CSR.
- Improve efforts to promote tolerance within society: Although campaigns to promote tolerance have been conducted, tension and mistrust between Catholic and Protestant communities persist. CSOs should ensure that their organizations have representation from both communities, and work to reduce duplicating the spending of public resources by similar organizations within both communities.

Conclusion

It is perhaps inevitable that, despite significant political achievements over the past decade, civil society still reflects the fragmented nature of Northern Ireland's society. There is no unifying agenda underpinning civil society's diverse efforts. However, it is important that all organizations within this sector seek to foster collective cross-community action and social tolerance. A strategy should be developed that engenders a sense of common purpose, informs key civil society actors, and encourages them to increase cooperation. Increased interaction will enable these actors to learn how their respective roles and activities influence one another and contribute to civil society's growth as a whole in Northern Ireland.

CSI Report

J.J. McCarron, *Civil Society in Northern Ireland—A New Beginning?: CIVICUS Civil Society Index Report for Northern Ireland* (Belfast, Northern Ireland: Northern Ireland Council for Voluntary Action, 2006).

Notes

1. The CSI assessment was implemented in Northern Ireland by the Northern Ireland Council for Voluntary Action (NICVA) from April 2004 to July 2005. This chapter presents the main findings of the CSI and is based on a comprehensive country report for Northern Ireland, which can be accessed on the CSI pages of the CIVICUS website at http://www.civicus.org.

Chapter 29

Orissa[1]

In Orissa, one of the poorest states of India, the state's role in service provision is declining, foreign aid and investment are increasing, and major industrial development is taking place. Thus, there is an increasing need for civil society to channel people's concerns into the governance system and to allow for people's participation in development initiatives. However, the extent to which civil society is able and ready to meet this challenge and become a catalyst in the state's development process is a topic of debate.

Table 29.1 Background Information for Orissa

Orissa, India	
Size of state (square km)	155,707
Population (millions 2001)	36.8
Population under 14 years (2005)	14.99%
Urban population (2003)	28.30%
Seats in parliament held by women (2005)	8.21%
Language groups	Oriya, English, Hindi, Telgu, Bengali, Santhali, and many dialects
Ethnic groups	62 indigenous tribal communities
Religious groups	Hindu 94.67%
HDI score and ranking	0.404 (11th of 15 major states of India)
Population living below poverty line*	47.15%

*The poverty line is calculated on the basis of kilocalories, not income.

Historical Overview

Orissa is one of twenty-eight states that make up modern India, and it is widely recognized as a cultural melting pot of eastern, western, northern, and southern India. Historically, civil society in Orissa has roots in the ancient traditions of collectivism, philanthropy, and religious duties.

Mostly based on an agrarian economy, Orissa's sizable peasant class has frequently been suppressed by rulers, and Orissa's history is replete with peasant uprisings against exploitation, such as the Khurda Paika, Keonjhar, and Nayagarh uprisings; the Ghumsur revolts; and the Rayat movement in Ganjam. In the early twentieth century, local movements merged with the mainstream pan-Indian independence struggle to demand social emancipation for the masses, following Gandhi's philosophy, which aimed to educate the rural poor, emancipate women, and remove "untouchability."

In the mid-1930s unionism gained currency among the working class. The Rice Mill Labour Association was established in 1935 and marked the formation of the first trade union in Orissa. In 1939 the Press Workers' Union became the first registered trade union, followed by the formation of other unions, particularly in the manufacturing and mining sectors. Various religious institutions, such as the *Mathas*[2] or *Bhagabat Tungis,*[3] existed in all villages as centers for collective action for religious enlightenment, education, and welfare activities aimed at helping the poor and those in need.

India achieved independence in 1947. However, well-defined class and caste structures remained a defining feature of society. The caste system was premised on social stratification. It determined livelihood opportunities and the organization of society, preventing social mobility and protecting existing power relations in society. As a result, by the 1970s, civil society in Orissa remained fragmented along caste lines and the corresponding professions. Various associations and committees represented caste interests, and a code of conduct often existed for the community that reinforced social norms and responsibilities. Despite the fact that one caste group or community may have dominated and subjugated another, each caste had an active civil society, particularly in the areas of education, culture, religion, and social harmony.

The period immediately following independence was also full of social optimism, and CSOs and the government were actively engaged in a broad range of development initiatives. The government's failure to deliver basic services to the population and meet its development aspirations led to growing citizen discontent by the 1970s. As a result, movements against the state government took shape in Orissa, paralleling national-level movements. Civil society became occupied with resistance activities, such as those in opposition to development projects that displaced locals and those demanding forest and environmental protection.

These and other social movements persisted throughout the 1980s and 1990s. The relationship between government and NGOs fluctuated between confrontation and cooperation. NGOs continued to contentiously pressure the ruling elite to instill a more responsive system of governance, especially with regard to service delivery and equal access to public services for all citizens. By the turn of the century, the state government of Orissa increasingly came to recognize civil society's potential role in development and explored modes of cooperation to jointly implement public programs. At the same time, globalization, liberalization, and privatization processes weakened the state's authority and rendered the need for an active citizenry as important as ever.

The State of Civil Society in Orissa

This section provides a summary of key findings of the Civil Society Index (CSI) project in Orissa, India. It examines the state of Orissan civil society along four dimensions—structure, environment, values, and impact—highlighting the main weaknesses and strengths.

The Civil Society Diamond (figure 29.1) visually depicts the CSI findings in Orissa. Civil society is relatively small and generally balanced in its four dimensions. The structure of civil society is rather weak because of a poorly organized and underresourced civil society sector. Despite a stable political context, the operating environment in Orissa remains somewhat unconducive and is impeded by unfavorable socioeconomic factors and inadequate relations between civil society, the state, and the private sector. The values of civil society are its strongest asset, with tolerance, nonviolence, democracy, and environmental sustainability well-embedded in its daily work. Overall, civil society's impact is assessed as relatively insignificant, with particular weaknesses in the fields of advocacy and monitoring the state and the private sector.

Structure (1.2)

The structure dimension examines the makeup of civil society in terms of the main characteristics of individual citizen participation and associational life. The structure of civil society in Orissa is

Figure 29.1 Civil Society Diamond for Orissa

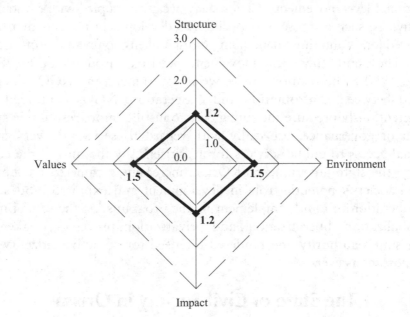

assessed as weak. This is primarily because of the underrepresentation of marginalized groups within civil society, as well as the poor organization and the weak financial sustainability of the sector.

Civil society's main structural asset is the rather vibrant and broad civic engagement of Orissans. Charitable giving and volunteering are particularly prevalent forms of civic activities. Findings from the CSI population survey indicate that 4 out of 5 citizens donate to charity regularly, particularly for religious and spiritual purposes. Volunteering is also widespread, with 9 out of 10 respondents to the population survey claiming to volunteer regularly, such as by helping neighbors or fellow citizens in need. The same survey reveals that a slight majority of respondents are members of a CSO, with religious organizations (22%), cooperatives (17%), and neighborhood village committees (15%) being the most popular types, while participation in urban and more modern types of CSOs is much less widespread. Thus, there are firmly rooted traditions of civic engagement in Orissa, which create a vibrant associational life, especially at the community level.

However, civil society is not free from power dynamics. The caste and patriarchal system of society reproduces itself in civil society's social makeup. Certain social groups—particularly women, rural people, religious minorities, and the poor—are underrepresented in civil society's membership and leadership, whereas the elite is overrepresented.

The level of organization of Orissa's civil society is underdeveloped. There are few networks, federations, or umbrella bodies for most types of CSOs, although networks among NGOs are more prevalent. Self-regulation in CSOs is also weak and few efforts are being made to establish a code of conduct or other means of self-regulation. Nearly 80% of stakeholders indicate that civil society's support infrastructure, such as resource centers and information hubs, is limited or does not exist at all. Similarly, only a limited number of Orissan CSOs have international linkages.

Communication among CSOs in Orissa ranges from weak to moderate. Numerous NGOs regularly work in the same district on the same issues but remain uncoordinated, resulting in duplicated efforts and inefficient use of resources. However, with the increased use of computers and internet access, information sharing and communication are expected to improve. In the meantime, inadequate coordination, networking, and communication will remain key obstacles for civil society's future growth.

A majority of stakeholders who participated in the CSI believe that financial resources in Orissa are inadequate for CSOs to achieve their goals. The primary sources of funding are membership fees (38%), government sources (27%), and donations (17%). Foreign funding only accounts for a small portion of budgets in Orissa (9%). Many CSOs appear to have the human resources required to achieve their goals, but a large majority of stakeholders view financial and technical resources as absent or limited.

The structure of civil society is rather weak. Although the findings reveal a rather strong citizen support base, organized civil society is poorly connected, resources are inadequate to achieve desired goals, and social composition is skewed toward the more well-off segments of society.

Environment (1.5)

The environment dimension considers political, legal, socioeconomic, and sociocultural contexts, as well as the relationships between civil society, the state, and the private sector. The external environment is somewhat disabling for the development of a vibrant civil society. Political rights and civil liberties are respected, but pervasive corruption, an indifferent private sector, and a problematic socioeconomic context pose challenges for civil society.

Orissa is a particularly poor state in India, where nearly 50% of the 37 million citizens live below the national poverty line. Similarly, literacy rates, infant mortality, and per capita consumption of electricity are also lower than the national average. These adverse socioeconomic conditions limit civil society's professional capacity and its ability to function effectively.

While the basic tenets of democracy and human rights are respected in Orissa, the state's governance practices feature a series of problems, including widespread corruption, an unresponsive and rather ineffective public administration, and occasional violations of the rule of law. The prevalence of corruption is a significant concern for both the government and the public. Of the twenty-eight Indian states, Orissa is ranked as the twelfth most corrupt; a recent study found that officials from eighteen of Orissa's twenty-five public sector units embezzled millions of dollars.

The state generally accepts the existence of an independent civil society and increasingly sees CSOs as key partners in its development programs. Still, the CSI stakeholder survey reveals that CSOs are occasionally subject to unwarranted government interference, which usually relates to issues of displacement and rehabilitation of local people, resulting from industrial developments; there may also be police interference during rallies and demonstrations. Dialogue between state and civil society is neither frequent nor balanced among the different types of CSOs, and mostly focuses on professional associations and certain civil society networks. Cooperation in the implementation of governmental programs is more widespread because the state increasingly draws on developmental NGOs and community-based organizations as partners in service delivery, and the state is therefore a significant funder of a large number of CSOs.

The relationship between civil society and the private sector is seen as weak. Findings from the media review and stakeholder consultations indicate a perception of private sector indifference toward civil society. Likewise, notions of corporate social responsibility (CSR) have not taken root in Orissa and many businesses disregard the negative social and environmental impact of their work. Corporate philanthropy to civil society remains limited although many firms contribute to small-scale community development activities. The study also finds a shortage of civil society initiatives to engage the private sector and promote changes in corporate strategies.

Values (1.5)

The values dimension examines the extent to which civil society practices and promotes positive values. Orissan civil society is based on a moderate foundation of positive values. Tolerance, nonviolence, and environmental protection are strong values for civil society, whereas gender inequity and a lack of transparency and democratic practices in CSOs constitute problematic areas.

Civil society in Orissa is quite tolerant, and citizens belonging to different social groups tend to be open and supportive of one another. Isolated groups within civil society, such as the *Naxalites*,[4] occasionally resort to violence, but violence is generally denounced by civil society at large. The activities of civil society to promote nonviolence mostly consist of campaigns and demonstrations for peace, and protest rallies opposing gender violence, child abuse, and violence against the *dalits*.[5]

Civil society is actively involved in environmental sustainability initiatives. Environmental activism is increasing; protests (such as civil society's campaign to prevent the displacement of people in the face of large-scale development projects) have caused the government to improve resettlement and rehabilitation policies, and to take caution when establishing new mineral-based industries. Overall, civil society is most active in protecting natural resources such as Orissa's lakes, mountains, and mineral deposits.

Specific weaknesses in civil society's values relate to internal mechanisms and procedures within CSOs. Issues of corruption, financial transparency, and legitimacy are seen as key challenges for the sector. Recently, following public debates on the legitimacy of advocacy CSOs, a House Committee of the State Assembly enacted legislation that obligates those CSOs that receive a majority of their funding from the state to disclose their accounts. While membership-based CSOs are generally regarded as involving their members in elections and organizational decisionmaking, other indicators of internal organizational practices—such as the rights and treatment of CSO employees—were regarded by CSI stakeholders as requiring significant improvement.

Another issue of concern is the extent of gender equality in civil society. Although the representation of women in the NGO sector is higher than in such CSO types as trade unions and professional associations, it is still considered limited. Interviews and consultations carried out as part of the CSI reveal that, because patriarchal attitudes and behavior are deeply entrenched in the cultural, social, and political systems of Orissa, civil society representatives are not sufficiently sensitized to the issue of gender equality within their organizations.

Impact (1.2)

The impact dimension assesses civil society's role in governance and society at large. Civil society's impact in Orissa is quite limited. Most predominantly, civil society's efforts to influence public policy are inadequate, particularly as regards social development issues and government and corporate accountability.

As a reflection of deep-rooted traditions of social empowerment, civil society in Orissa has been fairly involved in informing and educating citizens, empowering women, providing essential services, and supporting the livelihoods of those in need. Respondents to the population survey who had interacted with both types of institutions feel (by a ratio of 4 to 3) that CSOs are somewhat more helpful than state agencies. As a consequence, religious institutions (96%), NGOs (60%), and to a lesser extent, trade unions (40%) are rated as having very high to moderately high levels of public trust.

In contrast, civil society plays a very limited role in influencing public policy and state governance. Stakeholders generally regard civil society to be rather inactive and not successful in influencing key policies in the fields of human rights, education, and the national budget process. Although the CSI study finds isolated examples of civil society's advocacy work—for example, the work of the Centre for Youth and Social Development (CYSD) in monitoring and analyzing annual state budget allocations for social issues—experts highlighted as a major weakness the lack of systematic, concerted, vigorous advocacy efforts by civil society coalitions.

Civil society is even less successful in its role as a watchdog of state and corporate behavior. Between 80% and 90% of stakeholders found civil society to be neither particularly active nor successful in these fields. Although there are isolated examples of civil society mobilizations—for example, against the state government's initiatives on mineral-based industries that adversely affect the local population and environment—overall, civil society's watchdog role remains limited.

Recommendations

Participants from civil society, the government, and the media gathered at a CSI Workshop in May 2006 to develop recommendations for strengthening civil society in Orissa. Some key recommendations are listed below:

- Establish a mechanism for more regular and systematic interface among various civil society subsectors, such as NGOs, trade unions, tribal groups, and professional associations.
- Establish a common systematic framework to develop mechanisms for dialogue among civil society, the state, and the business sector.
- Improve CSOs' internal transparency to enhance civil society's legitimacy and social relevance.

Conclusion

The CSI assessment for Orissa found a civil society that, despite a long history of fervently struggling for social justice, emancipation, and democracy, seems to have lost momentum in recent years, in part because of the successful co-optation of many NGOs by the state. While civic engagement remains rather vibrant at the community level, the structure, organizational processes, levels of activity, and impact of organized civil society at the state level leave ample room for improvement. The hope is that the CSI assessment, by using a participatory approach to detect the most glaring weaknesses, will mobilize civil society to collectively work toward a stronger, more responsive, and influential civil society in the years to come.

CSI Report

Centre for Youth and Social Development, *CIVICUS Civil Society Index Report for Orissa* (Bhubaneswar, Orissa, India: Centre for Youth and Social Development, 2006).

Notes

1. The CSI assessment was implemented in Orissa by the Centre for Youth and Social Development (CYSD) from June 2004 to May 2006. This chapter presents the main findings of the CSI and is based on a comprehensive report for Orissa, which can be accessed on the CSI pages of the CIVICUS website at http://www.civicus.org.
2. *Mathas* are the secluded places where religious leaders and their disciples stay and where religious discourse takes place.
3. *Bhagabat Tungis* are community club houses where villagers come together for religious and social purposes.

4. *Naxalites* are revolutionary groups waging a violent struggle on behalf of landless laborers and tribal people against landlords and other representatives of the upper classes and ruling elite.

5. A *dalit* is a person whose ancestors were of the caste once called "the untouchables," who performed duties that were important to the well-being of society, but menial in nature.

Chapter 30

Poland[1]

Over the past decade and a half, Poland, like many transitioning countries, has undergone a period of tremendous political, social, and economic change, in which civil society has played an important role. Since the election of a conservative government in September 2005, civil society's position among the set of key public actors, particularly vis-à-vis the new critical government, has become more difficult. However, because the Civil Society Index (CSI) research activities were carried out before the 2005 election, the results presented here describe civil society's situation prior to this important shift in government.

Table 30.1 Background Information for Poland

Poland	
Country size (square km)	312,685
Population (millions 2004)	38.2
Population under 15 years (2004)	16.8%
Urban population (2003)	61.9%
Seats in parliament held by women (2005)	20.2%
Language groups	Polish (official), Ukrainian, German
Ethnic groups	Polish 98%, German 1%, other and unspecified 1%
Religious groups	Roman Catholic 90%, unspecified 8%
HDI score and ranking (2003)	0.858 (36th)
GDP per capita (US$ 2003)	$11,379
Unemployment rate (% of total labor force)	19%
Population living on less than US$2 a day (2002)	<2%

Historical Overview

The history of charitable activities dates to the medieval times in Poland. However, civic activism became more widely relevant during the Partitions of Poland (1795–1918), when the country lost its independence and associations played a crucial role in maintaining Polish identity. This legacy of strong associational life proved important during the period of regained independence (1918–1939), when a diverse group of associations supported the new and rather weak state in providing social services such as health care and education. During German occupation (1939–1945), civic organizations had to move underground and became important pillars of the resistance movement. After the end of World War II, Communist rule was installed in Poland, which led to the banning of independent civic organizations and the subsuming of all existing associations into Communist mass organizations closely linked to the ruling party. The Catholic Church was the only realm not penetrated by the Communist state. It not only engaged in charitable activities, but was also able to provide shelter to certain banned associations, thereby assisting in the preservation of the tradition of civic activism.

The year 1980 marked a crucial milestone in Polish history with the emergence of the first independent trade union, Solidarity. Solidarity began to challenge the party-state monopoly but was banned in 1981, forcing underground the wave of independent nonviolent civic action that had spread across the country. As part of the overall breakdown of Communist rule in Eastern Europe, in 1989 the Polish government agreed to roundtable talks with civic activists. This marked the onset of democratization. As a consequence of immediate reforms, many civic associations sprang up to engage in political reform and address key social needs. Similar to many transitioning countries, in Poland the development of civil society began to slow after the installation of a democratic government. While the NGO sector continued to grow and professionalize, the percentage of citizens engaged in voluntary activities dropped significantly. Thus, the growing NGO sector assumed the character of an enclave in Polish society, and became unable to fill the emerging vacuum between citizens and the state. However, as the CSI findings show, in recent years, civil society activists have become more aware of the need for civil society organizations (CSOs) to develop a social base, and for civil society to become the glue connecting the increasingly diverse Polish society.

Figure 30.1 Civil Society Diamond for Poland

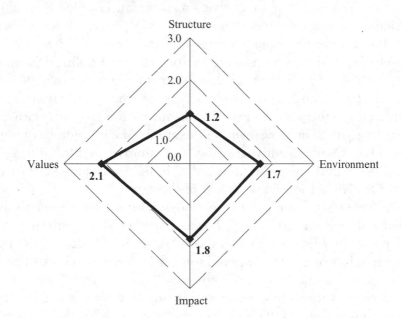

The State of Civil Society in Poland

This section provides a summary of key findings of the CSI project in Poland. It examines the state of Polish civil society along four dimensions—structure, environment, values, and impact—highlighting the main weaknesses and strengths.

The Civil Society Diamond (figure 30.1) visually summarizes the assessment's findings in Poland. The diamond shows a rather skewed picture of civil society in Poland. Civil society is characterized by a relatively weak structure (primarily because of a weak social base) and operates in a somewhat enabling environment, where political and legal factors are generally conducive. The lack of social capital and poor relations with the private sector present the most important barriers. Civil society has rather strong values and exerts moderately strong impact. This is weakened by civil society's limited role as watchdog monitoring state and private sector activities.

Structure (1.2)

The structure dimension examines the makeup of civil society in terms of the main characteristics of individual citizen participation and associational life. As is the case in many other post-Communist countries, in Poland the structure of civil society has a dual character:

a rather well-connected and well-structured organized civil society exists in the context of weak civic engagement. Low levels of citizen participation in public life are found in CSOs, in which fewer than 1 in 5 Polish citizens claims membership and only 1 in 3 members is actively engaged. This extends to various forms of political participation, with less than half of Polish voters turning out for the 2005 general elections, and only around 5% of the population having contacted a politician or civil servant during the last year. However, there are signs of improvement. For example, the percentage of volunteers in CSOs is steadily growing and almost doubled during the period from 2001 to 2004. Still, CSOs' limited social base clearly presents the main structural weakness of the sector.

A somewhat more positive picture emerges from the analysis of organized civil society, which boasts a rather strong infrastructure and good international linkages, and relies on effective systems of interorganizational cooperation. However, certain weaknesses can be detected, including the lack of umbrella bodies. Currently, only about 1 in 3 organizations belongs to a network or umbrella organization. Also, preliminary efforts at self-regulation, such as the Charter of NGOs, have been unsuccessful. Issues of civil society's accountability and transparency need to be addressed, particularly because the public's image of the sector is rather negative.

The resources available to Polish civil society are regarded as less than adequate, and civil society representatives are particularly concerned about limited and uncertain financial resources. Government and European Union (EU) funds are growing in importance, but are not accessible to the majority of smaller CSOs. In addition, civil society's human resources are often not sufficient to do the increasingly complex and specialized work demanded of CSOs. The process of professionalization of the sector needs to be supported, but not at the expense of civil society losing its flexibility, spontaneity, and volunteer support. Interestingly, research shows that a more professional staff provides strong incentive for people to get involved with CSOs as volunteers. This could, in turn, address the challenge of developing a wider social base for civil society.

Environment (1.7)

The environment dimension considers political, legal, socioeconomic, and sociocultural contexts, as well as the relationships among civil society, the state, and the private sector. The environment in which Polish civil society operates presents a mix of conducive and nonconducive factors. The overall political context, in terms of democratic rights and procedures, is clearly positive, although there are several problems regarding the implementation of these provisions. Corruption, disregard for the rule of law, and limitations in the state's effectiveness hamper good governance in Poland. However, CSI participants expressed the view that this is not only a consequence of an uncommitted and ineffective public administration, but also follows from the lack of civic initiatives advocating for better governance in the country.

In recent years, state–civil society relations have significantly changed, mainly for the better. The legal environment for CSOs with regard to registration, operation, and taxation is generally conducive, although room for improvement remains. Similarly, the rules of engagement between state and civil society have received significant attention and witnessed some positive changes in recent years. Examples of favorable change include the adoption of the Public Benefit Act that defines the rules of cooperation between CSOs and the government, the creation of the Public Benefit Works Council, and the strong presence of NGO representatives on various social dialogue bodies. Also, the scope of tasks handed over to CSOs and the corresponding financial support from the state is increasing, and long-term contracts are becoming more common. Because a positive framework for cooperation now exists, it is important for civil society to promote good practices and exert more effective pressure in cases where the state disregards its statutory obligations.

Civil society's relations with the private sector are also undergoing changes, but at a much slower pace than its relations with the state. Corporate social responsibility (CSR) is becoming a more widely discussed concept, and marketing campaigns more frequently appeal to social values. Also, nonfinancial forms of cooperation, such as volunteering options for company employees, are becoming increasingly popular. Still, the pace of these changes is unsatisfactory, perhaps because of the weak capacity of the organizations that mediate between civil society and the business community.

Last, the assessment of the sociocultural context for Polish civil society is relatively negative. For example, levels of interpersonal trust and public spiritedness in Poland are among the lowest of all the countries covered by the European Social Survey. The low levels of social capital have serious negative consequences on the propensity of citizens to become involved in civil society activities, and in public life in general.

The analysis of civil society's environment reveals a set of dynamic relations between civil society, the state, and the private sector. Although there are indications that attitudes and procedures are shifting in a positive direction, more systemic factors, such as weak sociocultural norms and the limited capacity of the state, are likely to remain barriers for the future development of Polish civil society.

Values (2.1)

The values dimension examines the extent to which civil society practices and promotes positive values. The CSI results indicate a relatively strong position for CSOs as defenders of such critical values as democracy, transparency, tolerance, nonviolence, gender equity, and poverty eradication.

For example, public opinion surveys show that a majority of Poles acknowledge the important role CSOs play in contributing to an effective democratic system. Civil society activities undertaken to fight corruption in the public sector enjoy particularly strong visibility (for example, the Anti-Corruption Program activities jointly overseen by the Stefan Batory Foundation and the International Helsinki Federation for Human Rights).

Different from the cases of most other Eastern European countries, in the Polish civic sector the issue of poverty eradication is well-entrenched and its significance is widely appreciated by Polish society at large. This is a likely consequence of the important role played by faith-based organizations in Polish civil society, as borne out by the fact that in 74% of all Polish parishes, charitable activities are part of the church's work. There are also nationwide campaigns to fight poverty, such as the Movement against Social Helplessness, supported by a range of CSOs and other institutions.

The exception to Polish civil society's strong values commitment is the issue of internal transparency. Civil society's track record with transparency is weak, both as a value to be practiced within CSOs, and as a value to be propagated in society at large. Existing efforts to improve transparency and accountability among CSOs have yet to yield a discernible impact. This weakness is reflected in public opinion. A majority of Poles agree with the statement that "abuse and self-interest are common in CSOs." Thus, without substantial improvement in this area, CSOs' authority to judge others will be called into question, the effectiveness of their activities will likely decrease, and the public's already weak trust in civil society will ultimately be put at risk.

The CSI study notes a discrepancy between the rather strong performance of civil society in practicing and promoting important values and the weakness of Polish society's value base. For example, while civil society is active in promoting tolerance, solidarity, environmental awareness, and other progressive values, these norms are not at all entrenched in society as a whole. Thus it seems that owing to its small size and niche character, the effects of civil society's value promotion cannot trigger any noticeable shift in the values of society at large.

Impact (1.8)

The impact dimension assesses civil society's role in governance and in society at large. Similar to the results of the structure dimension, the moderate score for civil society's impact is based on both positive and negative components. The assessment of civil society's role in interacting with society at large through educating the public, empowering citizens, providing services, and meeting needs is rather positive. This contrasts with civil society's limited role as a watchdog guarding the state and corporate sectors. However, as indicated in the results of the CSI's civil society panel survey, civil society leaders recognize this as an area in need of more attention.

Civil society makes a positive contribution to social welfare, particularly as regards the plight of marginalized groups, such as the homeless. However, the public perception of civil society's role indicates that the niche it occupies is small and that lacks public support. For example, a majority of Poles consider civil society to have little influence in solving important social problems, only 1 in 10 citizens know of a local CSO organizing social activities in their community, and almost one-third of Poles do not view CSOs as assisting people in need. Regarding the last point, a similarly negative assessment was made in relation to the state.

The main challenge for almost all of civil society's activities is to increase their scale, which will require growth in the numbers and capacities of the CSOs themselves. While CSOs are able to generate workable solutions for many key challenges, they are often unable to apply them on a larger scale. Thus, developing mechanisms for scaling-up workable solutions to social problems is one of the greatest challenges faced by Polish civil society. The predicted increase in financial resources available to the sector will be an opportunity, and may force CSOs to think on a different and larger scale, although this must be coupled with a focus on developing a stronger social base in terms of both volunteers and professional staff.

Recommendations

During the consultative meetings of the CSI, first and foremost the CSI National Workshop, the following primary recommendations were made for strengthening civil society in Poland:

- Pay more attention to civil society's limited social base: Polish citizens' weak involvement in civil society activities is an indication of a lack of civic engagement and social capital in Polish society. The government's draft National Development Strategy for 2007–2015 features a significant section on building an integrated community. This is one of six priorities in which civil society support is mentioned as a goal. It presents a unique opportunity for joint efforts by CSOs and public officials to mobilize and involve communities in the country's development. For example, an effective infrastructure should be developed to promote volunteerism, and civic education should be incorporated into school curricula.
- Improve civil society's relations with the state: Civil society needs to improve its own capacity and skills to interact effectively with public officials. This should be done by training NGO professionals and establishing more effective representative bodies and structures. Additionally, issues of accountability and transparency, such as stronger promotion of the Charter of NGO Codes of Conduct, require more attention. There should be more cooperation between the state and civil society in service delivery, but CSOs should be careful not to lose their unique features or give up their already limited role as a watchdog of state and private sector behavior.

Conclusion

Poland is still undergoing a process of profound change. While the CSI results point toward a range of positive trends—such as improving state–civil society relations, improved legal reforms, increased CSR and financial resources for CSOs, and professionalization of the civic sector—they have also identified a set of critical weaknesses. Key challenges are the low levels of social capital and civic engagement, which determine the niche role played by civil society in Poland. To meet these challenges, there is a set of relevant recommendations on how civil society can break out of its niche and improve its activities to become a more visible and relevant force in society.

Given the importance of and resources attached to civil society in the National Development Strategy for 2007–2015, it is hoped that the CSI will become a regularly used tool to map and track the future development of Polish civil society. In the assessment of the Klon/Jawor Association, the CSI is already seen as an excellent tool for developing a comprehensive picture of civil society's current state. Given the CSI's function as a structured data base on civil society, Klon/Jawor is considering making the project a permanent mechanism for collecting and analyzing data on civil society in the years to come.

CSI Report

Marta Gumkowska et al., *The Challenge of Solidarity: CIVICUS Civil Society Index Report for Poland* (Warsaw, Poland: Klon/Jawor, 2006).

Notes

1. The CSI assessment was implemented in Poland by the Klon/Jawor Association in 2005. This chapter presents the main findings of the CSI and is based on a comprehensive country report for Poland, which can be accessed on the CSI pages of the CIVICUS website at http://www.civicus.org.

Chapter 31

⟜—⟞

Romania[1]

Among the civil societies in post-Communist Europe, Romania has often been regarded as a particularly troubled and difficult case. Romanian civil society is characterized by low levels of civic engagement and social capital, coupled with foreign donor dependency and a number of institutional deficiencies. However, the Civil Society Index (CSI) assessment finds signs that the country is moving toward a stronger and more sustainable civil society.

Table 31.1 Background Information for Romania

Romania	
Country size (square km)	237,500
Population (millions 2004)	21.7
Population under 15 years (2004)	15.9%
Urban population (2003)	54.6%
Seats in parliament held by women (2005)	11.1%
Language groups	Romanian (official), Hungarian, German, and Roman
Ethnic groups	Romanian 90%; Hungarian, Roma, and four others 10%
Religious groups	Romanian Orthodox 87%, Protestant 8%, Roman Catholic 5%
HDI score and ranking (2003)	0.792 (64th)
GDP per capita (US$ 2003)	$7,277
Unemployment rate (% of total labor force)	7%
Population living on less than US$2 a day (2003)	12.9%

Historical Overview

Compared to other Eastern European countries, civil society traditions in Romania developed at a rather late stage. Prior to the mid-nineteenth century, there were no significant civil society activities. This stemmed from the country's geopolitical instability, prolonged foreign rule, the society's rural and agrarian nature, and the failure of the Orthodox Church to stress the value of charity in its theology.

During the second half of the nineteenth century, Romanian society underwent a period of modernization; by the interwar period of the twentieth century, the institutional basis for civil society had been established. The 1923 Constitution represented the first recognition of freedom of association, and the liberal constitutional monarchy that reigned during the 1920s and 1930s led to the emergence of a new, albeit fragile, civil society. However, these developments were halted by a series of authoritarian regimes during World War II.

Following World War II, the Communist government perceived civil society as a threat to its power and severely limited all voluntary associations. By the 1950s and 1960s, civil society was all but eliminated by the ruling party. However, by the 1970s and 1980s, an apolitical civil society began to develop, consisting mainly of sports and cultural associations. No organized dissident movements existed; instead the limited Romanian resistance to the regime was based on isolated individuals.

The reemergence of civil society after the collapse of the Communist system in 1989 was a lengthy and difficult process. Because the development of a strong civil society was considered essential for the positive post-Communist evolution of Romanian society, international institutions and foreign donors developed programs to support an emerging Romanian civil society. In the early 1990s, while the country was still struggling with its Communist legacy, Romanian civil society encountered difficulties in creating an autonomous public space outside the state.[2] In the middle to late 1990s, civil society's relations with political decisionmakers gradually improved, and civil society began to gain a stronger public profile and play a more important role in Romanian society. Civil society supported the victorious Democrat Convention Coalition in the 1996 elections, and many civil society organizations' (CSOs') leaders joined the new administration as advisors and government officials.

Because foreign donors regarded the democratic change in government in 1996 as a sign of the consolidation of Romanian democracy, foreign aid to civic organizations dropped significantly. Nevertheless, the number of registered NGOs increased during this period, but there was also a proliferation in the number of civil society corruption scandals. Against the backdrop of a national economic downturn and society's disaffection with public institutions, the public image of civil society also worsened.

Relations between civil society and the new social democratic government, elected in 2000, were strained. However, formal institutional dialogue between the state and CSOs improved, and civil society exploited the European Union (EU) requirements to advance its agenda. In 2004, another change in government was optimistically perceived by civil society. The new government was viewed as more cooperative, and the previously tense relations between both sets of actors eased significantly.

The State of Romanian Civil Society

In Romania, civil society generally refers to NGOs, without implying a diverse range of CSO types such as trade unions, professional associations, and political parties. This is in part because NGOs did not exist under Communism and their emergence was fueled by programs established by foreign donors, whereas trade unions, professional associations, and cultural associations are associated with the former regime. The National Advisory Group (NAG) used the broad definition of civil society proposed by CIVICUS, but excluded political parties (because of differences in their legal treatment compared to how other types of CSOs are treated).

This section provides a summary of key findings of the CSI project in Romania. It examines the state of Romanian civil society along four dimensions—structure, environment, values, and impact—highlighting the main weaknesses and strengths.

Romania's Civil Society Diamond visually summarizes the results of the assessment's findings (figure 31.1). The diamond indicates that civil society has a relatively weak structure, primarily because of CSOs' donor dependency and limited citizen participation. The environment is regarded as somewhat conducive for civil society's operations, but is hindered by high levels of corruption and rather problematic state–civil society relations. Civil society practices and promotes positive values to a relatively significant extent, and is an important agent for social change. The sector has a moderate impact on society at large, particularly in the area of service delivery. However, it only plays a limited role as a watchdog of the state and private sector.

Figure 31.1 Civil Society Diamond for Romania

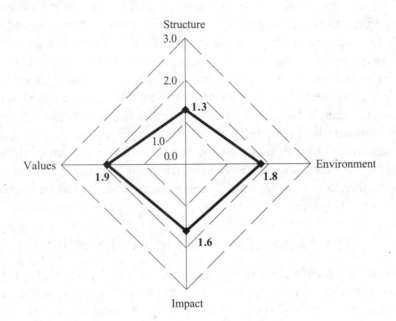

Structure (1.3)

The structure dimension examines the makeup of civil society in terms of the main characteristics of individual citizen participation and associational life. Low levels of citizen participation and the donor dependency of professional CSOs are the key factors inhibiting civil society's development.

Romanians' limited participation in civil society activities is at the core of the sector's structural weakness. Despite CSOs' attempts to mobilize citizens around issues of public concern, the population's response has remained lukewarm. For example, fewer than 10% of Romanians belong to a CSO and only 10% of respondents to a 2004 survey participated in a nonpartisan political action such as joining a demonstration or signing a petition. Similar to civic participation in other Central and Eastern European countries, involvement in Romanian community-based initiatives continues to be associated with the forced volunteerism of the Communist era. However, recent years have seen increased citizen engagement in important public issues. For example, devastating floods in 2005 affected large areas of western Romania, triggering a wave of solidarity in which many people donated money and goods to victims in the affected communities.

Limited citizen participation has negative implications for organized civil society, for it endangers civil society's financial sustainability and raises questions about the mandate for civil society's advocacy activities. In the context of a country struggling with difficult socio-economic conditions, individual charitable giving, state funding, and private donations remain limited. Romanian CSOs heavily rely on foreign sources of funding. Likewise, because civil society has limited local constituencies and inadequately represents marginalized groups, it is often viewed as driven by foreign donor interests. This is likely a key factor that contributes to its negative public image, which discourages increased citizen participation.

Dependency on foreign donors, which are gradually withdrawing from the region and will probably phase out their contributions after Romania's accession to the EU, compromises the long-term sustainability of Romanian civil society. The general mistrust among civil society actors combined with fierce competition for funding limits communication and cooperation within the sector. Only one-quarter of NGOs are organized into networks and, because of the reasons cited above, existing umbrella bodies are generally assessed as rather ineffective in voicing and addressing the needs of their members.

Environment (1.8)

The environment dimension considers political, legal, socioeconomic, and sociocultural contexts, as well as the relationships between civil society, the state, and the private sector. While the operating environment for Romanian civil society has improved in recent years, certain political and legal factors (such as corruption and the limited effectiveness of the state) constrain civil society's activities. The extent of cooperation between civil society, the state, and the private sector also remains low.

In the immediate post-Communist era, considerable progress was made in building viable democratic institutions. Civil society played a vital role in creating a positive legal environment and securing basic freedoms. Civil liberties and political rights are now generally respected, and there is open political competition. CSOs have little difficulty registering, and there exist no institutional barriers to advocacy or to CSO criticism of the government.

Against this positive institutional and legal backdrop, problems of corruption, a weak judiciary, weak administrative capacity, and inadequate state decentralization continue to impede civil society's work. Citizens have little confidence in the judiciary, primarily because of high levels of perceived corruption. The relationship between civil society and the state remains inadequate. Although mechanisms for institutionalized dialogue are in place, stakeholders believe the dialogue is not meaningful and only serves government's public relations interests. Similarly, the state's financial support to civil society is limited to certain social service NGOs, while most CSOs fear that a closer relation with the state may lead to a loss of autonomy.

Relations between civil society and the private sector also remain weak. Civil society has not developed a strategy to improve its relations with the business sector, while the private sector is generally indifferent to civil society and does not offer assistance in resolving social problems. Funding and donations from the private sector are limited and unevenly distributed to civil society. Comparatively, Romanian companies donate 0.4% of their average annual turnover, whereas companies in the United States donate 1.2% of their pre-tax income. A study by the Association for Community Relations (ARC) and Allavida in 2003 indicated that 61% of all surveyed businesses had never made a donation to charity. However, there are signs that the private sector is beginning to recognize its social role: large corporations are developing corporate social responsibility (CSR) strategies and are beginning to acknowledge the potential negative social and environmental impacts of their operations.

The lack of social capital is an additional weakness of civil society's environment, as indicated by widespread mistrust and low public-spiritedness in society. Approximately 90% of citizens agree that it is advisable to be cautious in interactions with other citizens. This is one of the highest percentages worldwide.

Although major advances in civil society's institutional and legal context have been made, significant obstacles remain. These obstacles relate to lack of enforcement of the institutional and legal framework, which is caused by the weak capacity and lack of political will by the state, and pervasive sociocultural norms of alienation, mistrust, and prejudice.

Values (1.9)

The values dimension examines the extent to which civil society practices and promotes positive values. In Romania, it represents the most positive dimension of the CSI assessment, indicating a generally strong value base for civil society. Yet practices of genuine transparency and accountability within CSOs are limited because CSOs are often reluctant to open themselves to public scrutiny.

Since the fall of the totalitarian regime in 1989, civil society actors have been actively involved in rebuilding Romanian society on the basis of democratic institutions and inter-ethnic tolerance. CSOs are regarded as rather well-governed institutions because they are typically seen as encouraging staff creativity and initiative, and as able to engage members and staff in decisionmaking.

However, issues of internal transparency and accountability loom large within the sector. Romanian NGOs are still affected by the stereotype frequently promoted by the media in the 1990s, which suggested that CSOs were primarily used for smuggling cars and receiving foreign donations to benefit their founders. Although there were many cases in which these accusations of fraud were valid, generalizing on the basis of such instances gave the entire NGO sector an undeserved bad reputation.

The perception of civil society as corrupt is still rather common. However, a 2002 public opinion survey showed the sector to be regarded as the least corrupt among all institutions included in the survey (with 15% of respondents seeing civil society as corrupt, while a majority saw Parliament as corrupt). While specific initiatives have been undertaken to encourage CSO transparency—such as a nationwide contest to select the best annual report—and while recognition of financial transparency and accountability is clearly growing within the sector, many CSOs still lack the capacity or political will to make this issue a priority.

Environmental sustainability and gender equity are not regarded by most Romanians as indigenous values; these therefore do not register strongly on the public agenda. However, the CSI reveals that civil society has been active in promoting these values, and that CSOs have become key partners of government and foreign donors, not least because of the heightened attention paid to these issues as a consequence of the EU accession process. Other values that do not receive strong public support are related to domestic violence and the fight to overcome poverty. Again, in both areas, civil society is leading the effort to raise public awareness and to provide services to the affected groups.

Impact (1.6)

The impact dimension assesses civil society's role in governance and society at large. Given the structural weaknesses of Romanian civil society, the findings reveal a higher level of impact than expected. However, closer analysis shows that much of the impact is focused on civil society's interactions with the government or marginalized groups, and rarely reaches society at large.

Over the past few years, important advances—for example, the adoption of legislation on access to public information and stronger public participation in government decisionmaking processes—have helped civil society become more involved in public policy processes. The CSI policy impact studies reveal that the voices of Romanian CSOs are heard and are most influential on those policy interventions in which they were backed by international actors. Additionally, the EU accession process has been an incentive for government to consult with CSOs on the adoption of policies and legislation.

Foreign support has also enhanced civil society's ability to provide social services to Romanians. Most social service NGOs provide direct services to particularly vulnerable groups, such as persons with physical or mental disabilities, people living with HIV/AIDS, institutionalized children, and the elderly. According to the CSI population survey, NGOs are seen as quite effective in delivering these services. They were rated second highest (with ratings of 56% approval), behind international organizations (62% approval) but ahead of religious institutions (54% approval), the business sector (48% approval), and the state (43% approval).

However, because of the focus on special groups and the donor-driven nature of their work, CSOs do not play a strong role in empowering entire communities or impacting the population at large. Their niche role, together with the disinterest of the media and the generally weak public communication efforts of CSOs, contributes to the fact that CSOs are not very present in Romanian society. As a result, public trust in NGOs, although growing, remains low (rating around 30%) and trust in trade unions has reached a record low of 18%.

Recommendations

Representatives of CSOs, the government, academic institutions, business, and the media gathered at the CSI National Workshop to reflect on the CSI findings in Romania. They identified the following recommendations to encourage the growth of Romanian civil society:

- Improve citizen participation by developing tools to educate citizens, and by publicly promoting the important role of civil society in the country.
- Improve civil society's relations with public authorities by strengthening genuine partnerships in fields such as social services.

- Increase cooperation within civil society by building inter- and intra-sectoral coalitions, networks, and groups to enable civil society to speak with a common voice.
- Strengthen CSOs' watchdog role by increasing their capacity to pressure government and address irresponsible actions and corruption by public and private authorities.
- Strengthen CSOs' advocacy capacity by adopting a more proactive role, and by being less reactive and responsive to foreign donor priorities.
- Improve civil society's public image by increasing transparency, improving annual reporting, and increasing civil society's presence in society. This will enable civil society to be more accessible and responsive to public interests.

Conclusion

Romanian civil society stakeholders believe the CSI assessment is an important initiative, which provides an informative description of the current state of civil society. By shedding light on the obstacles impeding civil society's development, the findings reveal that particular attention must be paid to finding new ways to involve citizens in civil society initiatives, build local constituencies for civil society's advocacy work, and thereby increase the public image and standing of civil society. The study generated a collectively owned assessment of civil society's strengths and weaknesses, which will provide a point of reference for future research and policymaking, and lay the groundwork for stakeholders to act upon the identified recommendations.

CSI Report

Civil Society Development Foundation, *Dialogue for Civil Society—Report on the State of Civil Society in Romania: CIVICUS Civil Society Index Report for Romania* (Bucharest, Romania: Civil Society Development Foundation, 2005).

Notes

1. The CSI assessment was implemented in Romania by the Civil Society Development Foundation (CSDF) from September 2003 to November 2005. This chapter presents the main findings of the CSI and is based on a comprehensive country report for Romania, which can be accessed on the CSI pages of the CIVICUS website at http://www.civicus.org.

2. From 1990 to 1993, civil society was typically perceived as the "public enemy" of new Romanian power structures. For example, then-President Ion Iliescu vocally reiterated the sentiment of the ruling party by labelling participants of the 1990 University Square protest movement "a bunch of hooligans and junkies."

Chapter 32

Russia[1]

Over the past five years, Russian civil society has found itself in an increasingly challenging situation. It is threatened by a government that is becoming progressively more authoritarian and wielding more economic and political power. In addition, civil society cannot count on widespread support from citizens, whose priorities are individual survival, personal well-being, and the country's overall stability and security, rather than civil liberties and involvement in public affairs. While it is unlikely that civil society will become stronger in the coming years, civil society is also sufficiently organized, resourceful, and resilient, to help it withstand any serious attacks on its existence. A potential scenario is a severely constrained civil society in constant danger of government co-optation. In this context, the implementation of the Civil Society Index Shortened Assessment Tool (CSI-SAT) is important for taking stock of the current state of civil society, with a view toward identifying future challenges and prospects for Russian civil society.

Historical Overview

Modern civil society activities in Russia date back to the late stages of the Tsarist state, which witnessed the emergence of independent citizen initiatives, particularly among the growing urban middle class. For example, private charities grew rapidly over the course of the nineteenth century. In the countryside, the establishment of *zemstva* (local councils) provided space for property owners' involvement in social affairs. In the late nineteenth century, initial attempts were made to organize trade unions among the urban working class. While largely autonomous in their work, associational life was tightly monitored and regulated by the state, which feared political mobilization and opposition.

Table 32.1 Background Information for Russia

Russia	
Country size (square km)	17,075,400
Population (millions 2004)	143.8
Population under 15 years (2004)	15.7%
Urban population (2003)	73.3%
Seats in parliament held by women (2005)	9.8%
Language groups	Russian (official), many minority languages
Ethnic groups	Russian 82%, Tatar 4%, Ukrainian 3%, Bashkir 1%, Chuvash 1%, Belarussian 1%, Moldovian 1%
Religious groups	Russian Orthodox, Muslim
HDI score and ranking (2003)	0.795 (62nd)
GDP per capita (US$ 2003)	$9,230
Unemployment rate (% of total labor force)	8.6%
Population living on less than US$2 a day (2002)	12.1%

In the early twentieth century, groups of urban revolutionaries and democrats began to challenge the supremacy and foundation of imperial Russia. After years of civil unrest and World War I, the 1917 revolution ushered in the socialist Soviet system, which was initially accompanied by a vibrant civic life in areas such as the workplace, revolutionary art, and theater groups.

With the deepening of totalitarianism in Soviet Russia, independent forms of associational life began to disappear. By the 1930s, all existing social organizations were fully controlled by the party-state regime and formed part of an elaborate social system of trade unions, women's and youth associations, and professional organizations. In the 1960s, following Khrushchev's "secret speech" denouncing Stalin's repression, unofficial associations focusing on leisure activities such as sports, hobbies, and music emerged and were not persecuted by the party. The dissident movement also strengthened, but after the 1968 Prague Spring in the Czech Republic it was actively suppressed by the state. As a consequence of Gorbachev's *perestroika* policies in the 1980s, a large number of CSOs began to emerge, focusing on a diverse set of issues, ranging from social and environmental concerns to political issues.

The collapse of the Soviet Union and the formation of the Russian Federation in 1991 ushered in vast social, economic, and political changes. During Yeltsin's presidency, economic production fell sharply and the state's social safety net eroded. The emerging political system was one characterized by volatility and co-optation by powerful economic and political interest groups. However, the opening up of the country also led to the expansion of civil society, mainly in the form of urban-based advocacy NGOs, which were heavily dependent on funding from foreign donors. In addition, many Soviet-style mass organizations transformed themselves and remained active in providing services to their members and constituents.

By the beginning of Putin's presidency (in 2000), civil society had not succeeded in establishing roots in Russian society. Since then the country has seen a period of economic growth and political stability as well as an undermining of the incipient democratic system of governance. While public officials pay lip service to the importance of civil society for Russia's development, in practice, the notion of an autonomous civil society representing popular interests is perceived as a threat to the state. Civil society's ability to operate independently is more and more curtailed through various mechanisms, such as restrictive legislation, regular checks by the public administration, and government co-optation of CSOs. As becomes increasingly clear, the short-lived phase of genuinely open public space that transpired in the mid-to-late 1990s has not led to the consolidation of a strong, independent, and well-organized civil society. Instead it led to a rather poorly institutionalized civil society situated in an increasingly hostile environment.

The State of Civil Society in Russia

The Russian CSI-SAT project examined civil society in its diverse manifestations, with the exception of political parties and uncivil elements of civil society. This section provides a summary of key findings of the CSI-SAT project in Russia. It examines the state of Russian civil society along four dimensions—structure, environment, values, and impact—highlighting the main weaknesses and strengths.

The Civil Society Diamond (figure 32.1) for Russia depicts a rather weak civil society, particularly with regard to its structure, which is marred by low levels of civic engagement and poor resources; it can, however, draw on a well-developed infrastructure for the civic sector. The operating environment for Russian civil society is somewhat disabling, particularly with respect to the political and legal context, which is characterized by various restrictive provisions and practices. A relatively strong feature of Russian civil society is its

Figure 32.1 Civil Society Diamond for Russia

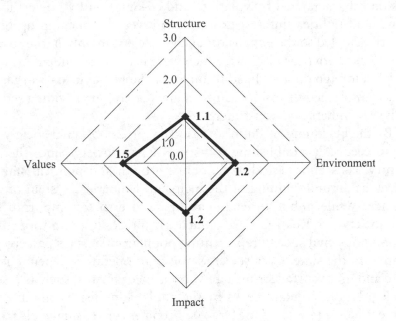

value base. While the internal practice of key values such as democracy and transparency is limited, CSOs are regarded as active promoters of these and other positive values in society at large. However, civil society's impact on politics and society is rather limited, particularly with regard to its policy and watchdog roles.

Structure (1.1)

The structure dimension examines the makeup of civil society in terms of the main characteristics of individual citizen participation and associational life. Similar to most other post-Communist civil societies, the structure of Russian civil society has a dual character. Low levels of civic activism are coupled with the well-developed infrastructure of a rather small civil society. The state of organized civil society remains particularly precarious, due to a lack of local financial, human, political, and moral support for its activities.

While public opinion surveys provide quite different results, most point toward a general disinclination of the Russian population to become involved in public affairs, particularly through organizations. Apart from trade unions, where membership is a formality, membership in CSOs remains very low and volunteering is not widespread. Despite this low level of participation, Russian civil society is rather diverse in terms of its social composition and geographical spread throughout the country.

Foreign donors' focus on building civil society over the past decade has created a rather strong infrastructure for organized civil society through resource centers, networks, communication channels, and international linkages. However, this top-heavy infrastructure has not been accompanied by increased organizational capacity or financial sustainability. Most CSOs remain highly dependent on a strong leader, without sufficient institutionalization of oversight boards or effective management systems. The widespread lack of financial resources threatens the long-term existence of many CSOs. Most professional NGOs are highly dependent on foreign donors, which, however, are significantly decreasing their support to Russian civil society. Due to the widespread civic disengagement of the population, individual financial support remains a negligible source of CSO financing.

As is the case in most post-Communist countries, Russian civil society has a rather strong layer of organized civil society at the national level, but this is weakly rooted in society at large, which poses major challenges for its organizational and financial viability and public credibility. Recent government actions that further discourage active civic engagement, such as the abolition of elections for regional governors and negative statements by various public officials about NGOs, are likely to further aggravate this trend.

Environment (1.2)

The environment dimension considers political, legal, socioeconomic, and sociocultural contexts as well as the relationships between civil society, the state, and the private sector. Russian civil society operates in a rather disabling environment, particularly with regard to its political, legal, and sociocultural characteristics.

The past few years have witnessed a significant deterioration in Russia's governance and human rights record. Infringements on political rights and civil liberties, the severe curtailment of independent media, and the concentration of political power in the executive branch indicate a trend toward an authoritarian system of governance. These authoritarian tendencies are reflected in state–civil society relations, in which the state seeks to strengthen its control over independent civil society. A recent manifestation of this trend is the expected implementation of the new NGO law. This law will restrict the setting up of unregistered CSOs and complicate the procedures for Russian and especially foreign CSOs to (re)register, leaving ample space for discretion and abuse by public authorities. Additionally, financial provisions are unfavorable for the development of civil society, particularly with respect to restrictions on charitable giving and work by foreign foundations and other donors.

The Russian government has attempted to engage civil society by putting in place a series of mechanisms for dialogue and consultative bodies. These, however, have received mixed assessments. For example, the high-profile Civic Chamber, set up in late 2005 and tasked with designing and proposing laws on social issues, is described by many activists as a weakly disguised attempt to tame NGOs and pay lip service to involving civil society in policymaking; others, however, see real value in this institution. However, mechanisms for dialogue at the regional and local levels are viewed as more conducive to providing civil society with an effective voice in the policy process.

The corporate sector is also not seen as supportive of civil society. In a recent poll, only 3% of NGO leaders agreed with a positive statement regarding corporate philanthropy. While corporate social responsibility (CSR) and corporate philanthropy are growing phenomena among multinational and other large companies in Russia, the lack of significant tax incentives for corporate giving limits the overall willingness of businesses to donate. Examples such as the state's harsh persecution (on dubious grounds) of Mikhail Khodorkovsky, who set up a foundation to support independent civil society, certainly do not encourage Russian businesses to support CSOs.

Similarly, the overall sociocultural context, characterized by widespread social mistrust, lack of public-spiritedness, and a focus on private life, limits the growth potential for civil society. For example, fewer than 1 in 4 Russians feel that most people can be trusted, signifying an overall lack of social capital in society.

Thus, the CSI's analysis indicates that civil society operates in a rather hostile environment, one in which civil society cannot count on any significant support from the state, the corporate sector, or citizens at large.

Values (1.5)

The values dimension examines the extent to which civil society practices and promotes positive values. The values base for Russian civil society is stronger than the other dimensions. However, while civil society is rather committed to promoting crucial values such as democracy, transparency, environmental sustainability, and gender equity, it is less prone to practicing these values in its own organizational contexts.

The flagship of Russian civil society's value promotion activities is environmental protection. Since the time of *perestroika,* a well-organized environmental movement has been at the forefront of raising awareness and mobilizing the population around environmental concerns. This contrasts with civil society's lack of attention to the issue of poverty. Despite growing poverty, unemployment, social inequality, and the state's attempt to cut back social security, civil society has not taken up poverty as a major social concern. A vivid example is the well-attended nationwide demonstrations by pensioners against reductions in social benefits, which were disconnected from organized civil society. As a consequence of paternalistic traditions and the current environment of fast-paced economic liberalization, it appears that Russian society, including its third sector, has embraced the principle of survival of the fittest, with little concern for the marginalized. When help is needed, it is usually provided by informal networks of extended family and close friends.

Russian civil society does not practice many of the values it promotes. While CSOs are active in advocating for democratic reform and government accountability in the public sphere, internal democratic and transparent practices by Russian CSOs are rare. During stakeholder consultations in Novosibirsk, many participants regarded principles of financial transparency as Western imports that should not be embraced by Russian CSOs. This reflects a society-wide phenomenon of corruption and clientelism as well as fear of government harassment when organizational activities and records are made transparent. Stakeholders estimated that only a small share of CSOs follow proper accountability and transparency standards, and that instances of financial irregularities, if not outright corruption, are rather frequent in the sector. While several initiatives to promote the principle of transparency have been established, such as a competition held by the St. Petersburg NGO Development Center for the best annual report, a more concerted sector-wide effort is required to improve civil society's record.

Another recent challenge for civil society's values is the growth of nationalist, xenophobic, and racist groups and movements. While civil society is quite vocal in its response to these widespread forms of uncivil society, such movements have not been contained and appear to be on the rise.

Impact (1.2)

The impact dimension assesses civil society's role in governance and society at large. Overall, Russian civil society's impact is rather weak. A 2004 opinion poll showed that three-quarters of Russians consider civil society's influence on life in Russia to be extremely insignificant.

The CSI assessment does not find any specific fields of activity, apart from civic education and awareness-raising campaigns, to be a significant strength of civil society. Civil society's advocacy, service provision, and empowerment functions all receive modest assessments. The reasons for civil society's limited impact relate to legal and political impediments, weak organizational capacities, and a lack of coordination among CSOs.

The extreme centralization of power in the executive branch of the government makes it more difficult for CSOs to access key policy-makers at the national level. Additionally, while the state has set up a range of mechanisms for dialogue with civil society, the attitude of the public administration toward civil society remains critical. At regional and local levels, this situation looks somewhat different, since there is a range of examples of civil society's successful involvement in social policy issues.

While CSOs are active in various social fields, providing services and capacity building to women, the poor, pensioners, the homeless, and other groups, their scale and societal impact remains limited. Despite recent reforms seeking to involve CSOs in service provision, CSOs' generally weak organizational and financial capacities have prevented them from successfully competing with state and business agencies.

Given civil society's limited role in society at large, it is not surprising that most Russians have never heard of CSOs. Of greater concern is that 3 out of 4 Russians are not interested in taking part in civil society activities. Thus, Russian society seems to have a strong preference for a state-centered model of development, which, when coupled with increasingly authoritarian tendencies, is unlikely to facilitate a greater role for civil society in the country's future.

Conclusion

As the CSI-SAT assessment shows, Russian civil society is poorly institutionalized, lacks influence on society at large, and shows deficiencies in embracing key value principles, such as accountability and transparency. This analysis has particularly highlighted the challenging environment in which civil society operates. Key domestic actors such as the state, the business sector, and the population lack a commitment to and interest in supporting civil society. The Russian authorities even actively obstruct the activities of independent CSOs. In addition, foreign donors, who have thus far been civil society's main allies, are in the process of scaling down their grant programs, with a few exceptions for such issues as human rights. The most viable, but still exceedingly difficult, option seems to be for civil society to actively reach out to citizens and convince them to become involved in civic activities, which would address civil society's challenges of financial sustainability, operational autonomy, and societal base. Most importantly, if civil society succeeds in the difficult task of building social roots and cultivating a strong citizen base, it will likely protect itself against further attacks on its independence and autonomy and also diminish the threat of co-optation by government.

CSI Report

L. Proskuryakova et al., *An Assessment of Russian Civil Society 2006: CIVICUS Civil Society Index Shortened Assessment Tool Report for the Russian Federation* (St. Petersburg, Russia: St. Petersburg "Strategy" Center, in cooperation with the Department of Public Policy at Moscow State University, 2006).

Notes

1. The CSI Shortened Assessment Tool was implemented in Russia by St. Petersburg "Strategy" Center, in cooperation with the Department of Public Policy at Moscow State University, from June 2003 to December 2005. This chapter presents the main findings of the CSI-SAT and is based on a comprehensive country report for Russia, which can be accessed on the CSI pages of the CIVICUS website at http://www.civicus.org.

Chapter 33

~~

Scotland[1]

Scotland features a strong voluntary sector, an active trade union sector, and other key components of a vibrant civil society. However, as the Civil Society Index (CSI) assessment highlights, these active subsectors usually do not come together under the umbrella of civil society. The implementation of the CSI project in Scotland provided an opportunity to stimulate greater engagement and cohesion among civil society's different components.

Table 33.1 Background Information for Scotland

Scotland	
Size (square km)	20,640
Population (millions 2004)	5.08
Population under 16 years	15%
Urban population	81.3%
Seats in parliament held by women (2006)	18.1%
Language groups	English, Gaelic, and Scots
Ethnic groups	White 97.99%, Asian or South Asian 1.09%, Chinese 0.32%, mixed 0.25%, black 0.16%, other 0.19%
Religious groups	Christian 65%, no religion 27.5%, not stated 5.5%, other 1.2 %, Muslim 0.8%
GDP per capita (US$ 2005)	$25,700
Unemployment rate (2005)	3.8%

Historical Overview

In 1707 Scotland, England, and Wales united to form the United Kingdom of Great Britain. As a result, the Scottish parliament was dissolved

327

and Scottish representatives were incorporated into the Westminster parliament. Historically, however, Scotland has always considered itself a separate country and has retained a unique national identity.

During the Scottish enlightenment of the eighteenth century, the Scottish education system flourished and philosophers such as Adam Smith, David Hume, and Adam Ferguson contributed to the country's vibrant intellectual life, including the intellectual history of the civil society concept. As cultural life thrived, numerous secular associations based on personal networks and friendships emerged.

In the nineteenth century, industrialization transformed Scotland. The emerging middle class asserted itself against the establishment by campaigning to reform local government and challenging the Scottish Church's deference to the political establishment in Westminster and Edinburgh. Through charitable organizations, the middle class engaged in philanthropy and allied itself with progressive sections of the new urban working class in campaigns to extend the franchise.

After World War II, civil society's development was affected by the emergence of the welfare state. As the state became the main provider of social services, the role of charities decreased and civil society was primarily represented by trade unions, professional associations, and local authorities. However, since the 1970s, new forms of civic initiatives have emerged around issues such as ecology, international development, and lifestyle.

In the last quarter of the twentieth century, a strong campaign to establish a Scottish parliament led to its formation in 1997. In 1999, the first parliamentary elections since 1707 took place, and the parliament was given substantial oversight of Scottish affairs, including control over the country's health and education systems. Scottish devolution generally increased civil society's influence on public policy. Other benefits of devolution included a new, more accountable, transparent, and accessible government and more positive relations between the Scottish parliament and civil society than traditionally existed with Westminster.

The State of Civil Society in Scotland

The term "civil society" is not commonly used in Scotland outside of policy and academic discourse. To emphasize action rather than organizational form, the National Advisory Group (NAG) modified CIVICUS's definition and defined civil society as "the act of associating to advance common interests and concerns, but not motivated by personal profit or

Figure 33.1 Civil Society Diamond for Scotland

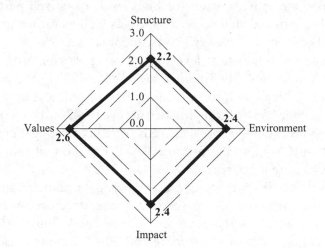

statutory obligations." The NAG agreed that Scottish civil society is not a cohesive sector, but is divided into constituent subsectors, each with its own umbrella body, political lobby, and internal communication mechanism. The primary subsectors of civil society in Scotland are the voluntary sector, charitable trusts and foundations, trade unions, faith-based organizations, professional associations, cooperatives, community councils, and academic institutions.

This section provides a summary of key findings of the CSI project in Scotland. It examines the state of Scottish civil society along four dimensions—structure, environment, values, and impact—highlighting the main weaknesses and strengths.

Scotland's Civil Society Diamond is a visual summary of the CSI findings (figure 33.1). The diamond reflects civil society's relatively strong structure, which is characterized by a well-organized sector. The environment is enabling and benefits from a particularly favorable political and socioeconomic context. The diamond illustrates a values-led civil society that promotes key values such as nonviolence, gender equity, poverty eradication, and environmental sustainability. The impact of the sector on society at large, particularly in providing services and empowering marginalized groups, is significant, although its record in holding the state accountable is rather weak.

Structure (2.2)

The structure dimension examines the makeup of civil society in terms of the main characteristics of individual citizen participation and associational life. The score for this dimension indicates a relatively strong structure, a result of high levels of citizen participation and a well-organized civil society sector, as well as rather strong relationships between civil society's constituent subsectors.

Scotland has significant levels of citizen participation in various civil society activities. The findings reveal that 65% of the population took part in at least one form of nonpartisan political action during 2002 and 2003, 85% of individuals surveyed in 2000 gave to charity in the previous month, 77% of citizens were involved in a civil society organization (CSO), and approximately 1.5 million citizens regularly engage in volunteer activities.

Umbrella bodies and infrastructure support organizations for civil society are cornerstones of the sector's strong structure. According to research conducted by the Scottish Council for Voluntary Organisations (SCVO), 40,000 of an estimated 50,000 voluntary organizations are connected to umbrella bodies. Churches share a parliamentary lobby through Action of Churches Together in Scotland (ACTS), forty-six trade unions and thirty-two trade union councils find representation through the Scottish Trade Union Congress (STUC), and cooperatives are linked through the Scottish Co-op and Cooperation and Mutuality Scotland. Civil society's support infrastructure is also well developed in Scotland. The sixty-one local councils for volunteer service and SCVO provide information support and management training to CSOs in the voluntary sector. Another sixty organizations, such as Voluntary Arts Scotland, Voluntary Health Scotland, Scottish Environment Link, and Youthlink Scotland, provide subsector-specific support.

Cooperation and communication between civil society subsectors takes place through alliances and collaborations, but generally on an ad hoc or project basis. The recent emergence of large-scale civil society movements is exemplified by Scotland's anti–Iraq War marches, anti-poverty initiatives, widespread response to the 2004 Asian tsunami disaster, and the high-profile civil society campaign during the 2005 G8 Summit in Gleneagles. Thus, whereas traditionally Scottish civil society consisted of well-organized subsectors, civil society as a whole is becoming more connected through less-formal, high-profile coalitions. Broad citizen participation and cross-sectoral cooperation between CSOs in these activities may serve as a foundation for increasing civil society's connectivity and influence in Scotland.

An ongoing challenge for civil society is the availability of resources to support its activities. There are serious concerns about low funding levels and short-term funding. SCVO's analysis finds that while the voluntary sector employs 5% of the workforce, it accounts for just over 1% of the national income, and the sector struggles to cope with its fast-growing staff. New, small, and rural organizations suffer the most from financial constraints. Despite the presence of peer-support networks, the effectiveness of available human resources was also assessed negatively. Availability of technical resources was regarded as slightly better, reflecting the widespread use of computer technology and other resources by CSOs. However, the CSI assessment highlighted a lack of skills necessary to use these technical resources.

Environment (2.4)

The environment dimension considers political, legal, socioeconomic, and sociocultural contexts as well as the relationships between civil society, the state, and the private sector. The CSI findings for Scotland indicate that civil society operates in a very enabling environment.

Scotland is part of a liberal democracy where no severe socioeconomic conflicts or crises exist. Since devolution, the government has become more transparent and accessible. A greater number of independent candidates and a larger variety of political parties have secured seats in the Scottish parliament than in the central UK parliament. With a devolved and effective legal system, basic rights and the rule of law are guaranteed to Scottish citizens. However, new restrictive laws introduced or proposed at the UK level (such as laws concerning terrorism, immigration, asylum, and identification cards), show an erosion of certain civil rights. These laws pose a potential threat to civil society's operating environment, but civil society continues to challenge such legislation. At the same time, devolution has meant that some restrictive laws enacted in England and Wales, such as those related to the incitement to religious hatred could be avoided in Scotland.

Registration requirements, tax benefits, and the nature of allowable advocacy for CSOs vary considerably between trade unions, charities, voluntary organizations, academic institutions, and faith-based groups. Overall, the legal environment for CSOs is conducive, although there is room for improvement. There are no substantial institutional barriers to civil society's operations, and CSOs are free to criticize the government. However, disincentives for advocacy work, such as the implications of government funding to CSOs, exist implicitly rather than explicitly.

The assessment of the relationship between civil society and the state is quite favorable. The Scottish parliament's public petitions process provides a direct line for civil society's influence on public policymaking. The 1998 Scottish Compact, an agreement between the Scottish Executive and the voluntary sector, allows for criticism without financial penalty and is a key instrument for dialogue between civil society and the state. As part of a wider agenda to improve public service delivery, the government launched the Future Builders of Scotland investment package, an £18 million program to invest in the voluntary sector in order to strengthen the sector's role in delivering public services. In contrast, the private sector's relationship with civil society requires improvement. Despite the high profile of corporate social responsibility (CSR), there is limited evidence of actual CSR activities, and direct private-sector funding to CSOs is low.

However, all in all, the challenges mentioned above should not detract from the overall conclusion that Scottish civil society functions in a generally very conducive external environment.

Values (2.6)

The values dimension examines the extent to which civil society practices and promotes positive values. The high score for this dimension reflects the positive values that Scottish civil society practices internally and promotes in society at large. Civil society is very active in promoting democracy, nonviolence, gender equity, poverty eradication, and environmental sustainability. Tolerance and transparency also scored relatively high in the CSI assessment; however, the practice of these values within the sector requires further improvement.

The findings reveal concerns in the media about the limited regulation of Scottish charities and how this lack of regulation may have contributed to a handful of high-profile charity scandals in 2003. However, the NAG pointed out that these concerns are likely to be alleviated by the establishment of the new Office for Scottish Charities Regulator. Nevertheless, high standards of accountability and financial transparency within Scottish civil society remain important factors in maintaining public trust and confidence.

Sectarianism in Scottish CSOs—particularly in relation to some football and faith-based groups—remains problematic. Some religious marches and parades were identified as instances of intolerance within civil society.

Despite the weaknesses mentioned above, civil society is a driving force in promoting positive values in Scotland. In addition to the more visible activities, such as the environmental movement and the anti–Iraq War campaigns, CSOs' efforts in lobbying against sectarianism and their strong role in community mediation, restorative justice, gender equality, and poverty reduction are highlighted by the CSI. Major corruption scandals are rare in civil society, and efforts are being made to increase gender equality within the membership and leadership of professional associations and trade unions.

The findings demonstrate that Scottish civil society is strongly value-driven. However, it is apparent that civil society does neither have a unified voice nor a set of shared values. While this diversity in values is seen by some as positive, there are notable clashes in the values held by different actors, such as those of lesbian, gay, bisexual, and transgender (LGBT) support groups and those of some faith-based organizations. Value conflicts primarily emerge around campaigns against religious sectarianism, animal liberation, and sexual orientation. Stakeholders felt that while one voice may not be desirable in a diverse civil society, the lack of consistently shared values dilutes civil society's ability to influence public and private sector policy.

Impact (2.4)

The impact dimension assesses civil society's role in governance and society at large. Scottish civil society's impact is assessed as rather strong. The sector is especially successful in empowering citizens, responding to social interests, and meeting societal needs; however, civil society is less successful in holding the state and the private sector accountable.

Civil society is relatively weak in monitoring state performance. In comparison to its strong record in influencing public policy, it is less active in checking the financial and legal accountability of the state. Similarly, while there is some evidence of activity by trade unions and environmental organizations to ensure private sector accountability, no signs of impact were recorded. In contrast, there are many examples of civil society successfully impacting public policy, especially since devolution. Civil society is loud and vocal, and has successfully pressured for legislative policy change for such issues as charity law, free care for the elderly, disclosure checks, protection of children, a smoking ban in public places, and free student tuition. However, it is difficult to assess the extent to which the content of specific policies is directly attributable to the influence of civil society lobbying.

The sector also conducts a wide range of activities to empower citizens and has a record of meeting a large number of social needs. LGBT, youth, minority, rural, and faith-based organizations successfully connect many constituents to other marginalized groups. Such CSOs manage to create a nonjudgmental public space for disenfranchised groups, resulting in increased confidence and empowerment for those communities.

In general, the state and civil society play complementary roles in service provision. Although the state plays a primary role in providing services to the population, civil society is effective in complementing existing service delivery and reaches groups and areas not otherwise reached by the state.

Recommendations

A series of seminars, with representatives from a range of civil society subsectors, such as faith-based organizations, the voluntary sector, trade unions, academia, and international NGOs, was convened by SCVO to reflect on the findings and put forward recommendations for the future of Scottish civil society. The following are the most crucial recommendations:

- A follow-up implementation of the CSI: Participants highlighted the importance of civil society's self-reflection on the processes and needs of the sector in order to improve its future impact.
- An outward-looking approach: Scottish civil society tends to be inward-looking. Participants emphasized the need to utilize the CSI assessment to study civil society through a wider lens. The global CSI findings should be used to learn about civil society experiences in other countries and thus strengthen Scottish civil society.

Conclusion

Scottish civil society is generally well-organized, active, driven by positive values, and effective at empowering citizens and meeting the needs of marginalized groups. A key challenge facing the sector is its relations with the state. To ensure a conducive operating environment, civil society needs to respond to restrictive UK legislation enacted in response to the global war against terrorism. It also needs to ensure adequate funding to continue meeting societal needs, since the UK government is proceeding with substantial reforms of the welfare state. This will likely place increased pressure on civil society, but it will also create certain opportunities for a stronger role for CSOs in service provision. Given civil society's current funding constraints (and the implications of large CSOs' increasing dependence on state funding), there is a danger of organizations being co-opted by the state. If CSOs are forced to work within the state's public policy priorities, they risk losing not only their autonomy, but also their grassroots connections and ability to meet certain societal needs.

Stakeholders believe that the acquisition of current data on the strengths and weaknesses of Scottish civil society and the corresponding recommendations will help increase the commitment of key actors to strengthening Scottish civil society. The assessment also provides an opportunity to focus on the state of civil society as a whole, and less on the different subsectors of Scottish civil society, such as the voluntary sector or trade unions. The findings identify issues of joint concern, which challenge all CSOs to work together on civic initiatives to improve participatory governance and social development in Scotland.

CSI Report

Ruchir Shah, *An Assessment of Scottish Civil Society: CIVICUS Civil Society Index Report for Scotland* (Edinburgh, Scotland: Scottish Council for Voluntary Organizations, 2006).

Notes

1. The CSI assessment was implemented in Scotland by the Scottish Council for Voluntary Organizations (SCVO) from December 2003 to April 2006. This chapter presents the main findings of the CSI and is based on a comprehensive report for Scotland, which can be accessed on the CSI pages of the CIVICUS website at http://www.civicus.org.

Chapter 34

❦❦

Serbia[1]

Compared to other Eastern European transition countries, Serbia went through a particularly long and protracted transformation process, which has yet to lead to a successful consolidation of democratic governance in the country. As a consequence, the development of a vibrant civil society has been severely hampered. In today's Serbia, civil society actors still lack public support, and, in some cases, are confronted with outright hostility from the state, the private sector, and the general public. The Civil Society Index (CSI) assessment identifies these and a range of other challenges for civil society. It also detects certain signs of positive change (found primarily at the local level) toward a stronger civil society working in a more enabling environment.

Table 34.1 Background Information for Serbia

Serbia	
Country size (sq km)	88,361 (excluding Kosovo)
Population (millions 2002)	7,498,001 (excluding Kosovo)
Population under 15 years	18.1%
Urban population	56.4%
Seats in parliament held by women	7.9%
Language groups	Serbian
Ethnic groups	Serbs 82.86%, Hungarians 3.91%, Bosniaks/Muslim 2.1%, Roma 1.44%, Croats 0.92%, Montenegrins 0.92%, Albanians 0.82%, Slovaks 0.79%, Yugoslav 1.44%
Religious groups	Orthodox 85%, Catholic 5.5%, Islamic 3.2%, Protestants 1.1%, undeclared 3.1%, nonbelievers 3.1%
GDP per capita (US$ 2005 est.)	$4,400
Unemployment rate (2005)	20.0%

Historical Overview

The origins of Serbian civil society date back to the eighteenth century, when the first charitable organizations were established in rural communities, under the influence of the Eastern Orthodox Church. While various forms of associational life sprung up during the late nineteenth and early twentieth century, they came under attack of the authoritarian regimes ruling Serbia during World War II. In 1945 the Communist regime of Yugoslavia integrated associations working in the fields of recreation, culture, athletics, and professional development, into the state-controlled system and closed down all independent organizations by nationalizing their assets. New associations were eventually allowed to form, as long as they did not challenge the regime's ideology and were apolitical in nature.

In the late 1980s, when the Yugoslavian state began to lose its control over society and showed its first signs of disintegration, independent citizen initiatives, such as the Yugoslavian Democratic Initiative, were founded to pursue a democratic future for the country. Democracy did not materialize, however. Instead, the 1990s were marked by the influx of internally displaced people and refugees, economic crises, an upsurge in nationalism, intolerance against ethnic minorities, and several violent wars related to the breakup of the old Yugoslavian state, which left Serbia and Montenegro as the only two members of the Federal Republic of Yugoslavia. In 1998 and 1999 violent clashes between Serbian forces and the Albanian minority in Kosovo led to a North Atlantic Treaty Organization (NATO) bombardment of Serbia. Subsequently, Kosovo became a UN protectorate.

However, the 1990s also saw the expansion of basic civil liberties, including the freedom of association, for Serbian citizens. In turn, organizations proliferated, mostly in opposition to the ruling authoritarian regime led by Slobodan Milosevic. The regime used the media to portray these often foreign-funded civil society organizations (CSOs) as undermining national interests by propagating foreign ideas. To a certain extent, this perception of CSOs still influences the way the public views civil society in Serbia today.

After mounting discontent with Milosevic's regime, a series of demonstrations and citizen mobilizations in 2000 led to the ousting of the authoritarian government and the installation of democracy. In the following years, civil society found it difficult to move from a critical to a constructive perspective of the new government; however, relations with the democratic government of Prime Minister Djindjic

Figure 34.1 Civil Society Diamond for Serbia

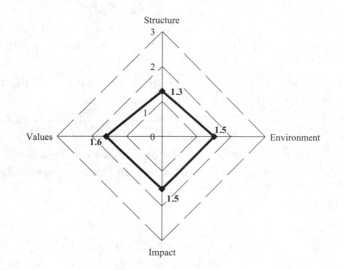

grew closer over time. The 2003 assassination of Djindjic was a turning point. A conservative minority government came to power relying on support from Milosevic's Socialist Party, which treats civil society with a pronouncedly less positive attitude—and sometimes with outright hostility.

The State of Civil Society in Serbia

The term "civil society" is not used in mainstream public discourse in Serbia. Only one-third of Serbs are familiar with the term. Its conceptual history is confined to the progressive elite, which used the concept in the 1990s as a normative ideal for the future development of society. Thus, the proposed CSI definition of civil society, including both positive and negative forms of civic action, was new and challenging for the Serbian project team.

This section provides a summary of the key findings of the CSI project in Serbia. It examines the state of Serbian civil society along four dimensions—structure, environment, values, and impact—highlighting the main weaknesses and strengths.

The Serbian Civil Society Diamond (figure 34.1) depicts a civil society of moderate size with balanced dimensions. The weakest component is civil society's structure, which is marred by low levels of citizen participation, as well as a weakly institutionalized and a rather poorly resourced organized civil society. Serbian civil society operates in an environment that features moderately enabling factors, such as civil liberties and positive socioeconomic conditions, and a range of disabling factors, such as the volatile political context and negative relations between civil society and the state, and civil society and the private sector. Similarly, civil society's track record in practicing and promoting important social values presents a mix of rather strong value commitments, such as nonviolence and environmental sustainability, and serious weaknesses, particularly in the fields of transparency and poverty eradication. The impact of civil society on governance and society at large is moderate, and is negatively affected by civil society's limited role in advocacy and policy formulation.

Structure (1.3)

The structure dimension examines the makeup of civil society in terms of the main characteristics of individual citizen participation and associational life. The structure of civil society in Serbia is somewhat weak. While Serbian civil society shares the problem of limited citizen participation with many other post-Communist countries, it distinguishes itself through equally poor levels of sectoral infrastructure, cohesion, and resources.

After a period of heightened civic engagement during the 1990s, which culminated in the widespread demonstrations against Milosevic's regime on October 5, 2000, the level of citizen participation in nonpartisan political actions dropped significantly. The CSI population survey revealed that while 39% of respondents participated in demonstrations during authoritarian rule, participation fell to 9% in the postauthoritarian period. Membership in CSOs seems to be growing and has reached 47% of the population. However, CSI participants pointed out that the share of active members is much lower. CSO types with the highest membership are trade unions (27%), political parties/movements (26.5%), NGOs and sports groups (both 19%), and tenants' associations (17%). Volunteering is rather common, but primarily relates to providing help to the immediate community, and volunteering for CSOs is rare. In addition, people's participation in collective community activities (21%) or meetings (17%) is not widespread and, according to civil society stakeholders, is mainly driven by political motivations rather than community-wide concerns.

In examining the structural features of organized civil society, one finds a markedly urban bias, with a concentration of CSOs in large cities. This corresponds to an underrepresentation of rural dwellers and poor people as members or leaders of CSOs. Despite significant and long-term support from foreign donors, civil society's level of organization and infrastructure receives a somewhat negative assessment. Sector-wide self-regulatory mechanisms are uncommon, and the coverage and operations of civil society networks are regarded as largely insufficient and rather ineffective. Stakeholders point out that cooperation is no longer widespread among Serbian CSOs, as it was in the 1990s when they were fighting a common enemy. In contrast, CSOs' expanding support infrastructure, such as resource and information centers, receives a more positive assessment.

A severe challenge to the sector is represented by the decrease in financial resources for many CSOs, due to foreign donors leaving the country. In 2001 31% of surveyed organizations assessed themselves as being in a good to excellent financial situation; this dropped to 15% in 2005. However, the departure of foreign donors might also end civil society's excessively donor-oriented objectives and will likely force CSOs to develop their own priorities.

Based on this assessment, the challenges for Serbian civil society lie clearly in the development of domestic resources and a larger citizen support base as well as in overcoming the barriers to effective cooperation among CSOs. As indicated by CSI participants, there are some positive signs of an emerging citizen-driven civil society grounded at the local level that need to be capitalized upon.

Environment (1.5)

The environment dimension considers political, legal, socioeconomic, and sociocultural contexts as well as the relationships between civil society, the state, and the private sector. Aside from the short period of Djindjic's government in the early 2000s, Serbian civil society has operated in a largely disabling political and legal environment, which is somewhat balanced by a respect for basic civil liberties and rights and an absence of major socioeconomic barriers.

Serbia's political arena and public life are characterized by fairly widespread corruption, disrespect for the rule of law, mistrust in public institutions, an inefficient state apparatus, and a deeply divided party system, which reflects a similarly divided society. These factors severely limit the political space available to independent civil society. Similarly, low levels of social tolerance and interpersonal trust represent severe barriers to the development of a civic culture.

An examination of the legal environment provides a somewhat more positive picture, since regulations regarding civil liberties, press freedoms, and information rights are in place, though there are certain gaps in these regulations regarding discrimination against religious or ethnic minorities and the implementation of the Access to Information law. CSOs operate under an unclear and inconsistent legal framework, leaving ample room for discretion by public officials. A new Law on Associations has been drafted, which received largely positive feedback from experts in civil society. In addition, existing tax laws are widely regarded as limiting the financial viability of many CSOs and the development of individual and corporate domestic philanthropy. CSOs are subject to all local taxes, including value-added and income taxes.

State–civil society relations are problematic, since large parts of the public administration have a negative attitude toward civil society, particularly advocacy NGOs and trade unions. Interference in critical CSOs' operations and negative branding of these organizations in the media by government officials are not uncommon. Since the state does not attach any importance to principles of consultation or partnership, dialogue between the sectors is rare and financial support to civil society is limited, constituting only 14% of the sector's funding, primarily for CSOs involved in social service provision.[2] However, examples of mutually beneficial partnerships between state and civil society are emerging at the local level and could provide an impetus for improving relations at the national level.

Similarly, the private sector's attitude toward civil society is seen as either suspicious (41%) or indifferent (36%) by CSI stakeholders. Local companies provide support to less than a quarter of CSOs and make up only 9% of the sector's financial contributions.[3] Examining this issue from the perspective of the private sector presents a slightly more positive picture, with 56% of local and 96% of international companies declaring to have a corporate social responsibility (CSR) strategy in place. However, rather than a systematic and planned approach to CSR, ad hoc charitable activities still form the core of these activities.

Values (1.6)

The values dimension examines the extent to which civil society practices and promotes positive values. While Serbian civil society receives a moderate rating for the values dimension, a closer look reveals a number of problematic areas, such as transparency and poverty eradication, as well as certain strengths, such as promoting tolerance and nonviolence in society.

Aside from gender equity, which is widely practiced within CSOs, but not strongly promoted in society, civil society's internal practice of key values did not receive better evaluations than its promotional activities. The low scores for civil society's transparency are of particular concern, since this norm underpins many other values and is of crucial importance for Serbian society as a whole. A review of 200 Serbian CSOs' websites (carried out as part of the CSI assessment) revealed that not a single one published its financial report on the internet. Also problematic is that corruption within CSOs is seen as rather common by stakeholders consulted during the CSI implementation.

Another weakness of Serbian civil society relates to poverty eradication, which is primarily seen as a responsibility of the state. While certain CSOs are active in this field through their involvement in the national Poverty Reduction Strategy, the rest of civil society remains largely unaware of these activities.

Despite these weaknesses, civil society shows a strong commitment to the promotion of a tolerant, nonviolent, and democratic society, and is regarded as a leading force in the public debate on these issues. However, in relation to democracy promotion, civil society is less active than it was five years ago and is described as tired, frightened, and disconnected from citizens. In addition, intolerant and violent groups within society, such as skinheads and nationalist groups, often do not encounter strong resistance from civil society at large.

Impact (1.5)

The impact dimension assesses civil society's role in governance and society at large. Serbian civil society is assessed as having a moderate level of impact, but, overall, occupying a rather marginalized position among key social forces in the country.

Civil society organizations play a moderately strong role in public education and service provision, particularly for marginalized groups; however, their role in governance (as policy advocates and watchdogs) is less developed. According to the CSI, key obstacles to increasing civil society's impact are CSOs' lack of advocacy skills and a government that does not see civil society's input into policy proposals as important. Similarly, the role as watchdog of the state and private sector is not widely embraced by civil society and remains a largely foreign concept.

Serbian civil society is rather active in providing a range of social services to marginalized groups. However, the state retains its dominant role in the overall welfare system. The CSI population survey found that by a ratio of 2 to 1, CSOs are seen as better service providers than state agencies, which may indicate that CSOs' competitive advantage in the social sphere is underutilized by the Serbian government. Interestingly, this positive assessment does not translate into significant public trust, which is rather low for NGOs (36%) and trade unions (19%), and presents a key impediment for a stronger public role for civil society. CSI participants noted such issues as negative media reporting, low CSO transparency, and CSOs' disinterest in promoting their work among society at large as factors contributing to public distrust.

Recommendations

Approximately eighty participants attended the CSI National Workshop to generate action-oriented recommendations from the CSI assessment. The following are some of the recommendations identified at this workshop:

- Public image: Civil society should cooperate with the media to present positive examples of its work to the public. CSOs should also address their weak internal accountability and transparency.
- Cooperation with the state: CSOs should work with the state at all levels to increase public funding and initiate joint projects and other forms of partnerships.
- Legal framework: There is a need for more enabling laws pertaining to the activities of civil society. NGO experts should be involved in drafting these laws and monitoring their implementation, to ensure appropriate and consistent application.
- CSO capacity: More focus should be placed on providing new CSOs with relevant information, services, and skills that support their work, such as a national database and exchange programs between established and new CSOs.

Conclusion

Civil society is a rather marginalized sector in Serbia. Its relationships with the state, the private sector, the media, and the public are problematic and sometimes even hostile. However, as the CSI assessment highlights, building trust with stakeholders will require that civil society address issues of accountability, cooperation, and professionalism, in order to be seen as a respectable partner. At the local level, the development of effective partnerships with the government and the private sector and early indications of locally driven forms of civil society are becoming evident. It will take considerable time for these developments to reach CSOs working at the national level; however, the bottom-up nature of this process points to first indications of a sustainable, citizen-driven, locally rooted civil society in Serbia.

CSI Report

Zdenka Milivojevic, *Gaining Legitimacy and Recognition in the New Millennium: CIVICUS Civil Society Index Report for Serbia* (Serbia: ARGUMENT, in collaboration with the Center for the Development of the Non-profit Sector [CDNPS], 2006).

Notes

1. The CSI assessment was implemented in Serbia by the research center ARGUMENT, in collaboration with the Center for the Development of the Non-profit Sector (CDNPS), from September 2004 to June 2006. This chapter presents the main findings of the CSI and is based on a comprehensive country report for Serbia, which can be accessed on the CSI pages of the CIVICUS website at http://www.civicus.org.
2. "Serbia," in *Nations in Transit 2006* (Freedom House: 2006). Accessed at http://www.freedomhouse.hu/nitransit/2006/serbia2006.pdf (accessed September 26, 2006).
3. Ibid.

Chapter 35

Sierra Leone[1]

Sierra Leone arguably has one of the most troubled legacies of violent conflict in the world. Decades of patrimonial rule incapacitated the state, followed by an extremely violent and insidious ten-year civil war in the 1990s. The country is still recovering from the immense physical, socioeconomic, and psychological devastation brought about by the war. However, since 2002, a period of peace, growing respect for human rights, and certain progress toward democratic governance indicates that Sierra Leoneans may have an opportunity to build public institutions and invigorate economic and social development processes. In this context, the role of civil society actors as crucial intermediaries between government and the people is of critical importance, and the CSI study highlights the main opportunities and challenges related to this role. The fact that such a participatory and comprehensive assessment of the state of civil society could even take place in Sierra Leone is already an achievement.

Historical Overview

The port of Freetown was founded by the British in 1787 and soon became the destination for freed black slaves from the United States. British colonial rule lasted about 150 years, until the country gained independence in 1961. After a short period of democracy, the shift to authoritarian government began in the late 1960s following two coups by rival parties. Prime Minister Siaka Stevens emerged victorious, and in 1971 installed a presidential system that increasingly turned into an authoritarian one-party state, ruled by his All Peoples' Congress. Widespread patronage and poor economic policies destroyed the rather healthy economy, impoverished the state, and brought the public sector

347

Table 35.1 Background Information for Sierra Leone

Sierra Leone	
Country size (square km)	71,740
Population (millions 2004)	5.3
Population under 15 years	42.8%
Urban population (2003)	38.8%
Seats in parliament held by women (2005)	14.5%
Language groups	English (official), Mende in South, Temne in North, Krio (English Creole)
Ethnic groups	Temne 30%, Mende 30%, other 30%, Creole (Krio) 10%
Religious groups	Muslim 60%, indigenous beliefs 30%, Christian 10%
HDI score and ranking (2003)	0.298 (176th)
GDP per capita (US$ 2003)	$835
Population living on less than US$2 a day (1989)	74.5%

to a virtual standstill. Key civil society institutions, such as labor unions and teachers' unions, were co-opted into the ruling class, while faith-based CSOs began to replace the state in its social functions of education and welfare.

In the early 1990s, the vulnerable state came under attack by the Revolutionary United Front (RUF), led by Foday Sankoh, which seized control over a considerable part of the country. A decade of civil war followed. After a brief military junta, and during continued fighting with the RUF, elections were held in 1996. Ahmad Tejan Kabbah of the Sierra Leone People's Party won the elections. An accord between the government and the RUF, signed in late 1996, quickly collapsed, leading to a coup d'etat by the RUF and its allies, again plunging the country into violence. President Kabbah returned to power in April 1998, backed by military troops from the Community of West African States (ECOWAS). Several months later, after a bloody onslaught by the RUF on Freetown, the capture of RUF leader Sankoh led to a disintegration of RUF forces and eventually to the signing of a peace accord in July 1999. After the peace accord was signed, a large UN peacekeeping mission was dispatched to the country. However, fighting continued until 2002. On January 17, 2002, the civil war was declared officially over, and on May 14, 2002, presidential and parliamentary elections were held, which elected incumbent President Kabbah to another term in office.

During the civil war, a number of civil society initiatives aimed for a peaceful solution to the conflict and a return to democracy during the brief military junta. The systematic campaign of noncooperation with the military junta and the RUF, launched by civil society, helped to bring about the return of democracy, which ushered in the democratically elected government of Ahmad Tejan Kabbah in 1996. Women's groups, teachers' unions, labor unions, and, particularly, religious groups, such as the Inter-Religious Council of Sierra Leone, played an important role and continued to do so after the peace accord was signed. They provided training and ran public education campaigns in relation to the Truth and Reconciliation Commission. Since the return to peace and democracy, professional NGOs, funded by foreign donors, have entered the scene, but they remain largely confined to the capital of Freetown.

The State of Civil Society in Sierra Leone

Sierra Leonean civil society is made up of a diverse range of associations, which are generally grouped into three categories: elite CSOs, which are part of, or have preferred access to, the ruling class, such as advocacy and service delivery NGOs and networks; socially embedded, membership-based CSOs, such as trade unions, religious organizations, and farmers' associations; and traditional and locally organized associations, such as credit groups, women's societies, burial societies, and parent-teacher associations. Although the CSI sought to analyze the entire range of these associations, in many cases the activities of urban-based NGOs were most visible and relevant for this study.

This section provides a summary of key findings of the CSI project in Sierra Leone. It examines the state of Sierra Leonean civil society along four dimensions—structure, environment, values, and impact—highlighting the main weaknesses and strengths.

The Civil Society Diamond (figure 35.1) for Sierra Leone portrays a rather weak civil society. Its structure features both strengths, such as the high levels of civic engagement in community-based civic activities, and weaknesses, such as the weakly organized and poorly resourced organizations of formal civil society. Civil society operates in a disabling environment, where immense socioeconomic, sociocultural, and political legacies impede the work of CSOs. Civil society's internal and public commitment to key values is moderate and generally mirrors society's value base, with particularly weak adherence to

Figure 35.1 Civil Society Diamond for Sierra Leone

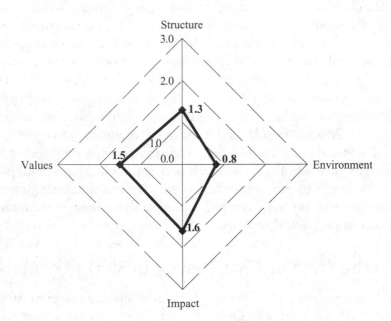

transparency and gender equity principles. In a context of an ailing state, CSOs have assumed many roles in social welfare and the fight against poverty. However, their impact on governance remains weak, due to internal weaknesses and an unresponsive state.

Structure (1.3)

The structure dimension examines the makeup of civil society in terms of the main characteristics of individual citizen participation and associational life. In Sierra Leone, civil society's structure is rather weak. Although there are significant levels of civic engagement in community-based activities, formal civil society is fragmented, loosely organized, and underresourced.

Sierra Leonean citizens are engaged in various community activities. Ninety-seven percent of the CSI population survey respondents either attended a community meeting or participated in a community activity during the previous twelve months. Similarly, despite pervasive poverty in the country, 2 out of 3 Sierra Leoneans donated money or goods, particularly within their communities, over the same period. CSO membership is prevalent, with 73% of population survey respondents being a member of at least one organization. Community-based organizations have high membership rates, for example cooperatives (24%), farmer/fishermen's associations (16%), and local business associations (10%). Other popular types of CSOs are professional associations (13%), youth groups (10%), trade unions (6%), religious organizations (6%), and women's groups (6%). However, the social composition of formal CSOs is rather skewed. Stakeholders view women, rural people, ethnic minorities, and poor people as severely underrepresented in CSOs, at both membership and leadership levels. Similarly, although informal forms of association are common throughout the country, organized forms of civil society are highly concentrated in urban areas, particularly Freetown.

There is a range of networks for different civil society subsectors, but their reach and effectiveness is rather limited. More than three-quarters of CSI stakeholders consider the level of communication among CSOs to be moderate or weak, and there are few examples of cross-sectoral cooperation. Support infrastructure for CSOs, such as resource and training centers, is almost absent and only provided by a small number of international NGOs and donors. Civil society's high level of fragmentation and lack of coordination is apparent in the fact that there are no serious efforts to establish a sector-wide system of self-regulation. Due to weak internal governance, limited constituency links, and donor dependency, the development of self-regulatory mechanisms for individual CSOs and the sector as a whole should be prioritized. Although membership-based CSOs rely on scant local financial resources, from membership dues and local contributions, most NGOs are highly dependent on foreign donors. Given the brain drain that took place during the civil war, human resource shortages are another challenge for civil society.

Civil society in Sierra Leone faces important structural challenges. There is a particular need to overcome the fragmentation between civil society in the rural areas, which is mainly informal and community-based, and urban civil society, made up of a rather small number of professionalized NGOs and professional associations.

Environment (0.8)

The environment dimension considers political, legal, socioeconomic, and sociocultural contexts, as well as the relationships between civil society, the state, and the private sector. Not surprisingly, civil society's environment is the weakest dimension in Sierra Leone, indicating formidable challenges, particularly in the political and socioeconomic contexts.

Decades of authoritarian rule and civil war have seriously impaired the social fabric of the country. Among the various social groups that suffered, the youth were exceptionally exploited by both sides during the civil war, as combatants or sex slaves. Today the youth remain traumatized, uneducated, disillusioned, and socially excluded. In general, social trust is rather low, with two-thirds of the respondents to the CSI population survey not trusting fellow citizens. The same survey found similarly low levels of social tolerance, particularly toward people living with HIV/AIDS, homosexuals, and people of a different race. Poverty is rampant, the economic reconstruction of the country has not progressed far, and large parts of the rural population live in a survival economy without any ties to urban centers.

The Sierra Leonean government has made impressive efforts to protect human rights, ensure free and fair elections, initiate an administrative decentralization process, and establish key democratic institutions. However, the limited ability and resources of the state to implement policies, enforce the rule of law, provide basic services, make government institutions work effectively, and address widespread patronage and corruption in the public sector are key weaknesses. In international surveys, Sierra Leone is ranked among the weakest countries with regard to rule of law, state effectiveness, and level of corruption. Public access to government information is extremely limited. Despite demands from civil society, no legislation exists to improve access to government information. Given the legacies of patrimonial rule, civil war, and a collapsed state, a culture of and mechanisms for public accountability are almost completely lacking.

The government generally respects freedom of association and CSOs are allowed to operate freely. Despite isolated instances of discrimination, the registration process for CSOs is assessed as generally conducive. A majority of CSI stakeholders consider registration to be simple, inexpensive, consistently applied, and following legal provisions. However, respondents were divided in their assessment of the speed of the process and feel that decentralizing the process would facilitate the registration of local-level CSOs. Even though civil society's autonomy is largely ensured, state–civil society relations leave ample room for improvement. A majority of surveyed stakeholders consider dialogue between both sectors to be limited. The government has begun to include civil society representatives on some consultative bodies, such as budget oversight committees, but civil society–state dialogue is generally ad hoc, with limited impact. A transparent and more institutionalized framework for state–civil society interactions is required.

Similarly, civil society–private sector relations are minimal. Due to civil society's limited role and capacity, the private sector, with the exception of beverage and telecommunication companies, is largely indifferent or even hostile toward civil society. Company officials who were approached as part of the CSI study were reluctant to divulge information on their company's activities, let alone discuss their corporate social responsibility (CSR) plans, since they feared their companies would be singled out for negative publicity by the media for failing to undertake CSR activities.

As highlighted by the CSI study, civil society's operating environment features a range of serious constraints and gaps, which limits its room to maneuver. In a country where the majority of the population is concerned with basic survival, where the social fabric is severely impaired, and a rights-based culture has not been established, collective citizen action for the public good is, understandably, rarely a priority for Sierra Leoneans.

Values (1.5)

The values dimension examines the extent to which civil society practices and promotes positive values. In Sierra Leone, the CSI study finds civil society to be a mirror of general social values.

An overall culture of secrecy and corruption also affects civil society. During CSI consultations, participants acknowledged widespread corrupt practices within CSOs, which they relate to most CSOs' lack of internal democracy, accountability, and transparency. Many CSOs are controlled by a founding director or set up as "ghost organizations" to attract foreign funding. In general, financial transparency and oversight mechanisms are weak. Participants stress the need for civil society to develop effective mechanisms of self-regulation, to ensure the transparency and accountability of CSOs and their adherence to an agreed code of ethics.

Women remain largely excluded from key government positions and key political and development processes. There are some CSOs that advocate for a greater role for women in public life, such as the 50/50 campaign, the Women's Action for Human Dignity (WAHD), and the Women's Forum. However, the civil society sector is home to the same discriminatory practices as society at large. According to the CSI assessment, women are significantly underrepresented in CSO leadership positions and three-quarters of CSI stakeholders could recall sexist practices within civil society. This situation has prompted calls for the promotion of gender equality within civil society.

Despite these weaknesses, a range of principles and values are strongly promoted by civil society. For example, civil society has been and remains a critical, though often overlooked, force in national reconciliation and peacebuilding. Human rights and faith-based CSOs have engaged in nationwide advocacy, training, and capacity building efforts for the Truth and Reconciliation Commission and the Special Court for Sierra Leone. They were also active in assisting with the disarmament, rehabilitation, and reintegration of ex-combatants into society. CSOs also played an important role in the democratization process, particularly in mobilizing resistance to the various antidemocratic forces during the civil war.

As democracy and peace are stabilizing in the country, a set of different and more complex principles is taking center stage, such as good governance, social accountability, and public transparency, although civil society's capacity as an effective promoter of these values has so far proven to be quite limited.

Impact (1.6)

The impact dimension assesses civil society's role in governance and society at large. In Sierra Leone, this dimension receives a medium-level assessment. Given the disabling political environment, it is not surprising that civil society's role in social development is more significant than its roles in policy and governance.

In the context of an incapacitated state, civil society, mainly in the form of development NGOs and community-based organizations, is very active in addressing the key social needs of the population, such as water, housing, health, and education. The CSI assessment finds that civil society has considerable reach in this capacity. Four out of five respondents to the population survey could remember a CSO promoting income-generation activities in his or her community and 87% see voluntary organizations as providing better services than the state. Correspondingly, public trust in faith-based CSOs (75%) and NGOs (66%) is significantly higher than trust in key state institutions, such as the police (24%), armed forces (27%), or central government (32%).

Civil society's involvement in advocacy is marred by difficulties. Advocacy CSOs are generally inadequately resourced, weakly trained, and poorly networked; in addition, they face an unresponsive government. As a result, they struggle to make their voices heard. Although there are a growing number of advocacy campaigns around issues such as the rights of children, gender mainstreaming, and mining policies, they have had little impact. Thus, the weaknesses of civil society's environment and structure clearly limit civil society's impact on key governance processes.

Conclusion

Even though there has been a noticeable expansion of civil society programs and activities in recent years, the full potential of nonstate actors to promote development and good governance in Sierra Leone is seriously marred by the legacies of a failed state, social alienation, and economic collapse. More importantly, civil society remains highly fragmented and lacks links between organized civil society in Freetown and rural community-based organizations. Similarly, due to resource scarcity, organized civil society is highly dependent on foreign donors and largely disconnected from the population's needs. This severely constrains the legitimacy and impact of these organizations. What emerges from the CSI study is the need to build civil society from the bottom up and give marginalized groups, especially women and youth, a stronger voice and representation. This would likely boost civil society's social power base and its ability to engage with the state on the key concerns of the country.

CSI Report

Campaign for Good Governance, *CIVICUS Civil Society Index Report for Sierra Leone* (Freetown, Sierra Leone: Campaign for Good Governance, in cooperation with Christian Aid, forthcoming).

Notes

1. The CSI assessment was implemented in Sierra Leone by the Campaign for Good Governance, in cooperation with Christian Aid, from 2005 to 2006. Although most project activities had been completed at the time of writing this chapter (September 2006), the CSI National Workshop had not yet been held and the country report had not yet been finalized. This chapter is therefore based on a preliminary version of the CSI country report for Sierra Leone as well as other studies on civil society in the country. Although the specific results reported in this chapter are not going to change, some indicator scores are still being validated.

Chapter 36

Slovenia[1]

Different from the development of civil society in many other post-Communist countries, the growth of the sector in Slovenia has been rather slow. However, in the last few years, civil society has improved its level of coordination to overcome its history as a collection of disparate organizations operating in isolation from one another. The public sector is also increasingly recognizing the valuable role of civil society, and the government and civil society are seeking to establish mutually beneficial relations.

Table 36.1 Background Information for Slovenia

Slovenia	
Country size (square km)	20,256
Population (millions 2004)	2
Population under 15 years (2004)	14.2%
Urban population (2003)	50.8%
Seats in parliament held by women (2005)	12.2%
Language groups	Slovak (official), Serbo-Croatian
Ethnic groups	Slovene 88%, Serb 2%, Croat 3%, Bosniak 1%
Religious groups	Catholic 58%, unspecified 23%, other 19%
HDI score and ranking (2003)	0.904 (26th)
GDP per capita (US$ 2003)	$19,150
Unemployment rate (% of total labor force)	6.6%
Population living on less than US$2 a day (1998)	<2%

Historical Overview

The first civil society organizations (CSOs) in Slovenia were established in the fourteenth century, when guilds were formed and faith-based organizations began to emerge. During this period, the Catholic Church played an active role in society through humanitarian activities that included the provision of cultural, educational, and health services.

By the first half of the nineteenth century, trade unions and other social movements emerged, but were persecuted under the absolutist Austro-Hungarian Empire. Among these movements, the most significant were referred to as "camps," where groups gathered in open areas to discuss public issues. Also significant were the cooperatives that formed to protect the interests of farmers, workers, and tradesmen against the emerging capitalist system.

In 1918 Slovenia joined with other southern Slavic states to form the Kingdom of Serbs, Croats, and Slovenians. In 1929, under a Serbian monarch, it was renamed the Kingdom of Yugoslavia, which fell to the Axis powers during World War II. Following World War II Slovenia became part of the Socialist Republic of Yugoslavia, whose civil society sector was severely restricted because its activities and goals were perceived to threaten the Communist regime. In 1974 the adoption of the Law on Societies opened up some space, and many CSOs arose to meet the social needs that government was unable to address. As the socialist system began to loosen its grip in the early 1980s, civil society continued to grow and more political forms of citizen action emerged, including the noncommercial FM radio station Radio Student, and the political weekly magazine, *Mladina*. The emerging Slovenian social movements often combined pro-democracy elements with nationalistic ones, and fought against the domination of the Yugoslav government in Belgrade.

After Slovenia's independence in 1991, the NGO sector that emerged was rather small, except in the fields of sports, culture, and social care, where a significant number of CSOs appeared. Advocacy CSOs were few in number; the more active ones often formed political parties and directly entered the political arena. Since Slovenia joined the European Union (EU) in 2004, the environment for CSOs has steadily improved. The public's perception of civil society has begun to shift and civil society's relevance is increasingly recognized. For example, a process is under way to establish more systematic dialogue between civil society and the government. However, largely because of limited resources and poor organizational capacity, Slovenian CSOs have yet to take full advantage of the opportunities created by accession to the EU, such as access to EU structural funds.

Figure 36.1 Civil Society Diamond for Slovenia

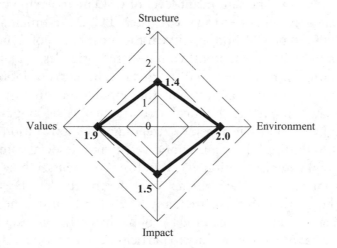

The State of Civil Society in Slovenia

This section provides a summary of key findings of the Civil Society Index (CSI) project in Slovenia. It examines the state of Slovenian civil society along four dimensions—structure, environment, values, and impact—highlighting the main weaknesses and strengths.

The Civil Society Diamond (figure 36.1) for Slovenia depicts a medium-sized civil society. Because of weak organization and a lack of resources within the sector, the structure is somewhat weak, despite rather widespread citizen participation. Civil society's relatively conducive operating environment and positive value base are potential assets for civil society's growth, but its impact remains moderate. Civil society plays a key role in delivering services and empowering Slovenians, but its advocacy record is weaker, and its influence in holding the state and private sector accountable is limited.

Structure (1.4)

The structure dimension examines the makeup of civil society in terms of the main characteristics of individual citizen participation and associational life. Overall, the structure of Slovenian civil society is somewhat weak because of an underdeveloped sectoral infrastructure and inadequate human and financial resources.

A distinguishable strength in civil society's structure is the rather widespread participation of Slovenians in civil society activities. According to the CSI population survey, charitable giving is practiced by a large majority of citizens (66%) and more than half are active in at least one CSO. The significant level of CSO membership correlates with the large number of formally registered CSOs (estimated at more than 25,000). The CSI findings reveal the most common type of participation to be in trade unions, volunteer fire brigades, and organizations of farmers, fishermen, and sports fans. In terms of more ad hoc forms of participation, almost half the population (46%) has taken part in some nonpartisan political activity, such as signing a petition, writing a letter to a newspaper, or attending a demonstration.

The CSI findings show a lack of diversity in the social composition and geographical distribution of CSOs. Rural residents, ethnic and religious minorities, and the poor are considerably underrepresented in CSOs. Thus, although there are many CSOs representing the interests of marginalized groups, the target groups themselves are underrepresented and have less opportunity to participate. Furthermore, CSOs are concentrated in the capital city of Ljubljana and other urban centers, while the presence of CSOs in rural areas is rather limited.

The Slovenian civil society sector remains underdeveloped and rather weakly organized. Communication tends to be informal, issue-based, and limited to CSOs operating within the same field. More than 90% of stakeholders believe the level of communication (such as information sharing) to be moderate (47%) or limited (45%). The extent of cooperation among CSOs is slightly stronger. Examples of alliances and coalitions exist, but they tend to be among CSOs operating in the same field. The umbrella bodies and federations in Slovenia include the Centre for Information Service, Cooperation, and Development of NGOs (CNVOS); the Association of Slovenian Societies (ZDOS); and the Association of Slovenian Foundations (ZSU). However, only a minority of Slovenian CSOs participate in networks because many CSOs do not see the benefits of such membership. Umbrella bodies tend to function rather effectively but would benefit from broader dissemination of information and closer engagement with their members. There is no code of conduct governing CSOs, although the government is drafting a new law on societies that is expected to include certain regulatory principles. A few NGO resource centers exist, but CSI stakeholders confirm that support infrastructure requires further development in order to enhance civil society's capacity.

A key impediment for civil society is the shortage of financial and human resources. The availability of these resources varies considerably among subsectors, but resources to cover core operational costs are generally scarce because most funding is tied to specific short-term projects. This also has negative implications for CSOs' ability to retain professional staff. Thus, even though there is a fairly diverse funding base for the sector, financial and organizational sustainability is a key challenge for many Slovenian CSOs.

Environment (2.0)

The environment dimension considers political, legal, socioeconomic, and sociocultural contexts, as well as the relationships between civil society, the state, and the private sector. Civil society's operating environment has improved in recent years and is relatively conducive. The largest weaknesses are found in the legal framework and in poor relations between most CSOs' subsectors and the private sector.

As a result of the 1990s' successful democratization and Slovenia's overall economic growth and stability, the political and socioeconomic environment is rather enabling for civil society. Basic freedoms and rights are respected and no major political obstacles impede the development of civil society. Unlike much of the rest of the former Yugoslavia, Slovenia was spared the experience of war and socioeconomic devastation that followed other independence struggles. Slovenia has a healthy economy, and has been a full member of both the EU and the North Atlantic Treaty Organization (NATO) since 2004.

Slovenia also enjoys a more favorable sociocultural context than the majority of post-Communist countries in Central and Eastern Europe. This is often attributed to the tradition of civic associations and the rule of law established during the Hapsburg Empire. Over the past decade, trust among Slovenians has grown to a moderate level; according to the CSI population survey, 36% of Slovenians feel that most people can be trusted. Society's level of tolerance is also fairly high, although there is a degree of intolerance toward homosexuals and the Roma population.

The legal environment is not as conducive as it could be. Although the CSO registration process is rather inexpensive and CSOs are entitled to perform any advocacy activity, tax provisions are not conducive for civil society's growth. Tax benefits for philanthropy are not widely promoted and the rate of reduction is not a substantial incentive. Although most CSOs are not subject to income taxation, this does not apply to CSOs' profit-oriented agenda, which often constitutes a majority of their activities. Like other legal entities, CSOs are obliged to pay a value-added tax (VAT); there are no tax exemptions for CSOs with public interest status.

As mentioned above, there are signs that relations between civil society and the state are improving, but existing relations are not highly institutionalized. The vast majority of stakeholders (98%) affirm that the extent of civil society's dialogue with the state is limited or moderate at best. In general, proper mechanisms for CSOs' participation in public decisionmaking are lacking. Comments are not properly recorded, there is no feedback, and inputs are usually not considered. Because of this lack of formal process, most CSOs resort to using personal contacts to interact with the state. According to participants in the CSI, the level of public financial support varies among ministries and municipalities, but is generally inadequate and biased because it favors CSOs operating in the area of social welfare.

Civil society's relations with the private sector are not conducive for strengthening civil society. A majority of CSI stakeholders feel that the private sector is indifferent to CSOs, and 3 out of 5 believe the private sector rarely participates in civil society initiatives. However, the CSI's corporate social responsibility (CSR) study reveals that all of the ten largest companies in Slovenia are either donors to or sponsors of CSOs, particularly in the fields of sports and culture, and 67% of smaller companies are involved in some sort of CSR activity. Stakeholders acknowledge increased awareness of CSR in Slovenia, but emphasize the bias of CSR activities toward sports and culture and the neglect of advocacy CSOs.

Values (1.9)

The values dimension examines the extent to which civil society practices and promotes positive values. The findings indicate that Slovenian civil society is built on a relatively significant foundation of positive values, particularly around the norms of nonviolence, tolerance, democracy, and environmental sustainability.

Violence is extremely rare in both Slovenian society and the civil society arena. Because public violence in society tends not to be a problem, civil society's activities focus on acts of domestic, sexual, and workplace violence. Whereas the CSI media review did not find any articles covering violent acts committed by civil society, stakeholders mentioned several isolated cases of intolerant behavior by civil society actors, such as the stance of religious organizations toward homosexuals, and the activities of a neighborhood association opposed to a transit home for foreigners and asylum seekers. However, these and other forms of intolerant behavior are usually strongly denounced by civil society at large.

Many CSOs are mandated to promote environmental sustainability. Stakeholders and the CSI media review confirm civil society's widespread activities in this area. The work of the Coalition for *Volvje Rebro* and the Coalition for Sustainable Waste Management is particularly noteworthy. Civil society is seen as particularly active in organizing educational activities and publishing educational material on environmental protection. Because environmental education is lacking in the school curriculum, civil society fills the gap, mostly by collecting and distributing information on issues of environmental sustainability.

Two separate issues—transparency and poverty eradication—require more cultivation in Slovenian civil society. Although transparency was not identified as a major problem for CSOs themselves, only a few CSOs are dedicated to promoting transparency in society at large. The majority of stakeholders (61%) could not recall any action by civil society to promote corporate transparency, and a majority of stakeholders (73%) believe civil society plays an insignificant role in promoting transparency. Similarly, civil society is somewhat inactive in campaigning against poverty, which is regarded as most effectively handled by the state. The social composition of CSOs appears to favor urban middle-class professionals, and often excludes the poor, which may lead to the sector not paying sufficient attention to the issue of poverty.

Impact (1.5)

The impact dimension assesses civil society's role in governance and society at large. Overall, civil society's impact is assessed as moderate. A more detailed examination finds its political influence and role as watchdog of government processes to be rather weak, while its social impact is more pronounced.

Civil society's record in influencing public policy is moderate, mainly because of its limited access to the policy process and lack of capacity to prepare policy inputs. The CSI policy studies on same-sex legislation and the status of asylum-seekers and citizens of the former Yugoslavia reveal that civil society is often active in raising awareness, lobbying, and engaging the government on issues, although this rarely translates into tangible impact on the policy outcomes.

Civil society plays a marginal role in holding the state and private sector accountable and in influencing the state budget. The sector undertakes some activities that involve monitoring the state, but the vast majority of CSI stakeholders (93%) describe these as fully or largely unsuccessful. Similarly, there is no discernible impact of civil society's limited efforts to monitor the private sector, with the sole exception of the work of environmental organizations.

The picture is different for civil society's social role, which is significantly more pronounced than its political function. Many CSOs are active in empowering the population. A recent example is the establishment of community foundations that mobilize local communities around their own needs. Civil society often fills gaps in services provided by the state and, based on public funding, addresses the needs of a range of such marginalized groups as drug users, persons with disabilities, victims of domestic violence, and the Roma people. Interestingly, 4 of 5 population survey respondents indicated that when requiring assistance, they regard CSOs as more helpful than state agencies. This extrapolates to higher, but still moderate, trust ratings for NGOs (51%) than for the central government (28%), major companies (36%), church organizations (24%), or political parties (4%). On the other hand, the Red Cross (34%) and trade unions (27%) do not enjoy much confidence from the Slovenian people.

Slovenian civil society's moderate impact is a consequence of its limited strength in terms of coordinated efforts, sectoral identity, resources, capacity, and public support. The sector's activities often respond to opportunities, particularly from the state, that make independent and adversarial advocacy and watchdog functions less of a priority.

Recommendations

During the CSI National Workshop and regional stakeholder consultations, participants from civil society, the government, and the media developed recommendations to strengthen Slovenian civil society. Some key recommendations that arose are listed below:

- Share infrastructure: CSOs working in the same geographical area could benefit from economies of scale by sharing infrastructure (for example by using common office space, research departments, and equipment).
- Encourage more cooperation and communication: CSOs should improve formal and informal linkages with one another, and develop electronic mailing lists, forums, and networks to increase the sharing of information.
- Diversify and lobby for financing: CSOs should advocate for state financing to CSOs to match the level of other EU countries. They should also lobby for balanced and unbiased distribution

of finances to CSOs performing activities for the public benefit, for the introduction of a law through which citizens could dedicate 1% of their annual taxes to a CSO of their choice, and for a more conducive tax structure to encourage philanthropy.

- Utilize the media: CSOs should develop a media campaign to promote CSR.
- Self-regulation: CSOs should develop and implement a code of conduct to improve civil society's accountability.
- Government and civil society relations: The government and CSOs should sign the 2005–2008 Agreement on Cooperation between NGOs and the Republic of Slovenia, to systematize and institutionalize their relationship and to enable effective dialogue.

Conclusion

The CSI assessment found that, in the light of a rather enabling environment, Slovenian civil society is a relatively minor force in society. The key weaknesses lie in the limited coordination and organization of the sector, which is a consequence of CSOs' preoccupation with immediate challenges of financial resources and organizational sustainability. In the years to come, Slovenian civil society therefore needs to strengthen its relations with key stakeholders in the government, the EU, the corporate sector, and citizens—particularly those outside the comfort zone of the urban middle class.

The first signs of stronger relations are already apparent. Slovenia's public sector increasingly recognizes the importance of civil society, as evidenced by the Draft Agreement on Cooperation between NGOs and the Government. In turn, the 2003–2008 Systematic Development Strategy for NGOs in Slovenia shows civil society's commitment to strengthening its capacity. In addition, the increasing engagement of Slovenians in civil society activities is another promising sign of the development of a more sustainable civic sector.

CSI Report

Matej Verbajs, *After Fifteen Years of Independence and a New Regime—Active, but Still Weak: CIVICUS Civil Society Index Report for Slovenia* (Ljubljana, Slovenia: Legal Information Centre for Non-Governmental Organizations, 2006).

Notes

1. The CSI assessment was implemented in Slovenia by the Legal-Information Centre for Non-Governmental Organizations, Slovenia (LIC), from February 2004 to November 2005. This chapter presents the main findings of the CSI and is based on a comprehensive country report for Slovenia, which can be accessed on the CSI pages of the CIVICUS website at http://www.civicus.org.

Chapter 37

~~~

South Korea[1]

Roughly twenty years after the advent of democracy, South Korea is experiencing a participatory revolution, driven by unprecedented growth in the number of civil society organizations (CSOs) and an explosion of various forms of citizen participation in the public sphere. As the findings of the Civil Society Index (CSI) assessment show, the crucial challenge is how to marry these two growth trends to create a vibrant, participatory, powerful civil society in the country.

Table 37.1 Background Information for South Korea

South Korea	
Country size (square km)	99,900
Population (millions 2004)	48.1
Population under 15 years (2004)	19.1%
Urban population	80.3%
Seats in parliament held by women	13
Language groups	Korean (official)
Ethnic groups	Korean
Religious groups	Buddhist 47%, no affiliation 46%, Christian 26%
HDI score and ranking (2003)	0.901 (28th)
GDP per capita (US$ 2003)	$17,971
Unemployment rate	3.5%
Population living on less than US$2 a day (1998)	<2%

Historical Overview

The modern history of South Korea began with the end of colonial rule, which included the Japanese occupation (1910–1945) and US military jurisdiction (1945–1948). It is also shaped by the establishment in 1948 of two separate nations—North Korea and South Korea—with opposing political, economic, and social systems.

South Korea's contemporary history was significantly influenced by the military dictatorships that lasted from 1961 to 1987, and by the rapid economic growth that accompanied this period. Since the 1960s, a distinct feature of South Korea's economic development has been the presence of the *chaebols*, or family-owned corporate groups, such as Samsung, LG, and Hyundai. Yet, until the late 1980s, South Korea's economic progress was not accompanied by similar advances in the areas of democracy and human rights.

South Korea's political history has strongly influenced civil society's development, particularly because successive authoritarian regimes did not allow for the establishment of independent groups. The forceful reemergence of civil society in South Korea was part of the late twentieth century's global surge known as the Third Wave of Democratization. The June 1987 uprising that toppled the authoritarian regime of General Chun Doo-hwan was a historical landmark for South Korean civil society. Subsequently, the democratization movement led by the *simin-undong* (civil movement) and by a social movement against corruption successfully mobilized around key political and institutional changes. A crucial transformation of civil society's role was triggered by an economic crisis between 1998 and 2001, which brought government leaders and civil society together in a war against poverty and unemployment. For the first time in South Korean history, CSOs were accepted as legitimate participants in the country's governance system.

Over the past few years, South Korea has experienced an unprecedented explosion of new CSOs. The number doubled within seven years and the country currently has approximately 22,000 CSOs. This growth is the result of the expansion of democratic space, the growing influence of organized CSOs, and the participation of ordinary citizens in the country's political processes through unorganized forms of civic engagement. Various government-funded civic and social programs also played a significant role in supporting civil society.

The State of Civil Society in South Korea

This section provides a summary of key findings of the CSI in South Korea. It examines the state of South Korean civil society along four dimensions—structure, environment, values, and impact—highlighting the main weaknesses and strengths.

Figure 37.1 Civil Society Diamond for South Korea

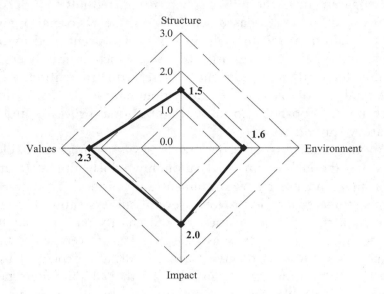

The South Korean Civil Society Diamond (figure 37.1) visually summarizes the CSI findings in South Korea. The diamond indicates that the current state of South Korean civil society is rather unbalanced among the four dimensions. The sector's structure, the weakest among the four dimensions, is rather limited because of inadequate financial and human resources. The environment is seen as somewhat enabling, despite relatively weak legal and sociocultural contexts. In contrast, the values dimension illustrates a strongly values-led civil society that is actively promoting democracy, gender equity, and sustainable development. Finally, the impact of the sector is assessed as relatively significant. Although civil society has been successful in influencing public policy and holding the government accountable, it has been less successful in its engagement with the South Korean population.

Structure (1.5)

The structure dimension examines the makeup of civil society in terms of the main characteristics of citizen participation and associational life. The most critical weakness relates to the gap between growing civic engagement and organized civil society.

The current proliferation of informal and unorganized South Korean citizen participation was accelerated by the boom of volunteers who supported the 2002 Soccer World Cup staged in South Korea and Japan, but has not led to increased giving, formal volunteering, or membership in CSOs. It appears therefore that South Korean citizens' engagement in the public sphere is spurred not by CSOs, but rather by ad hoc issues-based activities outside of formal organizations. In addition, membership in CSOs is concentrated in recreational and other apolitical organizations, which are rarely engaged in public life. A final impediment to increased participation in CSOs is the tendency of CSOs to be run by dominant leaders, who do not attach much importance to intra-organizational processes and participatory approaches.

Another critical issue is the low level of resources available for CSOs and the lack of financial autonomy, which ultimately affects CSOs' independence from government and business. Despite South Korea's strong economic progress, several surveys show that only a minority of the adult population give to charity on a regular basis, with donations amounting to as little as 0.4% of average net annual income. This low level of giving can be partially explained by the restrictive law on fundraising and the fact that, despite more people giving to charitable causes, they are donating smaller amounts through telephone, internet, and mobile phone drives.

Turning to the features of organized civil society, the CSI assessment finds it to be well organized through effective umbrella bodies and networks. However, although CSOs frequently cooperate with each other, their joint efforts rarely bring advocacy and service-oriented CSOs together. In addition, there is limited infrastructure for CSOs in terms of resource centers, information hubs, and other support functions. Nevertheless, the two main subsectors of service and advocacy NGOs emerge from the assessment as well coordinated and well equipped to wield considerable power in the public sphere.

Environment (1.6)

The environment dimension considers political, legal, socioeconomic, and sociocultural contexts, as well as the relationships among civil society, the state, and the private sector. The findings indicate that the environment is neither particularly favorable nor unfavorable for civil society in South Korea.

Since the democratic transition process that began in 1987, political rights and civil liberties have improved and expanded significantly. Previous regulations that had restricted the participation of labor unions and other civil organizations in elections were partially abolished in 1998 and 2002, respectively. However, several laws continue to constrain CSOs' activities and civil society in general. The laws on national security, elections, freedom of information, gatherings, and demonstrations restrict political expression. In addition, strict limits on available tax benefits and fundraising activities make many CSOs financially dependent on government contributions.

The relationship between the state and civil society in South Korea has improved since the democratization movement in 1987. Government now exerts little control and grants CSOs a high degree of autonomy in their work. However, due to the potential for unwarranted interference from authorities and a complex process, advocacy CSOs are often reluctant to register as a formal organization, despite its economic and legal advantages. The severe economic crisis of 1997, which brought together government leaders and civil society in a war against poverty and unemployment, also led to significant improvement in the quality of relations between government and civil society. Communication channels were institutionalized and new venues for dialogue were developed, including the Government Advisory Committee, the Public-Government Cooperative Project, and the Government Supported Public Foundation. However, the capacity and role of these mechanisms remain limited.

The relationship between business and civil society in South Korea is considered generally more confrontational than cooperative. Businesses often face severe criticism from civil society and the public at large. Furthermore, corporate social responsibility (CSR) in South Korea is also still in a nascent stage.

Not surprisingly, the socioeconomic context, which has steadily improved since the 1960s, is found to be particularly conducive to the development of South Korean civil society. The national rates of poverty (15%) and adult illiteracy (3.1%) rates are low; and higher education is widely available and accessible. In addition, more than 79% of the population is connected to ultra-high-speed internet services, making South Korea one of the most advanced societies with regard to information technology.

From colonialism through military dictatorship, South Korea's problematic legacy is reflected in its sociocultural context. Low levels of trust, tolerance, and public-spiritedness are a hindrance to the future development of South Korean civil society. For example, population surveys show widespread mistrust among South Koreans, with only 25% of the population feeling that most people can be trusted.

Taken together, the environment dimension presents a mixed picture. Overall, the past decades' socioeconomic and political development has provided positive conditions for civil society. However, a number of legal and operational factors—particularly those concerning civil society's relationship with the state and private sector—inhibit civil society from achieving its full potential.

Values (2.3)

The values dimension examines the extent to which civil society practices and promotes positive values. Its score indicates that South Korean civil society practices and promotes these values to a rather significant extent. In particular, the promotion of transparency, gender equality, democracy, and environmental sustainability are recognized as strengths of South Korean civil society.

South Korean civil society has played an exceptionally significant role in promoting democracy, and has made crucial contributions to the democratization process. The campaign of Citizens' Solidarity for the 2000 General Elections is symbolic of South Korean civil society's recent efforts at promoting democracy. The goal of Citizens' Solidarity was to oust antidemocratic politicians via electoral means. With the support of 900 CSOs, the campaign succeeded in defeating 59 of its 86 targeted candidates.

For the past two decades, advocacy CSOs have focused many of their activities on encouraging financial transparency within the public and private sectors. The activities have included monitoring central and regional governments' budgets, promoting freedom of information, and lobbying for the adoption of laws related to good governance. The 2005 Korea Pact on Anti-corruption and Transparency (KPACT) was such an advocacy activity. The KPACT aimed to eradicate corruption in all sectors of society, and won the endorsement of the government, political leaders, private enterprises, and civil society.

Despite civil society's strong role in promoting public transparency, its own track record remains somewhat problematic. The sector's degree of financial transparency is closely associated with CSOs' capacity to raise funds and improve their financial independence. Although the overwhelming majority of financially stable and independent organizations make their financial statements public, other CSOs are more reluctant because they are financially dependent and lack expertise in accounting.

South Korea's patriarchal social system has historically limited women's rights. The system was challenged in 2000 by the Coalition of Citizens for the Abolition of System of Head of Family, a broad movement of 113 CSOs. As a result of their long-term campaign, *hojuje*, or the system of head of family, was finally abolished in 2005. In 2003, 321 women's organizations established the Coalition of Women for General Elections. The coalition initiated activities to improve the electoral system and increase women's political representation. As a result, 13% of the members elected to parliament in 2004 were women, a twofold increase over the previous election, constituting the highest number of women ever elected to parliament in the history of South Korea.

Although the values dimension was generally assessed as positive, certain values require further development, such as civil society's role in promoting tolerance and nonviolence. South Korean CSOs fail to encourage a culture of tolerance with regard to minorities and groups espousing values at odds with the majority of the population. Social tolerance remains rather low. The percentage of South Koreans who are intolerant of homosexuals and persons living with HIV/AIDS is as high as 80%. Possible reasons for such high intolerance may be found in the suppression of ideological and cultural diversity that were part of South Korea's historical and political experience—Confucianism, Japanese colonial rule, and perhaps most important, the authoritarian militarism that predominated during the Cold War.

Impact (2.0)

The impact dimension assesses civil society's role in governance and society at large. It presents a fairly healthy state of South Korean civil society. Civil society's impact on public policy is particularly strong and evenly distributed among the five fields examined by the CSI, with the exception of social welfare where civil society's role is somewhat weaker.

Civil society's strength in the policy arena is a consequence of its focus during the past two decades on advocacy activities, such as holding the state and business sector accountable and promoting transparency. South Korean CSOs tend to utilize nationwide solidarity strategies for agenda-setting and political mobilization, which heavily depends on direct actions, such as campaigns, petitions, boycotts and demonstrations, which are successful in uniting hundreds of CSOs to advocate on social and political issues. Because of these campaigns' high levels of success, advocacy CSOs are among the most trusted institutions in the country.

Linked to its influence on public policy, civil society's activities in holding the state accountable were assessed as extensive and rather successful. An example is the Budget Watch Movement, a taxpayers' rights movement that monitors the effectiveness and transparency of central and local governments in budgetary planning and administration. As a result of civil society's lobbying around information disclosure, almost all local governments now disclose administrative information to the public.

While civil society is active as a watchdog of the state, its comparable efforts in the private sector are seen as somewhat unsuccessful. Civil society representatives feel that businesses tend to pay only lip service to CSR. For example, while *chaebols* have played a major role in South Korean economic development since the 1960s, they are criticized for lacking managerial transparency. During the 2002 presidential campaign, it was revealed that major *chaebols* made illegal political contributions. This reflects the fact that the country's democratization process in the political sphere has not been accompanied by similar advances in the economic sphere.

Civil society is playing a moderately effective role in empowering citizens and directly meeting social needs. A key weakness is the lack of cooperation between service and advocacy CSOs. As a consequence, service CSOs—heavily funded by government, and constituting an absolute majority of South Korean CSOs—do not play a role in advocating for the underprivileged or in empowering citizens.

The CSI assessment found that South Korean CSOs have effectively advocated for political reforms and have been successful in holding the state accountable. However, civil society has not played a strong role in meeting societal needs, building social capital, or empowering citizens—reflecting the gap between advocacy-oriented and service-oriented civil society activities.

Conclusion

Since the establishment of democracy in South Korea twenty years ago, civil society has gathered significant strength as an advocacy movement, has established generally positive relations with the state, and has succeeded in occupying an important position in the policy arena. Despite the tremendous growth in CSOs and citizen participation, the CSI assessment found that the current state of South Korean civil society is rather unbalanced among the four dimensions. The major strengths of South Korean civil society lie in its strong values and impact, mainly driven by the sector of well-organized advocacy CSOs. However, the structure and environment dimensions remain weaker. The structural problems facing South Korean civil society are mainly the result of limited financial resources and limited citizen involvement in CSOs. A number of laws impede the environment in which civil society operates. For CSOs to become financially sustainable, the relevant tax laws must be reformed. It is also incumbent upon CSOs whose composition is generally seen as somewhat elitist to reach out to those citizens who are currently engaged in informal civic activities in the public sphere. Successfully linking organized civil society with the increasingly active citizenry is likely to signigicantly enhance the foundation and social power of civil society in South Korea.

CSI Report

Sungsoo Joo, Seonmi Lee and Youngjae Jo, *The Explosion of CSOs and Citizen Participation—An Assessment of Civil Society in South Korea 2004: CIVICUS Civil Society Index Report for South Korean* (Seoul, South Korea: Third Sector Institute, Hanyang University, 2006).

Notes

1. The CSI assessment was implemented in South Korea by the Third Sector Institute (TSI) from July 2003 to September 2005. It was part of a larger research undertaking, "The Development of Korean Civil Society and the Role of NGOs." This chapter presents the main findings of the CSI and is based on a comprehensive country report for South Korea, which can be accessed on the CSI pages of the CIVICUS website at http://www.civicus.org.

Chapter 38

<div align="center">~~~</div>

Taiwan[1]

Taiwan has slipped off the global radar somewhat over the past few years, and its civil society has never received much international attention. The Civil Society Index Shortened Assessment Tool (CSI-SAT) findings show a rather influential and active civil society that plays a strong role in politics and society. Compared to its impact, however, civil society's structural foundations seem relatively underdeveloped.

Table 38.1 Background Information for Taiwan

Taiwan	
Country size (square km)	36,000
Population (millions 2004)	22,894,384
Population under 15 years (2004)	19.70%
Urban population (2003 estimate)	17,569,616
Seats in parliament held by women (2001)	22.2%
Language groups	Mandarin Chinese (official), Taiwanese (Min), Hakka dialects
Ethnic groups	Taiwanese 84%, mainland Chinese 14%, aborigine 2%
Religious groups	Buddhist, Confucian, and Taoist 93%, Christian 5%, other 2%

Historical Overview

In Chinese society, the culture of relationships, or *guanxi*, has influenced the development of social organizations. *Guanxi* refers to the dynamic of personalized networks of influence between persons or a group of contacts in the form of guilds, gangs, and clans. In Chinese history, folk organizations were based on kinship or interpersonal relationships and characterized by exclusivity and privacy. Citizens were often unwilling to trust social organizations other than those of their own clan. Hence, in pre–World War II China, not many organizations with a public character existed, which prevented the development of strong community values and a civil society.

From 1949 to 1987, during the period of martial law, the Kuo Min Tang regime (KMT) applied the Special Civil Society Organization Law, which forbade two organizations of the same nature from existing in the same area and severely limited the development of civil society organizations (CSOs). Therefore, the earliest CSOs in Taiwan came from abroad, such as the Red Cross, World Vision, the Christian Children's Fund, and various religious groups. These international NGOs served as a solid base for the proliferation of local CSOs in the late 1980s.

In the 1980s rapid economic development, a thaw in cross-strait relations, mainland China's open-door reform policies, and the decline of the KMT regime led to Taiwan's democratic transformation, which resulted in an increase in local associations and groups, such as the *Danwai* movement and a range of women's and environmental groups. After the demise of authoritarianism in the late 1980s, Taiwanese civil society continued to grow and began to exert influence on government and society. Today there are more than 20,000 NGOs registered with the Ministry of the Interior. Of these, 2,000 cooperate in some way with international NGOs. From underground social movements and the campaigns against one-party rule in the 1970s and 1980s, Taiwanese civil society has become a civic force with growing political influence in Taiwan and increased presence abroad.

The State of Civil Society in Taiwan

This section provides a summary of key findings of the CSI-SAT project in Taiwan. It examines the state of Taiwanese civil society along four dimensions—structure, environment, values, and impact—highlighting the main weaknesses and strengths.

Taiwan's Civil Society Diamond (figure 38.1) visually summarizes the CSI findings. Apart from the weaker structure dimension, the diamond reflects a well-balanced and relatively developed civil society sector. The weak structure of Taiwanese civil society is underscored by a lack of umbrella bodies, poor self-regulation, and rather limited

Figure 38.1 Civil Society Diamond for Taiwan

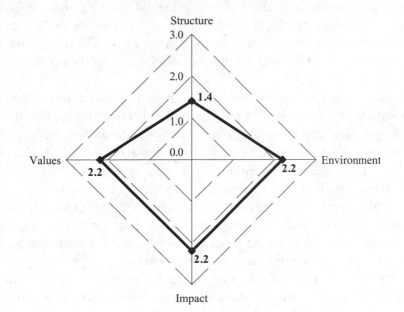

citizen participation. However, civil society's environment is relatively conducive; civil society benefits from cooperative relations with the state, although the private sector continues to lack interest in CSO activities. Civil society practices and promotes positive values to a significant extent, particularly democracy and tolerance, and its impact on society and governance is considerable given the sector's young history.

Structure (1.4)

The structure dimension examines the makeup of civil society in terms of the main characteristics of individual citizen participation and associational life. The CSI-SAT found that the structure of Taiwanese civil society is the biggest impediment to its growth. Having developed quickly over recent decades, the sector exhibits a low level of organization and limited citizen engagement. A more positive feature is the diversity of Taiwanese CSOs, which represent many different issues and social groups.

Civil society features underdeveloped self-regulatory mechanisms and lacks institutionalized forms of cooperation among civil society actors, with horizontal cooperation and integration among CSOs being particularly weak. The study's Stakeholder Assessment Group (SAG) frequently reiterated that the lack of mechanisms to facilitate networking among CSOs impedes the sector's growth and efficacy. A particular weakness is the lack of umbrella organizations bringing together a range of CSOs working across various issues. However, some networks do exist, such as the Union of Disabled Persons, the National Union of Taiwan Women's Associations, and the Green Citizen's Action Alliance.

Poor management and misuse of charitable donations following the major earthquake in 1999 are high profile consequences of limited self-regulatory mechanisms, which weaken donor confidence and public trust in the sector. Therefore, stakeholders highlight the importance of establishing self-regulatory principles within CSOs in order to encourage citizen engagement and charitable donations. As an important step in this direction, in September 2005 Taiwanese CSOs established the Union of Charity and Self-Regulation to promote rigid standards, including due diligence checks, financial transparency, and efficient CSO service delivery and management.

The sector also suffers from a scarcity of individual donations, low volunteerism, and limited civic engagement. Less than 30% of citizens have participated in some form of nonpartisan political action, such as signing a petition or joining a boycott, and only 28% are a member of a CSO. Similarly, in 2003 only 14.5% of citizens were reported to have volunteered for a civil society activity.

The long-term sustainability of Taiwanese civil society depends on strengthening the sector's structure. For citizens to participate in public affairs they need to be mobilized, and a system of self-regulatory mechanisms must be established to increase the sector's accountability and the public's faith in the sector. Umbrella bodies should also work to facilitate greater networking across civil society's diverse components.

Environment (2.2)

The environment dimension considers political, legal, socioeconomic, and sociocultural contexts, as well as the relationships between civil society and the private sector. Economic growth and democratization in Taiwan have facilitated a relatively enabling environment for Taiwanese civil society. The CSI found that the political context, basic rights and freedoms, legal environment, state–civil society relations, and socioeconomic conditions are conducive for civil society's development. The greatest weakness within the environment dimension is the weak relationship between civil society and the private sector.

Favorable factors, such as economic growth, rising income levels, and higher living standards, have created positive socioeconomic conditions in Taiwan. The transition from an aid to a donor country also created a sense of humanitarian responsibility in Taiwan and led to the establishment of various aid and development NGOs. Politically and legally, the environment regulating civil society does not provide any substantive obstacles. The CSO registration process is relatively friendly in terms of the speed and ease of the application process. Tax benefits for philanthropy enable domestic businesses to donate up to 10% of net income before tax. These various political, legal, and socioeconomic features form a solid base for civil society's future growth.

With respect to relations with the state, a study on civil society in the capital, Taipei, revealed that most CSOs have positive interactions with the central government. Certain problems, such as mutual mistrust and excessive oversight, were reported with regard to CSO interactions with the state at the local level. Overall, the degree of CSO autonomy from government is strongly influenced by the extent of public funding. Dialogue with the state in areas of mutual interest has also increased. Because of the difficult relationship between Taiwan and China, the government has diplomatic relations with only a few nations. As such, the interests of Taiwanese society abroad are increasingly represented by "people diplomacy" and the international activities of CSOs. In 1998, the Ministry of Foreign Affairs (MOFA) began to hold meetings to utilize the resources and expertise of Taiwanese CSOs in development projects, such as Taiwan's response to the Kosovo crisis in 1999. Among other government initiatives, the Taiwan Civil Union on Foreign Aid was created in 2000, under the leadership of MOFA. Twenty-five NGOs agreed to hold regular meetings to exchange ideas and resources regarding international humanitarian projects. At the same time, interaction with the state remains issue-specific and somewhat ad hoc, and dialogue would benefit from more institutionalized interaction. Nevertheless, the CSI findings reveal rather favorable stakeholder perceptions of the relationship between civil society and the state.

The relationship with the private sector is more problematic for civil society. In particular, corporate social responsibility (CSR) and charitable giving by businesses require cultivation in Taiwan. The concept of CSR is not entrenched in society, and stakeholders reported that most companies only pay lip service to CSR. Regarding corporate donations to ease civil society's financial shortcomings, a survey conducted among Taiwanese civic associations revealed that private sector donations and resources account for less than 20% of the total revenue for 70% of all associations surveyed. Thus, to date, the private sector's lack of CSR and limited corporate philanthropy are not conducive to civil society's growth.

Values (2.2)

The values dimension examines the extent to which civil society practices and promotes positive values. Taiwanese civil society received a rather positive assessment for this dimension. The CSI study found that democracy, tolerance, nonviolence, gender equity, poverty eradication, and environmental sustainability are all well-developed within Taiwanese civil society. However, corruption within civil society still exists, and financial transparency is not widely practiced among CSOs.

The value of transparency requires the most development in civil society. Historically, Taiwan's CSOs evolved out of family, clan, and personal networks, which tended to be insular, exclusive, and secretive. Given these traditions and the relatively recent formation of civil society, the concept of transparency is only now beginning to take hold. In the absence of adequate procedures for transparency and accountability, the majority of CSOs do not open their financial records to the public. There are also documented incidents of misappropriation of funds and embezzlement.

A majority of Taiwanese CSOs operate in a democratic manner and use participatory methods in their policymaking processes by encouraging members to freely share and express ideas. Civil society also actively promotes democratic principles in society, as exemplified by the work of the Taiwan Democracy Foundation (TDF), a government-sponsored NGO working to consolidate Taiwanese democracy and strengthen the government's commitment to human rights. In part, civil society's strong democratic values stem from historical factors, such as the country's special relationship with mainland China and civil society's important role in the democratic transition process. In addition, the ongoing political rivalry between Taipei and Beijing has encouraged the Taiwanese government to propagate CSOs' activities to promote democracy, as part of an approach to draw the attention of the international community to the differences between Taiwan and mainland China.

As a mostly democratic and peaceful sector, tolerance and nonviolence are entrenched in civil society. Instances of intolerance that do exist within civil society primarily stem from ethnic and ideological divisions, such as Taiwanese-mainlander disputes or independence-unification issues.

The CSI-SAT assessment shows that the strengths and weaknesses of values in Taiwanese civil society are largely related to civil society's historical and cultural development. The roots of many Taiwanese CSOs are embedded in the 1980s struggle for democracy and human rights; therefore, democratic values remain a driving force for Taiwanese civil society today. Civil society has strong commitments to tolerance, nonviolence, poverty eradication, and environmental sustainability. However, the somewhat close-knit and exclusive character of familial organizations in Taiwanese society has influenced the limited degree of transparency in civil society. Developing appropriate mechanisms to ensure transparency and accountability within CSOs should therefore be a priority, which would also stengthen public trust in civil society.

Impact (2.2)

The impact dimension assesses civil society's role in governance and society at large. The impact of civil society on society and governance is considerable, particularly given the fact that CSOs have only been legal since the end of martial law in 1987. The findings indicate that the sector is particularly successful in influencing human rights policy, responding to social interests, holding the state accountable, and empowering citizens by educating the public on social issues, building social capital, and empowering women. Civil society's ability to hold private corporations accountable is more limited and remains a primary weakness of the sector.

Civil society organizations, such as the Human Rights Foundation and the Taiwan Association for the Development of Human Rights (TADHR), are active in promoting human rights and influencing public policy. For example, TADHR investigates suspected human rights violations and monitors the government's human rights practices. TADHR's role paved the way for the establishment of the National Human Rights Council and the Human Rights Advocacy Union in 1999.

Civil society is also influential and successful in responding to public interests. For example, the Taiwan Home Keepers Union (THKU) responded to public demands for a cleaner environment by campaigning for government-sponsored recycling programs and by encouraging citizens to bring their own shopping bags. Civil society also formed the Eco-protection Alliance and the Anti-nuclear Action Alliance to limit pollution and oppose nuclear power.

Civil society has a positive record on empowering citizens. Women's groups, such as the Awakening Foundation, the Association of the Promotion of Women's Rights, Homemakers' Union and Foundation, and the Warm Life for Women Foundation, have worked to empower women and ensure gender equality. Faith-based organizations, such as Tzu Chi, Fo Guang Shan Monastery, and the Chinese Christian Relief Association, have been extremely active in supporting livelihoods by assisting low-income households, disabled and marginalized groups, and those affected by natural disasters.

Civil society is likewise active in monitoring the state. A recent survey of advocacy CSOs revealed that over 50% of Taiwanese advocacy CSOs have participated in some type of state monitoring activity. The Judicial Reform Foundation (JRF) is an example of an active watchdog organization around corruption, with its own system to monitor the police and courts. However, as far as monitoring CSR is concerned, civil society has less impact. Few Taiwanese CSOs aim to hold corporations accountable, with the Consumers Foundation Chinese Taipei the notable exception.

Though civil society's impact is relatively significant, challenges exist. For the state, the private sector, and the public to see the civil society sector as an important player, it must reach a greater level of maturity and cohesiveness at the national level and attract more widespread citizen participation to give more power to its advocacy activities.

Conclusion

Since the end of martial law, the rapid development of Taiwanese civil society has been remarkable. In a positive socioeconomic and political environment, CSOs have proliferated and civil society has actively responded to social interests, pushing for government accountability and empowering citizens through education and information programs. While Taiwanese civil society has undergone rapid transformation during the past three decades, the overall capacity of Taiwanese civil society is in its infancy. The structure of civil society is relatively weak, and it lacks institutionalized forms of cooperation and self-regulatory practices. According to the CSI study, stakeholders believe that by further developing relationships with international NGOs, the civil society sector will increase its knowledge and improve its level of organization. In addition, lobbying for increased financial support from the private sector and cultivating a culture of CSR will further expand civil society's influence in Taiwan.

CSI Report

Lin Teh-chang, *An Assessment of Civil Society in Taiwan—Transforming State-Society Relations—The Challenge, Dilemma and Prospect of Civil Society in Taiwan: CIVICUS Civil Society Index Shortened*

Assessment Tool Report for Taiwan (Taiwan: Center for International NGO Studies (CINGOS), National Sun Yat-sen University Kaohsiung, 2005).

Notes

1. The CSI Shortened Assessment Tool was implemented in Taiwan by the Center for International NGO Studies (CINGOS) at National Sun Yat-sen University, in cooperation with the National Youth Commission of the Executive Yuan, Republic of China, from March 2005 to July 2005. This chapter presents the main findings of the CSI-SAT and is based on a comprehensive report for Taiwan, which can be accessed on the CSI pages of the CIVICUS website at http:// www.civicus.org.

Chapter 39

Togo[1]

In August 2006, the Togolese government and opposition forces signed an agreement to install a government of national unity. This accord opened a new page in the history of the country and provides hope for national reconciliation, democratic governance, and respect for human rights. Togolese civil society has not been particularly active in the country's development or governance processes, but it is hoped that the Civil Society Index Shortened Assessment Tool (CSI-SAT) study can provide a springboard for a stronger role for civil society in this crucial phase of Togo's development.

Table 39.1 Background Information for Togo

Togo	
Country size (square km)	56,785
Population (millions 2004)	6.0
Population under 15 years (2004)	43.7%
Urban population (2003)	35.2%
Seats in parliament held by women (2005)	6.2%
Language groups	French (official), Ewe and Mina in south, Kabiyè and Dagomba in north
Ethnic groups	37 native African: largest and most important are Ewé, Mina, and Kabre
Religious groups	Indigenous beliefs 51%, Christian 29%, Muslim 20%
HDI score and ranking (2003)	0.512 (143rd)
GDP per capita (US$ 2003)	$1,696

Historical Overview

Various forms of civil society organizations (CSOs), such as self-help groups and village-based committees, existed in Togo long before the arrival of European colonizers in the sixteenth century. For many years, religious organizations associated with the Catholic and Protestant churches were in charge of the education of most of the population and delivered basic services, such as healthcare. They ran schools and hospitals, and worked in local communities by carrying out social activities aimed at supporting livelihoods in villages.

For centuries, the goal of Togolese community associations was to serve the interests of people coming from the same geographical area or belonging to the same tribes (such as the Ewé, the Kabiyè, and the Moba). Groups and associations representing different ethnicities constituted the bulk of Togolese civil society during the three successive colonizations by the Germans, British, and French. In the early to mid-twentieth century, Togolese society witnessed the strengthening of the colonial state structure and the simultaneous emergence of independence movements.

Throughout the 1950s, civil society groups spearheaded the popular movement that led to independence. For example, groups of women sent letters to the United Nations (UN), and the three-day general strike organized in 1957 by the trade unions significantly influenced the UN decision to hold a referendum to question French supervision. In 1958 a referendum was held, and the pro-independence cause, led by trade unions and political parties, won the popular vote. In 1960, Togo became independent.

In the first years of the newly independent state, national cohesion was a key priority for the government, particularly in light of ethnic tensions and territorial disputes. The struggle for national unity led to the centralization of political powers. The main social forces operating in the country—such as trade unions, political parties, and various other CSOs—were co-opted by the one-party state, which was instituted by Eyadéma in 1967. Gnassingbé Eyadéma would become the longest-serving president in African history (1967–2005). Women's organizations, youth groups, and some business associations became wings of the state party—the Rally of the Togolese People (RTP)—and the party's reach extended to neighborhood cells throughout the country, including remote rural areas.

After a series of attempted coups against Eyadéma, a democratic movement came to the fore in the 1990s and influenced the formation of NGOs working on various issues, such as human rights, the environment, the fight against poverty, and HIV/AIDS. Most of the NGOs that were established in this period were either branches of international NGOs or created by members of the elite, and therefore they often associated with specific religious or political groups. This elitist trait permeated civil society in Togo for years to come, and the transition to democracy was hampered by numerous obstacles and was never completed.

After Eyadéma's death in 2005, his son Faure took power by changing the constitution, a move widely condemned by the international community. In April 2005, Faure Gnassingbé won the presidential elections, with opposition parties claiming massive electoral fraud. However, Gnassingbé soon promised democratic changes and national reconciliation. In fact, a social dialogue between trade unions, the private sector, and government representatives gave way to a political dialogue between the government and the opposition. On August 20, 2006, a political accord was signed that called for the creation of a government of national unity—and free and fair parliamentary elections—in 2007.

The State of Civil Society in Togo

This section provides a summary of key findings of the CSI project in Togo. It examines the state of civil society in Togo along four dimensions—structure, environment, values, and impact—highlighting the main weaknesses and strengths.

The Civil Society Diamond (figure 39.1) visually summarizes the CSI assessment's findings in Togo. The diamond indicates that civil society in Togo has a rather weak structure and operates in a disabling environment, mainly due to the problematic political context and long-standing socioeconomic crisis. Consequently, civil society's impact on society and politics is insignificant, and, although civil society promotes some important values, the internal practice of these values is limited.

Structure (1.0)

The structure dimension examines the makeup of civil society in terms of the main characteristics of individual citizen participation and associational life. It shows that Togolese civil society is affected by poor interorganizational cooperation and limited citizen participation.

Togo's geographical configuration divides the country into five regions, each with its own economic, cultural, and social outlook.

Figure 39.1 Civil Society Diamond for Togo

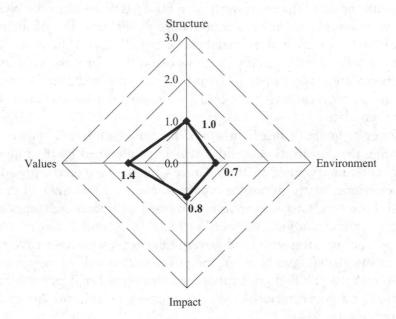

The differences between regions, including the ethnic distinctions between the main tribes, create significant divisions among the population and affect civil society's role, which remains limited due to inadequate outreach capacity, low citizen participation in nonpartisan political actions, and generally limited citizen involvement in civil society's activities.

Rivalries and lack of communication between organizations affect most CSOs operating in the country. Cooperation is unusual, and few CSOs share experiences and best practices. In general, individual CSOs are rarely organized into networks, and alliances are more common among international NGOs with branches in the country. Organized civil society is small and primarily funded by international donors, and the lack of cooperation leads to an exacerbation of rivalries between CSOs competing for limited financial resources. These resources have been declining since the 1993 presidential elections, when a number of donors suspended aid to the country in an attempt to force the government to democratize.

Most CSOs' human resources are inadequate and reveal the elitist tendencies of Togolese civil society, which is still affected by hierarchical structures, hegemonic leaders, and minimal representation of marginalized groups. Most CSOs are based in the large cities, and a disconnect exists between these organizations and the disadvantaged communities they are supposed to serve. In this regard, the CSI analysis highlights the importance of promoting citizens' involvement in CSOs' activities and bridging the gap between CSOs and marginalized communities.

Environment (0.7)

The environment dimension considers political, legal, socioeconomic, and sociocultural contexts, as well as the relationships between civil society, the state, and the private sector. In Togo, these factors pose significant obstacles for the development of civil society and severely limit the space for CSOs.

According to a UN report on the violence committed before and after the 2005 presidential elections, political rights are widely violated in Togo. Despite some political reforms that allow for elections, in practice, opposition parties are not free to conduct their activities, and the right of citizens to hold public demonstrations is severely curtailed. For example, an existing ministerial regulation forbids political gatherings or demonstrations on weekdays. The legal environment for CSOs is also extremely restrictive. CSOs are subject to significant government surveillance, and advocacy activities, although permitted under a 1901 law, are rarely carried out for fear of prosecution.

In terms of political competition, more than 90% of parliamentary seats are held by the RPT, which makes the country a de facto one-party regime. At the same time, the public sector fulfills its responsibilities only to a limited extent, since the state apparatus is relatively weak and patronage is widespread, especially at the local level. The socioeconomic crisis that has ravaged the country for the past two decades has weakened state bureaucracy even further, with many civil servants leaving their positions, which remain unfilled. It is estimated that half of the inhabitants of Togo's capital, Lomé, live in poverty, while the percentage reaches 79% in rural areas. Aside from widespread poverty and poor public service delivery, the socioeconomic context is further aggravated by the HIV/AIDS pandemic that affects around 5% of the population.

Although Togolese people show more peaceful and tolerant attitudes than citizens from neighboring countries, violent clashes between different tribes occasionally occur and are often fueled by political factions. For example, in 2005, various clashes between supporters of the opposition parties and the military followed Faure Gnassingbé's takeover as president.

In general, the negative operating environment is the main obstacle to civil society's growth in Togo. The political context poses many challenges—not only to civil society, but also to the protection of human rights and the promotion of democracy at large.

Values (1.4)

The values dimension examines the extent to which civil society practices and promotes positive values. Although in the case of Togo the values dimension is the strongest of the four dimensions, the CSI assessment reveals that Togolese CSOs are rather weak in practicing and promoting important social values. This aspect is particularly worrisome, considering that the long-term development of democracy in Togo will require a significant commitment from civil society.

The fight against poverty is the value that Togolese CSOs promote most wholeheartedly. Most NGOs, religious organizations, and trade unions have a number of activities and programs in place to improve the living conditions of Togolese citizens. In a country where poverty is widespread, income-generation programs are seen as a primary area of work for civil society. CSOs implement microfinance projects, train women in agricultural techniques, train youth in entrepreneurship, and run self-help initiatives aimed at strengthening the capacity of local communities. For example, many programs train communities in building dispensaries, forages, wells, and rural pathways.

The CSI found that Togolese CSOs do not carry out systematic activities to promote democratic values in society at large. In the run-up to the 2005 elections, some CSOs organized education campaigns and participated in public debates on radio and TV to inform the population about the rights and duties of citizens and to explain voting procedures. In general, most of these activities were donor driven and lacked both support from the population and public visibility.

Particularly after the clashes in 2005, a number of CSOs began to conduct activities to promote nonviolence and tolerance. Mainly through newspapers and radio programs, various types of CSOs—such as international NGOs, trade unions, and religious organizations—issued appeals to encourage tolerance and respect, and they conducted initiatives to educate people about nonviolent conflict resolution.

When it comes to the internal practice of these values, the CSI found an even less promising situation. Few organizations pay significant attention to internal democratic governance or transparency issues, and, when they publish their financial statements, they typically circulate the information to a select group of stakeholders to account to donors for their spending. This lack of attention paid to internal democratic practices and transparency is of greater concern when it is seen against the backdrop of the disconnect between most CSOs and the general population, which stands out as a key weakness of civil society's structure in Togo.

Impact (0.8)

The impact dimension assesses civil society's role in governance and society at large. Civil society's impact in Togo is weak—as is its influence on public policies—even though many organizations try to address the socioeconomic problems of the population.

In general, NGOs are more effective than the state in meeting the needs of marginalized groups. One-third of registered CSOs implement programs to build women's capacities, while a number of NGOs assist the disabled, people living with HIV/AIDS, orphans, and the mentally ill. Since the suspension of cooperation between Togo and the EU,[2] the state's budget has shrunk, and the economic deterioration and sociopolitical situation has made it particularly difficult for public authorities to address the needs of the population.

Many NGOs try to respond to these growing needs, but they are limited in number and often do not have the necessary expertise and financial support. Although CSOs have conducted several initiatives, especially in the area of microfinance, economic hardship and the lack of financial resources make it difficult for CSOs to organize long-term programs aimed at mobilizing the rural population to act collectively and generate income.

The CSI analysis reveals that the impact of Togolese CSOs on policy processes is virtually nonexistent. CSOs' human rights activities are limited and have no significant impact, and CSOs do not play any role in social policy or the national budgeting process. Only the Togolese League for Human Rights has some visibility in denouncing human rights abuses, and this is due mainly to an international alliance of like-minded human rights groups that disseminates their appeals worldwide.

Not surprisingly, the CSI did not record any civil society activities aimed at monitoring state institutions. The few CSOs (especially international NGOs) working on public accountability are mainly concerned with educating citizens on how to hold public officials accountable, but rarely address the state directly. Furthermore, there are no significant Togolese CSO activities that hold private corporations accountable.

It emerges from the CSI analysis that Togolese CSOs have only been able to exert an impact through programs aimed at supporting marginalized groups and responding to the overall socioeconomic crisis of the country. However, policy impact is almost nonexistent, mainly due to the very restrictive political environment.

Conclusion

Togolese civil society plays a marginal role in the development of the country. The CSI assessment shows that the ongoing political crisis and the twenty-year socioeconomic slump make it difficult for CSOs to carry out their activities and have any real impact on the lives of Togolese citizens. The CSI enabled Togolese civil society to reflect on its role in society at large and to try to address the key weaknesses hampering the development of civic activism in the country. It is hoped that a civil society that is aware of its strengths and weaknesses will be able to play a more significant role in helping Togo to move toward a democratic system of governance.

CSI Report

FONGTO and Plan Togo, *A Diagnostic Study of Togolese Civil Society: CIVICUS Civil Society Index Report for Togo* (Lomé, Togo: Plan Togo, 2006).

Notes

1. The CSI Shortened Assessment Tool was implemented in Togo by the Federation des ONGs Togolaises (FONGTO) in partnership with Plan Togo from July 2005 to March 2006. This chapter presents the main findings of the CSI-SAT and is based on a comprehensive country report for Togo, which can be accessed on the CSI pages of the CIVICUS website at http://www.civicus.org.
2. The EU suspended its cooperation agreement with Togo in 1993, due to human rights abuses and lack of democratic reforms. In 2005 the EU condemned Faure Gnassingbé's coup and threatened to impose sanctions.

Chapter 40

~~

Turkey[1]

Turkey is among the most dynamic countries in the world today, with one door opening to Europe and the other to the Middle East. Since the early 1990s, the country's democratic, political, economic, and social trajectories have been aligning toward future membership in the European Union (EU). Within this context, civil society has begun to enjoy a more enabling environment and is undergoing crucial processes of growth and professionalization. The Civil Society Index (CSI) project was conducted during this period of intense change and captures a sector that is increasingly asserting itself as an important facet of Turkish society, despite its relatively small size.

Table 40.1 Background Information for Turkey

Turkey	
Country size (square km)	779,452
Population (millions 2004)	71.7
Population under 15 years (2004)	29.5%
Urban population (2003)	66.3%
Seats in parliament held by women (2005)	4.4%
Language groups	Turkish (official), Kurdish, Arabic, Armenian, Greek
Ethnic groups	Turkish 80%, Kurdish 20% (estimated)
Religious groups	Muslim 99.8% (mostly Sunni)
HDI score and ranking (2003)	0.750 (94th)
GDP per capita (US$ 2003)	$6,772
Unemployment rate (% of total labor force)	10.3%
Population living on less than US$2 a day (2003)	18.7%

Historical Overview

While Islamic foundations have existed in Turkey since the Middle Ages, the evolution of modern associational life in Turkey can be traced back to the late Ottoman Empire era (1850–1917), when foundations and other philanthropic institutions emerged. Following the founding of the Turkish Republic in 1923, the state-centered modernization process left little space for civil society organizations (CSOs) and other non-state actors. During this modernization process, the Turkish state quickly became the most powerful actor in the political, economic, social, and cultural spheres, providing little space for CSOs and other non-state actors. State control steadily increased and peaked during three military interventions of 1960, 1971, and 1980, which severely disrupted the political development of the country. In addition, Islamic and Kurdish identity demands and their politicization during the 1980s resulted in heightened social tensions, which led the government to devise legal mechanisms to restrict freedom of association and assembly. During this time, many CSOs were shut down or restricted in their operations.

It was not until the 1990s that CSOs began to resume a more prominent position in Turkish society, due in part to Turkey's entrance into the global market economy and to domestic developments, such as the political and ethnic conflict in the southeast of the country. In 1996 the UN Habitat meetings held in Istanbul helped increase government acknowledgment and public awareness about civil society. In 1999 the Marmara and Kaynasli earthquakes, which led to the deaths of an estimated 20,000 people, mobilized CSOs and increased public interest and trust in civil society, as citizens participated in search-and-rescue activities through volunteering and donating to various CSOs. More recently, the acceleration of Turkey's EU accession process, the decentralization of government, and key reforms to civil society law have presented opportunities for civil society to operate more freely and visibly within the country.

The State of Civil Society in Turkey

In carrying out the CSI assessment in Turkey, it was not possible to give all civil society subsectors equal attention. While the CSI covered all types of CSOs—including trade unions, professional associations, and cooperatives—anecdotal evidence and discussions among stakeholders led to a particular emphasis on CSOs engaging in development, democracy, and rights-based issues.

Figure 40.1 Civil Society Diamond for Turkey

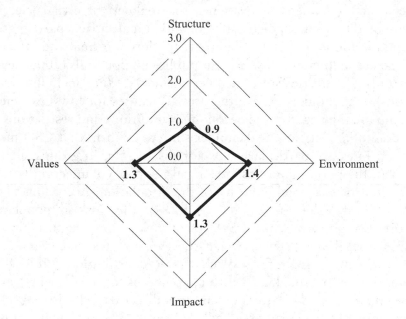

This section provides a summary of key findings of the CSI project in Turkey. It examines the state of Turkish civil society along four dimensions—structure, environment, values, and impact—highlighting the main weaknesses and strengths.

The Turkish Civil Society Diamond (figure 40.1) is a visual summary of the project findings and indicates a relatively underdeveloped civil society. The structure dimension is the weakest of the four dimensions, with particular shortcomings in the areas of citizen participation, CSO resources, and cooperation within the sector. Although recent reforms have created a marked improvement in civic freedoms, a legacy of government restriction continues to affect some aspects of the legal framework and practices governing Turkish civil society. Civil society plays a rather active role in promoting positive values, such as gender equity and environmental sustainability, but it is less successful in practicing these values internally. Civil society's impact is rather insignificant; the CSI assessment reveals that, while recent advocacy campaigns for legal reforms have achieved some success, there is a lack of civil society activities holding the private sector accountable and responding to key social interests, such as unemployment, inflation, and corruption.

Structure (0.9)

The structure dimension examines the makeup of civil society in terms of the main characteristics of individual citizen participation and associational life. Individual participation in formal and informal civil society activities is low. Recent public-opinion polls (2006) reveal that only 5% of Turks are members of a CSO (not including trade unions). Stakeholders believe the primary causes for low CSO membership are the negative socioeconomic conditions and restrictions on freedom of association. Stakeholder surveys confirm that CSO membership rates are particularly low for disadvantaged groups such as women, the poor, minorities, and rural people. Volunteering is similarly limited to a small minority of the population. According to the 1999 World Value Survey, only 1.5% of the Turkish population reported volunteering for a CSO. In contrast to low membership and volunteering levels, a more recent survey estimates that four out of five Turks make some form of charitable contribution. While 87% prefer to give to individuals—through religious forms of giving (*zekat, fitre, sadaka*)—37% of total giving goes directly to charities (broken down into 14% to religious-based CSOs and 23% to secular CSOs).

The level of organization within Turkey's civil society sector remains limited. Only trade unions and professional associations are organized under active umbrella organizations. Stakeholders also highlight the lack of voluntary codes of conduct among CSOs and identify the need to increase the number of resource centers available to help CSOs become more institutionalized and develop their human, financial, and technical capacities. Linked to this is Turkish civil society's weak level of connectedness—stakeholders report very low levels of communication, cooperation, and linkages among CSOs. However, some successful examples of cooperation within civil society subsectors should be noted, such as environmental platforms, women's groups' platforms, and various union federations.

As mentioned above, the civil society sector and a majority of CSOs are still in a stage of nascent formation. This presents a rather large number of limitations in terms of civil society's structure in Turkey. However, some strengths merit acknowledgment, such as the growing number of CSOs with strong infrastructures and capacities, which raise tremendous support from the public at large. Some CSOs even assist other countries with youth development, women's issues, poverty alleviation, and search-and-rescue operations. As the sector becomes more institutionalized, the formation of self-regulatory codes and common platforms will provide an important bonding function for CSOs. In addition, policy reforms and discussions with CSO alliances in the EU will likely result in an emergence of more organized Turkish CSO networks.

Environment (1.4)

The environment dimension considers political, legal, socioeconomic, and sociocultural contexts, as well as the relationships between civil society, the state, and the private sector. Over the past few years—especially since the beginning of the EU pre-accession political reform process—Turkey has undergone a significant transformation.[2] The Turkish government embarked on a series of reforms to align Turkish laws with international laws. Reforms to political rights (such as passing the Right to Information Act in 2004) and civic rights (such as the Association Law of July 2004 and the pending Foundations Law) mark important improvements for civil society's environment. Despite the successful adoption of these reforms, it is still too early to accurately assess implementation practices and their direct effects on civil society.

Even with improvements to civil society's regulatory frameworks, stakeholders still judge state–civil society relations as very limited or, where they exist, as sometimes outright hostile. Sixty-two percent of surveyed CSO stakeholders report limited dialogue with the state, and only 12% report receiving financial support from government sources. At the same time, Turkish civil society continues to feel that its autonomy is impeded by the state. A majority of surveyed stakeholders report that government continues to meddle with CSO activities—36% assess that these interferences are somewhat common, and 33% consider them to be quite frequent. The most common examples are CSOs (especially trade unions) being prevented from organizing protests or boycotts.

Given the relevance of Turkey's EU pre-accession process for civil society, the Third Sector Foundation of Turkey (TUSEV) added indicators to assess its impact and found that CSOs generally report a positive impact of the EU and pre-accession process, particularly on civil society's operating environment and CSOs' ability to promote democratic values and help disadvantaged populations such as women, children, and minorities. In focus group discussions, the EU was frequently mentioned as a panacea for the protection of rights and freedoms, funding for CSOs, promoting connections among

CSOs, enabling citizens to make better use of their civic rights, and increasing public awareness of civil society's importance in general.

Finally, low levels of trust between individuals (beyond close kin and friends) and limited social tolerance for diversity reveal concerns about the weak levels of social capital among Turkish citizens. This has negative implications for civil society, and CSI stakeholders suggest that CSOs would benefit from integrating trust-building measures into their programming efforts to play a role in bridging different communities in the country. However, this weakness is balanced with extremely high levels of helpfulness. According to a recent study on giving, the level of helpfulness is seen to have a positive correlation with the person's propensity to make charitable donations and actually help others in times of need.

Values (1.3)

The values dimension examines the extent to which civil society practices and promotes positive values. The score for this dimension is moderate, which reflects the fact that while some values are actively promoted by civil society, others, such as tolerance, have been—and, to some degree, remain—sensitive or taboo since they challenge ideologies about the unified identity of the Turkish nation-state.

These challenges are particularly evident in civil society's actions to promote tolerance. According to stakeholders, incidents of intolerance within civil society are seen as significant (45%) and several examples were provided, including the growing nationalist movement, mobilization around the headscarf issue, and tensions between ethnic and religious minorities. The low level of civil society activity in this area is likely a result of the negative consequences of civil society's advocacy work on minority issues. One example concerns CSOs that recently organized a conference to promote dialogue on the Armenian issue but were subsequently branded "anti-Turkish" for including speakers with different views on the subject, some of which challenged the status quo.

While CSOs are reported to be least active in the areas of promoting transparency in the state and the private sector, civil society seems to perform a more significant and visible role in practicing and promoting nonpolitical values such as environmental sustainability, gender equity, and poverty eradication. For example, Turkish CSOs actively promote gender equity through several activities, such as the recent penal code and civil code reform successes, efforts to increase women's representation in parliament, and campaigns to promote literacy for girls and women.

While CSOs are perceived to be rather active in promoting democracy at the societal level, the CSI identified problems with the internal practice of democracy within CSOs. Participants in the regional and national CSI forums stressed severe deficits in the practice of CSOs' internal democracy, particularly the limited role of members in organizational decisionmaking. These deficits could be due to negative societal and cultural contexts, the relatively immature stage of civil society's development, and the lack of information and skills regarding the effective governance of CSOs.

As discussed above, the values practiced and promoted by Turkish civil society closely mirror those of society at large and are strongly influenced by the overall political and cultural environment. Therefore, the relatively low score for this dimension may be linked to the threat of condemnation by society—and even by government—for promoting values that challenge the current societal value system. However, as Turkish society embraces more progressive norms, civil society may feel more at ease in advocating for certain sensitive values. Yet, regardless of external factors, CSOs in Turkey must take steps toward adopting and practicing values such as democratic practice and gender equity—both within their organizations and in the broader civil society arena.

Impact (1.3)

The impact dimension assesses civil society's role in governance and society at large. The CSI reveals that civil society's impact on politics, society, and the economy is limited but gaining momentum.

The rich case studies conducted by the CSI on human rights and social policy issues—such as the penal code reforms for women's rights—support the findings that Turkish CSOs have some impact, albeit limited, in key areas of the country's social and economic development. This is especially true for, but not limited to, rights-based discourse and reforms.

The long list of examples provided by stakeholders on how CSOs meet societal needs—especially for disadvantaged populations and women—was compelling, as was the surprising thematic diversity that characterizes civil society's work in serving the public. One of the areas where CSOs are most active is the field of public education. Examples include initiatives to inform and empower citizens about a variety of issues, including civic and consumer rights, education of schoolgirls, environmental issues such as genetically modified foods, and the EU accession process.

Turkish civil society is rather weak in responding to social interests (areas defined by public opinion surveys to be of the most importance to Turkish citizens—such as unemployment, inflation, and corruption) as well as holding the private sector accountable. However, when it comes to holding the state accountable and lobbying for better state services, CSI stakeholders are of the opinion that CSOs are at least somewhat active. Some examples mentioned by stakeholders were civil society's reactions to the Susurluk Scandal of 1996, in which a major government corruption scandal was exposed; the successful Bergama protests against a government decision to allow mining, which posed a danger to the local community; the response of CSOs to the lack of government support for the earthquake victims in 1999; and the recent reports of CSOs, which monitor the legislative activities of members of the Turkish parliament.

While civil society's accomplishments need to be acknowledged, the limitations inhibiting a stronger role in governance and development must also be addressed. CSOs need to focus more on service delivery, rather than on policy analysis and advocacy. While there is an increasing awareness of the importance of these activities, there is a lack of clarity on how to become more involved. Civil society lacks cooperation and joint advocacy initiatives, which weaken its ability to be effective. In addition, evaluation mechanisms to measure the impact of its activities are inadequate, and mechanisms to engage civil society in national, regional, and local policy formulation and monitoring are lacking.

The examples of human rights and social policy advocacy support the findings that Turkish CSOs have some impact, albeit limited, in key areas of Turkey's social and economic development. This is especially true for, but not limited to, rights-based discourse and reforms. Yet, the common theme among various facets of civil society's impact is that while such impact remains barely discernible, it has been increasing.

Recommendations

These recommendations are based on the opinions of a diverse range of stakeholders, such as civil society practitioners, government officials, media members, private sector representatives, and academics, who were consulted during regional consultations and at the CSI

National Workshop. The following are the most significant recommendations raised in these meetings:

- Turkish CSOs need to deepen and broaden their relationships with citizens to increase citizen participation, by promoting and strengthening volunteer outreach, recruitment, and management programs; developing fundraising strategies; and designing membership recruitment programs.
- To increase their capacity, Turkish CSOs should increase their institutional strength by improving internal governance through management training courses and training materials that can be widely disseminated within civil society.
- CSOs should promote stronger cross-sectoral collaboration.
- CSOs should diversify and sustain their funding through mobilizing domestic philanthropy and exploring alternative mechanisms for funding—such as community foundations that can enable interested individuals and institutions to make contributions— promoting best practices on grantmaking, and facilitating the strategic allocation of funds in the form of grants to CSOs.
- CSOs should increase their PR and media-liaison skills to better access the Turkish public. CSOs should find ways for their organizations and issues to achieve greater coverage by columnists, who are critical in influencing public opinion in Turkey.

Conclusion

Key developments during the last ten years have paved the way for a tremendous growth period for Turkish civil society. The picture of civil society documented by the CSI study was formed during a time of transition, a moment when a number of dramatic and mostly positive changes were taking place. Thus, while the CSI assessment finds a rather limited group of CSOs operating in a somewhat disabling environment, all indications are that this sector will continue to grow in size and impact.

The CSI assessment provides a set of concrete recommendations for how to capitalize on this generally positive trend. In terms of next steps, TUSEV will inform the public and key stakeholders of the CSI results, putting to use the recommendations with regard to effective use of media and organizing a series of launch meetings for the CSI report. TUSEV also hopes that the extensive data collected through the CSI will be utilized and further elaborated on by interested stake-holders in the future.

CSI Report

TUSEV, *Civil Society in Turkey (2005)—An Era of Transition: CIVICUS Civil Society Index Report for Turkey* (Istanbul, Turkey: TUSEV, 2006).

Notes

1. The CSI assessment was implemented in Turkey by the Third Sector Foundation of Turkey (TUSEV) from 2004 to early 2006. This chapter presents the main findings of the CSI and is based on a comprehensive country report for Turkey, which can be accessed on the CSI pages of the CIVICUS website at http://www.civicus.org.
2. In 2001 Turkey's process to join the European Community officially began with its acceptance of the Copenhagen Criteria, which requires a number of mandatory legislative reforms in order for Turkey to eventually be considered for full membership in the European Community.

Chapter 41

❦❦

Uganda[1]

Ugandan civil society is at a crossroads. As in many other African countries, Ugandan civil society organizations (CSOs) have overwhelmingly focused on service delivery activities and largely refrained from becoming involved in the more political terrain of advocacy and governance. However, taking a more dedicated approach to policy engagement and advocacy could prove crucial for civil society's sustainability and for the future of social justice in a country where multiparty democracy was only introduced in February 2006.

Table 41.1 Background Information for Uganda

Uganda	
Country size (square km)	241,038
Population (millions 2004)	27.8
Population under 15 years (2004)	50.4%
Urban population (2003)	12.3%
Seats in parliament held by women (2005)	23.9%
Language groups	English (official), Swahili, Ganda, many Bantu and Nilotic languages, Arabic
Ethnic groups	Baganda 17%, Ankole 8%, Basoga 8%, Iteso 8%, Bakiga 7%, Langi 6%, many other groups
Religious groups	Roman Catholic 33%, Protestant 33%, Muslim 16%, indigenous beliefs 18%
HDI score and ranking (2003)	0.508 (144th)
Unemployment rate (% of total labor force)	3.2%

Historical Overview

During the colonial period, Ugandan CSOs consisted primarily of cooperatives of export-crop producers and trade unions, missionary hospitals, educational institutions, and other charitable organizations. After World War II, trade associations and cooperatives increasingly engaged in political activism and the fight against colonialism. Following independence in 1962, a militarized state became central to Uganda's political economy. Peasant cooperatives and trade unions lost much of their autonomy and were co-opted by government, while associational life at the grassroots level centered on organizations operating along kinship lines or on a self-help basis. Legal restrictions severely limited overt civic and political participation during most of the 1970s and 1980s, thus confining citizen participation to covert or low-key activities. During this period, the most significant nationwide organizations were faith-based institutions, which focused their activities on education and health care.

When the National Resistance Movement (NRM)[2] came to power in 1986, CSOs initially found more space for their activities. However, new challenges arose, including potential co-optation by government. In February 2006, the movement system that had been in existence for twenty years in Uganda was abandoned, and the country held multiparty elections. This move was applauded by international donors, which have long seen Uganda as an important target for foreign aid; tangible gains for democracy and civil society, however, remain to be fully realized.

The State of Civil Society in Uganda

This section provides a summary of key findings of the Civil Society Index (CSI) project in Uganda. It examines the state of Ugandan civil society along four dimensions—structure, environment, values, and impact—highlighting the main weaknesses and strengths.

The Civil Society Diamond for Uganda (figure 41.1) visually summarizes these findings. It indicates a relatively strong civil society structure, with inclusive and widespread community-based organizations (CBOs) in rural areas being a particular strength. Ugandan civil society is operating in a rather disabling environment, constrained by socioeconomic problems and political restrictions. Civil society practices and promotes positive social values to a moderate extent, and its impact is significant, particularly in relation to the delivery of social services and citizens' empowerment, although it is significantly weaker (though growing) in advocacy work.

Figure 41.1 Civil Society Diamond for Uganda

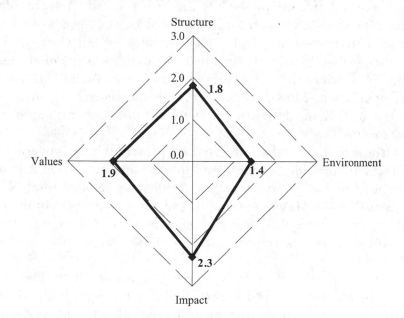

Structure (1.8)

The structure dimension examines the makeup of civil society in terms of the main characteristics of individual citizen participation and associational life. Citizen involvement in CSOs appears to be very extensive, partly because rural life in this largely agrarian country is often accompanied by membership in various forms of community associations, especially self-help groups and faith-based organizations, which are socially inclusive. Volunteering and other forms of community action are also prevalent. For example, the CSI population survey indicates that 81% of respondents provide support to members of their community on an unpaid basis.

However, probably due to the country's history of civil strife and repressive regimes, high levels of participation do not necessarily translate into equally high levels of activist political involvement. For example, only 16% of respondents to the population survey have ever taken part in a demonstration, signed a petition, or written a letter to a newspaper. Nevertheless, there are signs that some CSOs have recently become more active in claiming political space, and a relatively free press has created opportunities for criticizing government.

Aside from the large number of community groups, Ugandan civil society also features other forms of CSOs, including professionalized

NGOs with their networks and coalitions, trade unions, and professional associations. Many NGOs are urban-based and are often donor-dependent, with staff, vehicles, projects, and agendas that the average citizen does not easily associate with or feel close to. The NGO sector is somewhat fragmented and competitive, and accountability to donors often takes precedence over accountability to the local population. Most NGOs operate in the central region of the country, with Kampala hosting about a fifth of the total number of registered NGOs.

Although the number of organizations obtaining government contracts to provide services has grown rapidly, NGOs are still dependent on foreign aid, which amounted to 86% of total NGO revenues in 2003. However, these financial resources are not distributed evenly. A handful of NGOs receive the bulk of foreign funding, and CBOs survive largely on their own income, membership fees and local funding.

The analysis of civil society's structure in Uganda shows that community involvement in civil society activities is widespread, while it rarely takes the form of nonpartisan political activism. CSOs are diverse and spread throughout the country, although the most professionalized organizations are typically urban-based and highly dependent on foreign aid.

Environment (1.4)

The environment dimension considers political, legal, socioeconomic, and sociocultural contexts, as well as the relationships between civil society, the state, and the private sector. Of the four dimensions, the environment dimension receives the lowest score. This is mainly due to the current political and socioeconomic contexts, which are seen as rather disabling for civil society.

Although Uganda's success in poverty reduction is significant, it remains an extremely poor country, with a growing gap between the rich and the poor. The overall proportion of poor people increased from 35% (or 7.7 million people) in 2000 to 38% in 2003. Also, while progress has been made in addressing the spread of HIV/AIDS, its social and economic impact will be felt for years to come. The current estimate is that 6% of the population is HIV positive.

While the effectiveness of public services, particularly in the fields of health and education, has improved over the past two decades, corruption in the public sector remains high, and the rule of law is insufficiently entrenched, with police brutality, poor prison conditions, and domestic violence being particularly problematic. The government keeps a tight grip on public life, and under the guise of antiterrorist measures, violations of press freedoms and other civil rights are frequent. Uganda is also at serious risk of armed conflict and political instability, particularly in the northern part of the country, which has suffered from conflict for the past eighteen years, and where most of the local population is displaced or living in camps.

Historically, the relationship between the state and civil society has been characterized by collaboration or co-optation, rather than confrontation. Recently, the government has been opening further avenues for CSOs to be contracted to deliver services, especially at the district level. A 2003 survey revealed that 33% of surveyed NGOs had a Memorandum of Understanding with a ministry. However, NGOs are increasingly seeing advocacy work as a necessary and legitimate field of activity. Although donors support this move, the legal framework and government attitude impede these efforts. The lack of government clarity on what constitutes allowable advocacy activities for NGOs, especially when NGOs stray into the political arena, is a particular issue of concern. Participants in the CSI's regional consultations confirm that public authorities regularly interfere with the work of CSOs when the latter are involved in governance issues. Many stakeholders cited cases of harassment against organizations involved in advocacy for good governance and anticorruption campaigns. In addition, registration procedures for CSOs are cumbersome, and the tax laws do not include any conducive regulations. Less important than its delicate relations with the government is civil society's relationship with the private sector. CSOs are not particularly concerned with this relationship and currently do not benefit much from private sector funding.

In conclusion, the environment within which civil society operates is affected by a number of constraints related to a political system that has only recently opened up to multiparty politics and is controlled by a government that has not refrained from threatening a range of civil society groups. Moreover, the socioeconomic context is still affected by high levels of poverty and by the perennial armed conflict in the northern part of the country.

Values (1.9)

The values dimension examines the extent to which civil society practices and promotes positive values. Overall, it appears that Ugandan CSOs struggle with practicing values of internal democracy, financial transparency, and, to a lesser extent, tolerance, nonviolence, and gender equity. Among NGOs there often seems to be a gap between what organizations officially proclaim and their day-to-day practice. However, CSOs' initiatives focused on the promotion of democracy multiplied in the run-up to the first multiparty elections, which were held in February 2006. In war-torn areas, CSOs have established civil society–military cooperation centers to ensure freedom of movement and access to necessities for the affected populations. CSOs have also actively advocated for a peaceful resolution of the civil war in the north and have been instrumental in designing programs for the peaceful resolution of ethnic conflicts in northeastern Uganda.

Although cases of full-blown corruption within civil society are relatively rare, stakeholders lamented that when they do occur they can easily undermine CSOs' credibility, especially if highlighted by the media. This is further aggravated by CSOs' lack of financial transparency. Civil society organizations are often accused by government of not being transparent or forthcoming with information about their activities and budgets.

Civil society has also promoted gender equity and ecological issues, but with varying degrees of success. Some CSOs have carried out gender mainstreaming activities, but not campaigns, and some skeptics believe that the rush to focus on gender issues is only to attract donor funding. A number of organizations focus on environmental sustainability. They have been conducting campaigns on ecological issues, but broad-based support for these activities is yet to emerge.

Poverty eradication is a strong value for civil society in Uganda, and stakeholders could list numerous examples of actions reflecting the strength of this value. Poverty eradication corresponds to the historical role of voluntary organizations, and most CSOs currently see activities to address poverty as their primary purpose. However, CSOs' fight against poverty is not immune to skepticism and suspicion, especially when antipoverty NGO staff receive generous salaries and benefits, which is seen as potentially discrediting the commitment of civil society in this field.

Ugandan civil society promotes some important values, but not always wholeheartedly. Poverty eradication and, to a certain extent, environmental sustainability, are more effectively embraced than many of the other values addressed in the CSI assessment.

Impact (2.3)

The impact dimension assesses civil society's role in governance and society at large. The overall picture that emerges is one of intense

CSO activity—particularly by faith-based organizations—in service delivery and economic and social empowerment, rather than policy advocacy work. These are also the areas where CSOs exert the most significant impact.

Many civil society actors provide information and education to local communities. A number of CSOs are involved in supporting marginalized groups, and they focus on building local skills and knowledge, establishing specific social services for minority groups, empowering women, and developing peacebuilding activities to reduce conflicts between neighboring communities. Many CSOs target communities or groups living in conditions of extreme poverty. In the war-torn north, CSOs are active in providing services to refugee camps, and a number of CSOs work with street children throughout the country.

When asked to compare CSOs' and the state's roles in service provision, 71% of respondents to the population survey feel voluntary organizations are providing better services. Voluntary organizations have long been perceived by the public as closer to communities and, in their view, CSOs understand people's problems better than public administration officials.

As social problems continue to grow, it is becoming clear that civil society's overwhelming focus on service delivery cannot succeed in redressing social injustices unless it is linked with a more active advocacy role. However, local CSOs have mixed feelings about participating in the country's governance. Many feel that contributing to policymaking in the context of an unaccountable government is a corrupting process.

Although CSOs' advocacy role is relatively limited, there are some exceptions, and changes are taking place. Some CSOs have begun to participate in trilateral meetings with donors and government on policy priorities. In addition, civil society has increased its ability to hold government accountable and to make its voice heard on specific issues, such as human rights, HIV/AIDS, and basic services for marginalized groups and the poor. Some networks and coalitions are proving to be effective in providing members with forums through which the collective consensus of these networks can be expressed to policymakers and other relevant stakeholders.

One policy area where CSOs have a considerable impact is anti-poverty policies. For example, the Uganda Debt Network used evidence collected through independent research to influence policy and attract the government's attention. During the drafting of the budget, the Uganda Manufacturers Association regularly submits proposals to the Ministry of Finance, and the Uganda Law Society is rather vocal on issues pertaining to human rights. Aside from these examples, however, CSOs (especially church-based organizations) have been reluctant to move beyond service delivery and are often not willing to integrate advocacy and policy engagement into their ongoing work.

Recommendations

The following recommendations are drawn from the CSI National Workshop held in Kampala on June 7, 2006, in which approximately eighty individuals participated, mainly from NGOs:

- Strengthen civil society's structure: It is necessary to invest in training CSO personnel, for example in areas of fundraising and leadership. Support organizations need capacity building and collaborative mechanisms, such as networks and coalitions.
- Credibility and autonomy vis-à-vis government: CSOs need to strengthen their credibility in society in order to be more effective in interacting with government without losing their autonomy and independence. CSOs should improve their internal governance through self-regulatory mechanisms and mechanisms for transparency, such as the Quality Assurance Mechanism for NGOs, which is currently being developed.
- Reduce donor dependency: CSOs must develop a long-term collective strategy to reduce donor dependency. Where CSOs are involved in direct service delivery, every effort should be made to avoid creating dependency, through effective project research, design, and collaboration with other development actors.
- Strengthen civil society's advocacy: Civil society must strengthen its role in monitoring government policies and advocating for the independence of the judiciary and the media. To this end, CSOs should create mechanisms to share information and expertise.

Conclusion

Civil society in Uganda is very diverse and comprises national-level organizations as well as a myriad of community associations and groups. However, a clear fault line is reflected between a majority of CSOs that overwhelmingly focus on service delivery and a small minority that are involved in advocacy and policy.

Although CSOs are successfully assisting marginalized people and empowering the poor, the limited engagement in advocacy and policy work will likely constrain civil society's overall impact on social justice. In a sense, Uganda's civil society is at a crossroads. Will it confine itself to a somewhat docile role, focusing on service delivery and subcontracting for government? Or will it develop its capacity to question the crucial sociopolitical processes and strive to strengthen its autonomy, sense of independent identity, cohesion, and local ownership?

CSI Report

DENIVA, *Civil Society in Uganda: at the Crossroads? CIVICUS Civil Society Index Report for Uganda* (Kampala, Uganda: DENIVA, 2006).

Notes

1. The CSI assessment was implemented in Uganda by the Development Network of Indigenous Voluntary Associations (DENIVA) from 2003 to 2006. This chapter presents the main findings of the CSI and is based on a comprehensive country report for Uganda, which can be accessed on the CSI pages of the CIVICUS website at http://www.civicus.org.
2. The NRM is the main political organization in Uganda and is led by Ugandan president Yoveri Museveni. Before taking power, the NRM was the political arm of the National Resistance Army, the guerrilla faction that led the rebellion against the regimes of Milton Obote and Tito Okello.

Chapter 42

Ukraine[1]

In November 2004, Ukraine and Ukrainian civil society were at the center of global public attention. Through the Orange Revolution's peaceful mass actions, Ukrainian citizens successfully ousted President Kutchma's corrupt government, which led to high hopes for a democratic and prosperous future for the country. The Civil Society Index (CSI) was implemented before, during, and after the events surrounding the Orange Revolution. However, since the data gathering was completed by the end of 2004, this chapter provides a snapshot of the situation just before the overturn of the Kutchma government.

Table 42.1 Background Information for Ukraine

Ukraine	
Country size (square km)	603,700
Population (millions 2004)	47.5
Population under 15 years (2004)	15.4%
Urban population (2003)	67.3%
Seats in parliament held by women (2005)	5.32%
Language groups	Ukrainian (official), Russian, Romanian, Polish, and Hungarian
Ethnic groups	Ukrainian 78%, Russian 17%
Religious groups	Ukrainian Orthodox (Kiev Patriarchate, Moscow Patriarchate) Ukrainian Greek Catholic, Ukrainian Autocephalous Orthodox
HDI score and ranking (2003)	0.766 (78th)
GDP per capita (US$ 2003)	$5,491
Unemployment rate (% of total labor force)	8.6%
Population living on less than US$2 a day (2003)	4.9%

Historical Overview

The beginning of collective action in Ukraine dates to the Middle Ages, when rural communities established organizations for mutual self-help. The first signs of organized civil society emerged in the seventeenth century, when Ukraine was divided between Poland and Russia and the national liberation movement used charitable organizations for its mobilization. As in other industrializing countries, the nineteenth and early twentieth centuries witnessed the emergence of charities set up by industrialists, which, together with other independent organizations, were disbanded at the onset of the Soviet era.

The Soviet state did not leave room for independent organizations, and installed state-controlled mass organizations (MOs) in key areas of social life, such as youth, women, workers, and the elderly. In the 1980s, under Gorbatchev's *perestroika* policies, citizen organizations emerged, particularly around environmental concerns in the aftermath of the Chernobyl disaster and also to promote Ukrainian nationalist ideology. Many leaders of these early NGOs played an important role in Ukrainian politics after independence in 1991.

New civil society organizations (CSOs), fostered by Western aid, emerged in the first years of independence. However, their sustainability was tenuous, and CSOs often found it difficult to adapt to the new environment, which demanded specific expertise in service delivery and policy formulation. Interestingly, the old-Soviet style organizations were best equipped to survive in this competitive and volatile situation, due to their capital assets and political networks.

In the new millennium, the Ukrainian government's ineffectiveness, corruption, and widespread disregard for the rule of law led to the emergence of a citizen movement demanding free and fair parliamentary elections in 2002. This mobilization intensified around the presidential election in 2004, which produced Victor Yanukovych as winner; however, it turned out that the election was fixed. In what would later be called the Orange Revolution, a wide array of civic groups mobilized, and, through demonstrations throughout the country, demanded the elections be annulled. This eventually led to a call for a new election, which was won by Victor Yushchenko, a pro-democracy, Western-oriented candidate.

The significance of the Orange Revolution lies in the successful ousting of an authoritarian government and in the activation of various forms of civic action, which were deemed impossible among a citizenry often described as disengaged. However, the question was to what extent Ukrainian civil society would be able to capitalize on this outburst of civic activism.

The State of Civil Society in Ukraine

Civil society in Ukraine is highly segmented. An analysis of the key social forces in the country reveals that CSOs can be divided into three categories: (1) politically oriented CSOs, focused on influencing politics and government policies; (2) donor-oriented CSOs, whose agenda is highly dependent on international or local funders, and (3) member-oriented CSOs, which seek to address the needs and priorities of their membership. One often finds umbrella bodies for each of these three categories, and CSOs rarely cooperate across these categories. CSI participants generally felt that mistrust and competition, rather than cooperation and partnerships, characterize relationships within the sector.

An interesting feature of the Ukrainian CSI assessment was the decision by the National Advisory Group (NAG) to include political parties, which were an integral part of the civic movement during the Orange Revolution. This distinguishes the study in Ukraine from most other CSI studies in post-Communist countries.

This section provides a summary of key findings of the CSI project in Ukraine. It examines the state of Ukrainian civil society along four dimensions—structure, environment, values, and impact—highlighting the main weaknesses and strengths.

Figure 42.1 Civil Society Diamond for Ukraine

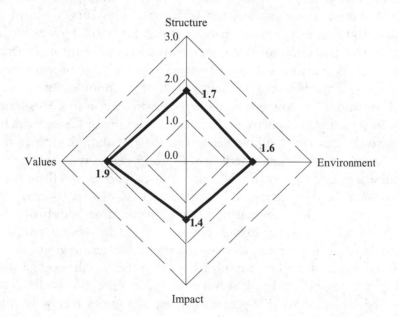

The overall state of Ukrainian civil society is visualized in the Civil Society Diamond (figure 42.1), which indicates a moderately sized civil society. It operates in an environment characterized by a dysfunctional political system and weak state, but favorable legal and socioeconomic contexts. Civil society has a strong record of promoting key values in society at large, but a much weaker performance in practicing them internally. Civil society's impact is assessed as somewhat weak, particularly with regard to its role in society at large. However, its role in the policy process has significantly strengthened over the last few years.

Structure (1.7)

The structure dimension examines the makeup of civil society in terms of the main characteristics of individual citizen participation and associational life. The structure of Ukrainian civil society is moderately developed.

Ukrainian civil society is characterized by a deep rift in terms of levels of citizen participation in different forms of civic activities. Large numbers of Ukrainians participate in demonstrations, strikes, and other forms of nonpartisan political action. Polls show that these figures more than doubled as a consequence of the Orange Revolution, from around 15% in 2003 to more than 30% in 2005. Other individual, nonformal types of civic activities, such as community involvement, informal volunteering, and charitable giving, are also quite common. For example, the CSI population survey found that 61% of Ukrainians give to charity on a regular basis. However, these high rates of participation are not mirrored in significant membership rates in CSOs. Various surveys estimate the percentage of membership in CSOs to range between 12% and 30% of the population.

The reasons for low levels of citizen participation in CSOs lie partially in the limited capacity and appeal of Ukrainian CSOs, which do not actively seek out the involvement of the population. According to government information, there are 143,655 registered CSOs in the Ukraine, a large majority of which are political parties and their various regional and local branches. NGOs make up 17% of all registered CSOs. There are also stark regional differences in the distribution of CSOs, which, due to a history of strong civic activism in the western part of the country, are stronger in the western than in the eastern regions.

Civil society's level of organization is moderate. Although a significant percentage (62%) of CSOs are united in umbrella bodies, coalitions, or informal working groups, these networks receive a mixed rating regarding their effectiveness. However, there is a tendency toward increased communication and cooperation among CSOs, particularly around issues of common concern, such as legal reform for CSOs. However, formalized and long-term partnerships that involve CSOs at all levels are rare. Other indicators of a sustainable civil society also show moderate but improving results. Plans for civil society's self-regulation are in place but are largely ineffective. Support organizations are expanding but are marred by limited capacity, ineffectiveness, and strong donor influence. Financial resources are generally tenuous, though increasing. The share of CSOs working with an annual budget of less than US$500 has decreased from 40% to 25% over the last few years. However, as is the case in most post-Communist countries, more than two-thirds of CSOs' income comes from foreign funders, and local philanthropic sources remain underdeveloped.

Although the key capacities of organized civil society are limited, there are signs of improvement. However, long-term strength and sustainability rely on civil society's ability to free itself from donor dependency and develop stronger roots within the citizenry. Thus, a key challenge for Ukrainian CSOs is to generate the skills, capacities, and political will to reach out to citizens and involve them in organizational activities as members, volunteers, or donors.

Environment (1.6)

The environment dimension considers political, legal, socioeconomic, and sociocultural contexts, as well as the relationships between civil society, the state, and the private sector. The environment dimension receives a somewhat positive assessment, which has improved since the project was completed in 2004.

The period of the Kutchma government, from 1994 to 2004, was marked by widespread disregard for the rule of law, basic liberties, and civil rights. The state took increasing control over public life, and the public administration was characterized by rampant corruption, ineffectiveness, and clientelism. In 2004 Ukraine ranked 122 among the 145 countries covered in Transparency International's Corruption Perception Index. Legal provisions safeguarding political and civic rights were in place but were frequently violated by state agencies, with the fraudulent 2004 presidential elections being a prominent example.

The legal provisions pertaining to civil society mirror the general gap between the de jure and de facto situations of rights and norms. Although registration procedures appear conducive, their application is highly dependent on the attitude of the respective local government.

Similarly, although the constitution stipulates widespread rights for citizens and gives civil society the right to be involved in the policymaking process, detailed provisions to operationalize these rights are missing or restrictive in nature. The legal situation is regarded as more conducive regarding tax benefits for CSOs and individuals as donors; however parliament is resisting passing a reform of the corporate tax law that would enable stronger corporate giving.

Particularly in the run-up to the 2004 presidential elections, state–civil society relations were riddled with tension. Public authorities used existing provisions to render the work of independent CSOs difficult. Of stakeholders surveyed for the CSI, 85% feel government's control increases during election periods. Also, mechanisms for dialogue between state and civil society exist but are used selectively. For example, only pro-government CSOs are invited to participate. In a similar vein, public financial support to civil society is selective, nontransparent, and generally limited. Only 11% of surveyed CSOs received significant support from government. Thus, the CSI assessment found clear, transparent, and coherent mechanisms for dialogue, interaction, and cooperation between state and civil society to be lacking.

In general, the Ukrainian corporate sector's interest in interacting with civil society is rather limited. Businesses prefer to give directly to people in need rather than via NGOs. Strategic approaches to corporate philanthropy and practices of corporate social responsibility (CSR) are lacking. When businesses support CSOs, they tend to focus on small donations to service-delivery organizations. Thus, civil society's relations with the private sector mirror that of the state. Both are dominated by piecemeal, selective, and once-off forms of engagement and lack a general strategy or framework.

The socioeconomic and sociocultural contexts present a mix of fairly conducive and problematic factors. While the gross domestic product (GDP) is growing steadily, so are poverty and social inequality. This indicates a developing economy that lacks an appropriate safety net. As in most post-Communist countries, levels of public spiritedness and tolerance toward minorities are limited. A specifically Ukrainian dimension of intolerance is the east-west cleavage within the country, which divides the pro-European, more tolerant west from the pro-Russian, less tolerant east. However, social trust, which was below 30% in 2001, has grown to almost 50% in 2005, most likely boosted by the successful social mobilization around the Orange Revolution.

Values (1.9)

The values dimension examines the extent to which civil society practices and promotes positive values. Although civil society's values receive the highest score among the four dimensions, a more in-depth analysis reveals crucial weaknesses. In general, there is a discrepancy between Ukrainian civil society's strong performance in promoting key values such as tolerance, gender equity, democracy, and environmental protection in society at large, and the rather weak performance of practicing many of these values internally.

As indicated by the various roles played by CSOs during the Orange Revolution—for example, voter education, election monitoring, legal advice, and citizen mobilization—civil society has become a key actor in promoting democracy and good governance. However, CSOs' record in practicing these same values internally is weak. Ukrainian CSOs have a minimalist approach to transparency and accountability, which is partly due to the general prevalence of corruption and informal networks in society, and the widespread shadow economy. The perceived corruption in NGOs is rather high. NGOs receive a score of 3 on Transparency International's 5-point corruption barometer, and 60% of regional stakeholder survey respondents assess instances of corruption in CSOs to be frequent or even very frequent.

A highlight of civil society's internal values is the practice of gender equity. Civil society is seen as a place where women can realize their potential. This is supported by survey data indicating equal representation of women in CSOs' leadership positions. An active women's movement in Ukraine is the driving force around key social concerns, such as human trafficking and domestic violence. Dating back to the successful mobilization of the public in the aftermath of the Chernobyl accident, addressing environmental issues constitutes another strength of Ukrainian civil society. However, a negative legacy of Communism is apparent in civil society's negligence of poverty and social justice issues. These are areas that are still considered the responsibility of government. Consequently, the majority of stakeholders consider civil society's role in the field of poverty eradication to be insignificant.

Civil society's lack of focus on social needs and the internal problems of transparency and accountability are likely to be major causes of the extremely low public trust and interest in the work of CSOs. This in turn limits civil society's impact on society at large.

Impact (1.4)

The impact dimension assesses civil society's role in governance and in society at large. The impact of Ukrainian civil society is assessed as slightly below average. Although its roles in advocacy, policy formulation, and empowerment of marginalized groups are rather well-developed, its level of interaction with, and influence on, society is quite limited.

Due to the centralized system of service delivery and a number of legal and financial provisions that give preference to public institutions, CSOs play a minor and complementary role to the state. Their performance receives a rather negative evaluation from the public. Whereas only 1% of respondents gave a positive evaluation, 58% rated NGOs' services as poor or very poor. However, this does not mean CSOs do not reach out to the population. There are impressive examples of public education, capacity building and empowerment initiatives, but they remain limited in scope and impact. The weak performance and penetration of CSOs into society translates into a mixed assessment of civil society's general role. Less than half of respondents consider NGOs to be essential or very necessary for Ukrainian society. Similarly, mistrust of NGOs is rather high at approximately 50%, but lower than that of political parties (83%), the president (75%), or government (63%).

A strength of the sector is civil society's involvement in advocacy and policy. In a 2004 survey, conducted by the Counterpart Creative Centre, almost 9 out of 10 CSOs indicated that they are involved in advocacy activities. Organizational capacities around advocacy have strengthened significantly, as signified by the improvement in the Capacity Index score between 2002 and 2004. Civil society was particularly successful in its advocacy efforts around the rigged 2004 presidential elections and government's overall social policy strategy. In contrast, civil society's work around the national budgeting process remains limited.

Ukrainian civil society's strong focus on political issues, at the expense of engagement with society, is apparent. Factors such as the Communist legacy, the current legislative and financial environment, and the limited capacity and quality of CSOs' services limit civil society's relevance for the day-to-day lives of Ukrainians. However, civil society is active and rather successful in its role in high-level governance processes.

Recommendations

The following recommendations were made by participants at the CSI National Workshop and other consultative meetings held as part of the CSI project. These recommendations might provide important input for the work the Ukrainian government began in 2005 on a framework of state engagement with civil society:

- Good governance: CSI participants suggested a number of policy proposals that focus on the development of more supportive and transparent rules of engagement between public authorities and civil society, including CSOs' stronger involvement in the delivery of social services and improved mechanisms for government accountability.
- Professional development: Civil society professionals need to strengthen their skills and capacities. This requires a coherent education system for CSO staff, which could be achieved in cooperation with the Ministry for Education and private universities.
- Financial sustainability: Due to a strong dependency on foreign donors, civil society's financial sustainability remains a key challenge. Proposals include the development of a domestic philanthropic base, improved tax legislation, the establishment of community foundations and social enterprise models, and greater outreach to the population at large.

Conclusion

With the Orange Revolution, Ukrainian citizens took a major step toward a democratic system of governance and a vibrant civil society. However, Ukrainian civil society remains moderate in size; it is characterized by several weaknesses and faces a number of crucial external challenges.

The new government has a more positive attitude toward civil society, but structural problems such as a weak state and divided party system remain. These problems are mirrored in a politicized and divided civil society, which is largely dependent on foreign donors, disconnected from the population, and marred by frequent cases of corruption and financial irregularities.

To become a driving force for positive change, civil society needs to reduce its external dependencies. Ukrainian CSOs should reach out to the population, which shows a high propensity for civic activism, and strengthen their social support base. Organizational governance, such as accountability and internal democracy, as well as organizational outputs, also need to be improved. Greater public support, financial and political independence, and stronger organizational capacities for Ukrainian CSOs would likely lead to the state taking civil society more seriously and would further open up avenues for CSOs' involvement in policymaking and service provision.

CSI Report

Svitlana Kuts, *Driving Engine or Spare Wheel for Change?: CIVICUS Civil Society Index Report for Ukraine* (Kiev, Ukraine: Centre for Philanthropy in cooperation with Counterpart Creative Centre, 2006).

Notes

1. The CSI project was implemented in Ukraine by the Centre for Philanthropy in cooperation with Counterpart Creative Centre in 2003 and 2004. This chapter presents the main findings of the CSI and is based on a comprehensive country report for Ukraine, which can be accessed on the CSI pages of the CIVICUS website at http://www.civicus.org.

Chapter 43

❧

Uruguay[1]

Uruguay is located between the giants of Brazil and Argentina. It was once considered the Switzerland of Latin America, due to its economic prosperity. However, a severe economic crisis in the early 2000s shook the foundations of the country. In its aftermath, a left-wing government was elected, ending two centuries of domination by traditional political parties and bringing with it greater attention to civil society issues. Thus, Uruguayan civil society is entering a new period, which could lead to positive changes in its relations with the state and its role in society as a whole.

Table 43.1 Background Information for Uruguay

Uruguay	
Country size (square km)	176,215
Population (millions 2004)	3.4
Population under 15 years (2004)	24.4%
Urban population (2003)	92.5%
Seats in parliament held by women (2003)	12.1%
Language groups	Spanish (official), Portunol or Brazilero (Portuguese Spanish)
Ethnic groups	White 88%, mestizo 8%, black 4%
Religious groups	Roman Catholic 66%
HDI score and ranking (2003)	0.840 (46th)
GDP per capita (US$ 2003)	$8,280
Unemployment rate (% of total labor force)	16.8%
Population living on less than US$2 a day (2003)	5.7%

Historical Overview

Civil society organizations (CSOs) and social movements have a long history in Uruguay. In general Uruguayan civil society seems less visible during times of socioeconomic prosperity, but its levels of activity and impact peak during times of crisis.

Organizations associated with the Catholic Church came into existence after the country's independence from Spain (1825–1830) and during the subsequent civil war. The British influence in the late 1800s, a result of the growth of international capitalism, brought the first business associations to the industrial and farming sectors. At the same time, the growth of the industrial sector gave momentum to the creation of the first trade unions and workers' organizations.

Over the course of the twentieth century, the consolidation of state bureaucracy and favorable economic development allowed for the establishment of a welfare state, which dominated political and economic life in the country. In the 1970s the crisis of this developmental model led to a rise of workers' and students' movements. Social turmoil and political polarization were fueled by the economic crisis and eventually ended in a period of military dictatorship (1973–1985).

In the 1980s the gradual process of democratization provided a fertile ground for new CSOs to come to the fore, particularly in the fields of human rights and gender issues. After the return to democracy in 1985, many CSOs were faced with challenges arising from the changing social, political, economic, and cultural environments that characterized the postauthoritarian society. While the country underwent a series of neoliberal reforms, which were strongly opposed by trade unions, other CSOs began to provide public services on behalf of state authorities. The victory of a left-leaning government in 2005 created a new situation for CSOs that is likely to provide a more positive operating environment and lead to further changes in civil society's roles.

The State of Civil Society in Uruguay

This section provides a summary of key findings of the CSI project in Uruguay. It examines the state of civil society in Uruguay along four dimensions—structure, environment, values, and impact—highlighting the main weaknesses and strengths.

Uruguay's Civil Society Diamond (figure 43.1) is a visual summary of the CSI findings and depicts a relatively balanced civil society.

Figure 43.1 Civil Society Diamond for Uruguay

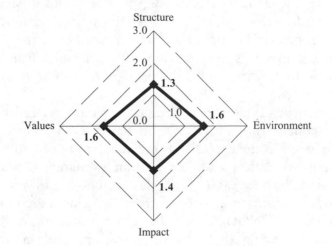

No dimension is particularly strong or weak. Civil society's structural foundation is assessed as somewhat below average, with a notable absence of an adequate support infrastructure. Civil society operates in a somewhat enabling environment, in which the positive political context and a good relationship with the state stand out as strong points. Good relations with the state also affect civil society's impact positively as well as negatively. One strength is its ability to partner with the state to provide services to the population; these ties, however, weaken civil society's role as a watchdog of state behavior. Civil society's value base is moderately well-developed, with particular strengths in promoting political norms, while social norms, such as environmental sustainability and gender equity, receive less attention.

Structure (1.3)

The structure dimension examines the makeup of civil society in terms of the main characteristics of individual citizen participation and associational life. This dimension receives the lowest score of all four dimensions. Limited citizen participation, a prevalence of urban-based CSOs, and poor support infrastructure for CSO activities are primary weaknesses in this dimension.

Low levels of citizen participation in collective community activities (less than 30%) and low membership in CSOs (less than 30%) indicate generally weak levels of civic engagement in Uruguay. Although a large number of individuals make charitable donations (more than 60%), the amount of donations is low in relation to personal income.

Civil society in Uruguay comprises many different types of CSOs, however, significant mass membership is only found in sports clubs (14.7%), trade unions (5.5%), and religious organizations (3.8%). Moreover, some significant social groups, specifically the youth, are largely absent in CSOs' membership and leadership. Rural populations, ethnic minorities, and poor people are also seen as severely underrepresented.

The civil society sector in Uruguay is characterized by a geographical concentration of CSOs in urban areas. Over 70% of CSOs are based in the capital, Montevideo, and only 30% in rural areas. Communication and information exchange is also rather poor. The only noticeable examples of cooperation are found among trade unions and cooperatives. In general, cooperatives, trade unions, and NGOs appear better organized than the rest of the sector in having umbrella organizations and implementing joint activities. There are also almost no civil society or governmental initiatives and entities devoted to the institutional strengthening of CSOs.

The strength of this dimension lies in the resources available to organizations. CSOs generally feel they have adequate financial, human, and technological resources to accomplish their goals. However, a significant amount of CSOs' funding comes from membership dues and national government grants, since most foreign donors have left the country because of its relatively advanced stage of development.

The CSI analysis indicates that civil society's structure is of moderate size and characterized by the absence of notable strengths and crucial weaknesses regarding individual and associational features of civic life in Uruguay.

Environment (1.6)

The environment dimension considers political, legal, socioeconomic, and sociocultural contexts, as well as the relationship between civil society, the state, and the private sector. The score for this dimension reflects a slightly enabling environment for civil society activities. The main strengths lie in the conducive political and sociocultural contexts, whereas the socioeconomic environment, private sector–civil society relations, and, to a lesser extent, the legal environment entail certain impediments to civil society's growth.

Uruguayan citizens have full freedom to participate in civic activities, and there is an open and competitive political process. However, the right to information remains constrained by a culture of secrecy:

the establishment and civil servants consider government information to belong to the state. Journalists also feel that libel laws limit the freedom of the press.

The absence of conducive tax regulations points toward the rather problematic legal framework for civil society. Legal provisions for registering a CSO are seen as neither quick nor simple. The legal registration procedures that have been in force for more than a century—since January 23, 1868—are outdated and in need of an overhaul.

The state–civil society relationship is mostly positive, even though cooperation is characterized by clientelism and some CSOs are overly dependent on the state, since the national government is a major funder of CSOs. In addition, dialogue between the state and civil society is limited, though recent initiatives, such as the creation of the Ministry of Social Development (MIDES) in March 2005, have aimed at addressing this problem. Following the establishment of MIDES, some umbrella organizations were invited to dialogue with the government on social policies, and agreements were signed with many CSOs within MIDES's programmatic framework. However, the information analyzed by the CSI study indicates a lack of institutionalized channels for dialogue between the state and CSOs, and stakeholders expressed the need for more stable relations and increased communication. In particular, the CSI assessment recommends establishing mechanisms for dialogue at the local level, to address the varying contexts in different localities.

The most problematic features of civil society's environment are the socioeconomic context and the relationship between civil society and the corporate sector. The negative consequences of the recent socioeconomic crisis, which strongly affected society, are still being felt. The gross national product in Uruguay fell by 18.6% between 1998 and 2002 and led to the devaluation of the Uruguayan peso, followed by a financial and balance-of-payments crisis, which impacted the entire economy and society. Poverty, unemployment, and immigration rates almost doubled, squeezing civil society's human and financial resources and requiring many CSOs to change their priorities to address the social crisis.

There is room for improvement in the relationship between the private sector and civil society. The degree of mistrust between these sectors means that business associations rarely participate in wider civil society initiatives. The private sector's attitude toward civil society is widely regarded as indifferent, and most CSOs receive little or no financial support from the corporate sector. No legislation exists to allow tax deductions for individuals or corporations making donations, except when donations are made to public schools or education centers. As a result, corporate social responsibility (CSR) is still incipient, and although some progress is being made, a great deal remains to be done.

Values (1.6)

The values dimension examines the extent to which civil society practices and promotes positive values. Together with the environment dimension, the value dimension received the highest score, reflecting a somewhat positive value base for Uruguayan civil society. The strengths of this dimension are the widespread practice of democracy and nonviolence. However, despite CSOs embracing positive values, their low public visibility in promoting positive values, especially around environmental protection and gender equity, remains a significant weakness.

The positive value base for civil society is characterized by strong internal democracy, as indicated by the fact that a majority (65%) of CSOs uses democratic elections for the selection of its leadership and that members are generally seen to have significant influence on organizational decisionmaking. However, there are only a few examples of activities undertaken by civil society to promote democracy within society at large.

The use of violence by civil society actors to express their interests is rare and usually restricted to marches, student protests, certain human rights advocacy organizations (escraches), football hooliganism, neo-Nazis, and street gangs. When violent actions occur, they are strongly criticized by civil society. Although a substantial number of Uruguayan civil society activities promote nonviolence in society, broad-based support and public visibility of such initiatives is lacking.

One challenge for civil society is the practice and promotion of transparency and accountability. Although cases of corruption in civil society are not common, financial transparency is not a widespread practice within CSOs. Many organizations do not publicly report their financial statements, and the small minority that are accountable do so to their members only, not to a wider set of stakeholders. There is a need for further introspection, and stakeholders suggest establishing coordinated actions for self-regulation and other accountability mechanisms for the sector.

The greatest weaknesses within civil society's values are its low level of activity in promoting environmental sustainability and its weak track record in practicing and promoting gender equity. Sexist practices within civil society are rarely denounced by civil society actors. Many (42.9%) CSOs have no written gender policies covering equal opportunities or equal pay for equal work for women. Civil society's actions to promote gender equity in society at large also have extremely low public visibility.

Thus, despite strengths in certain fields, civil society has overall only a moderate track record in practicing and promoting key social values.

Impact (1.4)

The impact dimension assesses civil society's role in governance and society at large. Uruguayan civil society is assessed as having a moderate level of impact, with service provision being a particular strength and its role as a watchdog of the state and the private sector being a clear weakness.

While a significant number of CSO activities in demanding accountability of state agencies (particularly at the local level) were detected in the CSI's media review, stakeholders assessed civil society's overall watchdog role as rather limited. This assessment is even more negative in relation to the private sector, where the few examples of civil society efforts to hold corporations to account are limited to industrial actions by trade unions.

The CSI assessment revealed that civil society has limited influence on public policies. Only a few CSOs, typically those with better standing, a strong technical profile, and a higher degree of professionalism, such as trade unions, co-operatives, and certain NGOs, have the ability to impact public policy. Although some of these CSOs have placed issues of human rights on the public agenda and have influenced the policymaking process, they have made little progress in many important policy areas, such as health, housing, education, unemployment, and the national budgeting process.

Uruguayan civil society is moderately active in engaging the population, for example, through empowering marginalized people and getting citizens involved in collective action. The most notable activities are public demonstrations, workshops, conferences and seminars, and the dissemination of information through the press, although these actions do not result in any substantial impact on the population.

Despite limited achievements in other areas, CSOs are seen as rather active and successful in meeting societal needs, especially those of marginalized groups. Providing food to the most deprived groups in society, for example, through community dining halls, is singled out by the CSI assessment as an area of significant activity and success. Civil society is also generally seen as responsive to the needs of society either through delivering relevant services or lobbying the state to provide services. Of the population survey respondents, 71.5% believe that civil society is better than the state in providing social services for the poor.

Recommendations

The CSI assessment provided an opportunity for a broad range of stakeholders to identify possible strategies for strengthening civil society. Recommendations made at the consultative meetings convened as part of the CSI suggest that civil society should concentrate on strengthening all four dimensions. The following are some specific recommendations:

- Foster greater participation within CSOs and encourage democratic practices by increasing membership and volunteering.
- Establish mechanisms to facilitate stronger information exchange and cooperation among CSOs, including the strengthening of networks and umbrella bodies.
- Build on the rather enabling environment. CSOs should increase their role and visibility in addressing the socioeconomic challenges facing Uruguay.
- Build better foundations for dialogue and engagement with government and the private sector to address structural deficiencies, such as the absence of laws encouraging corporate philanthropy and CSR.
- Streamline the sector's activities and visibility by practicing and promoting positive values, especially accountability and transparency. CSOs should implement self-assessments, develop quality certification mechanisms, and promote a culture of transparency and accountability within the sector to improve its legitimacy and promote greater citizen participation.

Conclusion

The current state of civil society in Uruguay is fairly balanced and indicates a moderate level of strength. Yet, a number of problematic areas persist, such as the sector's limited public visibility, minimal accountability, and weak watchdog and policy roles. Addressing these weaknesses will require the involvement of all stakeholders. Positive changes in the policy environment that encourage greater dialogue between the state and civil society have already been recorded since the new government took office in 2005 and established a Ministry of Social Development.

The hope is that this study, the first of its kind in Uruguay, will lay the foundation for actions and policies aimed at strengthening Uruguayan civil society and will increase its links with other sectors, thereby contributing to national development. The CSI in Uruguay has already raised a great deal of interest and is being widely distributed to interested stakeholders.

CSI Report

Instituto de Comunicación y Desarrollo (ICD), *The Brilliance and Imperfections of a Diamond: CIVICUS Civil Society Index Report for Uruguay* (Montevideo, Uruguay: Instituto de Comunicación y Desarrollo, 2006).

Notes

1. The CSI assessment was implemented in Uruguay by the Institute for Communication and Development (ICD) from June 2003 to December 2005. This chapter presents the main findings of the CSI and is based on a comprehensive country report for Uruguay, which can be accessed on the CSI pages of the CIVICUS website at http://www.civicus.org.

Chapter 44

Vietnam[1]

Largely unnoticed by the international community, Vietnam has undergone a series of profound economic, social, and even political changes over the last decade and a half. One of these developments has been the evolution of a rudimentary associational sector, although its main features are different from most other civil societies. The civil society concept has recently received growing attention in Vietnam, with the implementation of the Civil Society Index Shortened Assessment Tool (CSI-SAT) project being part of this trend.

Table 44.1 Background Information for Vietnam

Vietnam	
Country size (square km)	331,000
Population (millions 2004)	82.2
Population under 15 years (2004)	30.3%
Urban population (2003)	25.8%
Seats in parliament held by women (2005)	27.3%
Language groups	Vietnamese (official), English, French, and Chinese
Ethnic groups	Vietnam 85.9%, Chinese, Hmong, Thai, Khmer, Cham
Religious groups	Buddhist, Roman Catholic, Taoist, indigenous beliefs
HDI score and ranking (2003)	0.704 (108th)
GDP per capita (US$ 2003)	$2,490
Unemployment rate (% of total labor force)	2.1%

Historical Overview

Twentieth-century Vietnamese political and economic history has strongly influenced the contemporary character of Vietnamese civil society. Following the end of World War II, the Japanese surrender, and the 1945 August Revolution, the Communist-led Viet Minh took power in Hanoi and led the Vietnamese struggle for independence from French colonialism. In 1954 the ratification of the Geneva agreements by the French and Viet Minh led to the partitioning of Vietnam into the Democratic Republic of Vietnam in the north and the Republic of Vietnam in the south. In the north, socialist reform began with the introduction of a centrally planned economy, agricultural collectives, state-owned manufacturing companies and commercial sectors, and the integration of all autonomous associations into the Communist Fatherland Front. Mass organizations (MOs) for women, youth, and other groups, which were established in the 1930s, were converted into schools of socialism, and tasked with transmitting messages from the party to the people. After the end of the American War in 1975 and the country's reunification in 1976, socialist rule in Vietnam, including the system of MOs, expanded to the south.

In the mid-1980s, the *doi moi* reforms ushered legislative reforms toward a market economy with a socialist orientation. The role of MOs as intermediary organizations between the state and the people began to change. For example, trade unions increasingly represented the interests of urban factory workers, and the farmers' association voiced the demands of small-scale farmers. During this period, the space for autonomous civic organizations began to widen. Civil society organizations (CSOs) proliferated further in the 1990s, as a consequence of the Vietnamese economic boom, the passing of the 1992 reformist constitution, increased integration into the international community, and the overhaul of the administrative system. However, since the current political system can still be described as a Communist one-party system, the space for a fully independent civil society remains limited.

The State of Civil Society in Vietnam

In Vietnam, the term "people's organization" has historically been used to describe associations formed by Vietnamese people. However, these organizations are increasingly referred to as NGOs. Due to political circumstances, the concept of civil society is not part of mainstream discussions in Vietnam, and the associational landscape differs significantly from most other countries. In Vietnam, most associations are entangled with the state, and civil society is segmented into different types. These types differ in terms of mode of operation, relationship to the state, and public image. To conduct research on the state of Vietnam's civil society, stakeholders reached consensus on seven categories, which together make up civil society in Vietnam. Of these, four categories were considered in this study: MOs, professional associations, Vietnamese NGOs (VNGOs), community-based organizations, and other informal groups.

Mass organizations, such as the Women's Union, trade unions, Youth Union, and Farmers' Association, are intertwined with the state, though recent years have witnessed a trend toward greater autonomy. They also have extensive vertical networks connecting the center with local groups in rural communities. Professional associations, such as the Vietnam Union for Science and Technology Association (VUSTA), were established in the early 1980s to bring together people with similar professional interests. Issue-oriented organizations, or VNGOs, mostly emerged after the 1992 decree on the establishment of nonprofit science and technology organizations. Informal groups and community-based organizations (CBOs), such as groups for the elderly or microcredit associations, began to appear in the mid-1990s, but remain limited in number and scale. Although none of these types fully function independently from the state, some CSOs enjoy a greater degree of autonomy than others, such as the VNGOs and CBOs.

Thus, in Vietnam, associations often exist and operate as part of the party-state structure. However, since these organizations perform many important civic functions within Vietnamese society, such as aggregating and representing interests, empowering people, and providing services, they were included as part of civil society in this study. This is a unique feature that sets the Vietnamese civil society definition apart from the definition used in most other countries participating in the CSI and from the definition typically used in the literature.

This section provides a summary of key findings of the CSI project in Vietnam. It examines the state of Vietnamese civil society along four dimensions—structure, environment, values, and impact—highlighting the main weaknesses and strengths.

The diamond (figure 44.1) shows that Vietnamese civil society has an average structure, characterized by broad-based citizen participation, but a fragmented and weakly organized civil society.

Figure 44.1 Civil Society Diamond for Vietnam

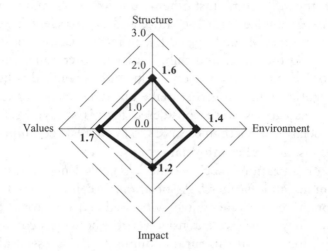

Civil society operates in a somewhat disabling environment because of restrictive relations with the state. The sector has mainly limited impact on politics and society. This is primarily due to its inability to influence public policy and hold the state and private sector accountable. Vietnamese CSOs focus their activities on poverty alleviation and other development initiatives, rather than on promoting more sensitive values, such as transparency and environmental sustainability. Thus, overall, civil society's values received a mixed assessment.

Structure (1.6)

The structure dimension examines the makeup of civil society in terms of the main characteristics of individual participation and associational life. After more than a decade of growth, Vietnamese civil society is broad-based, with widespread and diverse participation, including most social groups and a large number of organizational types and forms. Seventy-four percent of Vietnamese citizens belong to at least one CSO, and on average each citizen is a member of 2.3 organizations, reflecting a much higher rate of participation than neighboring countries. However, while approximately 65 of the 82 million Vietnamese citizens take part in civil society activities, the substance of participation is often considerably less profound than its breadth. In part, this is due to widespread membership in MOs, such as the 12 million members of the Women's Union, where not all members are actively involved in organizational activities.

The structure of civil society in Vietnam is defined by the four types of CSOs, each with its own unique organizational characteristics, external conditions, and financing model. Each CSO type is also subject to its own specific legal framework that regulates its formation and operations. Despite their close connection to the state and the party, MOs play a vital role linking local communities with the political center and constitute an important arena for civic engagement.[2] VNGOs are predominantly active in urban areas and tend to have narrower membership bases. They carry out projects in urban and rural areas, and provide services to disadvantaged groups, such as people with HIV/AIDS and Agent Orange victims. In rural areas, CBOs provide essential services to the population, and the number of community cultural and recreational groups is increasing.

Despite Vietnam's broad and diverse associational life, civil society is structurally segmented, and its defining features include poor networking and interrelations among civil society actors in general, and among the different subsectors in particular. Many organizations belong to umbrella organizations; however, many of these umbrella organizations do not function well. VNGO and CBO networks have only recently been established and are particularly weak compared to MOs and umbrella bodies of professional associations. In terms of organizational sustainability of the sector, the general lack of capacity, inadequate resources, and weak support infrastructure pose critical challenges for civil society.

Over the last fifteen years, a limited space for civic associations has opened up in Vietnam, and there are high levels of civic engagement at the local level. However, given the overall restrictive environment, the vibrancy and coherence of organized civil society remains constrained.

Environment (1.4)

The environment dimension considers political, legal, socioeconomic, and sociocultural contexts, as well as the relationships between civil society, the state, and the private sector. The examination of the environment in which Vietnamese civil society operates, generates a mixed picture of conducive socioeconomic and sociocultural factors, and less conducive legal and political conditions. Overall, the environment remains somewhat disabling, particularly given Vietnam's restrictive political and legal contexts and the problematic relations between civil society and the state.

Restrictions on basic freedoms, including civil liberties and press freedoms, impede autonomous citizen action in the country. Although international critics rate Vietnam in the lowest category of "not free" countries in the world, many local observers argue that accusations of political and other human rights abuses are infused with misunderstandings of the differences in Vietnam's political system and Vietnamese values. In Vietnam's one-party political system, there is no political competition. However, proponents of the regime refer to the people's strong confidence in the government, citing a 2001 opinion poll indicating that 97% of Vietnamese have quite a lot or a great deal of confidence in the government. However, despite the state's overall effectiveness, corruption remains rampant in the public sector, and the judiciary remains controlled by the ruling party. According to Transparency International's Corruption Perception Index 2005, Vietnam ranks 107 out of 159 countries. Despite divergent views about the Vietnamese political environment, it is clear that there is considerable room for improvement in the political context within which CSOs operate.

Complex, time-consuming, and restrictive laws shroud the legal environment regulating CSOs, making it difficult for new VNGOs to register. CSO advocacy activity is limited by the state, and there are no tax incentives for individual or corporate giving. Although MOs have direct access to institutionalized dialogue channels with the state, VNGOs and CBOs are not part of the organizational configuration of the state and must make their voices heard through public meetings and political pressure on local politicians.

The improving socioeconomic conditions in Vietnam, a positive sociocultural context, and a high level of state effectiveness are all favorable factors for civil society's development. From 1990 to 2005, the poverty rate fell drastically from two-thirds to one-quarter of the population, and citizens have been free from severe economic and social crises. Stemming in part from traditional Confucian family values, the level of trust is moderately high, with 41% of Vietnamese claiming to trust fellow citizens.

The economy and, to a much lesser extent, the sociopolitical arena have opened up since the *doi moi* reforms; however, the overall environment for Vietnamese civil society remains disabling. Although the space for civil society has increased, organizations still do not have significant room to maneuver. Given the overlap among the state, ruling party, and many CSOs, civil society in Vietnam cannot be conceptualized based on its independence vis-à-vis the state; rather, it must be seen as part of a contested area within the state sphere itself. However, autonomous civil society activities are increasingly taking place, in which people subtly practice daily protest due to dissatisfaction with the present conditions.

Values (1.7)

The values dimension examines the extent to which civil society practices and promotes positive values. This dimension received the highest score among the four aspects considered by the CSI in Vietnam. Civil society's activities in promoting values, such as poverty reduction, tolerance, and gender equity were seen as particularly strong.

Interestingly, democracy, transparency, and nonviolence are practiced more internally within CSOs than they are promoted externally, and done in accordance with specific Vietnamese cultural and ideological traditions. However, the extent to which civil society practices internal democracy varies among types of organizations. For example, while MOs are governed by centralized decisionmaking processes, there are fewer regulations guiding the internal operations of VNGOs, and the internal practices of VNGOs range from patronage to fully democratic practices.

According to stakeholders, the primary goal of the majority of CSOs is to contribute to poverty alleviation. This tendency is in line with the government's prioritization of socioeconomic development. Subsequently, considerable space has been granted by the government to civic organizations devoted to economic, social, and humanitarian development in Vietnam. In contrast, democracy and human rights issues remain politically sensitive, and, therefore, these values are much less frequently expressed by civil society.

Impact (1.2)

The impact dimension assesses civil society's role in governance and society at large. The impact of civil society in Vietnam is relatively limited and depends on the type of CSO. Whereas MOs continue to link people to the main organs of the state, VNGOs and CBOs primarily focus on service delivery and have been successful in empowering local communities. Together, the various types of organizations have had a relatively significant impact in supporting the poor and other disadvantaged groups, such as women, children, and people living with HIV/AIDS. However, only a few organizations reach the ethnic minorities in the northern mountains and central highlands.

Beyond civil society's direct impact on citizens, its influence on public policy and role as a watchdog of the state and private sector is very limited. At the national level, MOs have more direct access to policy debates than VNGOs or CBOs, but their impact remains limited. In general, civil society does not act as a watchdog of the state or private sector, since this role is not considered important or appropriate for civil society. However, recently there have been some notable but isolated examples of environmental and labor protests in response to unethical treatment of workers.

At the provincial level, MOs, professional associations, and VNGOs are exerting increasing influence, as the state gives civil society a larger role in service delivery. MOs are also an important link between the political administrative center and local communities and villages. At the grassroots level, various collaborative projects, by MOs and VNGOs, are carried out informing and educating citizens, building capacity for collective action, and supporting local livelihoods. CSO activities also contributed to the establishment of the Grassroots Democracy Decree in 1998, which ensures the right of the rural population "to be informed, to discuss, to carry out, and to monitor" government programs in their area. In general, the spread of participatory planning and stakeholder participation in the implementation of large-scale development projects has increased people's influence on their daily conditions.

It is important to note that the state remains the most powerful actor in Vietnamese society. Therefore, CSOs are assigned very limited and supplementary roles in service provision. Due to political restrictions, CSOs are extremely limited in pursuing advocacy and lobbying activities; however, there are some indications of a stronger policy and watchdog role for CSOs in this rapidly changing society.

Conclusion

Interpreting the exact degree of change in Vietnam's political environment since the *doi moi* reforms remains an issue of contention. However, it is clear that during the last fifteen years the space for civil society has begun to open up. CSOs have been able to make a contribution to poverty alleviation and the empowerment of disadvantaged groups. In contrast, civil society's level of activity beyond social and economic development is controlled by the state and remains extremely limited. In particular, advocacy around political and other rights remains a difficult area for civil society's involvement.

Major challenges facing Vietnamese civil society include internal fragmentation, poor networking, weak relations with the state, and an inadequate legal and political environment. However, the high levels of citizen participation in collective activities could become a favorable foundation for civil society's further development, if organizations can ensure a certain degree of autonomy and independence. Also, favorable socioeconomic and sociocultural trends, such as the pace of economic growth and rising levels of public spiritedness and trust among citizens, have positive implications for the prospect of a healthy and vibrant civil society. Thus, by further coordinating its activities, establishing more effective networks, and working with the state to develop a more conducive legal environment, civil society has the potential to further increase its role in Vietnamese society.

CSI Report

Irene Norlund, Dang Ngoc Dinh et al., *The Emerging Civil Society— An Initial Assessment of Civil Society in Vietnam: CIVICUS Civil Society Index Shortened Assessment Tool Report for Vietnam* (Hanoi, Vietnam: VIDS in collaboration with UNDP and SNV Vietnam, 2006).

Notes

1. The CSI Shortened Assessment Tool was implemented in Vietnam by the Vietnam Institute of Development Studies (VIDS), in close cooperation with the United Nations Development Programme (UNDP) and SNV from April to December 2005. This chapter presents the main findings of the CSI-SAT and is based on a comprehensive country report for Vietnam, which can be accessed on the CSI pages of the CIVICUS website at http://www.civicus.org.
2. Mass organizations are accused by some critics of being bureaucratic top-down organizations that are too closely linked to the party-state. However, in the national context, very few organizations in Vietnam can be considered truly independent from the state. Until the late-1990s, MOs represented the only organizations with connections to rural communities throughout the country.

Chapter 45

Wales[1]

The development of Welsh civil society has been shaped by the history of Wales, which has it its own distinctive features compared to its English counterpart. The term "civil society" is not commonly used in Wales, and the Civil Society Index Shortened Assessment Tool (CSI-SAT) was the first study of its kind in Wales. Although the CSI-SAT finds most civil society subsectors to be active and thriving, the study also indicates that civil society as a whole rarely comes together to discuss common issues or work on joint initiatives. It is hoped that the CSI-SAT implementation will highlight the need to address this void.

Table 45.1 Background Information for Wales

Wales	
Size (square km)	20,640
Population (2001)	2,903,085
Population under 17 years	20.1%
Urban population (% of total 2003)	68.0%
Seats in parliament held by women (2005)	48.0%
Language groups	Welsh and English (20% can understand, speak, read, and write Welsh)
Ethnic groups	White 97.9%, mixed 0.6%, Asian 0.9%, black 0.2%, Chinese 0.4%
Religious groups	Christian 71.9%, no religion 18.5%, Muslim 0.7%, other 0.8%, not stated 8.1%
GDP per capita (US$ 2003)	$20,838
Unemployment rate (2005)	4.60%

Historical Overview

The development of civil society in Wales has been intertwined with concepts of nationhood, nonconformist Christianity, and the labor movement. The growth of nonconformity accompanied the Industrial Revolution and led to the suffrage movement and campaigns to disestablish the Anglican Church.

Trade unionism came to Wales in the 1830s when Flintshire and Merthyr miners joined the Friendly Associated Coalminers' Union. In the early 1880s there was a marked growth in New Unionism, which resulted in the establishment of the South Wales Miners' Federation in 1898. The federation eventually attained a larger membership than any other secular institution in Welsh history. In 1890 the Labour Representation Committee was formed as a joint venture of trade unionists and members of socialist societies, and became the foundation for the Labour Party. More recently, the collapse of heavy industry and mining, as well as attacks on unionism by Margaret Thatcher in the 1980s, led to a steep fall in union membership.

Professional associations in Wales have been largely organized at the UK level, and, until recently, civil society infrastructure bodies were also dominated by UK organizations. A significant step forward occurred in 1998 when the Government of Wales Act put a statutory duty on the Welsh Assembly to form three partnership councils: one each for local government, business and employee organizations, and the voluntary sector.

There is also a long tradition of social movements in Wales. Welsh civil society has been active in affecting social change from the Merthyr miners' uprising in 1831 to a variety of Welsh language initiatives during the twentieth century. The Welsh home rule movements, the nineteenth-century mobilization by nonconformists, the championing of Welsh Liberalism, the founding of Plaid Genedlaethol Cymru (the Welsh National Party) in 1925, and the 1962 establishment of Cymdeithas yr Iaith Gymraeg (the Welsh Language Society) all contributed to the preservation of a distinct Welsh identity. Civil society's activities led to the establishment of the Welsh Language Board and played an important role in the recognition of Welsh as a core subject in the national curriculum. Although fewer people speak Welsh than did a hundred years ago, as a devolved nation, Wales currently has more powers of self-determination than it has had during the last 700 years.[2]

The State of Civil Society in Wales

"Civil society" is not a common term in Wales. Over the last two centuries, the domination of Welsh civil society, first by nonconformist Christian movements and then by the labor movement, made a common definition of civil society difficult. In relation to government, voluntary organizations are involved in the voluntary sector partnership council, while trade unions are included in the business partnership council. Traditionally, faith-based organizations, without wider public benefit, are excluded from the definition of voluntary organizations. Cultural differences between English- and Welsh-speaking communities also divide civil society, with parallel organizations often existing in one location. Within the context of these divides, the Wales Council for Voluntary Action (WCVA) sought to establish a consensus through the CSI-SAT assessment regarding the concept of civil society in Wales, and identify strengths and future prospects of Welsh civil society. The project advisory group adopted CIVICUS's definition of civil society and amended the list of CSO categories according to the Welsh context. Political parties, building and mutual societies, business federations, and chambers of trade were all excluded from the study and regeneration partnerships were included.

This section provides a summary of key findings of the CSI project in Wales. It examines the state of Welsh civil society along four dimensions—structure, environment, values, and impact—highlighting the main weaknesses and strengths.

The Welsh Civil Society Diamond (figure 45.1) visually summarizes the assessment's findings. The diamond indicates that civil society has a relatively strong structure, characterized by an active citizen base, and, due to strong state–civil society relations, it is operating in an enabling environment. The promotion and practice of positive values by civil society are significant and civil society has a substantive impact on society by redressing societal needs, holding the state accountable, and influencing policy.

Structure (1.9)

The structure dimension examines the makeup of civil society in terms of the main characteristics of individual citizen participation and associational life. This dimension receives the lowest score of the four dimensions. However, the score still indicates a relatively strong structure and reflects a high level of organization and widespread citizen participation.

Figure 45.1 Civil Society Diamond for Wales

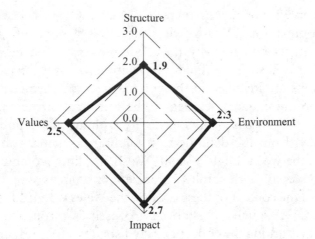

The strength of civil society's structure primarily stems from the diverse base of citizen participation. The European Social Survey revealed that 77% of citizens are a member, participant, or volunteer of a CSO. CSO membership is weakest among poor people; however, women, rural dwellers, and ethnic and religious minorities are fairly well represented. CSOs exist throughout Wales and have a higher density in rural areas. The Voluntary Sector Almanac indicates that there are at least 500 voluntary organizations in each local authority, ranging in density between 4.5 and 19 organizations per 1,000 Welsh citizens. Welsh civil society is also highly organized. A survey of community groups shows that over 60% of respondents are part of a network or umbrella organization.

Within this relatively strong structure, there remains room for improvement. Civil society needs to address its relatively low depth of citizen participation and inadequate resource base. Although 71% of adults donate money to charity, the average amount given is less than 1% of average adult annual income. Though the total income of the voluntary sector in 2003 was estimated at £1.12 billion and is well funded by international standards, CSO representatives feel they lack the necessary financial and human resources to achieve their goals and meet societal needs.

A large proportion of Welsh citizens belong to CSOs, and citizens demonstrate a willingness to donate both time and money to charity. However, the amount of time devoted by the average citizen to voluntary work remains limited, and there are concerns that CSOs are unnecessarily drawn into competition for funding and volunteers. In turn, resource vulnerabilities and financial insecurity may make organizations overly dependent on state support.

Environment (2.3)

The environment dimension considers political, legal, socioeconomic, and sociocultural contexts, as well as the relationships between civil society, the state, and the private sector. The assessment indicates that Welsh civil society is operating in an enabling environment. Civil society has healthy relations with the state; however, relations with the private sector are less developed.

Apart from operating under positive political, sociocultural, and legal conditions, the sector has particularly strong relations with the state. Dialogue takes place at all levels of government: between civil society and local government, public bodies, and the Welsh Assembly Government. For example, local authorities are responsible for community leadership and consult stakeholders on local strategies. There are also agreements or compacts between local authorities and the local voluntary sector. Nationally, the Government of Wales Act of 1998 introduced a voluntary sector plan and established the Voluntary Sector Partnership Council (VSPC), as well as biannual meetings between voluntary sector representatives and ministers of the Welsh Assembly Government. The VSPC exemplifies positive institutionalized dialogue between civil society and the state. The state's financial support to CSOs is extremely significant, with funding available from the local to EU levels, through a variety of funding mechanisms and plans. Estimates show that public funding of the sector is in excess of £400 million per annum, or between 30% and 35% of total CSO income.

Certain private sector organizations have made large contributions to civil society, particularly at the local level; however, the relations between big businesses and civil society are generally limited. Charitable donations and grants from businesses from 2002 to 2003 only amounted to £36 million. Likewise, corporate social responsibility (CSR) remains weak, and though many companies consider CSR to be an important part of business thinking, it fails to be an integral factor influencing business behavior.

Overall, Welsh civil society flourishes in a conducive external environment. As part of a liberal democracy, basic freedoms are protected and guaranteed, citizens participate freely in the political process, and there are high levels of public trust in the institutions of government and media. Legal and financial regulations and the socioeconomic context nurture CSO operations, and the quality of state–civil society relations is a particular strength of the external environment. In the future, the demographic shift to an increasingly elderly population and the corresponding strain on pension plans and health and social service provision may, however, put some pressure on the external environment of civil society.

Values (2.5)

The values dimension examines the extent to which civil society practices and promotes positive values. The high score for this dimension reflects civil society's significant practice and promotion of nonviolence, gender equity, poverty eradication, environmental sustainability, and internal democracy. Not all parts of civil society are equally active in promoting these values, but stakeholders believe that civil society has made significant contributions in these areas, and its practices have effected positive changes in public attitudes.

Civil society is particularly active in the struggle to alleviate poverty and sustain the environment. From 2002 to 2005, child poverty, defined as children living in households with less than 60% of the median UK income, fell from 31% to 22%. This drop is attributed to the improved economic landscape and government policy, and the wide-ranging efforts of CSOs. Local and national CSO initiatives, both for environmental sustainability and sustainable development of local communities, including local supplier networks and farmers' markets, are supported by the Welsh Assembly.

CSOs generally observe principles of democracy and accountability in their formal internal structures and are subject to legal and financial regulations limiting fraud and corruption. Most CSOs operate within the limits of peaceful action and lawful behavior and are working to achieve gender equality and social inclusion.

Impact (2.7)

The impact dimension assesses civil society's role in governance and society at large. This dimension receives the highest score of the four dimensions, and reflects the significant impact of civil society on society and governance. Key strengths include civil society's ability to meet societal needs, empower citizens, hold the state and the private sector accountable, and influence public policy.

CSOs are very active in monitoring and lobbying the government, and there is an abundance of high-profile cases demonstrating the power of CSOs to affect corporate behavior. Examples include environmental groups limiting the planting of genetically modified crops; campaigns to stop the fur trade and whaling; and campaigns to boycott banks that are known to invest in the arms trade, support oppressive regimes, or do not operate bilingually in English and Welsh.

In general, Welsh CSOs are influential in setting agendas and achieving tangible outcomes by influencing policies and debates on social, political, and economic priorities. CSOs engage in a wide range of educational and public information campaigns, and internet usage has increased the reach of such campaigns. Many of these activities are directed at special interest groups or marginalized groups excluded from society. In addition, most citizens view CSOs as making a positive and significant contribution to society.

Conclusion

There are no dramatic, overarching weaknesses within Welsh civil society, and the sector is balanced, healthy, and stable. Civil society thrives on widespread citizen participation, a strong organizational structure, and a favorable external environment, which is characterized by a healthy socioeconomic context and generally positive state–civil society relations.

The CSI-SAT revealed that Welsh civil society's strongest features include its positive value base and its strong impact on society at large. Civil society's ability to meet societal needs, empower citizens, hold the state and the private sector accountable, and influence public policy bodes well for the future of Welsh civil society. Civil society's significant practice and promotion of positive values reflects its long history in Wales, with its roots embedded in the labor movement, non-conformist Christianity, and the struggle for home rule. Given the history of political domination of Wales, and the recent devolution of legislative powers to Wales, Welsh civil society has its own character, distinguishable and unique from the rest of the United Kingdom.

Recommendations to further develop Welsh civil society focus on improving the sector's structure and deepening the existing levels of citizen participation, including the number of citizens taking part in collective community action, the portion of income donated to charity, and the securing of adequate financial and human resources for civil society to achieve its goals. Civil society also needs to encourage the adoption and practice of corporate social responsibility. The Stakeholder Assessment Group (SAG), set up to guide the CSI-SAT implementation, suggested that further links could be built among civil society actors. This would strengthen civil society and help it work together under a common banner that would be wider than the voluntary sector, trade union movement, or faith-based bodies.

CSI report

Bryan Collis, *An Assessment of Welsh Civil Society (2005): CIVICUS Civil Society Index Report for Wales* (Colwyn Bay, Wales: Wales Council for Voluntary Acton (WCVA), 2005).

Notes

1. The CSI Shortened Assessment Tool was implemented in Wales by the Wales Council for Voluntary Action (WCVA) in collaboration with the Department of Sociology, University of Wales in Bangor, from January to July 2005. This chapter presents the main findings of the CSI-SAT and is based on a comprehensive report for Wales, which can be accessed on the CSI pages at http://www.civicus.org.
2. The Government of Wales Act 1998 established an elected assembly of sixty members. The Assembly of Wales is responsible for education, health, social care, economic development, culture, and local government. Control of the police, courts, immigration, defense, and foreign policy remain with the UK parliament. Unlike the Scottish Executive, the assembly does not have tax raising powers.

Annex: Research Methods Implemented in Each Country

Country	Population Survey	Regional Stakeholder Survey and Consultations	Media Review	Desk Studies	Secondary Data
Argentina		x			x
Bolivia	x	x	x	x	x
Bulgaria	x	x	x	x	x
Chile*					x
China	x	x	x	x	x
Croatia	x	x	x	x	x
Cyprus, northern part of	x	x	x	x	x
Cyprus, southern part of	x	x	x	x	x
Czech Republic	x	x	x	x	x
Ecuador	x	x	x	x	x
Egypt		x	x	x	x
Fiji	x	x	x	x	x
Georgia*					x
Germany			x		x
Ghana	x	x	x	x	x
Greece*					x
Guatemala	x	x	x	x	x
Honduras	x	x	x	x	x
Hong Kong	CSO survey	x	x	x	x
Indonesia	x	x	x	x	x
Italy		x	x	x	x
Lebanon	x	x	x	x	x
Macedonia	x	x	x	x	x
Mongolia	x	x	x	x	x

(Continued)

Country	Population Survey	Regional Stakeholder Survey and Consultations	Media Review	Desk Studies	Secondary Data
Montenegro*					x
Nepal	x	x	x	x	x
The Netherlands					x
Northern Ireland	x	Online survey	x	x	x
Orissa, India	x	x	x	x	x
Poland	x	Online survey	x	x	x
Romania	x	x	x	x	x
Russia*	x			x	x
Scotland		Consultations with disenfranchised communities			x
Serbia	x	x	x	x	x
Sierra Leone	x	x	x	x	x
Slovenia	x	x	x	x	x
South Korea	x	x	x		x
Taiwan*					x
Togo*					x
Turkey		x	x	x	x
Uganda	x	x	x	x	x
Ukraine	x	x	x	x	x
Uruguay	x	x	x	x	x
Vietnam*					x
Wales*					x

*Countries that implemented the Civil Society Index Shortened Assessment Tool

About the Editor

V. Finn Heinrich is the Director of Programs for the global civil society network CIVICUS: World Alliance for Citizen Participation, based in Johannesburg, South Africa. Finn directed the CIVICUS Civil Society Index, an international action-research project on civil society, implemented in more than 50 countries. He has published widely on civil society issues, both in academic (e.g., *Journal of Civil Society, Voluntas, Development in Practice*) as well as in various practitioner journals. His research interests lie with comparative social research on macro issues such as civil society, governance, and democratization.

About CIVICUS

CIVICUS is an international alliance of civil society organizations dedicated to strengthening citizen action and civil society throughout the world. CIVICUS's mission is to nurture the foundation, growth, protection, and resourcing of citizen action throughout the world, particularly in cases where participatory democracy and freedom of association are threatened.

CIVICUS has worked for over a decade to strengthen civil society worldwide with the vision of a global community of active, engaged citizens committed to the creation of a more just and equitable world. This is premised on the belief that the health of societies exists in direct proportion to the degree of balance between the state, the private sector, and civil society. CIVICUS provides a focal point for knowledge-sharing, common interest representation, global institution-building, and engagement among these disparate sectors. It acts as an advocate for citizen participation as an essential component of governance and democracy worldwide. CIVICUS seeks to amplify the voices and opinions of ordinary people, and it gives expression to the enormous creative energy of the burgeoning sector of civil society. For more information about CIVICUS, please visit http://www.civicus.org.